Virginia Woolf

Virginia Woolf

REVALUATION AND CONTINUITY

A collection of essays

Edited, with an introduction, by

RALPH FREEDMAN

University of California Press / Berkeley, Los Angeles, London

Frontispiece drawing by F. Dodd, 1908.
Courtesy National Portrait Gallery, London.

University of California Press
Berkeley and Los Angeles, California
University of California Press, Ltd.
London, England

ISBN 0-520-03625-5
Library of Congress Catalog Card Number: 77-91745
Printed in the United States of America

1 2 3 4 5 6 7 8 9

Contents

Preface   *vii*
References   *ix*

Part One. PERSPECTIVES

1. Introduction: Virginia Woolf, the Novel,
   and a Chorus of Voices   RALPH FREEDMAN   *3*
2. Hunting the Moth: Virginia Woolf and the
   Creative Imagination   HARVENA RICHTER   *13*
3. Virginia Woolf's Narrators and the Art of "Life
   Itself"   JAMES HAFLEY   *29*
4. Forms of the Woolfian Short Story
   AVROM FLEISHMAN   *44*

Part Two. THE SEQUENCE

5. "Surely Order Did Prevail": Virginia Woolf and
   The Voyage Out   FREDERICK P. W. MCDOWELL   *73*
6. Enchanted Organs, Magic Bells: *Night and Day* as
   Comic Opera   JANE MARCUS   *97*
7. The Form of Fact and Fiction: *Jacob's Room* as
   Paradigm   RALPH FREEDMAN   *123*
8. *Mrs. Dalloway:* The Unguarded Moment
   LUCIO RUOTOLO   *141*
9. *To the Lighthouse:* Virginia Woolf's Winter's Tale
   MARIA DIBATTISTA   *161*

10. *Orlando* and Its Genesis: Venturing and
    Experimenting in Art, Love, and
    Sex   JEAN O. LOVE   *189*
11. Nature and Community: A Study of Cyclical
    Reality in *The Waves*   MADELINE MOORE   *219*
12. Nature and History in *The Years*
    JAMES NAREMORE   *241*
13. Woolf's Peculiar Comic World: *Between The
    Acts*   B. H. FUSSELL   *263*

    Contributors   *285*
    Bibliography   MARIA DIBATTISTA   *287*
    Index   *293*

Preface

This collection of essays grew out of a nucleus of papers read in 1974 at the English Institute meetings at Harvard. The theme of that section was the "revaluation" of Virginia Woolf; and indeed, the essays assembled both sought to revaluate her significance as a writer and to preserve traditional perspectives of her work. As the number and range of the articles in this volume has expanded, this dual task — to reassess her reputation and to preserve its continuity — has remained the dominant theme and purpose of the collection.

The authors and editor wish to thank all those who have contributed richly of their time and energy to make this volume a success. They include notably Ms. Cheryl Mares who has proofread the text with a watchful eye and prepared the index. Our thanks go out especially to Ms. Doris Kretschmer of the University of California Press, without whose devotion to Virginia Woolf and constant support our venture could not have borne fruit.

R.F.

Princeton, N.J.
July, 1979

References

The following texts are regularly cited throughout the book and will therefore be abbreviated. Dates of original publication, editions used, and code letters are listed below. In each case, the code letter(s) and page number, enclosed in parentheses, marks the reference.

All other references will be found in the footnotes.

	Code
The Voyage Out (1915) New York: Doran, 1920	VO
Night and Day (1919) New York: Harcourt Brace Jovanovich, 1973	ND
Jacob's Room (1922) New York: Harcourt, Brace, 1923	JR
Mrs. Dalloway (1925) New York: Harcourt, Brace, 1925	D
To the Lighthouse (1927) New York: Harcourt, Brace, 1927	L
Orlando (1928) New York: Harcourt, Brace, 1929	O
The Waves (1931) New York: Harcourt, Brace, 1931	W
The Years (1937) New York: Harcourt, Brace, 1937	Y
Between the Acts (1941) New York: Harcourt, Brace, 1941	BA
A Haunted House and Other Short Stories (1943) New York: Harcourt, Brace and World, 1944, 1963	HH

Part One

PERSPECTIVES

1. Introduction: Virginia Woolf, the Novel, and a Chorus of Voices

RALPH FREEDMAN

I

Virginia Woolf's renaissance is one of those unexpected events that have puzzled cultural historians. In one sense, of course, it need not be surprising at all. Woolf is too fine an artist, too secure in her imaginative range with a mind too subtly responsive to life outside and within to have been ignored forever. Still, in another sense it is surprising, for in her recent incarnation she has communicated aspects of herself which had seldom been noted in earlier years. Although she had shared the social and political ambience of Bloomsbury, and although her feminism was widely known, her essential reputation had been that of a highly accomplished writer of poetic prose. But now many readers take this latter role for granted and focus instead upon her sociopolitical stance, which they find equally innovative. They are raising important questions about Woolf's pivotal place between the fact and the vision of art.[1]

This turn in critical sensibilities may surprise the middle-aged critic, who has always found Woolf's genius most sharply etched in her well-wrought prose, in which interior lives are delicately displayed. But clearly this "new" reading of a familiar writer is rooted in the subtle interaction between the social and cultural needs of each generation and a writer's style. Milton had a great day at one time and not at another; Wordsworth was judged wanting during the 1940s and fifties but was restored in a

---

1. See, e.g., the relatively recent book by Alice van Buren Kelley, *The Novels of Virginia Woolf: Fact and Vision* (Chicago: University of Chicago Press, 1973).

4 RALPH FREEDMAN

different perspective during the sixties. And the great figures of "modernism" —Joyce, Yeats, Pound, Eliot, even Stevens — have been at best reinterpreted, at worst dismissed by fresh generations. But the reconsideration of Virginia Woolf in recent years has revealed a sharper edge: she has come to reflect a reassessment of our social and political life as a whole.

In this revision of Woolf's role as a principal on the stage of our intellectual history, she has often been alienated from the stance and milieu we usually associate with her and her work: the British upper class colored by Bloomsbury propensities, social generosity coupled with an intense artistic self-consciousness. It has seemed as though the slight, familiar figure were being suffused by a new and penetrating luminosity that revealed, as in an X ray, skeletons and structures that had never been perceived before. Clearly, this new fluorescence is connected with Woolf's role as a woman. Her re-emergence with the rise of feminist consciousness was appropriate and even inevitable. But important female writers have not been wanting in our time. Woolf was unique. Not only was she simply a writer par excellence, singled out by Leon Edel in 1955 as a pivotal proponent of a tradition that had culminated in Henry James.[2] She had also become a symbol for a much more far-reaching revision of contemporary society as a whole.

This turn in Woolf's reputation has given rise to questions about the reasons for differences between English and American critics, between middle-aged (and older) critics (both male and female) and men and women in their twenties and thirties who, in America at least, have been especially active in offering a fresh vision of her work. A closer look at the interplay of voices, which the present volume seeks to orchestrate, shows that the change in that vision may go deeper. The difference may not just lie in the fact that some critics have viewed Woolf as a self-consciously aestheticist writer while others have perceived her in a more ideological perspective; or that some like to see her, within the free-thinking limits of Bloomsbury, as fairly conservative, while others have thought her more radical. The crucial difference, in fact, may lie in her re-emergence not primarily as a storyteller or even a lyrical poet in prose, but as a soliloquist, a

2. Leon Edel, *The Psychological Novel: 1900–1950* (New York: Lippincott, 1955), pp. 190ff.

speaker whose words, even as they are couched in forms of fictional narration, are statements, possibly parables, but in any event projections of her self and thought delivered by the detached artist.

This new *angle of vision* points to a significant change in literary and critical sensibility in which the revaluation of Virginia Woolf, like that of several other writers, was caught. An analogy, though relating to audiences quite different in age and temperament, is the sudden flare-up in the popularity of Hermann Hesse twenty years ago, which is only now showing some signs of subsiding. That specifically European writer, until then largely confined to the German language and his origins in Germany and Switzerland, underwent an almost monstrous metamorphosis as he was caught in an American vogue. The responses his books evoked from American readers, leading ultimately to a complete rethinking of a writer's work which until then had not been taken too seriously, suggest that Hesse, like Woolf, served as a mirror — distorting as well as illuminating features that had up till then remained unperceived.

Both writers (after their deaths and therefore after all their work was "in") touched nerves in their respective audiences which led to their reinterpretation: youth and counterculture in one, a more mature radicalism in the other. But the analogy remains useful in discussing the source and dimensions of Woolf's role as it was conceived by many American readers. First, both writers developed a style that resembled the lyrical monologue in which consciousness displays itself and, second, both reflected an intimate connection between personal experience and narrative form. More than most modern writers, both Hesse and Woolf (however different they are in most other respects) displayed their consciousness with an immediacy which enabled them, as artfully formed personae, to function directly as models for their readers.

It may be useful to take this analogy a step further. For both writers there remains a serious discrepancy between their American reception and their original reputation. Both were transformed in their passage from the Old World to the New, and the reason for this transformation may be found in their conceptions as soliloquists and models. Moreover, as readers became impressed by the close relationships between their books and their biographical sources, they discovered in both writers new dimensions which underscored the predisposition to identify them with the figures in their works. Recent scholarship has not caused but deepened that development: it has lent it support. In the case of Hesse, little was known until recently in the English-speaking world about the personal life which was always assumed to be displayed on the pages of his books. When it came to light, it was used to reinforce an already existing image.

Similarly, in the case of Virginia Woolf, there is no way of measuring the impact that the Berg Collection in the New York Public Library, and its accessibility, has had on recent readings of her work. In addition, the publication of her diaries, of Nigel Nicolson's collection of her letters, of Leonard Woolf's memoirs, and, of course, of Quentin Bell's large biography have all contributed to a fresh biographical vision that is now used to telescope the person with the persona, the writer with her work. Quite apart from feminist and Marxist, Freudian or Jungian interpretations, the new *angle of vision* which has transformed the work of Virginia Woolf views her as a specifically fashioned *person*. This person has emerged from her books, but has seemed to verify the biographical evidence of letters and diaries. Paradoxically, for many important critics Woolf has become a model for thought and action beyond the frontiers of art, yet that model has been created by an artistry which continuously supports her role.

The line between a writer's person and her artistic persona may be gross or fine, but in Woolf's case it has been deliberately and purposefully trespassed. Here, then, a reappraisal of her work and self extends beyond her relationship with her readers and her craft and reaches toward a revision of modern life as a whole. A refusal to observe the line between narration and life, as between daily and artistic language, entails a revaluation of the relationship between social and artistic existence which has, for some time, been part of the American scene and has accelerated the decline of fiction.

Perhaps vocabulary can be a guide. The word that has been used in place of "poem" or "novel" in present-day critical language has been *text,* and, semantically at least, the act of criticism has become synonymous with an act of *interpretation.* Novels, stories, or poems may thus be part of a canon of texts which, as in the Bible, render statements or bodies of doctrine.[3] A rejection of "privileged language" may have derived its underpinnings from current theories of language and interpretation, but it is also rooted elsewhere: in an intense denial of artistic illusion and of the display of formal imagery, and in a search for the "truth of life." For a new generation of critics, illusion and fiction are appropriate mainly to the visual arts: the written word speaks either false or true. On that basis, writers have been either rejected as inconsequential or academic, or they have been turned into spokesmen for ideas capable of discursive statement, or they have been made into models molded by life. The story or poem has thus entered into the body of ordinary language: descriptive or exhortative alike.

Virginia Woolf is not just a survivor of the great age of Modernism who has been given artificial respiration.[4] She owes part of her renaissance to a reading of her texts beyond fictionality. This is by no means a negative criticism: a revaluation of that self-conscious artist as a radical and feminist model is partly a revaluation of fiction itself, an expansion of the language of narrative into the language of life. Betty Flanders, Clarissa Dalloway, Mrs. Ramsey, as well as many of Woolf's male figures, can be seen not as characters of fiction but as aspects and illustrations of a single consciousness envisioning and clarifying its themes. The revaluation of Woolf is based on a revolution in the conception of language, of reading, of literary art. It is one of Woolf's paradoxes, which this book seeks to lay bare, that the dissolution of artistic language and fictional characters into a sum of persons caught in the discourse of life has taken place in

3. See, e.g., the call by Avrom Fleishman, one of the contributors to this volume, for a return to "literary" criticism of Virginia Woolf as opposed to psychoanalytic, philosophical, or linguistic studies. "It is time for literary criticism to function," wrote Fleishman, "if Woolf is to be seen as one of the few transcendent modern masters"; "Virginia Woolf: Tradition and Modernity," in *Forms of Modern British Fiction*, ed. Alan Warren Friedman (Austin: University of Texas Press, 1975), pp. 133–163.
4. Jane Marcus, another contributor to the present volume, disputes that Woolf was an exponent of "modernism," i.e., a member of that illustrious company of Eliot, Joyce, and Pound. In a review of Avrom Fleishman's *Virginia Woolf: A Critical Reading*, she turned against the author's insistence on placing Woolf among modernism's classical writers. "When those saints come marching in," wrote Marcus, "she will not want to be part of their number"; "Putting Her in Her Place: New Approaches to Virginia Woolf," *Virginia Woolf Miscellany*, no. 4 (Fall, 1975).

the work of a writer who produced the most artful lyrical prose
of our time.

II

   Whatever its origins or avowed purpose, the "revolutionary"
reappraisal of Virginia Woolf, particularly in the United States,
has yielded a rich harvest. This volume brings together a variety
of voices, occasionally blending in harmony but more often
clashing as counterpoints. Many of the contributions reflect a
sense of that new language which has superseded the language of
fiction. In others, Woolf's language is viewed as privileged, and
her insight is seen as governed first by aesthetic and only then
by social perception. We can see evidence of a cultural gap,
created by different outlooks and generations. Yet in each essay
the writer also implies the opposite of what he or she asserts:
those who have written about Woolf's concern with community, about her social and sexual identity, come to assert her formal identity as an artist as well; and the reverse is true of the
critics who begin with an aesthetic perspective. Most striking is
the revelation that Woolf was almost all of the things attributed
to her in these essays: each interpretation and fact is, after all,
supported by ample evidence. She was both elitist and nonelitist,
playful and earthbound, self-conscious about her art and socially
conscious as well. If some critical opinion has become polarized
to reflect her own dialectic, this is precisely the symptom of a
condition that has returned her to the center of the literary stage.
Multivoiced as they are, the critics in this book stress her effectiveness both as an artful creator and as a discoverer of new
dimensions of our moral being. The paradox of the language of
art telescoped with the language of life remains one of the unifying themes in this "chorus of voices."
   The first section of the book presents a bird's eye view, intro-
ducing, with Harvena Richter's grace, the question of imagination as it has informed Woolf's sense of herself both biographi-
cally and artistically. Richter perceives the mental act, in both its
psychological and epistemological manifestations, as having
been caught in the image of the butterfly that constantly recurs
in Woolf's life and work. But for Richter (true to the design of
her *Virginia Woolf: The Inward Voyage*) Woolf's actions are still
located in the domain of fiction: the pageantry of her childhood

and the butterfly hunts she recalled are transcribed as those palpable figures of her imaginative consciousness that remained the core of her art.

Similarly, James Hafley's examination of the roles of Woolf's narrators, implementing the "art of life itself," moves both within and beyond the pattern he set in his book *The Glass Roof*. In that forward-looking work of the fifties Hafley scrutinized critically what was then taken for granted — Woolf's essential formality — but he examined it through her luminous awareness. In the process he took a large step toward a reading of Woolf as that very author of "life itself" whom in this paper he views in a formal context. The same markedly contrasting movement can be observed in Avrom Fleishman's meticulous essay on Woolf's short stories. Known, by self-description, as a formalist reader of Woolf's fiction, Fleishman offers a precise and unusually far-ranging analysis of Woolf's short stories, a form that has received far too little critical attention. But as he pursues the method of his recent book, *Virginia Woolf: A Critical Reading*, into this very special genre, Fleishman reveals the broad vistas that Woolf's sensibility opened up in a form which she had overturned and submitted to an extrinsic use of her own.

If greater diversity among critics appears in the second section — readings of the major novels in chronological sequence — Woolf's fusion of her aesthetic and moral identities furnishes some common ground. Frederick McDowell's detailed account of *The Voyage Out* sets forth both the literary and the psychological conditions for the "new" novel, which propelled itself outward through Woolf's varied use of the *Bildungsroman* toward that cosmic variant of the form, *The Waves*. McDowell's comprehension of death as a counterpoint to time adds a formal dimension to Woolf's most intimate tragic perception. A similar theme is sounded in my own reading of *Jacob's Room* as "fact and fiction," social comedy of manners and tragedy of life, which seeks to establish common, largely temporal, denominators for Woolf's interior journeys.

Time, in its personal and historical dimensions, has traditionally been recognized as one of Woolf's chief concerns. Yet many of the critics in this book have discovered that they have had to regard time in ways that would reflect Woolf's own ambivalence between visions of human mortality and dread of the historical moment. Lucio Ruotolo's exegesis of the "unguarded moment" in *Mrs. Dalloway* discloses the disjunction between the inward projection, in which Woolf's art excels, and its outward engagement. In a pivotal passage he makes clear that her heroine Clarissa is transformed, both in the process of composition and in the novel itself, from "an object of social satire to an existential heroine" through the very process of reshaping time, "whose kaleidoscopic movement continually uproots and transforms inwardness."

This projection of temporality into cosmic and tragic imagery is precisely the path that led Woolf from the experience of life toward her inward formality and thence back to life. James Naremore's analysis of *The Years* is particularly apposite, because it catches just that movement in an exegesis of a book that has been reclaimed as a major document of Woolf's politics. Yet he recognizes that this novel is also a formal event, a *Bildungsroman* on a historical scale which provides its own chronology as the framework for its form. Having dealt with Woolf's idea of self in his critical book *The World Without a Self*, Naremore conceives of *The Years* as yet another broadening of Woolf's self-consciousness and part of the development of human self-awareness in the continuum of modern history. Yet, though his objective is a sharp analysis of the social implications of *The Years*, Naremore ends with the observation that the novel demonstrates a faith "in beauty, simplicity, and peace," despite the ravages of historical time, "despite so much social and sexual frustration." Even in this clearly ideological reading, the two poles, aesthetic and moral, touch.

This apparent contiguity of Woolf's identities, within herself and among critics opposed to one another, can perhaps be most clearly illuminated by setting two seemingly contrasting readings side by side: B. H. Fussell's analysis of comic conventions in *Between the Acts,* and Jane Marcus' interpretation of *Night and Day* as comic opera. Both critics stress parody as a crucial ingredient in these works, which mark the beginning and end of Woolf's career. Both writers marshal compelling evidence to support their readings. Yet, quite apart from the difference between the two novels, the two critics diverge greatly in their manner of applying the notion of parody. Marcus views it as part of a political (feminist and socially conscious) statement: she illuminates *Night and Day* as a parody of Mozart's *Magic Flute,* as a feminist inversion of its freemasonry. Fussell, enlivening a very different book open to English history and its dramatic enactments, views the use of comic devices as part of that tradition which, for her, is both cosmic and formal. "Woolf," notes Fussell, "shared with Joyce his concern to make the personal narrator impersonal by various means of dramatic objectification." Marcus writes, hardly by contrast: "But the search for order which impelled Eliot and Joyce to shape their feelings of despair in ancient mythological structures was the same impulse which drove Virginia Woolf to shape *Night and Day* around the initiation, quest, and journey myths of *The Magic Flute.*" The thrust of each argument points in an opposite direction, but the two critics share a common assumption about Woolf's need for form and order.

In their different ways, the two epistemological and psychological essays in the book also convey simultaneously a sense of Woolf's importance as a feminist and socially conscious model, and the notion of her as the shaping spirit who has remolded these truths. Madeline Moore's description of Woolf's analogous vision of "nature" and "community" transforms *The Waves* into an orchestrated chorus in which, metaphorically, musical motifs have been replaced by the characters' perceptions of themselves and their society. The parallelism between epistemological and social relations, which Moore develops, becomes a formal analogy of imagination as well, since the latter is grounded in a similar dissection of consciousness. And as Maria DiBattista explores the psychoanalytic background of *To the Lighthouse* as a dream work, she adds to the familiar Freudian metaphor a specific context: *A Winter's Tale,* which represents the tradition that provides the spine of Woolf's "formal frame." In this way, DiBattista shows how an in-depth exploration of the impulses that govern the mind both tantalizes and disturbs the reader precisely because these impulses are grounded in formal assumptions.

In many ways, then, the perspectives from which the authors in this book have sought to illuminate different texts of Virginia Woolf converge, even as they diverge ideologically and critically. Formal analyses, like Fleishman's, for example, still respond to an outward pressure, turning to conventions that disclose "life itself." And ideological readings like Marcus' or Naremore's culminate in apprehensions of form with which Woolf's engagement in moral politics is nearly always identified.

One exception to this pattern is the psychobiographical story of Woolf's relationship with Vita Sackville-West, which played such an important part in the genesis of *Orlando*. Jean O. Love, whose *Worlds in Consciousness* developed a "mythopoetic" design for a critical reading of Woolf's novels, has documented the transformation of Woolf's private sexual experimentation into a public literary form. But even here a confluence of artistic and social conventions is discernible. By revealing the interaction between the formal convention of a historical setting and the autobiographical material on which Woolf drew, Love has given us a portrait of her subject as both artist and person.

These contiguities should not be trivialized. They express, as we have seen, the dialectical tensions within Woolf's life and work. In the same way, real differences divide the critics in this volume, even as they seem to touch in several important ways. As authors they are rigidly separate. They are not even consciously engaged as parties to a dialogue or to a convention in debate. Rather, they are like soliloquists on an identical stage, each turned in a different direction. Still, as each explores in depth, from a well-defined critical position, the complexities that haunt Woolf's texts, a composite picture is created. No author is fixed in time and place. The Chorus of Voices from which these divergent interpretations emanate is composed precisely of individual writers who accentuate their differences in nationality, age, sex, and professional commitment. They have explored many different facets of Virginia Woolf: the great writer, the woman, the suffering spirit, the sharp and satiric critical mind, the social critic, the probing philosopher of the psyche. Yet the meaning of these essays resides not only in their evident diversity but also in the profound unity which is their subject. In the English novel, relations between people determine the largest panorama, and it is this panorama in the end which pictures the nature and purpose of Woolf's work.

From this perspective, the following pages will record the revaluation and continuity of Woolf's reputation. They will show, I believe, how her ideological engagement took its meaning from its aesthetic incarnation, and how the aesthetic incarnations were fashioned by her ideological stance. It is in this sense — and in this sense only — that despite their diversity the authors here represented make a common statement that draws fitting outlines of the mind and stature of Virginia Woolf.

2. Hunting the Moth: Virginia Woolf and the Creative Imagination

HARVENA RICHTER

I

At the end of section V of *Jacob's Room,* the narrator assumes the guise of a hawk moth, hovering "at the mouth of the cavern of mystery" (JR, 120). What is Jacob like, the moth — an insect which is a member of the sphinx moth family and should certainly know the answer to all riddles — seems to ask. But the moth can only make up stories. "What remains," the narrator continues, "is mostly a matter of guesswork. Yet over him we hang vibrating" (JR, 121).

Jacob's Room was published in 1922, Virginia Woolf's third novel, and the first in which she introduces a specific symbol to represent the questing creative mind. The symbol is also a feminine one, for the sphinx is mistress of silence, mystery, the underground. Following that novel, over a period which embraces Woolf's finest work, the figure of the moth grows in importance and meaning. It becomes not only an emblem of her writing self, but of the act of imagination; in other words, not only the mind which creates but also the very process of creating. In the novel *The Waves,* which climaxes her concern with this theme, the public and private meanings of the moth symbol are fused, and the writer and her work become one.

The search for the meaning of the moth symbol leads into a labyrinth, a "cavern of mystery" which includes Virginia Woolf's childhood, her illnesses and personal relationships, and her scientific determination to understand her own creative process. *The Waves,* originally titled *The Moths,* is a little-explored section of the cavern. But as the thread of the moth symbol is followed, certain areas of the novel spring into light. This essay will attempt to hunt the sources of the symbol, trace its development through Woolf's writing, and show how the original vision of moths flying through a window turned into a book which deals, on one level, with the creative imagination. Finally, it will explain the connection between Rhoda, the "beautiful single moth" who metamorphoses into a girl, and Virginia Woolf herself.

Perhaps the best introduction to the complexity of the moth image occurs in Virginia Woolf's essay "Reading," which was begun about the time she started *Jacob's Room*. In the center of that essay — one which concerns the relation of both the writer and the reader to their own pasts, as well as to the literary work itself — there is a brilliant description of hunting moths.[1] It seems at first to have no relation to the essay. The narrator, the young Virginia Stephen, shuts the book she is reading on the Elizabethans. Grown-ups come in from the tennis court; the "swift grey moths of the dusk" come out; and a group of young people, armed with lantern, poison jar, and butterfly nets, go into the woods. As they leave the road for the forest, the narrator remarks that "it was the last strip of reality . . . off which we stepped into the gloom of the unknown."[2] The reader has the sense of entering some strange underworld in which everything is seen with heightened emotion and the vivid perception with which Orlando, in the later novel, glimpses the world "as if she had a microscope stuck to her eye" (O, 320). The light of the lantern alters the forest; everything looks different from by day. As the reader experiences its depths — the insects moving through the grass like "creatures crawling on the floor of the sea,"[3] the lantern flashing this way and that in the magic circle, the moths, lured by pieces of flannel soaked in sugar and rum, quivering their wings in ecstasy as they drink up the sweetness, and the final appearance of the great moth, the crimson underwing — the reader realizes that it is not only the forest, it is his own imagination. Even further, it is the mind of the writer,

---

1. The date 1919 appears in the essay as if set down at the moment of writing (*The Captain's Deathbed*). See *Collected Essays* (London: Hogarth Press, 1966), II, 26.
2. Ibid., p. 22.   3. Ibid., p. 23.

searching to pin down words and ideas that flit in the dark places of the brain — " 'the silver-grey flickering moth-wing quiver of words,' " as they are described in *The Waves*.

A third level of meaning hovers ominously at the edge of the scene. The great moth with the scarlet underwing is captured, subjected to the poison pot, imprisoned in glass. He composes himself "with folded wings." At the moment of death, a "volley of shot" rings out; it is a tree, fallen in the forest.[4] The reader is aware that there has been a subtle change, a shift in focus from the hunter to the hunted, to the great moth itself, a victim in its search for sweetness and for light. There seems no rational explanation for "the little shock" the reader feels, the "queer uneasy moment" when the moth is taken and the tree falls. As T. S. Eliot has said of Hamlet's grief, the emotion is in excess of the fact. Several pages later, after a discussion of Sir Thomas Browne and his exploration of the soul, "the microcosm of my own frame," as he puts it, the narrator comments on the "importance of knowing one's author." "Somewhere, everywhere, now hidden, now apparent in whatever is written down is the form of a human being."[5] Somewhere in the essay, Virginia Woolf is trying to say, is the presence of herself. She is not simply the young girl reading the Elizabethans or Sir Thomas, not only the grown writer searching in the forest of the unconscious; she is the crimson underwing.

If we search for the origin of the moth symbol, we can find it, at least in part, in the many butterfly- and moth-hunting expeditions which Quentin Bell, in his biography of Virginia Woolf, describes the Stephen children as taking until they were quite grown.[6] Although perhaps dramatized for the essay, the reminiscence seems genuine. However, it is doubtful that the young Virginia Stephen would have felt the symbolic relationship between the death of the moth and the fall of the tree. Something intervened between the years of hunting moths and the writing of the essay, something which made the synchronicity of the two events significant to her. For the young Virginia, the moth hunt must have embodied a sense of exploration, excitement, penetration into the unknown. For Virginia Woolf, writing in 1919, it

4. Ibid., p. 25.   5. Ibid., pp. 28–29.
6. Quentin Bell, *Virginia Woolf: A Biography* (New York: Harcourt Brace Jovanovich, 1972), I, 33–34.

involved a sense of being pursued, being destroyed by unknown and hostile forces.

One thing that intervened was a series of five mental break-downs between 1895 and 1920–1922 when *Jacob's Room* was written. Another, perhaps closely related, was the death of her brother Thoby. There are three novels in which the tragic aspect of the moth occurs, and in all three it is connected with her grief over Thoby's death. The first is *The Voyage Out*, in which Rachel, the heroine, dies from typhoid fever as did Thoby. The moth appears in the center of the book soon after Rachel and Terence have discovered they were in love — a love which is doomed — and later, in a nearly duplicate image, at the end of the book after Rachel dies.[7]

The Voyage Out may have been an attempt by the then Virginia Stephen to accommodate herself to the reality of her brother's death. Virginia is Rachel, but also the dying Thoby. In the jungle scene, which foreshadows the dreamy deep-sea atmosphere of the night forest in "Reading," crimson and black butterflies circle near the lovers, and one is reminded of the crimson underwing.

In *Jacob's Room,* the death of the moth and the fall of the tree are linked directly with Jacob. Jacob collects *lepidoptera;* at least eleven varieties of butterflies and four of moths are mentioned in the novel, including the death's-head moth. Another is a mysterious moth which Jacob discovers at midnight in the forest and cannot accurately identify in Morris' book on moths. That same night "the tree had fallen," sounding like "a volley of pistol shots." A brief reprise of the longer scene in the essay is given, together with a mention of the red underwing which, however, "flashed and had gone" and Jacob never saw it again. In the following chapter the images of the death of the tree and the volley of pistol shots recur, a sound echoed just before Jacob dies (JR, 32, 33, 49, 300). Jacob, it should be noted, travels to Greece, where Thoby had contracted the fatal typhoid. But unlike Thoby, Jacob Flanders is killed in World War I and is ironically "collected," like one of the specimens in his butterfly box, in

---

7. ". . . a large moth which shot from light to light . . . causing several young women to raise their hands nervously and exclaim, 'Someone ought to kill it!' " (VO, 183). "A young woman put down her needlework and exclaimed, 'Poor creature! It would be kinder to kill it' " (VO, 370).

Flanders Field, where so many perfect specimens of young manhood were gathered.[8]

In *The Waves,* in which the unseen character Percival is modeled after Thoby, a similar image occurs. Rhoda, who loves him, feels after his death that " 'an axe has split a tree to the core' " (W, 162). The image of the death of the tree, refined and synthesized over the years, suggests both Percival's death and the grief which Rhoda feels, an axe which "splits" the core of her being.

There is another possible source for the moth symbol, one which again lies at the heart of Virginia Woolf's childhood. It is her sister Vanessa, whose name signifies a genus of butterfly. That Virginia Woolf knew this is obvious from the number of butterflies mentioned in her works which belong to the tribe Vanessidi. They include red admirals, tortoiseshells, commas, the peacock butterfly, and one which must have seemed particularly to belong to Vanessa, who was an artist: *Vanessa cardui,* the painted lady.[9] Although the relationship between the sisters was unusually affectionate, Quentin Bell notes a touch of rivalry. Virginia, for example, competed with Vanessa to the extent of having a desk made where she could stand erect to write as Vanessa did at her easel to paint.[10] If Vanessa had a butterfly of her own, as it were, it should not be surprising that Virginia would then adopt the image of the butterfly's nocturnal sibling, the moth.

It had been decided quite early between them that Virginia would be a writer, Vanessa a painter.[11] In other words, Virginia would be concerned with what went on in the dark forest of the imagination, Vanessa with light, color, and shape. In the early novels especially, certain men and women characters tend to come under either the moth or butterfly rubric. Katharine Hilbery in *Night and Day,* Rachel of *The Voyage Out,* and Rhoda of *The Waves* closely resemble their author and are moth or night

---

8. "The battleships ray out over the North Sea . . . With equal nonchalance a dozen young men in the prime of life descend with *composed* faces into the depths of the sea; and there impassively . . . suffocate *uncomplainingly* together" (JR, 265, italics mine here and below). Compare with the crimson underwing who "*composed* himself . . . with folded wings" or the small day-moth in the essay "The Death of the Moth," who "now lay most decently and *uncomplainingly composed*"; *Collected Essays,* I, 361.

9. E. B. Ford, *Butterflies* (London: Collins, 1945), p. 76.

10. Bell, *Virginia Woolf,* I, 22–23, 73.

11. Ibid., p. 23.

people, connected to intuition and darkness. Characters associated with light, such as Jacob, Ralph Denham of *Night and Day,* and Lily Briscoe and Mr. Ramsay in *To the Lighthouse,* are butterfly or day people, concerned with the search for knowledge and outward form. Lily Briscoe, the painter, who like Vanessa was absorbed in light and color, twice expresses her vision of color as the "light of a butterfly's wing" (L, 75, 255). As Virginia Woolf's work develops, the concern with the outer or butterfly aspect of art drops away and a concentration on questions of inward form and the creative imagination becomes apparent.

II

So far, certain sources for the moth symbol have been suggested which have their genesis in Virginia Woolf's childhood. But the allusion has been mainly to outer events. There were also the inner happenings: " 'the presence of those enemies who change, but who are always there; the forces we fight against,' " to quote Bernard (W, 240).

A symbol for oneself is not arbitrarily chosen. It appears to rise spontaneously from some deep inner necessity, as images arise in dreams, and it tends to change or develop as the needs of the self change. After *Jacob's Room* and the essay "Reading," the moth symbol appears to lie quiescent. Then, as Woolf is finishing *To the Lighthouse,* she refers in her diary to "tapping my antennae in the air vaguely" before getting down to work each morning. Twenty-five days later her diary records "an impulse behind another book," one which would, several years later, become *The Moths* or *The Waves.* [12]

An undated entry just before the "antennae" note may reveal a possible cause for the surfacing of the moth symbol: it tells of experiencing "a whole nervous breakdown in miniature." But the connection between her illness (one of " 'those forces we fight against' "), the moth symbol, and her writing is not given until September 10, 1929, when she looks back on the long illness which followed the completion of *Mrs. Dalloway* five years before:

> These curious intervals in life — I've had many — are the most fruitful
> artistically — one becomes fertilised — think of my madness at

12. *A Writer's Diary* (New York: Harcourt, Brace, 1954). Entries dated Sept. 3,
    5, and 30, 1926, pp. 98, 100; Apr. 29, 1930, p. 155.

Hogarth — and all the little illnesses — that before I wrote the *Light-house* for instance. Six weeks in bed now would make a masterpiece of *Moths.*

In February of the following year, 1930, the connection be-tween illness and the "chrysalis stage" of the moth is made:

Once or twice I have felt that odd whirr of wings in the head, which comes when I am ill so often . . . If I could stay in bed another fortnight . . . I believe I should see the whole of *The Waves* . . . I believe these illnesses are in my case — how shall I express it? — partly mystical. Something happens in my mind. It refuses to go on regis-tering impressions. It shuts itself up. It becomes chrysalis. I lie quite torpid, often with acute physical pain . . . Then suddenly something springs . . . Two nights ago . . . I felt the spring . . . and all the doors opening; and this is I believe the moth shaking its wings in me. I then begin to make up my story whatever it is.

In the essay "On Being Ill" — published in the same year, 1930, by Hogarth Press — a similar image appears of a creature with wings rising out of bodily pain, followed by a reference to a sedative as "that mighty Prince with the moths' eyes and feath-ered feet."[13] With these might be placed a sentence from *Orlando* which occurs just before Orlando is delivered of her child: " . . . sleep, sleep . . . water of dimness inscrutable, and there, folded, shrouded, like a mummy, like a *moth,* prone let us lie on the sand at the bottom of sleep" (O,295, italics mine).

Illness, the unconscious, dreams, the waters of sleep — taken together they suggest the period of gestation necessary for the birth of an idea, the waiting time during which the concept develops in the waters of the unconscious. With Virginia Woolf's dramatization of this period as the chrysalis stage, the final synthesis of the moth symbol is complete. What began as a persona or mask of her own difficult artistic self has widened into a symbol representing the cycle of the creative imagination: conception, gestation, birth. Or, in metaphorical terms, the creative trinity of larva, chrysalis, and winged moth.

This widening of the symbol into what might be called a re-productive cycle implies certain things about the creative imag-ination: that it is not merely an isolated process occurring within the mind but one bound up with natural biological rhythms, alternating cycles of energy and fatigue, differing body tempera-

13. *Essays,* IV, 194–195.

tures (Mrs. Woolf had long periods of fever while writing), states of physical and mental hiatus which have their meaning even as does the dormant period for a seed.

In *The Waves* a good deal of attention is given to this aspect of the imagination, a procreative and re-creative element common to all living things which, in the last analysis, is mystical rather than scientific. Mrs. Woolf continually used the term "mystical" in her diary when speaking about both her illness and the projected novel (that is, *The Moths* will be a "mystical eyeless book . . . if I write *The Moths* I must come to terms with these mystical feelings").[14] Two major themes in the novel are related to this "mystical" sense. One is the archetypal pattern of death and rebirth or resurrection, carried out in the many mythical allusions to the vegetation gods of the ancient Middle East, and imaged in the moth cycle with the womb or tomb of the chrysalis and the ascended moth. A second theme is the eternal struggle of the mind to bring ïdeas to light, just as the moth reaches toward the flame. The yearning of the six friends for Percival (who represents a mystical sense of consciousness or light); the many references to the tearing of the veils; Bernard's search for words or phrases to reveal the reality of things — all are variations of the striving of the creative mind to express itself.

III

The years over which the moth symbol became synthesized are those, significantly, in which Virginia Woolf's works concerned with the creative imagination were written. The first glimpse of *The Waves* came, as mentioned earlier, while she was finishing *To the Lighthouse,* which deals with the need for the creative feminine element within the artistic mind. At that time, sensing an idea about to surface, Mrs. Woolf wrote that she wanted to watch "how the idea at first occurs. I want to trace my own process" — in other words, watch her mind as it is making up a book. Some eight months later (June 18, 1927) images are set down for a possible opening for this book, which she calls *The Moths:* a man and a woman, night, "the arrival of the bright moths," and the woman letting in "the last great moth."

---

14. *A Writer's Diary,* Nov. 7, 1928, p. 134.

Two years later there appears to be little progress; the diary gives much the same image: "a current of moths," a woman opening a window and letting in a "beautiful single moth."[15] But in the meantime Virginia Woolf had written *Orlando* and *A Room of One's Own,* both of which deal with the creative feminine imagination. And the image of the moth has kept haunting Mrs. Woolf's diary. She speaks of her mind as "the most capricious of insects — flitting, fluttering." She refers to "some nervous fibre, or fanlike membrane in my species" which records sensory impressions. When, she finally asks, will she begin *The Moths*? "Not until I am pressed into it by those insects themselves."[16] It is not until the symbol is complete toward the end of 1929 that, after several false starts on the novel, she is somehow free to write. Interestingly, at this time the waves — which, like the moths, suggest the unconscious and creativity — take over the book. The title changes. And the moths retreat into the background.

But they have not entirely disappeared, they have merely changed shape. The current of moths, "flying strongly this way," has become the motion of the "phantom waves," as they are at first called. And of those moths, six have remained to become the characters of the novel.

Briefly, *The Waves* is the story of these six characters, carried out in nine sections that go from the dawning of consciousness to death. The events of their lives are interior rather than exterior and belong more to the dark forest than to the lantern which goes exploring. The lantern itself to which the six are attracted is an unseen character, Percival — the mystical seventh — around whom the friends hover like moths about a flame. He is a transfiguring element, and as such unifies the six friends, three men and three women, who appear to represent different aspects of a single androgynous being.[17] They also suggest various facets of

15. We might stop for a moment and see what, in terms of the creative imagination, this means. A man and a woman: the two sexes in the mind necessary for the creative act (cf. *A Room of One's Own*); night: the unconscious; the bright moths: creative ideas; the woman letting in the "beautiful single moth": Mrs. Woolf herself and the concept of a book; the open window: the mind open to reality and the imagination.

16. *A Writer's Diary,* Feb. 18, 1928, p. 121; Aug. 12, 1928, p. 128; Sept. 22, 1928, p. 131. See also Feb. 11, 1928, pp. 120–121; Nov. 7, 1928, pp. 132–135.

17. See my *Virginia Woolf: The Inward Voyage* (Princeton: Princeton University Press, 1970), pp. 120–121 and appendix.

the imagination, its diverse processes, its conscious and unconscious areas. Passing through stages of mental development,
Bernard, Neville and Louis, Susan, Jinny, and Rhoda illustrate
collectively the struggle of idea from conception to birth. Seen in
Jungian terms, they may be said to symbolize the individuation
of the creative self.

Of these six friends whose soliloquies make up the novel, two
represent conscious aspects of creativity, four unconscious; thus
two-thirds of the creative process is placed in the "under-mind,"
as Mrs. Woolf called it in "The Leaning Tower," or in her diary
referred to as "the deep water of my own thoughts navigating
the underworld."[18] Bernard and Neville belong in the conscious
realm, though not exclusively so. Bernard, the phrase-maker, is
involved with words that " 'bubble up,' " indicating their origin
in those deep waters. Neville, in love with Percival, is clarity,
one of the properties of light; he expresses the ordering power of
the imagination. Louis, the Australian, who symbolically comes
from the continent "down under," is the male counterpart of the
feminine unconscious. His roots go down; he sees women
" 'carrying red pitchers to the Nile.' " (W, 66, 95). Thus he is the
sense of history and time from which the creative imagination
draws images, as he himself draws from those deep levels of the
Nile whose rising and falling waters figure in the fertility myths.

The three women are involved mainly in nonconscious aspects of the creative imagination. Jinny is sexual force, her
" 'imagination is the bodies' " (W, 128). She creates on the sensory and motor level and is associated with fire, energy, and
especially dance, the last being an analogy of the act of creation.[19] She does not dream. Susan is the earth mother who
croons "sleep." Her nurturing qualities are shown in the way she
is " 'spun to a fine thread round the cradle, wrapping in a cocoon
made of my own blood the delicate limbs of my baby.' " (W,
171). She nets over the strawberry beds, stitches " 'the pears and
the plums into white bags to keep them safe.' " She may be
called the gestation or chrysalis period of the creative cycle. As
such, she loves Bernard, whose emblems of bee, seed, and grain
link him to the fertilizing force. The emblem of the dove (the
Holy Spirit) belongs to them both.

18. *Essays,* II, 166; *A Writer's Diary,* June 27, 1925, p. 78.
19. J. E. Cirlot, *A Dictionary of Symbols* (New York Philosophical Library, 1962),
p. 73.

It is Rhoda, whose " 'shoulder-blades meet across her back like the wings of a small butterfly,' " (W, 22) and whose movement is always described in terms of flight, who is the "beautiful single moth" of the diary notes. Her body " 'lets the light through' "; her " 'spine is soft like wax near the flame of the candle.' " A girl in a white dress who cries to a star, " 'Consume me,' " she flutters against a background of dark like a white moth against the night forest. With her echoing " 'I dream, I dream,' " her eyes like " 'pale flowers to which moths come in the evening,' " she is related to the Egyptian Isis, goddess of the moon.[20] Water and moonlight are associated with her, and the swallow sacred to Isis; she sees " 'pools on the other side of the world reflecting marble columns' " — " 'dark pools' " in which " 'the swallow dipped her wings.' " Her emblems are the tree, cavern, and fountain; her leitmotif " 'the nymph of the fountain always wet.' " Thus she is the dreaming imagination as well as the psychic springs of creativity to which Mrs. Woolf refers in her diary.[21] She and Louis, of time and the Nile, are conspirators, but she is closest to Percival. The tone of her elegy upon his death in section V is somehow the narrating tone of the novel, the endless feminine mourner, the prophetic invisible chorus.[22]

For Rhoda has " 'no face.' " The reader sees her always from the back (traditionally her unconscious), gazing toward the other side of the world, as if Virginia Woolf, who admitted her close connection with this character, did not wish to reveal herself and hid in Rhoda's " 'clumsy . . . ill-fitting body.' "[23] Rhoda is the unstable element in the imagination: her mind leaves her body; solid objects fall apart, distorting her perceptual world. Totally of the mind, the physical is repugnant to her; she leaves Louis, with whom she is having an affair, and finally kills herself. Ber-

---

20. The opening sentence of the first ms. notebook of *The Waves* (New York Public Library, Berg Collection) is: "An enormous moth had settled on the bare plaster wall. As the wings quivered, the purple crescent in the dark border made a mysterious hieroglyph, always dissolving." The crescent is the young moon, symbol of Isis. The "mysterious hieroglyph," an attempt at communication, is related to the hawk moth at the cavern of mystery.
21. "After 6 weeks influenza my mind throws up no matutinal fountains" (*A Writer's Diary*, Feb. 18, 1922, p. 45). "I have been for the last six weeks rather a bucket than a fountain" (*A Writer's Diary*, March 22, 1928, p. 122). Note also Mrs. Ramsay as fountain.
22. In a small notebook Woolf kept while writing *The Waves*, which can be seen in the Berg Collection, she wrote: "Rhoda has the entirely visionary or ideal sorrow."
23. *A Writer's Diary*, March 17, 1930, p. 153; also May 28, 1929, pp. 139–140.

nard, speaking of her death, could " 'feel the rush of the wind of her flight as she leapt.' " In several ways she is related to Septimus Smith, the schizophrenic sufferer in *Mrs. Dalloway* whom Virginia Woolf admitted patterning after herself and who also leaps to his death.[24]

The problem of writing about oneself, even by "distancing," as Woolf did through the character of Septimus, is evident in the difficulty she had with the mad scenes in *Mrs. Dalloway*. The difficulty seemed to recur with *The Waves*, whose notebooks appeared to her at times like "a lunatic's dream."[25] If one looks at Rachel, the unconscious suicide of *The Voyage Out*, then at Septimus (whose hawklike image is related to the hawk moth), then at Rhoda, one sees a serial depiction of her destructive double which comes progressively closer to, and finally merges with, her own theriomorphic symbol.[26] In *The Waves*, Rhoda's mental deterioration is shown when the six friends meet, in late middle age, at Hampton Court — mirroring perhaps the author's own fear, as she approached fifty, of being engulfed by mental illness.

Although Rhoda appears as the lone surviving moth of the early version, other characters have clinging to them shreds of the original image. Bernard, in the final chapter, sees himself as " 'a little stout, grey, rubbed on the thorax.' " Memories of friends who are part of himself flit through his mind " 'like moths' wings' " or send him " 'dashing like a moth from candle to candle' " (W, 242, 268, 293).

Two aspects of the moth survive in Louis, one connected with the laughter of imagination and fantasy glimpsed in " 'his laughing eye, his wild eye' " (W, 92). This meaning is suggested by the curious passage in the preceding novel *Orlando*, in which the moths say, "Laughter, Laughter!" and breathe "wild nonsense" in listening ears when they come at evening (0, 271). The second aspect of the moth connected with Louis is concerned with the mythic imagination, a sense he shares with Rhoda and which is illustrated in the dinner for Percival when he and Rhoda see the

24. Both Rhoda and Septimus are sexually cold, exhibit perceptual distortion, fear falling into gulfs of fire, tend toward dehumanization (i.e., Rhoda hears voices "like trees creaking in the forest"). See also my *Virginia Woolf*, p. 88.
25. *A Writer's Diary*, final entry of 1929 (Rodmell — Boxing Day), p. 147.
26. The images of the hawk and the sun, used with Septimus, suggest the Daedalus/Icarus legend which mythicizes the artist and his soaring flights of imagination. Icarus flying near the sun is parallel to the moth attracted by the light.

celebration in terms of the mystic meal observed in the rites of Attis. Louis describes the other diners as having " 'become nocturnal, rapt. Their eyes are like moth's wings moving so quickly that they do not seem to move at all' " (W, 140). This level of the imagination — seeing mythically — seems to draw on archetypes of the collective unconscious, on mental processes of transformation and time manipulation.

Another attachment of Louis to this mythic level appears in the nightmare image of anxiety which haunts him long after his childhood: the sound of the beast's foot *stamping* on the beach. The beach, the no-man's area between land and water, may be analogous to the state of consciousness between waking and sleeping. Although the beast is identified on the following page as an " 'elephant with its foot chained' " (W, 10), perhaps a symbol of racial memory forcibly separated from its source, there is another more ancient image from Teutonic mythology which hovers around it, the nightmare figure cited by Jacob Grimm as the *Stempe*, or stamper, which tramples children to death. The movement of stamping or treading is traditionally connected with nightmares, and Jung notes the word's supposed derivation from the Old English *mara*, or "ogress, incubus, demon."[27] Whatever the private source of Louis' nightmare image, it appears obscurely linked to what might be termed certain perils of the imagination. Virginia Woolf in her diary (September 5, 1925) mentions her life as "hag-ridden . . . by my own queer, difficult, nervous system." A similar fear of the dangers of the creative unconscious is reflected in Faust's dread of going to the realm of the Mothers, the guardians of forms and images in the "cavernous deep" — a place reached only by the act of *stamping*.[28]

Even closer than Louis to the world of nightmares is his conspirator Rhoda, who comes at midnight to his attic rooms (as dreams come to the mind), who rides the darkness as do the nightmare and hawk moth. " 'I sink down on the black plumes

---

27. Jung also notes that in the Czech language the word *mura* stands for both nightmare and hawk moth, so called because they come in the darkness; C. G. Jung, *Symbols of Transformation: An Analysis of the Prelude to a Case of Schizophrenia*, trans. R. F. C. Hull (New York: Harper, 1962), I, 249–250.

28. Mephistopheles to Faust: "Bear down with might and main: Stamping you sink, by stamping rise again"; Johann Wolfgang von Goethe, *Faust*, pt. 2, act 1, "Dark Gallery," lines 6303–6304, trans. Philip Wayne, ed. E. V. Rieu (Baltimore: Penguin, 1962), p. 79.

of sleep; its thick wings are pressed to my eyes. Travelling
through darkness I see the stretched flower-beds' " (W, 27) — the
same gardens where earlier in the chapter Bernard, Jinny,
Neville, and Susan (but not Louis and Rhoda) have been skim-
ming their butterfly nets. Always feeling pursued, by people, by
nightmares, by unknown fears, Rhoda can be seen, together
with Louis, as involved in the darker, myth-haunted precincts of
the imagination.[29]

As to the association of the moth with the remaining characters, the chrysalis has been connected with Susan, and one of the
first things Susan notices as a child is " 'a caterpillar . . . curled
in a green ring' " (W, 9). Percival is remembered by Bernard
from their schooldays " 'burrowing' " in his blanket " 'like some
vast cocoon' " (W, 84). Neville spins thoughts into a cocoon of
meaning.[30] The relation of Jinny to the moth image had always
eluded me, save for the fact that her affairs are consummated at
night — " 'night traversed by wandering moths' " — just as the
creative mind, which contains both the masculine and the feminine, "celebrates its nuptials in darkness," as Virginia Woolf
writes in A Room of One's Own.[31] The most puzzling part was that
the name Jinny is a diminutive of Virginia; no character in The
Waves is less like her author. It was not until the section on the
essay "Reading" was studied that the relationship became clear.

Crimson is Jinny's main color. Operating at night, signaling
with a " 'moth-coloured scarf,' " she is the restless search of the
feminine imagination to find union in darkness (that is, union
with the masculine element of the mind), to take pleasure from
the moment as the moth lights in ecstasy on the sugared flannel.
In section IV of The Waves Jinny says: " 'My body goes before
me, like a lantern down a dark lane, bringing one thing after
another out of darkness into a ring of light' " (W, 129), a description reminiscent of the moth-hunters in the forest. If Rhoda
metamorphosed from the "beautiful single moth," so did Jinny
from the crimson underwing with which Virginia Woolf iden-

---

29. The small Waves notebook suggested dreams for both Rhoda and Louis.
30. "This room to me seems central . . . outside lines twist and intersect, but
   round us, wrapping us about . . . Thus we spin round us infinitely fine
   filaments." Compare with what she says of Henry James's characters, who
   "live in a cocoon, spun from the finest shades of meaning"; "Phases of
   Fiction," Essays, II, 81.
31. A Room of One's Own (New York: Harcourt, Brace and World, 1929 [paper-
   back edition]), p. 108.

tified herself in the earlier essay. Jinny is the joyful eye, the necessary sensory link with the world of objects which furnish images to thought. And being the crimson *under*wing, she suggests that hidden aspect of the unconscious or "under-mind" which comes into play only in flights of imagination.

Still another aspect of Jinny connects her to the crimson underwing, and coincidentally to the fall of the tree. She represents sacrifice. The act of the harlot or Magdalen is traditionally sacrificial, an earthly parallel of Christ's self-sacrifice on a tree (or Attis' sacrifice beneath it). The giving of the body is an act of love, like creation; and creation is not possible without sacrifice. The ancients sacrificed people, then animals, to insure the fruitfulness of their fields — and Jinny refers to herself as " 'Little animal that I am.' " The mother, as Susan makes clear, gives her blood and body to her unborn child. Virginia Woolf experienced illness and pain during the creation of her work; after each novel was published she suffered a breakdown, which can be likened to postpartum depression.

Curiously, after *The Waves* the moth image disappears from Virginia Woolf's writing. Perhaps the sacrifice of the moth was necessary to the creation of the work. But the death of the symbol so closely related to herself signaled the beginning of her decline as a writer.

To sum up the meaning of the moth, it is not merely a symbol of the creative process; it is both the imagination and what it feeds upon — fears and anxieties, emotional relationships, pains and joys — that piece of sugar-and-rum-soaked flannel. In an allegorical sense, it is the moth brought back from the forest who "composed himself" within the glass "with folded wings": it is the *completed work.*[32] So the moth symbol includes not only the subjective cycle of creation but its object, the work of art. It is probably not accidental that the verb to *compose* also means to create a musical or literary work, as well as to set type. And having founded the Hogarth Press with her husband Leonard, Virginia Woolf was especially familiar with that latter extension of the creative process.

The moth, then, like other symbols in Virginia Woolf's writing, assumed many roles. For her, it was the means by which she managed to wring survival out of disaster. For the reader, it is a

---

32. Can we not follow the allegory further and see in the "folded wings" the image of a book, open at the center?

way of suggesting the very motion of creativity, the stirring of
ideas as they rise into consciousness, the sense of sudden discovery as the mind's lantern peers into dark areas of the forest and
glimpses objects of creation never seen before. In a more general
manner, the moth embodies the continuous struggle of the mind
to bring form out of chaos: the universal and often desperate
condition of the artist. In Virginia Woolf's essay "The Death of
the Moth," a simple account is given of that struggle to formulate and understand in the figure of a small day-moth which
battles out its life against a windowpane. An "insignificant little
creature," it is nevertheless a "bead of life," a "vital light,"
heroic in its role. When one remembers that the mind for Virginia Woolf was the room, the window, and the moth, asking
for more light (as did Goethe on his deathbed), one can feel the
power of the image which was not only to aid its author but to
open, for the reader, a window on the creative mind.

3. Virginia Woolf's Narrators and the Art of "Life Itself"

JAMES HAFLEY

"The story ends without any point to it."
— "Mr. Bennett and Mrs. Brown"

I

"The String Quartet," the fifth story in *Monday or Tuesday* (1921), seems arranged to contrast life and art in consciousness. For the most part, life is perceived as unanswered question and fragmented dialogue; art as sustained description and narratory assertion; life as public, social; art as private, individual; life as reported occurrence; art as created experience; life as discordant and uncertain; art as achieving an order that is finally so sure and delimiting that after a time the relative chaos of life is welcomed as a release from it. The blocks of the story that represent life concern time before and after the performance of a string quartet (said by one listener to be early Mozart) and in between its four movements; the blocks representative of art are fanciful reactions by the speaker to each movement of the quartet as it is being performed.

I suspect that no musicologist would approve of this story's narrator, whose voice clearly enough suggests the quartet's musical structure (allegro, andante in A-B-A pattern, minuet with trio, and final allegro) but responds to that structure in extramusical equivalents of the most shamelessly impressionistic type.[1]

---

1. The opening allegro begins with "Flourish, spring, burgeon, burst!" The andante starts "The melancholy river bears us on." The minuet starts "These are the lovers on the grass," and its trio section starts "But to return," oddly enough. There is, extraordinarily for Mozart (but this isn't definitely

But for anyone interested in literary imagery the impressions are instructive indeed. The first movement evokes imagery that starts as centrifugal and that emphasizes, therefore, a deep inward source of the values suggested by the music heard: imagery of flowering, fountain, depth, proceeds then recedes inward to a vital center of raw energy, maelstrom, from which fresh spiral and ascent emerge. The second movement evokes similar imagery but adds to it that of fusion of opposites in unifying patterns. In the minuet, the element of story harmonizes the oppositions as dance, courtship, and assault, culminating in ascent, contentment, escape. The fourth movement combines story and scene toward and to a celestial city, paradoxically airy and solidly, even stolidly, enduring. But as confusion and chaos — flux and change — yield to a heavenly fixity and absolute order, the speaker seeks and welcomes a fall back to desert and chaos. The idea of a happy fall from perfection that is death-in-life to imperfection that is potentiality and freedom — this idea is underscored as the speaker greets an applewoman (Eve) beneath the starry night. The union of lovers sharply contrasts with the last lines of the story, in which two persons go their separate ways. The ideal, exactly as in Keats's Grecian urn ode, has penalties that come to throw the advantages of the flawed into attractive relief.

But chaos and confusion — life and living that are outside the created world of aesthetic experience — have an order and pattern of their own in this story. For all the questioning, the fragmentation, interruption, and discontinuity that characterize the dialogue, it is organized, for it is constantly concerned with encounter, location, and identification: namings. The motif of direction controls the story from beginning to end; and I think one's sense of this story comes after a time to be more and more a sense of analogous systems rather than, as at first, of order versus disorder. Composition, that is to say, characterizes both the life and the art dramatized here; and the speaker's voice is ultimately not only a common denominator but the creator of both worlds as one world wholly imagined, whether as life or art. The opening of the story, with its conditionals and its directed addressee(s), shows the narrator as instant arranger, of dubiety as well as of certainty.

Mozart), no break between minuet and the final allegro signaled by those impossible horns. The pattern is reasonably but not exactly that of sonata. Interruptions between movements would coincide with the fairly customary pauses for retuning of instruments then. But it is surely not probable that an audience would congregate this way to hear only one quartet before dispersal.

One thing this means is that the story exhibits not a contrast between objective and subjective modes but a mode 99.44 percent subjective: what is presented as overheard has been chosen, sorted, aligned in its supposed variety so as to provide a texture as seamless as that of the private fantasies of the listener to music. Everything is music; everything is, has been, selected in private caprice. And surely this is an odd string quartet: with horns in the last movement. Mozart himself has been thoroughly invented: the indoor pause from an outdoor journey is played finally according to the narrator's eccentric rules, and the story could as easily be titled "Three String Quartets": Mozart's, the narrator's version of Mozart's, and the narrator's version of the other-than-Mozart that is life.

II

The aesthetic questions raised by this story — of relationships between ideality and reality, art and life, subjective and objective, personal and societal, expression and imitation, fiction and fact — are all familiar to Virginia Woolf's readers. And though I have arranged them here as sets of dualities, romantic oppositions, nevertheless her solutions to them seem to me far more empirical than romantic. Just as in "The String Quartet" what are apparently two realities are seen at last to be one, to have the same creator working in the same way — selectively out of personal norms and needs — so elsewhere, I suggest, Virginia Woolf's narrators are creators and not reporters real or supposed; they do not tell the stories as much as the stories tell *them;* it is they who are the central drama, the central fiction. The abstract and general, the objective and true, are in this art to be located only in the concrete, specific, subjective, and invented. Reality is invention, and God only knows any meaning other than what each voice invents in its own image and likeness. The relationship between abstract vocabulary in Virginia Woolf's essays and the narrative voices of her fictions comes to be one of identity.

Surely everyone who has read the questioning essay "Modern Fiction" and the answering one "Mr. Bennett and Mrs. Brown" has noticed and been to some degree puzzled (in my case unnerved) by her habits of abstract or generalizing vocabulary there. What is this materialism in "Modern Fiction"? What in this essay does the word "spiritual" mean? What is the human spirit and what is this notion of spirit versus body? What is the "soul" of fiction? What is "the true — the enduring," and what "life or spirit, truth or reality," what "the vision in our minds" and "brain or spirit," what clod of clay versus purity of inspiration, what life "itself" as a spirit "varying, unknown and uncircumscribed"? What, perhaps most insistently, is the difference between the self embracing and the self creating what is outside and beyond it? Is this some world of dualistic *débat,* of conventional Christian oppositions or Zoroastrian pairings? What's this kind of vocabulary doing here?

Now in "Mr. Bennett and Mrs. Brown" — written before "Modern Fiction" but providing some answers to its questions — the same kind of word occurs: "create," "telling the truth," "vision" versus "convention" versus "reality," "spirit" and "life itself." But here we have solutions to my questions too: we have a narrator telling a story; and the narrator is also "Virginia Woolf herself" and the story a "true" one. The narrator has a penchant for accounting for fellow passengers (a paradigmatic situation in Virginia Woolf's art), and accounts for an old lady by two strategies: naming and plotting. "I will call" the elderly lady "Mrs. Brown." Naming and plotting are of course together in that act. The narrator says that Mrs. Brown (real, true, objective name unknown) is, in English literature, insight and eternal human nature changing only on the surface; that, more broadly, Mrs. Brown is an impression, a figment of imagination, and "the spirit we live by, life itself." There, in that predication, we have it. Spirit and life itself are creations; each human being is, or can be, a creator; the absolute is relative — or, if indeed absolute, is unknown, perhaps unknowable, and apparently not worth the price of admission. Telling the truth is telling about oneself alone; is telling a version based on brief observation. Meaning, or better "significance," must therefore be largely reflexive: an elderly lady and a man exist, but they are Mrs. Brown and Mr. Smith only as Virginia Woolf has named them; in fact, they are almost certainly not Mrs. Brown and Mr. Smith, and in fact their story is almost certainly not her version. Yet the stimulus, casual and passing, vanishing, provokes a version that becomes not a means but an end in itself: the models vanish, the story does not function in any relation to them, the story remains "complete in itself . . . self-contained." The world of art, then, is autonomous; it can be related to that outside art only as a created, imagined version, and not as a means for general understanding or universal regulating; it is expressive alternative and not mimetic reproduction.

Consider Ruskin in *Modern Painters:*

> High art . . . consists neither in altering, nor in improving nature; but in seeking throughout nature for "whatsoever things are lovely, and whatsoever things are pure"; in loving these, in displaying to the utmost of the painter's power such loveliness as is in them, and directing the thoughts of others to them by winning art, or gentle emphasis. . . . Art . . . is great in exact proportion to the love of beauty shown by the painter, provided that love of beauty forfeit no atom of truth.[2]

Not so for the creator of Mrs. Brown. For her, as for Wallace Stevens, the imagination alone is reality in a world that is imagined; the story is never about its subject but always, unavoidably, completely (or so nearly completely that exception is trivial) about its teller. Embracing what is beyond it, the self is and can only be creating: the gesture of embracing, the centripetal action toward an arbitrary center, is the gesture of narrative in Virginia Woolf. Abstraction and generalization are conditions of infinitely various individuality. Life may be art, but art is not about life; art is about art.

III

The eight fictions of *Monday or Tuesday* are of widely varying merit and degree of success; yet each is an experiment in narrative voice, a working toward the achievement of narrators that are dramatic insofar as they are creating, created embodiments of value. And it seems clear that in each of these fictions the narrative voice, as language, is of central importance, above and beyond all importance of conventional subject or story. It would be difficult to find another collection — so brief, so similar in theme — in which so many varieties of narrative voice are to be discovered, from third-person impersonal to third-person personal to first-person personal to first-person impersonal. The one kind of variety in this volume is variety of narrator, and in a serious way the stories are different from one another only because their narrators are. To look at a few of them is to see how supposed dualities are empirically one.

---

2. John Ruskin, *Modern Painters* (London: George Allen, 1901), III, 38.

The first of the stories, "A Haunted House," was appropriately chosen by Leonard Woolf, when he collected Virginia's
short fictions, to provide the title for that volume. In every way
it is an apt introduction to her art. And it is much more interesting, I think, than a story like "The String Quartet" because it
presents fusion and confusion — the conventional antipodes of
art and life — as clearly one from the start, rather than as apparently layered. It is a barrage of confusing, fusing pronouns, and
their pattern (seeming lack of pattern) is perhaps what first
strikes any reader of its opening: from "you" to "they" to "she"
to "he" to "we" to "them"; and then from a "you" with a
different understood referent to an "us" similarly alien — so that
haunters and live inhabitants of the house are confused into
fusion — to "one," to "I" and "my." And the ending pattern,
from "their" to "my" to "I" to "your," is similar. Location in
time and space are blurred by this ruse to dramatize the past/
present, dead/alive, house/inhabitants blurrings that create the
felt meaning of experience for the first-person narrator. Repetitions in threes enact the systole and diastole of heartbeat (displaced to be that of the house itself) without the illusion of
doubles that patterns in twos would create. Pulse and light, the
dominant images of the piece, are cunningly related in its final
sentence to insist on the interior, subjective location of all supposed transcendence, as the pronouns at the same time are cir-
cumscribed to an absolute with "the": "The light in the heart"
(HH, 5). This is the solution of Coleridge's "Dejection" ode,
but here it is triumphant rather than terrified in its relativity: the
absolute as relative, the one light that accounts for beam and
burning, moonbeam and lamp beam, that effects the union of
"their light" and "my eyes," located in the emotive-sensuous
center of the heart and in no objective realm whatsoever — in no
outside not created by the narrator.

Reality as imagination, as creation, is not more effectively
shown here than by the statements that "we see no lady spread
her ghostly cloak. His hands shield the lantern" (HH, 4). Language alone can at once assert and deny; can produce the lady in
"we see no lady"; and it works its handsome miracle here of
realizing the ideal — the light in the *heart* — and at the same time
keeping it truly ideal and beyond realization — the *light* in the
heart. Buried treasure found but buried still. The enactment is of
language — narrative voice — as a complete world where miracle

occurs and yet is mundane: when Lily Briscoe later on sees Mrs. Ramsay risen from the dead we have the apotheosis of this sacred trick. There, as here, everything is of this world; but because this world is a creation of the narrator and cannot exist without that voice (has no extra-aesthetic meaning at all), miracle is event, mystery is located in history; it is a world of Joyce's green roses and of Virginia Woolf's own roses blooming in December.[3] Not only death is overcome. This is the world, too, of Wallace Stevens, where the rabbit is king of the ghosts; or one where real ghosts, not cats, are kings of rabbits. Here, in "A Haunted House," the snails of "The Mark on the Wall" and "Kew Gardens" do not exist even as points of departure; the spiral action of "The String Quartet" is accomplished without a taking leave of or a reentering the atmosphere of the homely quotidian; the fiction is here quite self-contained, complete, as Virginia Woolf had hoped for art to be in "Mr. Bennett and Mrs. Brown." The treasure is buried in the narrator's sensibility and has its beginning and ending there, beneath the surface rather than behind the glass. Time and place are created here from nothing and thereby escaped; it is, in Hardy's phrase, a moment of vision.

I must add that although the narratory voice is "I," and one of "us," it is neither masculine nor feminine. And this is the androgynous mind. How far from the mark is a reading that identifies (often without thought) the "I" with a woman because a woman wrote the story — or worse with Virginia Woolf because she wrote it — and then looks to the voice's subject as to some revelatory "idea" or "message." Nothing, evidently — not even the explicitly male narrator of *Orlando* — will stop this kind of misreading; and yet of course the only unfortunate consequence is that to read this way is to lose (I surely believe) all the art — to end up with one snail on one wall. A literary escargot.

In "The Mark on the Wall" the snail is just as important as the elderly lady before she has been named Mrs. Brown; and she herself has been no more important in her own right than it is. Actually, the narrative voice here is not at all dissimilar to Vir-

---

3. My dreadful rhyme of mystery/history is a vulgarization of language from the first sentence of the "Prelude" to *Middlemarch*. With its conflict between the demonstrable and the vital unknowable, as well as its omniscient-fallible point of view, that great novel is obviously a source for the technical developments of Conrad (in *Victory*, for example) and Virginia Woolf.

ginia Woolf's own in her essay, and I have seen this fiction classed as an essay — understandably, because this is one of the fictions in which the creation is shown happening, as would occur if a magician slowed down or demonstrated even his preparations before and dispositions after the show.

The art of the inconclusive — of process as result (or result as stalemate) and indeterminacy as freedom — is clearly enough demonstrated by "The Mark on the Wall," an exercise in an associationistic tradition with which Wordsworth and Keats (especially the early Keats) have made us familiar. Fancy resists fixity (in the language of the first paragraph), the cycles of "perpetual waste and repair" that circumscribe linear time resist history and rule, and "nothing is proved, nothing is known." Precisely as in Stevens' poems like "The Poems of Our Climate" (a superb analogue for Virginia Woolf's method), the condition of imperfection is the ideal because it permits that license to re-create, to assemble but then disassemble and thus be allowed to reassemble, that alone exercises one's humanity. And in the fluidity of potential arrangement — the human climate — this narrator can shuck as well any arbitrary and delimiting sense of self, even to such an extent as permits vicarious experience of the cold feel of insects' feet upon a tree. This venture toward otherness ("some existence other than ours") can be attempted only if the perceiver resists prolonged formulation (static self-consciousness, or consciousness of a static idea of self) precisely as does the world perceived. The last pages of this story dramatize an assimilation of apparent otherness that is characterized by depth imagery similar to that in "The String Quartet." And, as in that story, the moment of vision ends with the intrusion of genuine otherness: another person and dialogue.

The external identity of the mark on the wall comes almost as afterthought, so unimportant is it to the internalization that has got merely a start from it. The snail as snail has no more vitality than do Jacob Flanders' shoes. For the story has focused on all sight as insight, each vision as an envisioning — a sense of things as aesthetically practicable as it is logically, or ethically, impossible.

Nonetheless, it bears noting that this art, whatever self-completion it may possess, is after all not free from relatedness, or even application, to our lives outside it. It is not escape or what is called mere decoration; it is not, I think, by anyone's standards irresponsible: inconclusiveness is freedom to come to the richly various and contradictory conclusions that are works of art, but it is also suggestive of a way life can be (and in this art clearly ought to be); and its very divorcement from lasting commitment to one version of experience has implications not inconsistent with, let us say, the political convictions of Virginia Woolf as we know them to have been.

"An Unwritten Novel," more nearly than any other fiction in *Monday or Tuesday,* deals with the narratory condition used as exemplum in "Mr. Bennett and Mrs. Brown." Here history is the *Times* and soon dispensed with, mystery, the forever dissoluble that remains absolutely insoluble, is much more about life than the newspaper as "my great reservoir of life." Both motive and reason are creations of fancy, and as subject to change as all else seeing or seen. "Whether you did, or what you did, I don't mind; it's not the thing I want" (HH, 13). Interruption is vitality — the allowance for change of course — and it is the concrete and multiple that sap, in due time, all credibility from the abstract One. Again as in "The String Quartet," the happily temporary state of perfect certainty is celebrated as a moment of lone ascent in sight of "the moon and immortality," but then "I drop to the turf" (HH, 15). There are "the vista and the vision," a fleeting sense of "the blue blot at the end of the avenue" (HH, 19) (compare Mallarmé's *azur* but also Stevens' "palm at the end of the mind") — meaning both plentiful and fugitive — but then comes what's paradoxically even more satisfying: the holocaust, the inevitable moving on and consequent demolition of the world that has been created, the catastrophe that alone makes possible the awareness of novelty, freshness, and the unknown with which this story ends. The last sentence once more offers the image of embracement, assimilation to and thereby discovery of a center of self; and "adorable world" exhibits the same empirical identification of noumenon with phenomena as did "the light in the heart."

The story is clearly "about" its narrator, whose voice literally creates itself out of the mere raw material that is its subject. That the voice of "Kew Gardens," say, is third-person ought not to obscure the fact that there too that voice, that narrator, is the true subject of the story. Toward the very end:

> It seemed as if all gross and heavy bodies had sunk down in the heat motionless and lay huddled upon the ground, but their voices went wavering from them as if they were flames lolling from the thick waxen bodies of candles. Voices. Yes, voices. Wordless voices, break-

ing the silence suddenly with such depth of contentment, such passion of desire, or, in the voices of children, such freshness of surprise;
breaking the silence? But there was no silence . . . (HH, 35– 36)[4]

Not what is described, but the act of describing, carries the
tune here, bears the watching. "Voices. Yes, voices," and
"breaking the silence?" emphasize the nature of the drama: a
discovery of self by self through the means of what is perceived
but in the creative act of how it is perceived. This is exactly the
narrative style of *The Years*. The speaker in "An Unwritten
Novel" had asked, "But when the self speaks to the self, who is
speaking?" (HH, 19). In these stories Virginia Woolf is always
answering that question, defining, characterizing, dramatizing the
"who" that is speaking. Hence the speech to the self so often
emphasized by the interruptive device of another speaking to the
self, or others speaking and overheard so as to break in upon
dialogues of the mind with itself, or soliloquy of the self for itself.
In the purest instances of this method — as in most of the later
novels — the sex of the narrator is insignificant: the voice is androgynous, a linguistic structure at once directly human and
human only by inference, achieving the same double existence as
the seen woman unseen in "A Haunted House." In *The Waves* it
may be said to project itself into both masculine and feminine
sexuality from the unified center of its basic speech structures:
"said Neville," "said Rhoda," and so forth — which, with the
italicized passages, most directly figure it as itself.

But before making some concluding suggestions about narrators in the novels, I do want to call attention to one additional
story, not from *Monday or Tuesday:* "The Shooting Party," composed in 1937.[5] Here again Virginia Woolf uses her familiar device: one passenger's creation of another (and hence of self) during a journey, with only the germ of a few externals to provoke
the most lavish conclusions. But what is of special delight in this
elegant story is its comic emphasis of the seam: of the threshold
between a decently probable fiction made by the narrator in the

4. I have treated the story "Moments of Being" in somewhat similar fashion in
an essay called "On One of Virginia Woolf's Short Stories," *Modern Fiction
Studies,* II, 12– 16.
5. Virginia Woolf advised the starting novelist to try writing the opening pages
of a novel, then look to see how apparently effortlessly Jane Austen had done
so; the opening pages of *Emma* remain a stunning example of complex narratory voice, blended almost imperceptibly from time to time with created
interior monologue, distant otherwise and fully knowing.

attempt to explain an experience, and one that is outrageously improbable and brings about its own downfall by its utter departure from any common sense (shared awareness). Here also the primary inventor is a "she" other than the narrator, so that both "she" and the narrator indulge in this drama of imagination as explanation. In fact, the conventional distance between narrator and "she" (inventing person) in this story is, amusingly, blurred out — narrator becoming character as invention builds — precisely as is the distance between the "she" and the other woman in the train who prompts her flight of fancy into the profound reality, sublime profound, of the tale told. The woman with a suitcase monogrammed M. M. (Memento Mori?) is assimilated into the "she," and the "she" in turn becomes one with the narrator. Everything converges to a center of the Omniscient Temporary.

All is enormously detailed, substantial, beyond a reasonable doubt, as the two purely imaginary ladies, Miss Antonia and Miss Rashleigh, have their luncheon and then sip their sherry afterward. The "she" and the narrator positively disappear, so convincing, so probable, is the eidetic narrative they are creating from a few "obvious" inferences at the outset. In fact, the scene of the invention can shift from indoors to out, from the ladies to the shooting party, as effortlessly as in a piece of Victorian realism. It is as if "she" and the narrator have given assurance that they can be trusted, that their version is *the* version, the truth, the very truth. There is only one suggestion of the fabulous — a mermaid carved in plaster on the fireplace — to remind anyone who notices it that this is a fish story.

What first disturbs the pattern of probability is that after luncheon, with butler and footman in attendance, Miss Antonia takes the carcass of the pheasant on which the ladies have fed and tosses it under the table to the pet spaniel. This incident thumbs its nose at common sense not only for the greasy mess it would inflict but also because cooked pheasant bones would be almost certain death to the dog. And when Miss Antonia raises her sherry glass to the mermaid in a toast, the fabric of probability starts rapidly coming unraveled — which is to say that the narratory imagination goes overboard. Through an "immensely high door" the hunters enter fresh from the hunt; that is strongly to be doubted. Their three big hunting dogs enter as well; and that dogs fresh, or rather gamey, from the hunt would be allowed not only indoors but into a room of antiques and of

antique ladies is beyond the pale. Finally, "the floor of the gallery
waved like a wind-lashed forest with the tails and backs of the
great questing hounds. They snuffed the table. They pawed the
cloth. Then, with a wild neighing whimper, they flung themselves upon the little yellow spaniel who was gnawing the carcass under the table." Calamity ensues, the hounds mauling the
spaniel, the Squire with his taws lashing not only a vase of
flowers but even Miss Rashleigh, who accidentally with her
stick brings the Rashleigh shield crashing down from over the
fireplace and falls, herself, into the ashes. "Under the mermaid,
under the spears, she lay buried" (HH, 66). A tree falls outside;
King Edward in a silver frame falls too. Down once more from
the sighted Heaven to the emberbed of plain facts. The scene is
again the train; the woman whose looks and accoutrements have
brought forth this elaborate fancy now seems ghostly, only her
visionary eyes agleam (for she may have her vision, too). Her
eyes are like will-o'-the-wisps moving over the graves in a
cemetery. "An absurd idea? Mere fancy! Yet after all, since there
is nothing that does not leave some residue, and memory is a
light that dances in the mind when the reality is buried, why
should not the eyes there, gleaming, moving, be the ghost of a
family, of an age, of a civilization dancing over the grave?" (HH,
67). But in the last paragraph those eyes are closed, buried like
the reality, buried like poor Miss Rashleigh under the mermaid.

IV

   The art of Virginia Woolf is a celebration of the unfinished, of
contradiction, of the discontinuous, of something always breaking in and nothing ever getting settled (save during the moments
in and out of time so prized but so pernicious if unchanged).
The paradox of fallible omniscience suits that art perfectly, is
that art, and Monday or Tuesday is a collection of tales telling
tellers, versions inventing their inventors, "every one of those
impressions . . . the impression of the individual in his isolation, each mind keeping as a solitary prisoner its own dream of a
world . . . a single moment, gone while we try to apprehend
it," in the well-known and beautiful words of Walter Pater,
whose "Conclusion" to The Renaissance can be called upon to
gloss Virginia Woolf's fictions.[6] I mention it now mainly be-

---

6. Studies in the History of the Renaissance (London: Macmillan, 1873), p. 209.

cause it is a reminder that the sense of life to be seen in the fictions I've been mentioning can evoke poignant, frightened, and despairing responses as well as exhilarated, optimistic, or comic ones. Virginia Woolf's novels move from the former to the latter sorts of response, albeit never ignoring what could be called the dark side of freedom between acts or the pathos of the mutability of acts themselves, however splendid.

The Voyage Out is a novel of the inconclusive that stresses, almost completely, that dark side and pathos in a study of relativity of perspective, relationship, and proportion. Its very first sentence establishes a personalized-omniscient narrator who significantly advises going on a journey single file rather than abreast; but the rest of its first paragraph, in Dickensian mode, stresses farcical rather than tragic results of eccentricity. The proportion there is not that of the novel as a whole, goodness knows, and the narrative voice itself changes like a boy's at puberty into a pretty steady bass accompanying Rachel's sadly arrested voyage. This narrator doesn't seem to me at all to foretell those of *Monday or Tuesday* or the novels after *Jacob's Room;* and it is in what gets said, not in how it gets said, that we have to settle for "meaning" here, by and large. When Hewet asks "do we really love each other, or do we, on the other hand, live in a state of perpetual uncertainty, knowing nothing, leaping from moment to moment as from world to world?" (VO, 127), he may be describing what goes on in the later fiction, but this novel is telling rather than showing it, in a mode perfectly accomplished and respectable, but not Virginia Woolf's own. Again, sometimes the sense of things gets illustrated, as at the dance: "There was a pause, and then the music started again, the eddies whirled, the couples circled round in them, until there was a crash, and the circles were broken up into separate bits" (VO, 152). But the novel as a total structure doesn't work that way because its narrator changes only in the clumsy fashion I mentioned earlier, and is otherwise consistent and logical in the same manner as the realities here. Hewet says again, "We're all in the dark. We try to find out, but can you imagine anything more ludicrous than one person's opinion of another person?" (VO, 218). Hewet speaks those sentences; the narrator of *Jacob's Room* of course enacts them.

And meanwhile *The Voyage Out* takes an increasingly dim view of inconclusiveness; at one point it seems to Helen Ambrose "that a moment's respite was allowed, a moment's make-believe, and then again the profound and reasonless law asserted itself, moulding them all to its liking, making and destroying" (VO, 263). This is a passage that bears some looking at, not least because Helen's sense of things here dominates the last part of the novel. The passage plays with the counters of the later stories and novels, but plays a different game. "Make-believe" is less than factual reality here, and the wish is less for freedom than for reasonable law, I should think. So, although the tension between creativity and fixity is established, the values of each are quite other than they will be. In *Jacob's Room*, for all its ending also with the untimely death of an attractive human being, the sequence has changed from the "making and destroying" of *The Voyage Out* to the much more typical "perpetual waste and repair" of "The Mark on the Wall." In *Mrs. Dalloway*, Septimus Warren Smith has great weight as embodying Helen's sense of things, but so also has Clarissa to the contrary. And in *The Waves* Rhoda's suicide puts in controlled perspective this dark side of freedom: her, and Percival's, life-to-death progress is easily diminished by the death-to-life one.

But if *Jacob's Room* does enact a predominantly affirmative sense of the inconclusive, and if its narrator performs accordingly and is of central dramatic importance and interest, nevertheless she does so in the first person and therefore in a limited, a pointedly limited, manner. What Virginia Woolf needed was a third-person narrator, derived from the traditional omniscient voices of English realism and nonetheless signifying and dramatizing perception and narration as creation rather than transmission. That is the narrator of "Kew Gardens" or *The Years* — speaking beyond the confines of personality and yet speaking for a self alone — and that is the ideal correlative for this sense of experience. Among other things, it is a voice famous for disappearing into the other voices it creates, especially in interior monologue, in a sublime refinement of Jane Austen's *Emma*, too well known to need illustration here. It is triumphant in *Mrs. Dalloway* or *To the Lighthouse;* I find it most subtle in *The Years;* many others do in *To the Lighthouse* or *Between the Acts*. Whatever one's preference, it is mostly for a third-person voice: the first-person voice of *Orlando,* so similar a device to that of *Jacob's Room,* seems limited indeed, a minor voice, compared to the others.

What Virginia Woolf did was dramatize the truth of the relative and mutable with the authority of the absolute unquestionable. There is only one consciousness defining itself by inventing order out of the chaotic suggestiveness of a maze of facts; but that one consciousness seems to be consciousness itself. It is contradiction as diction, and diction as benediction. Least optimistic, but not less than beneficent in its created acceptance of how things are, is *The Years,* surely inspired by Hardy's great lyric "During Wind and Rain"; the raindrop and tombstone, the raindrop as plow. In that lyric both work together in contradiction as do the butterfly's wing and bolts of iron in Lily Briscoe's theory of art in *To the Lighthouse,* and as does the fragile indomitable narratory voice Virginia Woolf came to fashion for her world, where, as Jinny says in *The Waves,* "beauty must be broken daily to remain beautiful" (W, 174). To fix the moment, not to abide by any fixed moment, to accept death as the mother of beauty, is the supreme creative performance in this world, and the narrators are the supreme performers — yes, of notes toward a supreme fiction.

"And this, Lily thought, taking the green paint on her brush, this making up scenes about them, is what we call 'knowing' people, 'thinking' of them, 'being fond' of them! Not a word of it was true; she had made it up; but it was what she knew them by all the same" (L, 258). And more significantly, by far, it is what she herself is known by, given the power of art to produce her created version of the Rayleys for all the world to read; and the narrator is known by created versions of Lily and the others. That narratory voice seems itself to be a lighthouse; and so it is — like the Lighthouse, an arbitrary measure and integration, a self to provide the centering that only each self can, but to the reader a Lighthouse as Mrs. Ramsay is for Lily and her painting, a veritable center as Shakespeare's sonnet is for Mrs. Ramsay in her turn, or Scott's novel for Mr. Ramsay. "As if" — to use that phrase repeated overwhelmingly on the last pages of *To the Lighthouse* — as if a center, as if a line in the empty center, as if conclusive: "it is finished."

4. Forms of the Woolfian Short Story

AVROM FLEISHMAN

I

The standard format for a critical study of Virginia Woolf is a series of chapters on the nine longer fictions, one after the other. The body of her short stories tends to be neglected, except as quarry for the longer works. In contributing to a revaluation of Woolf's achievement, I take up these stories to discover what is distinctive in their form and, by implication, their innovations within the development of the modern short story.[1] In this way, one can approach an estimate not merely of their contributory role in the Woolf canon but of their signal importance in the fictional tradition.

The place of Woolf's stories within the modern history of the genre deserves a study of its own. It is readily apparent that she was among the bearers of the Chekhovian example into England. The Hogarth Press published Chekhov's *Notebooks* in a translation by S. S. Koteliansky and Leonard Woolf in 1921 and earlier had published Katherine Mansfield's first breakthrough in story form, "Prelude" (1918). Current practitioners, like the English writer Elizabeth Taylor, attest that the Chekhov-Mansfield type represents a distinct strain in an age-old genre, and critics of Mansfield have from the first seen Woolf engaged in a similar, and mutually influential, enterprise.[2] Though it has

1. Among the few treatments of the innovative methods of Woolf's stories is: Erika Dölle, *Experiment und Tradition in der Prosa Virginia Woolfs* (Munich, 1971); see chap. 2 on the varieties of narrative perspective in the stories.
2. See Miss Taylor's remarks in "The International Symposium of the Short Story," pt. 3, *Kenyon Review,* XXXI (1969), 469–473. For Woolf's role, see

long been recognized that the stories of Chekhov, Joyce, Mansfield, Woolf, and a variable number of later writers constitute a loose but inevitable grouping, this critical commonplace remains untested by the usual historical and stylistic evidence for generic developments.

While an inductive definition of the story type must await the still unwritten critical history of the genre, some chronological notes may help to place Woolf's achievement in perspective.[3] The inception date can be taken as 1904, at least for English literature: in the year of Chekhov's death, Joyce sketched his theory of "epiphany" in *Stephen Hero,* then began writing the stories that were to make up *Dubliners.*[4] The last and greatest of these, "The Dead," was not completed until 1907, and the collection remained unpublished until 1914, but between those dates Mansfield was engaged in bringing out her earliest stories (1909) and her first volume (1911). It was only after the war had begun, however, that she wrote "Prelude," her first distinctively modern story. Here the decisive date is 1916, for in that year of Mansfield's initial version ("The Aloe"), Constance Garnett's comprehensive translation of Chekhov's tales began to appear, to ever wider dissemination.

It is not clear that one, both, or neither of these books inspired Virginia Woolf, but in the next year she published her first story, "The Mark on the Wall" (along with one by Leonard Woolf, in *Two Stories*), scarcely distinguishable from an imaginative essay, yet bearing the traits of the fictions to come. In the succeeding

---

Sylvia Berkman, *Katherine Mansfield: A Critical Study* (New Haven: Yale University Press, 1951 [1935], pp. 168–169, 175–176.

3. The closest approximation presently is: T. O. Beachcroft, *The Modest Art: A Survey of the Short Story in English* (New York: Oxford University Press, 1968). The line of stories in the Chekhov tradition has been well studied in Eileen Baldeshwiler, "The Lyric Short Story: The Sketch of a History," *Studies in Short Fiction,* VI (1969), 443–453.

4. A number of qualifications must quickly be made: there is no question of direct influence, Joyce having denied that he read Chekhov before writing *Dubliners* (quoted in Richard Ellmann, *James Joyce* [New York: Oxford University Press, 1959], p. 171); according to Frank O'Connor (*The Lonely Voice: A Study of the Short Story* [Cleveland and New York: World, 1963], pp. 37, 39), Joyce may have been preceded in his use of Irish subjects by George Moore, in *The Untilled Field* (1903); and Joyce had been writing epiphanies since perhaps 1900, according to the editors of his notebooks: Robert Scholes and Richard M. Kain, eds., *The Workshop of Daedalus* (Evanston, Ill,: Northwestern University Press, 1965). Nevertheless, the 1904 date has a significance in the passing of experimental impetus from the Russians to the English and Irish.

years, while Woolf reviewed further Garnett translations of Chekhov, she advanced her own methods and produced her first short masterpiece, "Kew Gardens" (1919).[5] By the twenties, as Mansfield's work established her preeminence in the field (*Bliss*, 1920; *The Garden Party*, 1922), Woolf brought together her first collection, *Monday or Tuesday* (1921). After this, the streams of influence and variegation become too diffuse to trace; among others, Hemingway, Anderson, and A. E. Coppard entered the field with their first story collections (indeed, *Winesburg, Ohio*, dates from 1919). Woolf began a new venture, her Dalloway stories, in 1923, the year of Mansfield's death, but with a view to an integrated form that would have the unity and mass of (and that eventually became) a novel. Although this form — a grouping of short stories in a synthetic but nonsequential fiction — remained unachieved, one can inquire into her smaller forms as independent contributions to the tradition.

II

Given the widespread contemporary "shame of form," it may be necessary to apologize for a formal study of Woolf with Geoffrey Hartman's dictum: "There are many ways to transcend formalism, but the worst is not to study forms."[6] There is no need, at this late date, to justify formalist methods by their utility in seizing the critical object, and a cool draft of formalism should prove bracing in the currently moist atmosphere of Woolf criticism. It is important, moreover, to recall that the emergence of the modern short story is almost synonymous with the *formal* experimentalism of Chekhov, Joyce, and their successors. It requires no formalist predisposition to recognize that form is at a high premium in short fiction, especially in dealing with modern materials. Lukács recognized this desideratum from the outset of his critique of modernism:

5. "Tchehov's Questions," *Times Literary Supplement*, May 16, 1918, p. 231; "The Russian Background," *TLS*, Aug. 14, 1919, p. 435. In these years, Woolf also reviewed collections of stories by Turgenev, Tolstoy, Dostoevsky, Conrad, James, Dreiser, Max Beerbohm, L. P. Jacks, and three lesser Russian writers. Her somewhat barbed statement on Mansfield, "A Terribly Sensitive Mind" (*New York Herald Tribune*, September 18, 1927), did not appear until well after the latter's death, and it reviewed the journals, not the stories.

6. *Beyond Formalism: Literary Essays, 1958–1970* (New Haven: Yale University Press, 1970), p. 56; cf. p. 358.

> In the short story, the narrative form which pin-points the strange-
> ness and ambiguity of life . . . lyricism, must entirely conceal itself
> behind the hard outlines of the event . . . The short story . . . sees
> absurdity in all its undisguised and unadorned nakedness, and the
> exorcising power of this view, without fear or hope, gives it the
> consecration of form; meaninglessness *as meaninglessness* becomes
> form; it becomes eternal because it is affirmed, transcended, and
> redeemed by form.[7]

While Lukács' view of the short story's objectivity may be open
to amendment when applied to Woolf and others, there is no
gainsaying the quest for formal controls in making commonplace events, chance, and meaninglessness available to artistic
"redemption."

If we press critical theory for an account of the process by
which story forms master the unpromising materials of modern
dailiness, we are driven back into philosophic tradition. It is not,
however, necessary to pursue the matter back to Aristotle's
Metaphysics, for George Eliot's "Notes on Form in Art" anticipates, toward the end of one century, the problems of the next.
Since much new-critical formalism is weighted with Cole-
ridgean organicism, it is well to be reminded by Eliot that form
is not only wholeness but uniqueness:

> Form, then, as distinguished from merely massive impression, must
> first depend on the discrimination of wholes & then on the discrimi-
> nation of parts. Fundamentally, form is unlikeness, as is seen in the
> philosophic use of the word Form in distinction from Matter; & in
> consistency with this fundamental meaning, every difference is
> form.[8]

If we bring this point to bear on the special conditions of the
short story, we discover the discriminative rather than the inte-
grative function of form intensely at work. We do not expect

---

7. Georg Lukács, *The Theory of the Novel* . . . trans. Anna Bostock (Cambridge, Mass.: MIT Press, 1971), pp. 51–52.

8. *Essays of George Eliot,* ed. Thomas Pinney (New York: Columbia University
Press, 1963), pp. 432–433; the quotation below is from p. 435. It should be
noted that this manuscript of 1868 goes on to reaffirm the organicist for-
mulas of unity: "But with this fundamental discrimination is born in necessary antithesis the sense of wholeness or unbroken connexion in space and
time . . . And the fullest example of such a whole is the highest example of
Form: in other words, the relation of multiplex interdependent parts to a
whole which is itself in the most varied and therefore the fullest relation to
other wholes . . . The highest Form, then, is the highest organism . . ."

to find multiple connections and a synthesis of particulars in a pervasive unity, although some Joycean stories achieve such integration, but instead a sharply drawn sketch, a highlighted association, a precisely poised relationship. These pictorial terms suggest the effects of modern stories in marking off small areas in the flux of experience and rendering them integral and distinct.

George Eliot's shift of emphasis from unity to differentiation goes hand in hand with an awareness of what may seem to be the very opposite of formal integrity. In pursuing the subject into poetic form, she goes on to offer some strikingly prescient notions of repetition, a subject that has engaged critical attention increasingly of late:

> Poetic Form was not begotten by thinking it out or framing it as a shell which should hold emotional expression, any more than the shell of an animal arises before the living creature; but emotion, by its tendency to repetition, i.e. rhythmic persistence in proportion as diversifying thought is absent, creates a form by the recurrence of its elements in adjustment with certain given conditions of sound, language, action, or environment.

The beginnings of this sentence in well-known doctrines of organic growth and form/content homology should not obscure the novel ideas that ensue. Eliot is framing here a theory of form as repetition and rhythm which deserves more elaboration than she gives it. The sequence of stages in the evolution of form would appear to be: emotion — repeated emotion — recurrent emotion under "given conditions" of language and context — rhythmic persistence of these "given conditions" — form. The movement from repeated emotion to rhythmic language is by way of a transition that Eliot does not name: she must be referring to the articulation of emotion in speech, both as a phonological and as a semantic system ("given conditions of sound, language, action, or environment"). In the latter two terms, however, there is a suggestion that fictional events, "action" and "environment," can become part of the rhythmic articulation. This neglected essay of a Victorian novelist may provide a clue to some of the theoretical cruxes of the modern short story: unity of effect, epiphany, and plotlessness.

Although George Eliot is speaking of poetic form, where the phonological repetitions of prosody are as prominent as the semantic structures, there is much to be gleaned here for a theory of story form. Recent stylistic studies have directed attention to the importance of closure in generating unity, significance, and dramatic effect in the realm of poetry.[9] Much of this technique is unavailable to fiction, lacking as it does not only conventional prosody but also several other formal structures of verse. Yet there are features which short stories and lyric poems will forever share: they are made of relatively small numbers of words, and words can be and are repeated. Stylistics has lately (long after Empson and Wilson Knight) begun the study of "key words," defined by their frequency and thematic prominence, which when repeated toward the end of poems become "summative," that is, resume the course of the theme through the poem, especially by gathering together the sounds of words which have previously conveyed it.[10] The "summative" effect is not restricted to the operations of alliteration and rhyme; repetition of whole words or groups of words can function to tie poems and stories together at the close. When one thinks of the endings of some canonical instances of the latter genre, one recalls not only symbolic objects — like the snow in Joyce's "The Dead," or the aloe and manuka plants of Mansfield's "Prelude" and "At the Bay" — but the reiterated words which mark a dramatic finale and formal completion, as in the conclusion of Joyce's story or of Mansfield's "The Doll's House."

From the inception of critical discussion of the short story, the theory of its form has not moved much beyond Poe's notion of the unity of effect to be realized in a genre of limited means. While problems of subject (plot or no plot?), theme (point or no point?), and narrative (telescoping . . . exposition . . . development) still persist, the question of form has never approached resolution. The usual byway down which this trail leads is epiphany; since the most prominent of modern stories come accompanied by the theory of epiphany, it was inevitable that Joyce's term has been used in lieu of a concept of form. A recent study of epiphany recognizes the laxity of such usage; despite Joyce's emphasis on the suddenness of the epiphanic

9. See Barbara Herrnstein Smith, *Poetic Closure: A Study of How Poems End* (Chicago: University of Chicago Press, 1968).
10. Dell H. Hymes, "Phonological Aspects of Style: Some English Sonnets," *Style in Language,* ed. T. A. Sebeok (Cambridge, Mass.: MIT Press, 1960), pp. 109–131.

moment, "it has been fashionable to speak of one or another of his entire works as 'an' epiphany . . . If an epiphany is 'sudden,' as it is, then works as long as the average short story — and certainly any novel — simply cannot 'be' epiphanies, for they cannot be 'experienced' or apprehended immediately." The story, short or long, is not a single event but a form extended in time and, conceptually, in space as well.[11]

If short stories are not unitary events but extended forms, they involve sequences of phenomena, verbal or representational. Morris Beja's definitions of epiphany are useful in defining story form, for he goes on to discriminate another frequent element of short fiction, the leitmotif. In the epiphany, Beja writes,

> [T]here has to be some such revelation — and it is here that we must beware a common misconception that confuses Joyce's epiphany with the leitmotif, the obsessive image which keeps coming back into the consciousness of a character or into the work as a whole but which at no single time involves any special, sudden illumination.[12]

This apt distinction between a series of repetitions and a salient event unfortunately avoids stating a possible relationship between the two: the epiphany may appear at the end of a sequence, either as a term that stands outside the "obsessive" chain and suddenly emerges to cap it, or as the final and crowning instance of the repetition itself — that is, either a new motif, like the coin of success and betrayal in Joyce's "Two Gallants," or a definitive statement of an established one, as in the protagonist's return to isolation in his "A Painful Case."

In this way, one can better appreciate the repetitiveness that appears so widely in modern literature — witness Pound, Eliot, Faulkner, Proust — but nowhere more strikingly than in the short story. What Frank O'Connor somewhat facetiously calls Hemingway's "elegant repetition" (on the model of "elegant variation") may be only a mannered extension of the repetitive patterns that mark the stories of Joyce, Mansfield, and Woolf.[13]

11. Morris Beja, *Epiphany in the Modern Novel* (Seattle: University of Washington Press, 1971), pp. 73–75.
12. Ibid., p. 75. Beja engages in an ultimately irreconcilable argument with Joseph Frank on literature as a temporal art. Compare *The Widening Gyre: Crisis and Mastery in Modern Literature* (Bloomington: Indiana University Press, 1963), pp. 9–10. See also Sharon Spencer, *Space, Time and Structure in the Modern Novel* (Chicago: University of Chicago Press, 1971).
13. Frank O'Connor, *The Lonely Voice*, p. 159.

In their work, repetition is divested of both its psychic compul-siveness and its ritualistic miming of life rhythms, and can be seen instead as a formal property. Indeed, in fiction considered as narrative, repetition may be of the essence, as theorists of folk tale (Propp) and of epic (Lord) have observed: not simply in keeping the story going (providing cues to the narrator) but in getting to the end of the story—which can be defined as the point at which repetition ceases. Above all, repetition may be a means of discovery: by returning to what begins as a chance remark or shout in the street, the story may find at last the "right" word, or a context or setting for that word, which lifts it out of its mundane origins and establishes it as the articulation of the entire tale.[14]

Two general patterns can be adduced to describe the most frequent sequences of the repetitive process. In one, a series of terms or represented objects, often including repeated ones, is passed through until the clinching or decisive motif or word is found; in this case the discovery marks the end of a *linear* form. Alternatively, an initially given word, phrase or represented ob-ject, thereafter absent or only occasionally presented, is made at the end the summative term for all that has gone before. In this case, a *circular* course is traced, finding its way back to where meaning was latent all along. In the linear form, there is a leap of novelty, an access to something not initially given or known, a sense of freedom and intuitive discovery—which may account for the mystical claims and analogues that have been presented in some descriptions of epiphany. In the circular form, on the other hand, there is a return to the familiar, a ritual of reenactment that can offer assuagement of tension—though it is sometimes ac-companied by a disturbing sense of the uncanny, classically associated with the Freudian account of the *déjà vu*. What is common to both these forms, however, is their closure value: they fulfill the expectation and need of an ending, either as a final term of a series or as the return to a starting point, which supplies the demarcation of a unique fictional work. Addition-ally, both forms create a distinctiveness which has variously been

14. The most remarkable extended study of the function of repetitions—of sounds, for the most part, but ultimately of words—in reinforcing meaning through a story, but also in revealing meaning at the close, is: Margot Peters, "The Phenomenological Structure of James Joyce's 'Araby,'" *Language and Style,* VI (1973), 135–144.

called significance, climax, or epiphany, but which we can recognize as the much discussed (and often found wanting) *point* of
the modern short story. The point in this sense is the period, the
ending, the closure of a story; but a point may be rounded by
circular form, becoming a point of origin to which the story
returns, rather than a sharp stab at a new truth.

The marked ending, pointed or rounded, need not create a
resolution of tension, feeling, or action; indeed, it is consistent
with what has come to be called "open" form. The latter is most
often not a formal but a material openness; the action is projected
into the future, but the language in which it is conveyed may
well have distinctive closure. Such tales as A. E. Coppard's
justly famous "The Higgler" achieve their circular form by returning to the fumbling dialogue of the inept lovers, while their
situation is acknowledged as irrevocably changed from its initial
possibilities (the concluding lines even suggest that the courtship
is to go on in future relations, yet the protagonists' linguistic
failure has been permanently established). Coppard was not
speaking for himself alone when he expressed his need to "know
the solution — if it had that! — before beginning to write." For
story differs from novel perhaps as simply as he claims: the story
writer "has to find the character or characters most likely to
bring it to successful issue," rather than those most likely to
generate extended narratives.[15] So compelling is the impulse toward closure that open endings can be achieved through closing
gestures; a recent, comprehensive study of story forms cites instances in which a problematic open ending ("problematisch-
offener Schluss") is achieved by a lapidary final sentence
("lapidaren letzten Satz").[16]

---

15. "The Higgler," originally published in *Fishmonger's Fiddle* (1925), is included
    in *The Collected Tales of A. E. Coppard* (New York: Alfred A. Knopf, 1948).
    My quotations are from Coppard's autobiography *It's Me, O Lord!*
    . . . (London: Methuen, 1957), pp. 215, 216. A more systematic statement
    of similar propositions is: Boris M. Eichenbaum, "O. Henry and the Theory
    of the Short Story," *Readings in Russian Poetics: Formalist and Structuralist
    Views* (Cambridge, Mass.: MIT Press, 1971), pp. 231–233.
16. Ludwig Rohner, *Theorie der Kurzgeschichte* (Frankturt: Athenäum, 1973), pp.
    247, 249. This remarkable book, in summarizing the results of more than
    twenty-two German monographs and dissertations, proliferates typological
    distinctions beyond the bounds of manageability. Nevertheless, its listings of
    Formtypen (p. 54), beginnings (pp. 141ff), and endings (pp. 246ff) suggest
    the limits of any distinction as simple as that between linear and circu-
    lar form.

III

Virginia Woolf's short stories can be broadly divided into those that are formally linear and those that are formally circular.[17] Another word on terminology here: the adjectives "linear" and "circular" are obviously metaphoric and, just as obviously, spatial. The use of these terms implies no exclusive disposition toward "spatial form" in Woolf: one might just as easily use the terms "progressive" and "returning," though these would emphasize the ongoing temporal flow of the narrative. *Linear* or *progressive* forms are those that start at one place or time or motif or verbal cluster and move through a number of others, arriving at a place, time, motif, or verbal cluster distinct from those with which they begin; while *circular* or *returning* forms are those which begin and end with the same or similar elements.

The earliest writing in *A Haunted House,* the main collection of Woolf's stories, is "The Mark on the Wall." This piece, without action, characterization, or setting, vividly raises questions about the demarcations of Woolfian prose: is it a story, an essay, or a prose poem? As the present analysis does not depend on these generic distinctions, I include "The Mark on the Wall" at least provisionally among the stories. The piece takes the form of a train of speculations on the character of a poorly perceived stimulus, an amorphous mark; this is a sequence of efforts in one direction, toward identifying something which is disclosed at the end of the sequence. This linear process begins at a particular time, "the middle of January in the present year," and moves through various later times at which hypotheses are framed: that the mark "was made by a nail," was not "made by a nail after all," "is not a hole at all," and "may have been caused by some round black substance"; that it is more prominent than a spot, "seems actually to project from the wall," and is perhaps the "head of a gigantic old nail," or alternatively "a rose-leaf, a crack in the wood" (HH, 37–44). Having moved beyond seeing the

---

17. These terms are also applied to Virginia Woolf in Jean Alexander, *The Venture of Form in the Novels of Virginia Woolf* (Port Washington, N.Y.: Kennikat Press, 1974), where "circular" implies a tendency toward totality of vision, while "linear" emphasizes historical vision. Compare the distinction between the "tragedy of life," presented in an epic form of historical narrative, and the "comedy of manners" or the drama of vision in the present tense, in Ralph Freedman's essay in the present volume.

mark as an indentation, then as a flat surface color, to seeing it as
a projection, and after running through a number of more or less
probable projecting objects, the conclusion is reached: "Ah, the
mark on the wall! It was a snail." Those who know and love this
piece will agree that my account of its form leaves out the rich
and humorous meanderings of the prose, in which the narrative
"I" moves from uncertainties and desires ("I wish I could hit
upon a pleasant track of thought") to a declaration of indeterminacy ("No, no, nothing is proved, nothing is known"), and on
to a final set of thoughts which the speaker describes as "wor-
shipping the impersonal world" (HH, 43– 46). It would require
further analysis to determine the form created by the interweaving of these subsidiary tracks, but it should already be clear
that "The Mark on the Wall" is not "free association" but a
controlled linear form.

    Another way of looking at the form of "The Mark on the
Wall" is to see it as the *progressive definition* of a term, by interpretation of an ambiguous sign, the mark. Other Woolf pieces having this linear form are "Solid Objects" and "The New Dress."
"Solid Objects" begins with a similar, undefined visual
stimulus: "The only thing that moved upon the vast semicircle
of the beach was one small black spot." The story does not go on
to examine the spot but instead supplies a series of references for
the pronoun "it," by which that small black spot is designated.
The second sentence reads: "As it came nearer to the ribs and
spine of the stranded pilchard boat, it became apparent from a
certain tenuity in its blackness that this spot possessed four legs;
and moment by moment it became more unmistakable that it
was composed of the persons of two young men." The initial
reference of "it" is thus to human beings, or at least to their
bodies: "nothing was so solid, so living, so hard, red, hirsute
and virile as these two bodies for miles and miles of sea and
sandhill" (HH, 79). After setting out the tale of one protagonist's infatuation with a piece of glass found on the beach,
and his progressive obsession for collecting other *disjecta membra,*
a climax is reached upon his discovery of a "remarkable piece of
iron" to which he (or the teller of the tale) attaches cosmic significance. Seen as a meteorite, "alien to the earth," this object
now becomes the main reference for the pronoun, "it": "It
weighed his pocket down; it weighed the mantelpiece down; it
radiated cold." A final turn in the fate of this pronoun is given at

the denouement, when the second protagonist tries to fathom his friend's obsession, which has caused the loss of his parliamentary career and his withdrawal from society: " 'What was the truth of it, John?' asked Charles suddenly, turning and facing him. 'What made you give it up like that all in a second?' 'I've not given it up,' John replied" (HH, 84, 85). For the man-of-the-world Charles, "it" is simply worldly success, but John clearly has another ideal in mind — though it remains unclear where that value lies. The pronoun thus begins with the "solid" bodily life of two friends, moves on to the metaphysical implications clustered around the solitary being of ordinary objects, and finally comes to rest in a suggestive juxtaposition of worldly and more profound values. Form here is a significant elaboration of the story's initial verbal donnée.

Another story formed as a series of identifications of the pronoun "it" is "The New Dress" — this time with associations closer to the jazz-age sobriquet for sex appeal. The story begins with the frumpy heroine's arrival at Mrs. Dalloway's party and her uneasiness about her new dress: "it was not right . . . No! It was not *right*." The dress is, however, only the first of the protagonist's shortcomings to be designated by "it" in the course of the story: "Everybody knew why she did it — it was from shame, from humiliation." When Mabel tries to play the game of social intercourse, the pronoun reaches a watershed: "Ah, it was tragic, this greed, this clamour of human beings . . . it was tragic, could one have felt it and not merely pretended to feel it." "It," then, is not simply Mabel's dress or her inadequacy, but the entire emotional life in which she fails to participate. And yet, she remembers "divine moments" in her life when she has said to herself " 'This is it. This has happened. This is it!' " At this point of elaboration, a climax is reached: Mabel envisages a future in which "she would become a new person. She would be absolutely transformed . . . and it would be always, day after day, as if she were lying in the sun . . . It would be it!" (HH, 47–56). Articulating this ultimate self-identity, the action concludes as Mabel makes her departure. The form of the story emerges as a progressive widening of the key term from direct reference to the new dress, to a broad indication of possible lifestyles, and on to an even more suggestive association with some integral state when, at the peak, "It would be it."

These prose pieces represent a simple form of linear organization in which a given, often insignificant term becomes a repetitive pattern, and is then subjected to a series of modulations and enhancements — mainly by shifting the context so that the key term enters into new relations and opens up varied possibilities. When the key term is so simple a thing as a mark on a wall or a neutral word like "it," the form of the story is, as it were, a making of something out of nothing — or, as a similar process is described elsewhere in Woolf, a "building it up."

A related group of stories takes a form similar to this gradual expansion or emergent creation, but in such a group there is no single term which moves through a sequence. Instead, a *series* of items is set out, the final item emerging as the key one. The most famous instance of such an organization is the well-known "Kew Gardens," in which eight beings or kinds of being are observed as they saunter through the botanical gardens. First comes the general class: "men and women." There follow a married couple remembering the past; a snail (who appears three times in all); a mystical and somewhat disturbed old man and his younger companion; "two elderly women of the lower middle class," looking for their tea; a young couple, also thinking of tea amid the glow of their romance; a group of aerial beings, including a thrush, butterflies, and an airplane; and finally, the voices. After lulling us with what seems a random and casual series of passers-by, the story reaches a new level of intensity at its final paragraph:

> It seemed as if all gross and heavy bodies had sunk down in the heat motionless and lay huddled upon the ground, but their voices went wavering from them as if they were flames lolling from the thick waxen bodies of candles. Voices. Yes, voices. Wordless voices, breaking the silence suddenly with such depth of contentment, such passion of desire, or, in the voices of children, such freshness of surprise; breaking the silence? But there was no silence; all the time the motor omnibuses were turning their wheels and changing their gear; like a vast nest of Chinese boxes all of wrought steel turning ceaselessly one within another the city murmured; on the top of which the voices cried aloud and the petals of myriads of flowers flashed their colours into the air. (HH, 35– 36)

This crescendo of the repeated word "voices" emerges as the final and triumphant term in the series of elements presented by the story. The voices are, indeed, a chorus of all the beings who have trooped through Kew Gardens, those named and all the others that might have been listed — come at last to expression and united in a common life. It is difficult to distinguish form and content in this beautiful piece; even the simplest description of the form verges on an interpretation of the content, and I must content myself on this occasion with singling out the linear progression by which "Kew Gardens" reaches its heights at the close.

Three other stories follow the "Kew Gardens" form of serial presentation, with a significant final term. "An Unwritten Novel" in some respects resembles "The Mark on the Wall" as a succession of speculations on the identity of an unknown being, in this case an elderly lady sitting in a railway carriage, but it also builds up to a peak by adding one item after another in an imaginative construction of a human identity. This peak is the discovery that the little old lady is not a spinster on her way to visit her brother and sister-in-law, where she will be victimized and unwelcome, but that she is instead the mother of a son who comes graciously to meet her at the station. The movement from novelistic imaginings to the hard kernel of reality is paralleled by the movement of the train which carries the observer and the observed. It begins (presumably) in London, passes Lewes (Virginia Woolf country), and arrives at Eastbourne and a view of the sea: "Grey is the landscape; dim as ashes; the water murmurs and moves. If I fall on my knees, if I go through the ritual, the ancient antics, it's you, unknown figures, you I adore; if I open my arms, it's you I embrace, you I draw to me — adorable world!" (HH, 21). We might consider this an example of *parallel* linear form, in which the spatial sequence and the perceptual sequence move along together to a joint arrival.

"Together and Apart" is a simpler exercise, merely following the course of a conversation in which two middle-aged and typically self-absorbed people try and fail to communicate. The conversation takes the form of a set of variations on the verbal motif "Canterbury," interlaced with other repetitive verbal patterns (like Miss Anning's self-rallying phrase, "On, Stanley, on"). I give only a few of the exchanges: " 'Do you know Canterbury yourself?' Did he know Canterbury! . . . To be asked if he knew Canterbury . . . all had centered in Canterbury . . . 'Yes, I know Canterbury' . . . 'It's odd that you should know Canterbury' " — and so on. This is Virginia Woolf at her satirical best, but the form is perhaps too simple: the party guests come

together, go through their travesty of conversation, and reach a
peak of absurdity in the final line: "whatever they may do, they
can't spoil Canterbury" (HH, 138–142).

The last story I would classify among the linear forms is "The
Man Who Loved His Kind." As in "Together and Apart," a
party conversation leads here to mutual hostility and separation,
but the formal sequence is somewhat different. The movement
of action and language is entirely unremarkable up to the final
page; then, in the last four paragraphs, the phrase from which
the story draws its title is employed four times. Miss O'Keefe
resents Mr. Ellis' penchant for self-congratulation, saying to
herself, "no one in the whole world ought to tell a story to
prove that they loved their kind," and "the Prickett Ellises
would always say how they loved their kind"; then he says, "I
am afraid I am one of those very ordinary people . . . who love
their kind"; and the narrative voice concludes, "these two lovers
of their kind got up, and without a word, parted for ever" (HH,
118–119). There are other linear movements at work, among
them repeated references to the humanitarian anecdotes the interlocutors thrust upon one another, but the story achieves a clear
direction only in the last phase, where the repetition of the key
term signals a height of satirical dismissal.

It will be observed that three of the seven stories described as
linear are of the Mrs. Dalloway's Party group, which has recently
been established as a unit by publication in a separate volume.[18]
The group contains none of the best of Woolf's stories, and some
of them are decidedly sketchy, as is suggested by their having
remained in manuscript; but their appearance as a group gives
rise to reflections on the compositional order of Woolf's stories.
Of the twenty-three pieces published in collected volumes, five
were composed in 1925, making this the year of most intensive
short-story writing in Woolf's career. For the hypothesis that
this intense activity also marked a turning point in her mode of
composition, the following facts can be considered: all of the
seven linear pieces date from 1925 or before, while all but three
of the thirteen stories to be described as circular are of the period

---

18. See Mrs. Dalloway's Party: A Short Story Sequence, ed. Stella McNichol (New
    York: Harcourt Brace Jovanovich, 1973). An eighth story and a fragment
    of a ninth belonging to this group are mentioned in James Hulcoop,
    "McNichol's Mrs. Dalloway: Second Thoughts," Virginia Woolf Miscellany,
    no. 3 (Spring, 1975), p. 3.

1925 and after. (Two others among the latter group are difficult
to date, but Leonard Woolf's Foreword to *A Haunted House*
suggests treating them among the later stories.) There is no
evidence of a concerted change, but only of a gradual shift in
Woolf's characteristic form from the linear to the circular
model.[19]

The simplest kind of circular form is the return at the close of a
story to the prominent use of a significant *word* which has been
introduced at or near the outset. Three stories conform to this
model. "The Duchess and the Jeweller" sums up its opening
account of a posh West End jeweller's career with an extended
metaphor: "Imagine a giant hog in a pasture rich with truffles;
after unearthing this truffle and that, still it smells a bigger, a
blacker truffle under the ground further off. So Oliver [Bacon]
snuffed always in the rich earth of Mayfair another truffle, a
blacker, a bigger further off." After the jeweller is duped by the
duchess and by his own social-climbing, he looks at the fake
pearls he has bought: "This, then, was the truffle he had routed
out of the earth! Rotten at the centre — rotten at the core!" (HH,
96, 102). The note of irony does nothing to enhance the comic
extravagance of the initial use of the metaphor, but it brings off
the conclusion roundly.

Similarly, "Lappin and Lapinova" opens and closes with a
definition of the imposing term "marriage." "They were married," it begins. "The wedding march pealed out" (HH, 68).
After a poignant account of the couple's imaginative personifica-
tion of each other as rabbits, and after the stern rebuke to imagination delivered by their upper-middle-class milieu, the dream
and the relationship come to an abrupt end: "So that was the end
of that marriage" (HH, 78). We have learned nothing significant
about the nature of modern marriage, but the form of the story
has been neatly rounded off.

The third of these word-closed stories is "The Legacy"; as in
many another tale, the title acts as the controlling focus
throughout, but it is mentioned only at the beginning and end.
When a widower discovers his wife's fifteen diary volumes, he

19. In what follows, I omit discussion of the two stories not republished from
Monday or Tuesday, and of "Mrs. Dalloway in Bond Street," since it raises
special problems, being an early draft of the opening of a novel. Briefly, one
can notice that the circular movement of the novel's opening section — from
the protagonist's home and back again — replaces the story's linear movement from home to a set of encounters at a glove shop.

values them as endowing him with something of herself: "So she had left it him, as her legacy. It was the only thing they had not shared when she was alive" (HH, 127). The diaries reveal, of course, that they have failed to share a good deal else, and in particular the passions of love and death aroused by her affair with another man. When the widower discovers all, the concluding paragraph simplifies the matter, perhaps too starkly: "He had received his legacy. She had told him the truth. She had stepped off the kerb to rejoin her lover. She had stepped off the kerb to escape from him" (HH, 135). The only pleasure the reader can take from this oversimplification lies in the neat closure effected by the repetition of the title-word.

A more elaborate use of this simple circular form is evinced in four stories, each of which opens and closes with approximately the same *sentence*. The most obvious instances of this type are the sentences "People should not leave looking-glasses hanging in their rooms" in the story "The Lady in the Looking-Glass," and "Slater's pins have no points" in "Moments of Being." Such stories do not gain their force merely from the repetition of an ironic understatement or a disconcerting irrelevancy. In the former case, the looking-glass is a continuing focus throughout. The action consists mainly of the changes in a room in the course of a day, as recorded by a passive but knowing field of vision, a mirror. Revelation comes when the lady of the house is brought under the mirror's relentless scrutinizing power, and is seen as starkly as the objects of her house: "At once the looking-glass began to pour over her a light that seemed to fix her; that seemed like some acid to bite off the unessential and superficial and to leave only the truth . . . She stood naked in that pitiless light. And there was nothing. Isabella was perfectly empty" (HH, 93). It is at this point, after the addition of a few more scarifying details, that the initial sentence returns to draw the irony out of its broad generalization: "People should not leave looking-glasses hanging in their rooms." It should be noted that the opening sentence of the story continues: ". . . any more than they should leave open cheque books or letters confessing some hideous crime." This does not alter the force of the repetition or the effect of the closure.

In "Moments of Being," the reappearance of the opening sentence in the final paragraph is considerably more complicated than in the story of the mirror. For one thing, the sentence is

repeated in two other forms: once as the epigraph of the story
(with capitals and quotes, as in a motto) and again in the course
of the text, with an altered verb form: "Slater's pins having no
points . . ." This pattern interweaves with a number of others in
a way so complicated as to make this one of the most interesting
of Woolf's stories. One of the patterns is the time scheme, which
begins with present action, introduces a past report on an even
earlier state of affairs (Miss Kingston's information about Julia
Craye's early life), fills out the portrait of Julia with brief images
of her at other times of life — meanwhile adding other notes on
the protagonist's recent encounters with Julia — and finally returns to the present for a momentary vision of the subject which
takes in the whole past: "All seemed transparent, for a moment,
to the gaze of Fanny Wilmot, as if looking through Miss Craye,
she saw the very fountain of her being spurting its pure silver
drops. She saw back and back into the past behind her . . . She
saw Julia —" (HH, 110–111).

This temporal pattern cannot be assimilated to the circle traced
by the repeated references to Slater's pins, unless we face up to a
subject that seems to have been avoided in discussions of this
story. For there is one other significant action at the close: the
elderly piano teacher kisses her young pupil on the lips, at the
precise moment of her vision of Julia's being. It seems crass to
labor the point, but this intuition of homosexuality is part of the
total vision of Julia which Fanny achieves. Throughout the narrative, numerous statements have underscored Julia's independence, especially of marriage, and indeed her separation from
other people, with the exception of her brother: "there was in
Miss Kingston's voice an indescribable tone which hinted at
something odd; something queer in Julius Craye; it was the very
same thing that was odd perhaps in Julia too." The next sentence
associates this insight with the pin: "One could have sworn,
thought Fanny Wilmot, as she looked for the pin, that at parties . . . [Miss Kingston] had picked up some piece of gos-
sip . . . which had given her 'a feeling' about Julius Craye."

Later, when Fanny speculates on Julia's repeated rejection of
offers of marriage, a perception of her sexual preferences is again
accompanied by the search for the pin: "The setting of that scene
[of rejecting a suitor] could be varied as one chose, Fanny Wilmot reflected. (Where had that pin fallen?)" (HH,108). Finally,
the moment of vision is triggered by Fanny's finding the pin and

her simultaneous discovery of Julia's self-sufficient happiness: "Fanny Wilmot saw the pin; she picked it up. She looked at Miss Craye. Was Miss Craye so lonely? No, Miss Craye was steadily, blissfully, if only for that moment, a happy woman." What seems clear from this repeated association of the search for the pin and the revelations of Julia's sexual disposition is that an arbitrarily chosen object has achieved symbolic status by the time it is repeated at the close. (Or is a pointed and elongated object, capable of linking and of pricking, once kept in hand but presently lost, chosen entirely arbitrarily?)

What is much less clear is the continued activity of the pin. At the opening, the pin has fallen from Fanny's dress, where it held a rose. When Fanny finds the pin and sees Julia in ecstasy, Julia is holding a carnation upright in her lap. Immediately after Julia kisses Fanny, the following sentences occur: " 'Slater's pins have no points,' Miss Craye said, laughing queerly and relaxing her arms, as Fanny Wilmot pinned the flower to her breast with trembling fingers" (HH, 111). Which flower and whose breast? We are not told. Only the emphatic repetition of the motto stands out clearly in this disturbing, but highly formal, finale.

Another story in which an initial sentence figures in the conclusion may be mentioned in passing: "Ancestors," one of the newly published Dalloway stories, opens with a reference to an overheard remark: "Mrs. Vallance, as she replied to Jack Renshaw who had made that rather silly remark of his about not liking to watch cricket matches, wished that she could make him understand . . ." After prolonged reflections on all she has lost in life through the absence of her parents, the protagonist returns to present realities: "she would have been oh perfectly happy, perfectly good, instead of which here she was forced to listen to a young man saying — and she laughed almost scornfully and yet tears were in her eyes — that he could not bear to watch cricket matches!"[20]

The major example of a story formed by the return of its opening lines at the end is "A Haunted House." Here the repetition is far from exact, and the complex pattern suggests another category of form, in which a *group* of elements is returned to at the close. But I shall treat "A Haunted House" as a borderline case of sentence repetition. The sentence in question begins not

20. *Mrs. Dalloway's Party*, p. 44– 47.

the first but the second paragraph: "Here we left it," says one of the ghostly presences in the house. After the previously discussed cases, we should have no trouble in deferring curiosity about the reference of "it" until the final paragraph, when the same voice says, "Here we left our treasure." If this seems insufficient to designate the object of their search, the following sentences go further: the wakened sleeper exclaims, "Oh, is this *your* buried treasure? The light in the heart." To sum up the sequence: the past inhabitants of the house return to seek some treasure they have left and discover it as "their light lifts the lids" of the sleeper's eyes. The place called "here" by the searchers becomes localized as the body of the sleeper; they discover their past happiness still alive in her eyes and heart, and the sleeper recognizes her happiness as the buried treasure left by the past inhabitants. The metaphoric element by which this transfer of feeling is effected is the medium of light: the presences shine their light into the sleeper's eyes, and the latter declares the treasure to be the light in her heart.

So much is established by the subtle shifts of implication in the closing paragraph. Other strains of language and imagery considerably thicken the texture. In addition to the quoted statements of the presences and the first-person narrative of the sleeper, another being is quoted in the story: the house itself. "'Safe, safe, safe,' the pulse of the house beat gladly." "'Safe, safe, safe,' the pulse of the house beat softly." "'Safe, safe, safe,' the heart of the house beats proudly." And finally: "'Safe! safe! safe!' the pulse of the house beats wildly." These repetitive strands set up interweaving connections with other chains, such as the relation between the heart of the house, which beats and pulses, and the sleeper's heart, which contains the light of the presences. These are only the beginnings of a complete account of the brilliantly elaborated form of this story, but what stands out is the trend of all these patterns toward the final discovery of value in the heart or consciousness with which the story begins (HH, 3–5).

It is apparent, even from this curtailed description of "A Haunted House," that we are on the verge of another sort of circular form, in which not one sentence merely but a *cluster* of elements is used to introduce a story and later to close it. Four stories, at least, fall into this category, the best known of which is the title story of Woolf's first collection, "Monday or Tues-

day." This piece marks the closest approach in Woolf to the
prose poem — if not to the condition of music — but even here
form has significance, while conveying little paraphrasable content. The piece begins: "Lazy and indifferent, shaking space easily from his wings, knowing his way, the heron passes over the
church beneath the sky. White and distant, absorbed in itself,
endlessly the sky covers and uncovers, moves and remains." The
last sentence takes up the elements of the first in the same order,
although in compressed expressions: "Lazy and indifferent the
heron returns; the sky veils her stars; then bares them." Between
the opening and closing sentences, four short paragraphs establish a pattern suggesting a persistent search for the truth of
experience: "Desiring truth . . . for ever desiring . . . for ever
desiring . . . for ever desiring truth . . . and truth? . . . and
truth? . . . truth?" It is to this internal sequence, as well as to the
opening evocation, that the closing sentence responds. Truth
here, as in the use of a similar bird symbol by Yeats, lies in the
perfect equipoise of dynamic elements: over, beneath; covers,
uncovers; moves and remains; veils, then bares. The finale of
"Monday or Tuesday" comes not merely with the reverberation
of a previously heard chord but by the reestablishment of a prior
condition; the dynamic equilibrium broken at the beginning sets
in again as language dies away at the close (HH, 6–7).

While the complex of elements returning at the end of "Monday or Tuesday" is a set of images, somewhat different elements
are to be found giving form to "A Summing Up," "The Shooting Party," and "The Searchlight." In "A Summing Up," one of
the Dalloway stories, the elements are place designations. The
story begins with the movement of the protagonist and her inter-
locutor from the Dalloway house into the garden, from which a
sense of the city beyond the garden walls is caught. In the midst
of the narrative, the relation of places is altered, the conversing
pair clambering up to peer over the garden wall at "the vast
inattentive impersonal world" around them, and then looking
back at "the dry, thick Queen Anne house" where they are being
entertained. The spatial relation is changed again at the conclusion: at the point when the interlocutors turn to reenter the
house from the garden, London is behind them, disturbingly:
"At that moment, in some back street or public house, the usual
terrible sexless, inarticulate voice rang out; a shriek, a cry." Between these three clusters of place, two images are repeatedly

introduced: between the beginning and middle, a "golden shaft" is seen as running through the protagonist, and her imagination evokes a tree or tree branch dripping gold. Between the middle and end, these images reappear as a "cloud of gold" and a "field tree" in the primeval marsh that preceded the building of London. The protagonist also sees her soul as an "aloof" and "unmated" widow bird perched on that tree, and in a coda to the final cluster of places that bird takes wing, describes wider and wider circles and becomes remote as a crow. Obviously, the imaginative construction in "The Summing Up" overflows beyond the form traced by its place designations, but those viewpoints of social position serve as a grid upon which the freer images of self are poised (HH, 144–148).

In "The Shooting Party," the clusters that provide formal order are parts of a conventional framing device. This story of the gentry's degeneration hinges on the discovery of a sexual taint in the scion of a smug county family. The opening scene (part of the frame) reveals a woman in a railway carriage, who is designated only by the initials "M.M." on her luggage, who carries a brace of pheasants as if from a shoot, and who utters only the sound indicated by the letters "Chk." Before she re-appears in the closing frame, M.M. is revealed in the course of the narrative as Milly Masters, the housekeeper and the mistress of the squire, whose illegitimate son is twice described as "the boy who cleaned the Church." The sound "Chk" is also elaborated in the body of the narrative, being twice uttered by one of the squire's spinster sisters. Before the story returns to that framing scene, the staid life of the gentry suffers an upheaval in the narrative as the squire and his hounds burst into the drawing room and thrash about wildly. But a more effective signal of the end of a class's heyday is given in the closing frame. The figure of M.M. becomes etherealized, a mist, "eyes without a body"; and her state of existence is suggested by the question, "since there is nothing that does not leave some residue, and memory is a light that dances in the mind when the reality is buried, why should not the eyes there, gleaming, moving, be the ghost of a family, of an age, of a civilization dancing over the grave?" (HH, 67). The return of the woman at the close now carries with it the ghostly presence of the aristocracy. The entire framing cluster — including even the "Chk Chk" of the last sentence — serves as a point of repair from which to take a distant perspective on the past, on a country house, its decorous manners and decadent morals.

The last of this group of stories with returning clusters is "The Searchlight," another of those which overflow their form yet gain strength from their firm underpinnings. Again a frame situation is established, this time of the Conradian type, in which a speaker in purportedly present time delivers a tale of the past; the story later returns to this narrative situation and its distant perspective on the past. In "The Searchlight" the speaker is a socialite entertaining her guests — at a dinner party during which a searchlight repeatedly sweeps the sky — with the legend of her great-grandparents' courtship. Between the initial presence of this light and its final appearance, there is an interruption of Mrs. Ivimey's narrative by a return to the present, during which the searchlight is described as "sweeping across the sky, pausing here and there to stare at the stars." This peculiar description of a searchlight's action is associated with the content of the narrative, which traces the great-grandfather's boyish infatuation with a telescope. At first he uses it only to look at the stars — and as Mrs. Ivimey describes this, her guests feel that "the boy was looking at the stars with them" — but later he discovers that telescopes can be used on terrestrial objects. The boy sees a girl come out of a house and kiss a man, who then departs; the boy races over hill and dale until he reaches her, eventually making her his wife. This narrative is clearly only a sketch, and Mrs. Ivimey fails to fill in the details, even when one of her guests asks what happened to the other man. But she concludes her tale with a further reference to the light, which, she says, "only falls here and there." After this, the final paragraph offers only the information that "the searchlight had passed on"; but we are not left entirely in the dark. The interweavings of the searchlight in the frame situation and the telescope in the narrative have established a fusion of the two kinds of vision, so that a further fusion of the narrator (seeing by searchlight) and her ancestors (seeing and being seen by telescope) is brought about: "A shaft of light fell upon Mrs. Ivimey as if someone had focussed the lens of a telescope upon her. (It was the air force [who were shining the searchlight].) She had risen. She had something blue on her head [like her great-grandmother] . . . 'She was my —' she hesitated, as if she were about to say 'myself.' " Thus, through the careful recomposition of the framing elements, an imaginative fusion of considerable subtlety and beauty is effected (HH, 124–125).

Only two more stories need be included among those with circular forms: "The String Quartet" and "The Introduction." "The String Quartet" has perhaps the most elaborate and independently interesting form among Woolf's short stories, but it is constructed so clearly as an exercise in form per se that it cannot be considered among the most important tales. "The String Quartet" is what we may call an exercise in *imitative* form, in which Woolf's prose follows the phases of experience that make up a chamber music concert so as to resemble the music itself. First comes a sketch of the audience assembling, then a freely imagined description of the Mozart quartet being played, then a reverie in which the listener imagines a little love story unfolding — it is not clear where, but the scene is set in a society like that in which the music was written. Abruptly, the imaginative description of the music returns, and at last the audience is described filing out. If we were to put this in the way musical themes are labelled, the form would be A-B-C-B-A. The circularity of form may be said to be concentric, with the daydream of romance in a past age forming the inner core, but never developing significant relations with the outer and middle circles (HH, 22–27).

Finally, a slight variation on the form in which a cluster of elements appears at beginning and end is offered by the Dalloway story "The Introduction," in which the transition is from *middle* to end. A young lady attains a sort of initiation into society at the middle of the story, only to reach a further turn in her development at the close. The midpoint climax is couched in these terms: "all made her feel that she had come out of her chrysalis and was being proclaimed what in the long comfortable darkness of childhood she had never been . . . this butterfly with a thousand facets to its eyes, and delicate fine plumage, and difficulties and sensibilities and sadnesses innumerable: a woman." At the close of the story, these elements are reassembled and their symbolic valence is reoriented: "she felt like a naked wretch who having sought shelter in some shady garden is turned out and made to understand (ah, but there was a kind of passion in it too) that there are no sanctuaries, or butterflies, and this civilisation, said Lily Everit to herself . . . depends upon

me." The coming out is replaced by a turning out in nakedness
from an Edenic state; the butterflies with their fine plumage are
suddenly withdrawn, and the "comfortable darkness of childhood" gives way to a world without sanctuaries. Yet this series
of negations is accompanied by a consciousness of connection
with the ongoing life of mankind. As a family friend puts it in
the story's final line, ". . . like all the Everits, Lily looked 'as if
she had the weight of the world upon her shoulders.' "[21]

IV

Having said this much about the kinds of form observable in
Virginia Woolf's short stories, what can we say about the structure of the collection as a whole? There is as yet no complete
edition of the stories. The most substantial collection was arranged by Leonard Woolf in an apparently symmetrical way: six
of the eight from *Monday or Tuesday,* followed by six published
in magazines, concluding with six unpublished pieces. (The true
figures are a bit altered by the fact that "Moments of Being" had
been previously published, as Woolf himself suspected.) The
seven pieces collected in the volume called *Mrs. Dalloway's Party*
approximate a structural conception that Virginia Woolf entertained in 1922: "a short book consisting of six or seven chapters,
each complete separately. Yet there must be some sort of fusion!
And all must converge upon the party at the end." Clearly, no
such conception can hold all her stories together — although it
may do so for the Dalloway pieces — nor is there any requirement to think of the collection as a totality. But I suspect this
body of prose has more structural unity than has yet been
acknowledged.

When the datable stories are related to the above analysis,
Woolf's performance shows a steady tendency toward circular
form. By 1921, she had already written three such stories, "A
Haunted House," "Monday or Tuesday," and "The String
Quartet." If the latter is merely an exercise in circular form, the
other two are seminal works in the canon. From "A Haunted
House" proceed all the tales based on a return to the opening
lines of a text; from "Monday or Tuesday" come all the pieces

---

21. Ibid., pp. 37, 43.

which repeat a cluster of thematic or verbal elements at the close. As Woolf's explorations continue (after passing through a period of writing Dalloway stories), the quest for form reaches a point of high fulfillment in the late twenties with "Moments of Being" and "The Lady in the Looking-Glass." There follow a number of further explorations in the late thirties, none of them producing outstanding achievement.

What should be most apparent from this formal analysis is the persistence of certain kinds of meaning in close association with particular forms. The stories described as circular are those that come back to their origins, reestablish an equilibrium, or discover the nature of what is already there. They are "moments" of being not only in the temporal sense — flashes of insight at an instant of time — but also in the dialectical sense, as philosophers in the Hegelian tradition have used the term. In the dialectical moment, a being takes a turn in its development that unfolds what is potential all along. It comes into its own, as we say; it reveals itself as in itself it really is. Such a manifestation of individual selves occurs in stories like "Moments of Being," "The Lady in the Looking-Glass," and "The Summing Up." In "A Haunted House" and "The Searchlight" the manifestation is somewhat more complicated, involving the identification of one self with another, especially with past selves. In other instances, particularly "The Shooting Party" and "Monday or Tuesday," the revelation is not of a person but rather of an overarching condition — sociological in the one case, what we can only call metaphysical in the other.

If circular stories can be said to engage themselves entirely in what is initially given, linear forms can be described as leading beyond the given to what is scarcely known or controlled. In "Kew Gardens," for example, the series of ordinary and apparently easily-known passers-by in the park ends in a final term, the voices, which is composed of known elements (the sounds of the city), yet is presented as an existence beyond the confines of the park, beyond even what is ordinarily known as life. "The Mark on the Wall" and "An Unwritten Novel" pursue something like the same course, moving from what seems to be easily grasped to what is tenuous and ultimately unknowable — even though it seems to be controlled when a name is assigned it (as when the mark is named a snail). The shift in Woolf's habitual practice noticed above — from the linear to the circular, broadly speaking — represents a tendency to return to the given, rather than to pursue the unknown and possibly unknowable. But it also marks a return to what has been latent all along, the meaning of the given, discovered in the act of repetition. It is in this sense that Woolf's rounded stories, like Slater's pins, can be acknowledged as having "no points."

Part Two

THE SEQUENCE

5. "Surely Order Did Prevail": Virginia Woolf and The Voyage Out

FREDERICK P. W. McDOWELL

I

Virginia Woolf's *The Voyage Out* (1915) was the result of agonizing efforts spread over ten years. She destroyed seven preliminary versions, and the novel is, of course, the result of great care, whatever its aesthetic merit. Obviously, she could not have perfected in it her experimental method, and the book owes much to the innovative psychological fiction of George Eliot and Henry James. Yet there is also a close authorial identification in *The Voyage Out* with the inner state of her characters — with their sensibilities, as with their rational motives — which takes the book, in its peculiar intensities and in its stress upon feeling, beyond the fiction of her two predecessors. The infusion into Rachel Vinrace, Terence Hewet, St. John Hirst, and Helen Ambrose of Virginia Woolf's own sensibility reveals a degree of probing into the reaches of personality as yet unusual for fiction in 1915.[1]

---

1. Only recently has *The Voyage Out* begun to achieve the recognition that it deserves. See James Naremore, *The World without a Self; Virginia Woolf and the Novel* (New Haven: Yale University Press, 1973), pp. 50–59; Alice van Buren Kelley, *The Novels of Virginia Woolf: Fact and Vision* (Chicago: University of Chicago Press, 1973), pp. 7–33; Jane Novak, *The Razor Edge of Balance* (Coral Gables: University of Miami Press, 1975), pp. 67–85; and Avrom Fleishman, *Virginia Woolf: A Critical Reading* (Baltimore: Johns Hopkins University Press, 1975), pp. 3–21.

Her preoccupations were much the same in her first novel as in her later ones; it is only the techniques that were subtilized, beginning with *Jacob's Room* (1922) and with some of the short stories and sketches immediately preceding that work. In *The Voyage Out,* she utilized a nineteenth-century longhand by which she conveyed inclusively the social environment of her heroine, Rachel Vinrace, and the people who surround — and crowd about — her, together with an extended analysis of the motives of her main characters. Virginia Woolf's twentieth-century "shorthand," used to re-create instead of to describe emotional, mental, and spiritual states, is present mostly in embryo. But the fact that she is on her way to achieving the shorthand "notation" present in the later fiction is one of the novel's chief fascinations. With this interesting and aesthetically substantial novel, she heralds, moreover, many of the insistent themes, situations, character types, and methods of presenting the subjective life that are prevalent in her books of the 1920s and 1930s.[2] In the most perceptive account of the book to date, Avrom Fleishman maintains that it is "one of the finest first works by any author," and I must agree.[3] In *The Voyage Out,* perhaps her most traditional novel, Woolf's vision is closer, I believe, to that expressed in *The Waves* (1931), her masterpiece and her most consciously experimental work, than it is to that found in any other of her novels; and I shall compare the two books at a number of places in order to demonstrate the closeness of their affinities.

The book is too long, however, and many episodes and characters are extraneous to the main action or expanded at too great length. For example, in chapter 7, Mr. Pepper's reflections on the English settling of Santa Marina in South America are superfluous, as is in chapter 19 the detailed presentation of Miss Allen, who is only tangentially involved with Rachel. In Woolf's later fiction she minimizes the development, or the number, of characters who do not reflect some aspect of her own psyche or who are only externally seen, or drops them after allowing them to illuminate some facet of the fully developed personae. What

2. Harvena Richter, *Virginia Woolf: The Inward Voyage,* p. 93. Richter concludes rightly that *The Voyage Out* contains illustrations of all the forms of Woolf's subjective method of discourse that she was later to refine more radically.
3. Fleishman, *Virginia Woolf,* p. 21.

conveys fullness for the milieu presented in a novel — what Woolf defined, with reference to her purpose in *The Voyage Out,* as the desire to present "a stir of live men and women, against a background" — is often irrelevant to the probing of the depths of personality.[4] Of this group of supernumeraries only Evelyn Murgatroyd is a memorable creation — the extrovert who is distracted by her emotions and by her inability to sort them out in any way that gives her peace.

Among these supernumeraries, Susan Warrington and Arthur Venning, though not altogether compelling in themselves, are more important than most of the other hotel residents at Santa Marina. As robust people they comment implicitly upon the less vigorous but more discriminating Rachel and Terence. One of the most effective scenes, a scene unusual in Georgian fiction for its frank eroticism, occurs when Rachel and Terence come upon Susan and Arthur making love on Monte Rosa and watch with loathing and fascination. A minute or two later, St. John Hirst and Helen Ambrose view the embracing lovers. Hirst and Helen only hint at their feeling for one another in contrast to the forthright Susan and Arthur.

Already Virginia Woolf was developing her own way of apprehending experience and recreating it. Statements about the characters or events were given a Woolfian habitation and a name by her quintessentializing of them, on the one hand; and by her use of unusual images, on the other hand, to give them an indelible identity. Rachel's and Terence's tendency to lose themselves in reverie and to become immersed in the fluidity of existence — and so to become quintessentialized — will be evident later. But some examples of Virginia Woolf's dramatizing of situation and personality by means of vivid images can now be cited: Rachel's fear of sex, transliterated into a dream in which she is enclosed in a vault with a deformed man; red cut flowers lying on the cold ledges in village churches, summarizing for the voyagers all that is magical in the England that they are leaving; and Rachel's thoughts about the discomfort of first seeing her relatives the Ambroses, projected into the annoyance caused by "a tight shoe or draughty window." The Dalloways are seen conventionally, satirically presented almost entirely from with-

4. Letter to Clive Bell, Feb. 7?, 1909, *The Letters of Virginia Woolf,* ed. Nigel Nicolson and Joanne Trautmann (New York: Harcourt Brace Jovanovich, 1975–1977), I (1888–1912), 383.

out. Yet in describing them Virginia Woolf suggests through the
arresting image more than a traditional exposition could convey,
when Rachel, for example, sees Richard as one who seems to
"come from the humming oily centre of the machine where the
polishing rods are sliding, and the pistons thumping" (VO, 47).
Rachel's deepening relationship with Terence is cast into this
arresting image as she thinks of the ease in communicating with
him: "those thorns or ragged corners which tear the surface of
some relationships being smoothed away" (VO, 212). Another
instance of a character presented in striking visual terms occurs
when Hirst is seen against a magnolia tree in Helen's presence,
the great waxen blossoms and glossy leaves suggesting Hirst's
exotic attributes, his aura of artifice, his aesthetic sensibilities, his
exclusiveness, and his alienation. What Virginia Woolf has not
yet evolved is her technique of repeated and interlocking images;
an elaborate but elusive symbolism based upon them; and a
density of texture that can result from such profuse yet controlled composing.

II

    In no other book does Virginia Woolf trace with the minute-
ness of *The Voyage Out* the progress to maturity of a protagonist;
and the fact that the book is a form of *Bildungsroman* allies it to
many nineteenth-century novels. In this kind of novel the emphasis had been placed upon the re-creation of the protagonist's
growth, especially in terms of his or her interaction with social
milieu, whereas the attenuation of such milieu in the interest of
directness and economy characterizes Woolf's later work. But
even in *The Voyage Out* there is a greater emphasis upon the
psychic aspects of the heroine's development than on her social
environment.
    As a result of her "voyage out," Rachel develops substantially
beyond the constricted individual she was at the outset. Somewhat predictably, the ship symbolism reinforces Woolf's view of
Rachel. The name Euphrosyne, one of the graces, implies a
sophistication that is lacking from the earlier, awkward Rachel
and a worldliness and spiritual depth that she will attain as a
result of life on board ship and in Santa Marina. At one point the
ship is likened to a bride going to her husband, as it travels all
day before an empty universe: such is the trajectory of Rachel's

own life, as she goes on a long and problematic journey to meet her lover. She is a psychic and spiritual virgin as well as a physical one, but she attains maturity as a result of a voyage that takes her not only outward, away from England, but inward into the deepest reaches of the spirit. Truly, hers is a "metaphysical education," as one commentator has observed.[5] Rachel is under the tutelage of a worldly but sensitive aunt, Helen Ambrose, who helps her to a point after overcoming a distaste for her naïveté.

Rachel's development flows mostly from her vibrant relations with Terence Hewet, an Oxford-educated writer and man of leisure. She is indeed Virginia Woolf, the tremulous sensibility, ready to respond to all the experiences, sensory and intellectual, that crowd in on her. Terence is Virginia Woolf, too, the dedicated yet still immature artist, who attempts to give order to perceptions of reality (for Terence it is easy to conceive incidents, but difficult to put them into shape). Rachel and Terence are united in their sensitivity, so that their connection deepens mutually their emotions, sensibilities, and intellects. St. John Hirst, Terence's university friend, is Virginia Woolf, the disillusioned, skeptical, and independent Bloomsbury initiate. His mild alienation was typical not only of his creator at times but of the Edwardian age as well. In temper he evinces, besides, some of the fastidious elegance and brusque iconoclasm of that Bloomsbury exemplar, Lytton Strachey; and his physical revulsion from women suggests Strachey's homosexual disposition. In this first novel Virginia Woolf is already isolating aspects of her psyche into separate characters, who also maintain their integrity as personae in a fiction. Indeed, the characters are effective to the extent that they thus mirror aspects of Virginia Woolf's being and uninteresting to the extent that they are seen from the outside.

For Helen Ambrose, Rachel is an unintegrated person rather late in their relationship, though Helen also realizes that this young woman has the capacity, in the acuteness of her senses, to become "formed": she is "on the whole, a live if unformed human being, experimental, and not always fortunate in her experiments, but with powers of some kind, and a capacity for feeling" (VO, 207). Her openness to sensory experience is, in fact, her chief grace. She has, accordingly, Virginia Woolf's own

---

5. Fleishman, *Virginia Woolf*, pp. 3, 9.

susceptibility to the impressions of sense and illustrates, like her creator, "the importance of sensation in an age which practices brutality and recommends ideals."[6]

Helen as her mentor is convinced that Rachel can only become an arresting presence by the development of her native powers, a process more instinctual than rational. Helen's task is, therefore, to educe what is there: "if Rachel were ever to think, feel, laugh, or express herself, instead of dropping milk from a height as though to see what kind of drops it made, she might be interesting though never exactly pretty" (VO, 25). The image of the dropping milk — unusual, original, vivid, and absolutely right in context — heralds the artist of the 1920s and 1930s who capitalizes upon the unusual concretion to convey or reinforce the concept she may wish to communicate. If in this first book Virginia Woolf does try, as in her others, to enclose experience in "a semi-transparent envelope," and to that extent etherealizes it, still her literary genius also expresses itself through vivid particulars. Perhaps this faculty of giving unmistakable and individual life to the concretions of our experience was what Clive Bell had in mind when he singled out in this early work Virginia Woolf's "power . . . of lifting the veil and showing inanimate things in the mystery & beauty of their reality."[7]

Rachel herself realizes the primacy of feeling and cultivates it in her room aboard ship through music or excited reverie. Her capacity to feel soon achieves quasimystic proportions as the objects she fastens upon become radiant in themselves, or else as inanimate things outside the self become invested, seemingly, with the attributes of life. As she sits in her room, her gaze focuses upon a ball in the ship's railing, with the result that her mind at that point becomes identified "with the spirit of the whitish boards on deck, with the spirit of the sea, with the spirit of Beethoven Op.112, even with the spirit of poor William Cowper there at Olney" (VO, 37). Her mind becomes, in essence, a "ball of thistle-down" as it rises and falls with the motion of the air, the ship, and the waves, kissing the sea repeatedly until it disappears from sight. Early in this journey to South America and to spiritual integration, Rachel is frustrated at the thought of life ebbing from her before she can experience to the

---

6. E. M. Forster, "Virginia Woolf," *Two Cheers for Democracy* (New York: Harcourt, Brace and World, 1951), p. 252.
7. Letter to Virginia Stephen [Oct.? 1908], Quentin Bell, *Virginia Woolf*, I, 208.

full such moments of illumination and can develop her inner self to its fullest dimensions: "her life that was the only chance she had — the short season between two silences" (VO, 82). She is upset by the transiency of life, by the notion that human beings may be only "patches of light" in a universe composed of "vast blocks of matter" (292–293), that "those black arrows of shivering sensation" (W, 251), celebrated by Bernard in *The Waves* as the basic reality, may perhaps too seldom pierce her being.

All intensity is thus comprised in the present moment, to which all one's past converges and from which all futurity streams away. Accordingly Rachel, and Virginia Woolf through her, reflect the Paterian point of view as they hold sacrosanct the instant that is to be apprehended through the senses. Like Pater, Virginia Woolf regarded the abstracting tendency of the mind as an impediment to fulfillment in the senses, though she, except in *The Waves,* opted for a less isolated provenance for the psyche than did Pater. Thus the whirling impressions in Rachel's mind after the dance convince her that, above all else, she should welcome "the present moment, with its opportunity for doing exactly as she liked" (VO, 173). In this mood of heightened sensitivity she notes along her path a tree, emblematic presumably of male sexuality. It seems to encapsulate the wonder of this time for her and will enshrine it in her memory forever: "Dark was the trunk in the middle, and the branches sprang here and there, leaving jagged intervals of light between them as distinctly as if it had but that second risen from the ground. Having seen a sight that would last her for a lifetime, and for a lifetime would preserve that second, the tree once more sank into the ordinary ranks of trees . . ." (VO, 174).

Rachel sees the tree in the transforming light of her sensibility, but later such an object as the willow tree in *The Waves,* while emblematic of something eternal in our lives, also mocks for Bernard, in terms of its objective permanency, the subjective (and mortal) life of the individual. Still, as Mrs. Ramsay and Lily Briscoe in *To The Lighthouse* would attempt to "make of the moment something permanent" (L, 241), and just as Jinny in *The Waves* finds there is no past and no future, "merely the moment in its ring of light, and our bodies; and the inevitable climax, the ecstasy" (W, 252), so Rachel becomes entranced by the powers of her sensibility to heighten the keenly apprehended moment. She is thus the prototype of Jinny, who is described in

terms that also fit Woolf's first major heroine — except that
Rachel is not completely unspeculative — as one "who was
without future, or speculation, but respected the moment with
complete integrity" (W, 265). Soon after Rachel's vision of the
tree, she finds also that the words of Gibbon have become transfigured, as have the images of her two friends, Hewet and Hirst:

> Any clear analysis of them was impossible owing to the haze of
> wonder in which they were enveloped. She could not reason about
> them as about people whose feelings went by the same rule as her
> own did, and her mind dwelt on them with a kind of physical plea-
> sure such as is caused by the contemplation of bright things hanging
> in the sun. From them all life seemed to radiate; the very words of
> books were steeped in radiance. (VO, 175)

Rachel herself becomes a vessel for the life energies, even if at
first she is only finding her way. Though death overpowers her
in a few months' time and takes her from a sentient existence
toward a world where the individual self is obliterated, still she
belongs, in the conspectus of the book, as much to the forces of
life as to those of death. By the time she is stretching toward
Terence, she embodies the potency of sex, though she may
hardly be aware that she exerts any attracting force. At the hotel
dance she becomes the mistress of the revels, an encourager of
Dionysian abandon, as she plays the piano for the others to
dance when the orchestra quits. Though she knows little popular
music, she has adaptive powers within her and makes compelling dance rhythms out of the classical compositions that she
plays so consummately, rhythms that excite a fascination over
the other guests as they yield themselves to their influence and
dance improvisations to them, culminating in a ritual of fellow-
ship, the great round dance. Here is an instance of the fellow
feeling, celebrated in Madeline Moore's essay on The Waves later
in this volume, fellow feeling which results in a dynamic community with others and which provides a pattern opposed to the
more impersonal mystical illuminations derived in particular
from a close rapport with nature.

When Rachel modulates into a more solemn music and puts
her soul into it with a lack of self-consciousness as yet unusual in
her, she commands the whole group and lifts them to her own
level of exaltation: "They sat very still as if they saw a building
with spaces and columns succeeding each other rising in the
empty space. Then they began to see themselves and their lives,

and the whole of human life advancing very nobly under the direction of the music. They felt themselves ennobled, and when Rachel stopped playing they desired nothing but sleep" (VO, 167). For the moment as they respond to the ecstatic sound, they become component parts of, and participants in, an order that reaches beyond their individual selves, many of them for the first time experiencing this sense of inner enlargement. Though the great moment cannot last, yet all is different for them because of its once having been. In any event Rachel at this time fully embodies "the indomitable vitality" of other Woolf protagonists, even though she later becomes the victim of death.

As a vessel for the life energies, Rachel becomes, by the completion of her inner voyage, a formidable influence in her own right. She impresses others — above all, Terence — by her intuitive understanding and her capacious sympathies. She is unique, he feels, in grasping what is said to her; and he is impressed by "the extraordinary freedom" which characterizes his relationship with her. Her gifts are real and comprehensive, making for both pleasure and pain, in other words for fullness and completeness of experience. "Curiosity and sensitivity of perception" are qualities in Rachel that secure Terence's approbation, attention, and love and are worth far more to him than the benefits that she may add to them later through living and reading. He sees that she has the capacity for spiritual greatness by virtue of the powers within her, once latent but now expressing themselves ever more expansively if still somewhat fitfully.

It is love, Woolf demonstrates in *The Voyage Out,* that can raise the inner being to its highest point: love is either a transcendent experience or else holds the key to such great moments, leading the individual at once to unimaginable depths within the psyche and outward to a commingling with the cosmic energies that govern existence. Even before she knows that she is committed to love for Terence, Rachel has undergone the enlargement of soul that will come to mean love to her: "She was conscious of emotions and powers which she had never suspected in herself, and of a depth in the world hitherto unknown" (VO, 224). The presence of the two young men, Terence and Hirst, inspires in her "an extraordinary intensity in everything, as though their presence stripped some cover off the surface of things" (VO, 200). With Rachel and Terence, the sensations brought on by their contact with each other lead to overpowering emotion, to Rachel's realization, in particular, that everything else is but a distraction from this central experience. The beating of her pulse, symptomatic of the intensity of her involvement, "represented the hot current of feeling that ran down beneath," and her body became "the source of all the life in the world" (VO, 258), triumphant against all the people and the forces that would repress it. But love is also a mystery as well as an intensity. The yellow butterfly which Rachel sees the night after the dance seems to signify all the magical elusiveness of her new state, its strength, too, as well as its fragility; and in itself the butterfly seems to her to pose the question, "What is it to be in love?" Even the cynical and reserved St. John Hirst is convinced by the example of Terence and Rachel; and he is able, with some exertion of his will, to tell them finally that love " 'seems to me to explain everything' " (VO, 312).

Rachel and Terence, who reflect most fully the Woolfian ethos and temperament, feel the most intensively after they achieve their understanding in the jungle on the expedition to the back country. James Naremore has extensively analyzed the jungle scene, emphasizing the imagery used (it is predominantly sexual), the hesitations and uncertainties of the two lovers, the racing rhythms present, and the couple's dazed and dreamlike demeanor. All these aspects of the scene contain implications, Naremore maintains, that a sexual encounter has taken place; and Fleishman regards the tropical forest as a Garden of Eden in which sexual experience means the loss of innocence and the acquiring of knowledge.[8] I agree that the rapprochement in the forest should be interpreted in this way, though Woolf's reticence is extreme.

It is possible that sexual encounters also take place the next day in the jungle, when the lovers are conscious of "a new feeling" within them, or the next night when on the deck of the steamer they peer at the stars: "The little points of frosty light infinitely far away drew their eyes and held them fixed, so that it seemed as if they stayed a long time and fell a great distance when once more they realised their hands grasping the rail and their separate bodies standing side by side" (VO, 289). The previous night they had sat on deck at the opposite ends of a circle of people and had felt a mysterious communion with one another that "left

8. See Naremore, *The World without a Self*, pp. 42–54, and Fleishman, *Virginia Woolf*, p. 8.

them sitting perfectly silent at the bottom of the world" (VO, 276). At that point "occasional starts of exquisite joy ran through them," as a preliminary, among other things, to their wide gazing into space the next night and to their possible exploration then of the depths of each other's bodies and souls.

As in D. H. Lawrence, the intensities of sexual emotion become, at their most ecstatic, a bridge to a still more ecstatic state beyond them. Accordingly, the relationship with Terence has forever changed Rachel, and the world now seems different — larger and fuller of meaning, simpler, more certain than it did before. Yet love now leads her to a peace that is not love, but a peace that she would never have known, except, paradoxically, through love, to a mystical impersonality that is akin, in some respects, to death. She is, in short, independent of Terence, though without her having known him her present assurance and insight would never have existed: "Nevertheless, as St. John said, it was love that made her understand this, for she had never felt this independence, this calm, and this certainty until she fell in love with him, and perhaps this too was love" (VO, 315). She is thus led from the self to "a world seen without a self" such as Bernard encounters at the climactic point in *The Waves*, though for her at first this awareness seems a blessed rather than a formidable experience. This rapture is for Rachel also induced by art, specifically music. Her music gives her this sense of inner completion; and for others sensitive to her artistry, her music leads them to a transcendent plane of emotional intensity and spiritual insight.

And yet ecstatic emotion, if greatly positive and vital, is sometimes negative in effect and influence. Pain or suffering are aspects of the inner life because emotion can wane as well as wax, because the world with its claims may intrude on a relationship, and because the very intensity of pleasure may bring it close to its opposite. Thus even in the jungle when the lovers attain their fullest understanding, Rachel wonders "why was it so painful being in love, why was there so much pain in happiness?" (VO, 285). Woolf may have absorbed some of the attitudes toward love current in the later nineteenth century: the nearness of ecstasy to pain and, more especially, the nearness of fulfilled eroticism to death. At the death of Rachel, Terence finds himself lulled "into perfect certainty and peace," contrary to the physical desire for her which beats so strongly in his conscious self. As he gazes on the dying woman, he finds in the moment a spiritual completeness that goes beyond love, though it has been inspired by love.

This awareness is akin to the timeless, disembodied emotion Rachel had achieved earlier through Terence even as it had left him behind. In their union, the lovers experience that state of transcendence which both the intensity of life and the finality of death can bring. It is a union in which they feel an interchanged identity with one another, an identity, moreover, that cannot be separated from either life or death. It is the kind of union that Catherine and Heathcliff experience in *Wuthering Heights,* a union in which the lovers most completely mingle in a state beyond life, when each one can exchange identity with the other. The Brontë novel is one of Rachel's favorites and has evidently been formative upon her. At her death Terence seems to be Rachel as well as himself, and seems, indeed, to have entered a world beyond time wherein Rachel now seems to reside. There he feels the intensest communion with her, participating in a Wagnerian "love-death," and finding now "what they had always wanted to have, the union which had been impossible while they lived" (VO, 353).[9] Only he does not die; and as this moment of illumination passes and he realizes the actuality of her death, he shrieks with agony at his loss of her. Incidentally, the inception, general movement, and meaning of *The Voyage Out* are essentially romantic and Wagnerian (especially Wagner of *Tristan*), in contrast to what Jane Marcus demonstrates as the germinal influences shaping Woolf's second novel, *Night and Day:* eighteenth-century classicism and, above all, Mozart (especially Mozart of *The Magic Flute*).

Rachel is increasingly conscious of her intrinsic worth and expresses in her thoughts Virginia Woolf's own high valuation of individuality: "The vision of her own personality, of herself as a real everlasting thing, different from anything else, unmergeable, like the sea or the wind, flashed into Rachel's mind, and she became profoundly excited at the thought of living" (VO, 84). There is, too, a not wholly tame side to Rachel, as this passage

9. As Fleishman points out, Rachel has been both attracted and repelled by Wagner's *Tristan* earlier in the novel; *Virginia Woolf,* p. 15. For a brilliant analysis of the literary allusions in the novel, all of them portending Rachel's death (Antigone, Shelley, Emily Brontë, Hardy, Milton, and Whitman), see ibid., pp. 13–21.

would indicate. She is the romantic individualist and is unconventional in tendency, despite the fact that she is, superficially, a
paragon nurtured by Victorian convention and evasiveness. This
is the forthright Rachel who at the beginning can decline a talk
with Helen in preference to this expressed intention: " 'I'm
going out to t-t-triumph in the wind' " (VO, 23), the woman
whom Clive Bell once saw as "mysterious & remote, some
strange, wild, creature who has come to give up half her
secret."[10]

III

The narrator's comment upon the relationship between Terence and Rachel sums up Virginia Woolf's views on personal
relationships that are important yet difficult to manage and con-
solidate: "they could never love each other sufficiently to overcome all these barriers, and they could never be satisfied with
less" (VO, 303). Love is, especially, a perilous state because one
is then dependent on another, yet the other person may be un-
reliable or else fate may intervene to remove that person or to
cause misunderstandings. In this novel Virginia Woolf, at least
by implication, values greatly the achievement of rapport with
another individual and understanding with him or her.

Yet Terence and Rachel both know that it is not easy to attain
communication with another person. At one time Rachel observes that " 'It's very difficult to know what people are like' "
(VO, 82); and she seems, for example to foreshadow Bernard's
despair expressed in *The Waves* at ever getting to know well the
friends that he loves: "Our friends — how distant, how mute,
how seldom visited and little known. And I, too, am dim to my
friends and unknown; a phantom, sometimes seen, often not"
(W, 275). At another time, Terence, thinking of Evelyn Murgatroyd and her problems, realizes also how immense are the obsta-
cles in relating to another person: "Why was it that relations
between different people were so unsatisfactory, so fragmentary,
so hazardous, and words so dangerous that the instinct to sym-
pathise with another human being was an instinct to be
examined carefully and probably crushed?" (VO, 194). Terence's
views are also near those of Bernard in *The Waves,* who feels

10. Letter to Virginia Stephen [Feb. 5? 1909], in Bell, *Virginia Woolf,* I, 210.

compelled to achieve identity with his friends but who discovers, too, how baffling the reaching of such understanding can be: "I to whom there is not beauty enough in moon or tree; to whom the touch of one person with another is all, yet who cannot grasp even that, who am so imperfect, so weak, so unspeakably lonely" (W, 267). As Madeline Moore demonstrates in her discussion of *The Waves,* the attainment of social solidarity and of meaningful community with others exists in Woolf's universe more as a wished-for state than as one possible of full attainment, otherwise than symbolically, in our imperfect world.

An emblem of the loneliness of human life, the ship *Euphrosyne* betokens the conditions under which the individual works out his destiny; personal relationships mean much, but they can take one only so far, and beyond that point one is alone. In the midst of life, one is still solitary with the self; so concludes Hewet in conversation with Hirst when he says, " 'The truth of it is that one never is alone, and one never is in company' " (VO, 108). Strong emotion, which ought to unite people into powerful unity, more often serves to sever them. Such is one of Rachel's earliest insights when she had found it difficult to secure rapprochement with her aunts: "To feel anything strongly was to create an abyss between oneself and others who feel strongly perhaps but differently" (VO, 36). It is no accident, then, that Woolf in this first novel stressed the divisions among people rather than the forces that unite them.

Rachel's powers truly do expand, mostly as a result of her love for Terence. In Santa Marina she feels herself immersed in life, half passive to the powers molding her, half active in wishing to gain something that will truly be her own:

> For the methods by which she had reached her present position, seemed to her very strange, and the strangest thing about them was that she had not known where they were leading her. That was the strange thing, that one did not know where one was going, or what one wanted, and followed blindly, suffering so much in secret, always unprepared and amazed and knowing nothing; but one thing led to another and by degrees something had formed itself out of nothing, and so one reached at last this calm, this quiet, this certainty, and it was this process that people called living. (VO, 314)

In its emphasis upon the need to follow one's inmost spirit, despite personal inadequacies and despite the inability to know

in advance whether an experience will yield pleasure or pain, this
passage summarizes the quality and the very process discernible in the musings of Clarissa Dalloway and Peter Walsh in
Mrs. Dalloway or of Mrs. Ramsay and Lily Briscoe in *To the
Lighthouse*. Even more striking is the resemblance between the
process just described for Rachel's reveries and the thought patterns which the six personae in *The Waves* exemplify. In *The
Waves* mysterious psychic forces stimulate the characters who
then follow them, without much sense of free will but with
entire sensitivity and receptivity, to an end that provides a degree
of certainty, security, and satisfaction when conflicting forces are
reconciled, even if this psychic harmony is at best only tenuous.
In *The Voyage Out* the description of Rachel's life in the mind is
authentic also for Woolf's later novels, though Rachel dwells
there less tenaciously than do most of the later figures. In *The
Voyage Out* Rachel has at least attained command of the self,
moral authority, and spiritual authenticity by the end of her
journey.[11]

Both Terence and Rachel often feel that life is unaccountably
strange. In a Woolfian passage, similar in effect to that deriving
from Mrs. Ramsay's musings as the beams of the lighthouse fall
upon her, Rachel ponders the mystery of life, its inexplicability,
her own strangeness in a world that is at once fascinating and
refractory, a world capable of arousing exalted emotion yet
finally ephemeral:

> The sounds in the garden outside joined with the clock, and the small
> noises of midday, which one can ascribe to no definite cause, in a
> regular rhythm. It was all very real, very big, very impersonal, and
> after a moment or two she began to raise her first finger and to let it
> fall on the arm of her chair so as to bring back to herself some
> consciousness of her own existence. She was next overcome by the
> unspeakable queerness of the fact that she should be sitting in an
> armchair, in the morning, in the middle of the world. Who were the
> people moving in the house — moving things from one place to
> another? And life, what was that? It was only a life passing over the
> surface and vanishing, as in time she would vanish, though the furni-
> ture in the room would remain. Her dissolution became so complete

---

11. Fleishman convincingly argues that Rachel's "voyage" extends beyond a
mere invitation to partake of a heroic quest. He regards her experiences on
board ship and in South America as "trials"; and he sees in her death not a
denial of her initiation but a confirmation of it and an enlargement of her
understanding; see *Virginia Woolf*, pp. 9–14.

that she could not raise her finger any more, and sat perfectly still, listening and looking always at the same spot. It became stranger and stranger. She was overcome with awe that things should exist at all . . . She forgot that she had any fingers to raise . . . The things that existed were so immense and so desolate . . . She continued to be conscious of these vast masses of substance for a long stretch of time, the clock still ticking in the midst of the universal silence. (VO, 124 – 125)

Responsive to the rhythms of life and recognizing that all mental and sensory experience is fluid, Rachel becomes intrigued with the mystery of existence to the point of uncertainty as to her own identity. The act of raising her finger establishes her reality as a person, but this momentary vital sense of the self becomes lost in a bemused identification with a spiritual force that flows through her. A heightened excitation of the self leads to the virtual extinction of the self in a cosmic power that is neither near nor remote, clear nor obscure, but unmistakably there and emblematic of truth and reality, even if to the reason it may seem at times to be arbitrary. This cosmic power gives us striking intuition into the quality of our existences, at the same time that it mercilessly holds them in control as Rachel and her fiancé discover at the end of the novel. At a later point in the novel, Rachel again voices her conviction about the uncertainty yet the perennial fascination of experience when she says that " 'there are things we don't know about, and the world might change in a minute and anything appear' " (VO, 145).

Once more Rachel speculates concerning the mystery and wonder of life, as do all the central figures in Woolf's fiction, when she examines one inch of South American soil; next she set an insect on the utmost tassel of one specific blade of grass, and then "wondered if the insect realised his strange adventure, and thought how strange it was that she should have bent that tassel rather than any other of the million tassels" (VO, 141). In turn, Terence feels that there is nothing fixed about life, for we " 'live in a state of perpetual uncertainty, knowing nothing, leaping from moment to moment as from world to world' " (VO, 127). In such disjunctions and incertitudes, then, lies the challenge of life, and our task is to reconcile and harmonize them. Our only certainty is, in effect, life's unpredictability; our only recourse in moments of disillusion is to cultivate, as Bernard does in *The Waves* "the sense of the complexity and the reality and the strug-

gle" (W, 294) when the stranger in the restaurant brings him
back to the here and now after he has dwelt for some moments
in the transcendent and impersonal "world seen without a self."

If the world is capable of being transfigured for Rachel and
Terence, it is basically sinister and its laws operate inexorably.
Virginia Woolf's view from the beginning was a darkened one,
and the only slightly mitigated pessimism and the rigor of vision
informing *The Waves* are present in almost as stark a form in *The
Voyage Out*. The universe of this first novel is one in which
chance predominates, in which the unpredictable can result in
tragedy as well as in spiritual insight and ecstasy. It is a universe
in which nature, if beautiful, is also remote and impersonal and a
universe in which natural laws cannot be bent to insure the
welfare of any one human being. It is for Helen Ambrose a
universe in which insecurity alternates with a natural deter-
minism to minimize the power of the individual: "Her sense of
safety was shaken, as if beneath twigs and dead leaves she had
seen the movement of a snake. It seemed to her that a moment's
respite was allowed, a moment's make-believe, and then again
the profound and reasonless law asserted itself, moulding them
all to its liking, making and destroying" (VO, 263).

Later, Helen's pessimism is more radical still, when she thinks
of human destiny in general. She has then a Joblike view of
humanity in a world that is impersonal and malignant. She is
incredulous of the alleged beneficence of the cosmos and is convinced, rather, that Fatality is unkind to people in proportion to
their having been deserving: "She was not severe upon individuals so much as incredulous of the kindness of destiny, fate, what
happens in the long run, and apt to insist that this was generally
adverse to people in proportion as they deserved well" (VO,
221). It is Rachel's death, certainly, that provides the most significant expression of Woolf's pessimism: her death gains impact
not merely because it is a senseless waste of spiritual power but
because of its symbolic dimensions. One can argue that the arbitrary demise of the woman built up through the entire novel is
a flaw because this person's importance is thereby undercut.
Rachel's inner expansion and development come to seem pointless, perhaps, when she meets such an arbitrary end.

From another point of view, however, the sequence provides
Virginia Woolf with a metaphor for her deeply pessimistic world
view. That the good die young, that the potentially great are cut

down the most relentlessly, was illustrated for her in her brother
Thoby's pointless death from typhoid in 1906 when he was
twenty-six. Her tragic view of life was prophetic and in accord
with the disillusion engendered by the senseless destruction and
carnage characterizing the Great War which broke out soon after
Virginia Woolf had finished her final revision of the book. Even
the music that Rachel plays at one of the high points in the action
is sad rather than gay, melancholy rather than joyous, elegaic
rather than exultant. In Rachel's own view, the effect of her
music had been "one of passionate regret for dead love and the
innocent years of youth; dreadful sorrow had always separated
the dancers from their past happiness" (VO, 165). Once we
know Rachel's fate, it is almost as if she had been playing her
own requiem. The cause of Rachel's fever is left open: it could be
a disease contracted in the unhealthy surroundings up the river,
or it could be the result of the servants' failure to cook the
vegetables thoroughly at Helen's South American villa.

When Rachel comes down with fever, Terence experiences a
sense of cataclysm that had never before entered his consciousness. Spiritual distinction matters little in a Darwinian universe
which to Terence, in light of Rachel's agony, seems to be entirely
sinister and hostile. The realization is borne in on him, too, that
life is not at all malleable and is marked by ceaseless struggle; the
basic reality appears to be the pain which lies concealed beneath
our daily existences and which is a force always ready to devour:
"he seemed to be able to see suffering, as if it were a fire, curling
up over the edges of all action, eating away the lives of men and
women" (VO, 345). He illustrates, in his progressive awareness,
that he has gained a knowledge similar to that of Bernard in *The
Waves*, who, in his radical moments of self-confrontation,
realizes what he has learned by growing into maturity: "satiety
and doom; the sense of what is inescapable in our lot; death; the
knowledge of limitations; how life is more obdurate than one
had thought it" (W, 269).

Although Virginia Woolf begins by describing Rachel's illness
flatly ("The separate feelings of pleasure, interest, and pain,
which combine to make up the ordinary day, were merged in
one long-drawn sensation of sordid misery and profound bore-
dom [VO, 335]), she soon goes on to actualize it in the sensory
and imagistic mode that was to be at the heart of her later manner. Rachel's revulsion against her normal existence is expressed

in a dream in which ugly women in a subterranean tunnel under
the Thames obliviously play cards and represent for Rachel
vague figures of menace. In Woolf's elaboration of the fever's
progress, Rachel's horror at her illness and her traumatic withdrawal from life center in the images of a woman cutting off a
man's head with a knife and of severed heads rolling downhill;
her moments of semiconsciousness are lived in a "deep pool of
sticky water" at the bottom of the sea, with its booming sound
heard faintly from a distance; and her moments of consciousness
are charged into the image of her own bestriding the top of a
wave or becoming a patch of melting snow on a mountainside.[12]
In this sequence, Woolf's sensitivity to the nuances of feeling
comes to the fore. Eddies of calm in Terence alternate with
intense grief, a nihilistic peace with a total despair; Rachel reacts
to Terence's presence with aversion because he brings her back to
an unwelcome reality from the peace with which approaching
death now entices her; and she has, in fact, been so far in spirit
beyond the confines of life that she is only mildly interested in
contact with him when her mind clears at the moment of death.
The voyage charted in the novel is not only a voyage of psychic
discovery but also the longest and most absolute voyage of all,
the journey to death and to extinction in an implacable cosmos
wherein only the human gestures of protest against fate seem to
have meaning.

IV

The vision attained by the lovers in *The Voyage Out* is similar
to, even if less completely articulated than, that of Bernard
in *The Waves*. Woolf's quintessential diarist sums up the experiences charted in that novel. Having always treasured the
intensities of the moment and the possibility of transcendence
within it, Bernard realizes that these intensities are not possible
without a perceiving consciousness, and he confronts squarely

---

12. At the beginning of her delirium, Rachel sees "the glassy, cool, translucent
wave," identified with the nymph Sabrina, lapping at the foot of her bed,
and later she feels borne aloft by it. Rachel, beleaguered by death, is similar
to the beleaguered lady in *Comus* who calls upon Sabrina for help; but Rachel
finally dies, just as the would-be savior Sabrina drowns as a result of per-
secutions by Gwendolyn, her hostile stepmother and a force of death. See
Mitchell Leaska, "Virginia Woolf's *The Voyage Out*: Character Deduction
and the Function of Ambiguity," *Virginia Woolf Quarterly*, I (1973), 18–41.

the possibility of his becoming "a man without a self." In *The Voyage Out*, Rachel is more content, it seems, to rest in an impersonal sphere beyond the self than is Terence, who is rapt yet appalled by his entrance into a world beyond the human. In *The Voyage Out* these differing views toward the ineffable are embodied in two characters, whereas in *The Waves* Bernard is conscious both of mystical ecstasy and of horror at the prospect of self-extinction. Like Bernard, who resists mysticism because of his acute sense of the concrete, the actual, and the social, Terence shrinks from the loss of the self. Bernard had been obscurely conscious since childhood of an enemy lurking in the shadows behind even the strongest moments of vision, and in maturity he senses the full reality of an antagonistic principle in the universe — the impersonality of the cosmos, the final provenance of death. Or what he realizes is in fact what Terence discovers in *The Voyage Out*, the closeness of the moment of ecstatic exaltation — which becomes mystical and impersonal — to death itself, which is also a loss of the self and so impersonal. A heroic stance in face of the adversary death is the only response possible, as we see in Terence's embittered resignation to Rachel's loss and in Bernard's charging his opponent like a knight in the concluding sentences of *The Waves*.

Order, yet an impersonal order, finally does persist, since the rhythms of existence go on eternally: social life in Santa Marina in *The Voyage Out* haltingly begins anew after Rachel's demise and the waves in *The Waves* continue to swell and fall. But this modicum of order has been secured at a great price. Has the price been too great? This question seems to have nagged at Virginia Woolf throughout her career, and it is dramatized graphically in her first novel in the spiritually needless destruction of Rachel Vinrace, as it was to be in *The Waves* in the suicide of Rhoda — who would place squares on oblongs as a symbol of an attained internal harmony — and in the denuding of Bernard, who yet does find in a "world seen without a self" that his being is yet "immeasurably receptive, holding everything, trembling with fullness, yet clear, contained . . . It lies deep, tideless immune" (W, 291). Something of value is yet retained, even at the cost of self-extinction, some intuition into the eternal that is expressed either in the depths of our souls, in art, in love, in our sense of the beauty and rhythms of nature, in human community, or in the courageous confrontation of the "enemy" that would despoil human existence.[13]

The pessimism expressed in *The Voyage Out* is deep-reaching and seems at Rachel's death to all but obliterate Woolf's belief in a transcendent reality that encompasses life, a belief expressed elsewhere in the book. Though life may seem pleasant, as Bernard says in *The Waves,* nevertheless after a time we sense that Monday follows Tuesday with a difference, deriving from our realization that eternity and doom are commingled, and that such order as exists has to be measured in impersonal rather than in personal terms. Yet order does exist, and an affirmation of such order informed Virginia Woolf's life as an artist. In this utterance dating from the end of her life, we see how the interpenetration of the outward and the inner to form a compelling pattern characterized her philosophy as an artist:

> it is a constant idea of mine; that behind the cotton wool is hidden a pattern; that we — I mean all human beings — are connected with this; that the whole world is a work of art; that we are parts of the work of art. *Hamlet* or a Beethoven quartet is the truth about this vast mass that we call the world. But there is no Shakespeare, there is no Beethoven; certainly and emphatically there is no God; we are the words; we are the music; we are the thing itself.[14]

In *The Voyage Out* as in *The Waves* Woolf contemplated the horror of the withdrawal of the self and the attenuation of our sense of the metaphysical importance of human existence. In both books her central faith that the world is a work of art grows dim. Yet even in them she emphasizes the presence of an order (or an intuition thereof) beyond the self; and so she could miti-

---

13. In Woolf's universe there is a constantly projected duality between self and the mystical obliteration of the self in transcendent experience. The way to the impersonal is through the personal, the way to the not-self is through the self, with its intense life in sensation, its aspirations in art and love, its feeling for nature and the cosmic processes, its restlessness and heroic defiance of death, and its discernment of a pattern in personal relationships. I agree with Madeline Moore in her essay on *The Waves* about the existence of this conflict in Virginia Woolf's fiction, though I feel that an illuminated social community is but one of the aspects of subjectivity that may be opposed to mystical and impersonal otherness.

14. "A Sketch of the Past," *Moments of Being: Unpublished Autobiographical Writings,* ed. Jeanne Schulkind (New York: Harcourt Brace Jovanovich, 1978), p. 72.

gate the pessimism, to some degree, that she had dramatized in these two spiritually related books.

In *The Voyage Out* both Rachel and Terence have felt the provenance of order encompassing them, although Rachel is still living at the time of these affirmations. They are, for that reason, easier to make than they would be if the circumstances of her future death could be known in advance. After the night of the dance, Terence, for example, realizes now that "there seemed to be at once a little stability in all this incoherence" (VO, 185); and later when he talks to Rachel, he reveals to her that "there was an order, a pattern which made life reasonable, or, if that word was foolish, made it of deep interest anyhow, for sometimes it seemed possible to understand why things happened as they did" (VO, 299).

Before the trip up the river, Rachel achieved similar insight, in her perception that the random events of life do coalesce into an evolving figure and an evolving meaning. Thus her life with her aunts, her life with her father, the visit of the Dalloways, and her present voyage add up to significance: "Perhaps, then, every one really knew as she knew now where they were going; and things formed themselves into a pattern not only for her, but for them, and in that pattern lay satisfaction and meaning" (VO, 314). This point of view amounts, as Rachel discerns, to a total acceptance of one's situation and the vanquishment of fear from one's universe. With Rachel's illness and death, such affirmations are shaken radically for Terence; and for him a frightening pattern emerges, in the peace, reconciliation, and fusion of all dichotomies and discontinuities in death.

Although Terence is not on hand to offer any affirmation (and long years would have to pass before he could make one), Mrs. Thornbury can do so. Her horror at Rachel's death is genuine and is symbolized in the tumultuous storm the night after, which disturbs all the hotel residents but brings them calm in its passing. Mrs. Thornbury perhaps most fully reflects Virginia Woolf's own eventual valuation of what has happened to Rachel. Mrs. Thornbury's is the final voice along with St. John Hirst's. Rachel's death is for her a tragic waste of spiritual power, as she thinks of what she herself would have missed if she had perished at Rachel's age: "unimaginable depths and miracles" that are precious and ineffaceable despite the suffering that life may also bring with it. Her horror remains, but she is able to affirm life,

for underneath the welter of existence — in spite of chaos, accident, and death — pattern and order do exist, she feels: "There
was undoubtedly much suffering, much struggling, but, on the
whole, surely there was a balance of happiness — surely order
did prevail" (VO, 360). And the cynical, worldly St. John supports Mrs. Thornbury by concluding that Rachel's death, terrible and senseless as it has been, does not represent the end of the
world. The assembled guests for the first time since her illness
strike him now as themselves forming an evolving and meaningful pattern before his eyes. The forces of life emerge again after
the holocaust of Rachel's death, but they only just manage to do
so. The fact that peripheral characters, with some hesitation, at
the end express an affirmative view reveals how tentatively
perhaps Virginia Woolf embraced it in her first novel.

Such is the precarious balance maintained between the life
energies and the death forces in *The Voyage Out*. And this is the
same ambiguous vision charted in *The Waves*. In the last haunting paragraph of that magnificent novel, Bernard as a charging
knight throws himself upon Death, his antagonist, though he
will surely be worsted in his struggles just as surely as the passive
Rachel was. Still, there is something great in Bernard's resolute
strength that engages the adversary, just as there is something
infinitely bracing in the self-conscious way in which Rachel
resists death in *The Voyage Out*.

So even if death may be physically victorious, the human race
still triumphs in the very fact of incessant struggles against a
remorseless opponent; and the human story cannot be as it
would be if Rachel Vinrace and Septimus Warren Smith, Jacob
Flanders and Mrs. Ramsay, Bernard and Rhoda and Percival had
never been. Mrs. Thornbury's "surely order did prevail" is
closely related to the closing sentence of *The Waves*: "The waves
broke upon the shore." The motions of an impersonal universe
go on without the presence of any one individual human presence or sensibility; but sentient life, if transient, has also contributed to the emergent, growing, ever-developing patterns
present in an organically envisioned universe. How death impinges upon and threatens life and how life is resolute and firm
before death and continues on despite the destruction of valued
individuals — some such notion informed the composition of
The Voyage Out (and all of Woolf's subsequent fiction), if we
can believe her when she described what she tried to do in this

initial work: "to give the feeling of a vast tumult of life, as various and disorderly as possible, which should be cut short for a moment by death, and go on again — and the whole was to have a sort of pattern, and be somehow controlled."[15] A like effect was the one she wished to achieve in the concluding ambiguous passage of *The Waves,* if we can judge by this diary entry concerning Bernard's last words, which will "show that the theme effort, effort, dominates; not the waves: and personality: and defiance."[16] To consider the two books is to see how *The Waves* is contained in *The Voyage Out* and how *The Voyage Out* suggests in embryo *The Waves.* In both books the sting of death is almost overwhelming. In both books some sense, painfully acquired by the individual, of a permanent, if inchoate and residual, order not unrelated to our experience as human beings in an otherwise impersonal cosmos, mitigates that sting but does not blunt it.

15. Letter to Lytton Strachey, Feb. 28, 1917, *The Letters of Virginia Woolf,* II (1912–1922), 82.
16. *A Writer's Diary,* ed. Leonard Woolf (New York: Harcourt, Brace, 1954), p. 159.

6. Enchanted Organs, Magic Bells: Night and Day as Comic Opera

JANE MARCUS

I

Critics have not been kind to *Night and Day*. Even female critics, who might perhaps be expected to respond approvingly to the feminist content of the novel, have found it unsatisfactory. "A lie in the soul," said Katherine Mansfield. "An academic exercise," said Virginia Woolf herself. When a work by a major artist is so generally deplored, and when it is formally unlike those works which are admired, then one is surely justified in asking whether indeed the hostile critics have looked for the right things.

I think that *Night and Day* is an extraordinarily interesting novel. It is a natural daughter of the Meredith novel, a minor masterpiece, a pleasure to read. The disappointment of contemporary readers — like E. M. Forster, Clive Bell, or Katherine Mansfield — was, I think, largely due to outrage felt at the audacity of using the comic form in a novel written during the war and published in 1919. But the search for order which impelled Eliot and Joyce to shape their feelings of despair in ancient mythological structures was the same impulse which drove Virginia Woolf to shape *Night and Day* around the initiation, quest, and journey myths of *The Magic Flute*.[1]

I suspect that those who reject the novel do so from two different points of view. Some, with Forster, Bell, and Mans-

---

1. See Robert Moberly, *Three Mozart Operas* (New York: Dodd, Mead, 1967); Brigid Brophy's *Mozart the Dramatist* (New York: Harcourt, Brace and World, 1964); and Robert Craft's essay in the *New York Review of Books*, Nov. 27, 1975.

field, find the comic mode impertinent in wartime and Woolf
out of character stylistically and temperamentally.[2] Modern critics do not hear the "authentic" voice of Woolf in this novel and
find it mannered. But *Night and Day* can be read as the Dreadnought Hoaxer's Merry Pranks. Woolf described this adventure
in "A Society" as part of the effort of a group of young women
to discover why men could not achieve "the objects of life,"
namely, "to produce good people and good books" — one of the
themes of *Night and Day*.[3] The female hoaxer (Rose, who later
turns up in *The Years*), dresses up as the Prince of Abyssinia
(with no apologies to the author of *Rasselas*) and violates *The
Dreadnought*, a secret man-of-war. The masquerade managed to
attack the British patriarchy at its most vulnerable point so effectively that Sylvia Pankhurst chose the motif as a rallying title,
first for her socialist feminist newspaper *The Women's Dreadnought*, then, at the founding of the British Communist party,
The Workers' Dreadnought.[4]

Allusively, then, Woolf is engaged in serious play with the
history and ideology of her culture, with biography, autobiography, and with the way in which literature shapes our expectations of life as individuals, couples, families, and generations.
The tone of serious playfulness, the structure of the book as
lively/deadly game, links *Night and Day* with *Orlando* and *Flush*,
the least admired of her books. They are certainly as experimental in form as her major works. As satirical comedies, they all
challenge the fundamental myths of patriarchal society. They are
melodramatic, operatic and flamboyantly visual. They "strike
the eye," as she said, and as such they annoy some literary
purists. Looking back from the thirties, Woolf told the com-

---

2. For a critical response, see *Virginia Woolf: The Critical Heritage*, ed. Robin
   Majumdar and Allen McLaurin (London and Boston: Routledge and Kegan
   Paul, 1975).
3. *Monday or Tuesday* (New York: Harcourt, Brace, 1921), p. 14.
4. Sylvia Pankhurst is revered in Ethiopia, where her statue stands to com-
   memorate her work for independence. Leonard Woolf also espoused this
   cause. Woolf's criticism of the suffrage movement in *Night and Day* should
   be seen in the light of the socialism and pacifism which always underlay her
   feminism. Her work for the cause of "adult suffrage," like that of Sylvia
   Pankhurst and many leftist intellectuals, must be seen as an alternative to the
   feminism of those women like Sally Seale to whom the "cause" was a
   personal religion which specifically did not include working men. For a
   discussion of Woolf's feminism see my "No More Horses: Virginia Woolf
   on Art and Propaganda," *Women's Studies*, Virginia Woolf Issue, 1977, and
   "Art and Anger," *Feminist Studies*, Feb. 1978.

poser Ethel Smyth that *Night and Day* might well be her best
book, and that the vision which accompanied its composition
was the key to her creative life.
Night and Day depends structurally on Mozart, stylistically on
Jane Austen, and thematically on Ibsen. *The Magic Flute, Pride
and Prejudice*, and *The Master Builder* may seem to be an odd
combination of sources for a twentieth-century novelist. But all
three had a special appeal for the consciously feminist and consciously female writer's imagination. The novel's structural relation to Mozart is what concerns me here.

Actual "evidence" that my reading of the novel is not completely in the realm of fantasy may be grounded for some readers
in the fact that Virginia Woolf saw a great deal of Goldsworthy
Lowes Dickinson during the composition of *Night and Day*
(1917–1920). Quentin Bell has pointed out to me that Dickinson
was writing *The Magic Flute: A Fantasia* at the time. Whether she
saw the manuscript or not, Woolf must have heard some discussion of the subject, which in Dickinson's version, far more than
in Mozart's, was bound to raise the eyebrows of any female,
feminist or not. While it took courage, Rebecca West has said,
for Virginia Woolf to affront natural male vanity in her novels,
she was only "chastised with whips;"[5] the homosexual intellectuals of her set "chastised her with scorpions." Dickinson's *Fantasia* is a rather puerile "Greek" vision of patriarchy, the quest,
and Sarastro's band of pure men. I find it comic but am sure it
was not meant to be. He makes Tamino not Oriental but English, fair and original Angle/Angel; the magic flute is not the
gift of the Queen of the Night (in Mozart she is Muse and
Mother, of his music and his masculinity), but one of his ancestors (from an old English house, no doubt) had gotten it from
Sarastro. The Queen of the Night is robbed of her stars and her
crown: she is Chaos incarnate,

> Death in life, and life in death,
> Passion's most authentic voice,
> Foe of reason and of choice,
> Secret urge behind the will,
> Now to gender, now to kill![6]

5. Rebecca West, "Autumn and Virginia Woolf," *Ending in Earnest* (Garden
   City: Doubleday, Doran, 1931), pp. 212–213.
6. G. Lowes Dickinson, *The Magic Flute: A Fantasia* (London: George Allen and
   Unwin, 1920), p. 9. See also *The Autobiography of G. Lowes Dickinson*, ed.
   Dennis Proctor (London: Duckworth, 1973).

Dennis Proctor read the *Fantasia* as an antiwar pamphlet; Forster concentrated on its exaltation of reason and mysticism and the introduction of Jesus and Buddha, who are not in Mozart's libretto. Since an earlier *Fantasia* was performed in Roger Fry's Omega Workshops, this one was undoubtedly familiar to the same circle of friends.

E. M. Forster praised the *Fantasia* as being beyond Mozart: "[the] slight pantomime of Tamino and Pamina is exalted into a mythology of Wagnerian scope"; the fire is the war, the water twentieth-century doubt, the castle of Sarastro the modern mind.[7] He found it a "lovely book"; modern readers would perhaps find it as priggish and smug as the institutionalized genteel homosexuality it represents and be glad that it inspired in Virginia Woolf not anger but the warm, light-hearted, realistic response to life and work she made of *Night and Day*.

II

"I went to *Tristan* the other night," Woolf wrote to Barbara Bagenal in 1923, "but the love making bored me. When I was your age I thought it the most beautiful thing in the world — or was it only in deference to Saxon? I told many lies in Covent Garden opera house. My youth was largely spent there. And we used to write the names of operas in books."[8]

But the same audience who recognized the antiwar theme in Lowes Dickinson would have recognized it in Woolf. The brilliant Cambridge Dent / Clive Carey revival of *The Magic Flute* in 1911 appealed to the imagination of the Apostles. There were Masons among the founders of the secret society and traces of Masonic ritual, especially the ark, in its ceremonies. Parsons and Spater have pointed out that Leonard Woolf was especially intrigued by these rites. This led to a London production during the war, greeted by a full page leader in the *Times Literary Supplement* praising the opera as pacifist; and young men wrote from the front saying that they did indeed feel like Sarastro's band of pure young men, and that the Prussians were Monostatos and his followers, representing chaos and militarism. Virginia Woolf recorded in her diary the feeling that Lowes Dickinson and his young friend, who were sitting in the same row with her, had an

7. E. M. Forster, *Goldsworthy Lowes Dickinson* (London: Abinger ed., Edward Arnold, 1973 [1934]), p. 147.
8. Lola L. Szladits, *Other People's Mail* (New York: New York Public Library and Readex, 1973).

instinctive ease with the opera, which escaped her. Her novel, then, is a feminist-pacifist's answer to masculinist-pacifism. Olive Schreiner, who shared her views, was a great admirer of *Night and Day*. That the first principle of Bloomsbury-Cambridge pacifism was hatred of women did not escape Woolf.

The Magic Flute is patriarchy's most glorious myth of itself as civilization. It tells the story of the transition from matriarchy to patriarchy, the maintenance of the male moral order by forcing the daughter to reject her mother. Anthropologically accurate, it stresses the key role of the uncle in maintaining the incest taboo and structuring the patriarchal family by seeing that the daughter marries a foreigner or stranger.

The 1911 Cambridge *Magic Flute* was a direct response to the political upsurge of militant feminism. *Night and Day is* an anti-war novel: it is against the "sex war," the most important political issue in Edwardian England, and it is against the misogyny of Cambridge-Bloomsbury culture, which appropriated the classics and music as male property.

Some interesting notes by Woolf on the opera (1906) in the Monks House Papers, Sussex, suggest a debate within herself over the question of a state opera house. Unlike Shaw, she feared cultural controls but liked the idea of the military protecting the opera house. Covent Garden appealed to her because of the conjunction of cabbages and kings, squalor and splendour, though her 1909 essay on Bayreuth suggests a conversion due to the marriage of nature and art achieved in Wagner's opera house.

Woolf has written the names of operas in her book and even composed *Night and Day* as a modern *Magic Flute*. But more to the point is the confession that she lied in Covent Garden opera house. Mansfield said that *Night and Day* was a lie and I think other critics feel this as well: they see "the truth" in the tragic visionary novels, *To the Lighthouse, The Waves, Between the Acts*. But comedy does not always lie, as Meredith tells us; it is most hampered from telling the truth when relations between men and women are unequal. Perhaps this is the source of the strain in *Night and Day*. Perhaps, like Tolstoy, Woolf only told the truth about men in *Three Guineas,* when she had one foot in her watery grave. Nevertheless, since all fiction lies in order to tell the truth (though we may at times prefer the tragic lie to the comic lie), let us look at Virginia Woolf in her costume as Covent Garden liar. One of *The Magic Flute's* finest themes is lying, comically repeated in *Night and Day*.

Woolf's achievement in *Night and Day* was formal. Actually to
write of such high, moral, and serious subjects with such aban-
doned and yet controlled gaiety was a demanding task which she
set for herself. But to write so comically (the scene in the zoo,
the engagement ring between owners rolling to "father's" feet)
seemed almost sacrilegious while Western culture was destroying itself on the battlefield.

To imitate Mozart, to mock Shakespeare and Henry James, to
poke fun at her own passionate commitment to the feminist
movement, to turn Ibsen's tragedies upside down, was daring
enough for a woman. But it is the tone which shocks. The utter
self-confidence of the impersonal female narrator of the story
makes us as secure as children in our mothers' arms. God and the
narrator, as in Jane Austen, may be as distant as the stars which
demand Katharine's gaze, but they have an order of their own.
We are sure she knows what she is doing.

The tragic icons, Lily Briscoe's triangle and Bernard's "fin in a
waste of waters," have often seemed more significant than the
comic harmony of the circle which shapes *Night and Day* as an
eighteenth-century opera. One is disconcerted to find women's
suffrage exposed by such a comic touch — especially that a novel
which manages to curtsey so gracefully to the past can manage a
stiff little nod in the direction of Ibsen and the future.

Its thirty-three chapters circle the subject of initiation into
society, courtship, and marriage. The characters are engaged in
an elaborate ritual, like an eighteenth-century dance. Mozart's
Magic Flute is invoked as William Rodney's model for a new
poetic drama. And Cassandra plays Mozart throughout the second part of the novel while the music both kindles and calms the
emotions of the characters. But *The Magic Flute* was based on the
symbolism of Masonry; it is about initiation into patriarchal
society, the preservation of which demands the quelling of the
forces of evil represented by the Queen of Night. Woolf reverses
the terms and demands no ritual patricide. Night and Day are
more in harmony than in opposition. The upset to the patriarchal order takes place at twilight and on the thresholds of lighted
rooms and dark streets. The twilight of the old gods is extin-
guished not by Brunhilde's torch but by the light in Mary
Datchet's room which represents "something impersonal and
serene in the spirit of the woman within, working out her plans
far into the night — her plans for the good of a world that none
of them were ever to know" (ND, 506).

Brigid Brophy said that Virginia Woolf brought to English prose an ear that was "quite outstandingly defective."[9] Obviously, she had never read *Night and Day*. For *Night and Day* is the perfect libretto for a classical opera in the comic but melancholy mode of Mozart, with some appropriately modern stylistic dissonances. One wishes that Virginia Woolf's friend Ethel Smyth had composed a score for it. Their shared feminism, love of England, and respect for the formal and classical harmonies was combined with an outrageous sense of humor and a modern visionary sense that alienation could be both expressed and controlled by artistic experimentation.

The magical bells of *The Magic Flute* ring out in the novel in praise of the marriage of those magical Bells, Vanessa and Clive. But the joyful peals of its praise have an undertone of irony. For when Virginia Woolf wrote *Night and Day* the marriage of the Bells had expanded to include other members, most notably Duncan Grant. And Virginia Woolf's admiration for their domestic bliss was aroused by awe at the sheer number of works of art it produced.[10]

That primitive instrument the glockenspiel, which is so effective in the opera in summoning love and controlling rebellion, is in Woolf's hands a magic wand. It is a kind of blessed baton (in the opera it was a parting gift from the King of Day to the Queen of Night) which creates splendid music on an eternal theme.[11] Woolf makes her "Four Passionate Snails" dance to the tune of "an enchanted organ" (her phrase for the prose style of her aunt, Lady Ritchie, who was the prototype of Mrs. Hilbery).[12] But as they conclude the figures of this ancient courtship

9. Brigid Brophy, *Don't Never Forget* (New York: Holt, Rinehart and Winston, 1966), p. 183. She continues: "with the result that onomatopoeia cannot make good the imprecision of her images." Brophy is very interesting on Mozart as a dramatist: "The literature in opera is like a well-contrived exhibition of landscape gardening or architectural town-planning: it *arranges* the vistas down which we glimpse the objects" (p. 112). The same might be said of the structures of the *Magic Flute*, the Masonic "square on the oblong" and the Dantean circle which arranges our perceptions in *Night and Day*.
10. In the novel Katharine and Mrs. Hilbery are trying to write the biography of the great Victorian poet; Mr. Hilbery is writing about Shelley; Ralph, as his assistant, is writing about law but really wants to write the history of the English village; Cassandra Otway's sister is helping her father write his autobiography; her brother, Henry, has written half an opera; Katharine is writing mathematics; William is writing a poetic drama and delivers a paper on Shakespeare; Mary is writing "Some Aspects of the Democratic State," as well as feminist pamphlets with Mr. Clacton and Sally Seale.
11. In the opera it represents the ordinary nonheroic man as well.
12. Woolf described Lady Ritchie's style: "Her most typical, and, indeed, inim-

dance, the happy couple realize that their happiness is made possible by those who are excluded from the dance. Mary Datchet, Sally Seale, and "old Joan up at Highgate" have worked and will work so that Katharine and Ralph can love one another.[13] The spirit of Virginia Woolf's feminism was as strongly, although perhaps unconsciously, at work in *Night and Day* as the "masculinism" of Masonry was in Mozart's *Magic Flute*.

No reader of the first volume of Virginia Woolf's letters can fail to realize that she educated herself in Covent Garden and that her primarily visual imagination found much stimulation there. As Robert Moberly explains it, the staging of the second act of *The Magic Flute* reflects a Masonic structure which is visually apparent. Pyramids of nines are placed on eighteen seats with a great black horn encrusted with gold. Behind them are palm trees. Sarastro and his priests march in carrying palm branches.[14] In Woolf's version it is Mrs. Hilbery who carries armfuls of palm, since it is she and the female tradition which inform the novel.

---

itable sentences rope together a handful of swiftly gathered opposites"; *Collected Essays*, IV, 74. She quotes her aunt: "the sky was like a divine parrot's breast" (p. 75), and *Night and Day* is full of references to parrots, a tribute to Lady Ritchie as well as Papageno.

13. The theme of sisterhood is strong in the novel. Mary's sister cares for their father, making it possible for Mary to live and work in London. Cassandra's sister serves the same function at Stogdon House. Joan will manage to fulfill Ralph's responsibilities at Highgate so that he can be free as well as married to Katharine. Mrs. Hilbery is indebted to her own sisters; Katharine to her aunts, and to her cousin Cassandra, who frees her from her engagement to William and plays "angel in the house" to Mr. and Mrs. Hilbery, charming them by playing Mozart so that Katharine can slip away to discover whether she loves Ralph. Katharine also acknowledges her dependence on Mary and her work. While to Ralph Katharine is the "star-flaming queen," to Katharine that role is played by Mary: the light in her room symbolizes the serious work for socialism and feminism that can make possible marriages like that of Ralph and Katharine, and they recognize their indebtedness in the last scene of the novel.

14. Robert Moberly explains the visual pattern as a pyramid:

	Virtue	
Discretion		Beneficence
Truth	Beauty	Purity
Reason	WISDOM	Nature
Patience	Strength	Friendship

Craftsmanship		Justice
Hard Work Arts		Forgiveness Good Will

Three Mozart Operas, pp. 262–263.

The point I would like to make is that there is a connection between Mozart's and Woolf's uses of these Masonic structures. She was inspired by his music and the visual representation of it in Covent Garden Opera House in the same way that Mozart was inspired by the mysteries and harmonies of Masonry. When Rhoda fantasizes in *The Waves* that "the players take the square and place it upon the oblong. They place it very accurately; they make a perfect dwelling-place" (W, 163), she is visualizing a moral and social structure formed by the patterns of the music, but she is also saying that the greatest art makes the reader or listener feel he has come home. Katharine's "square boxes halved and quartered by straight lines" (ND, 306) are part of the same imaginative process and quite different from Ralph's vision of "a little dot with flames around it," which is the emblem the Sun-King gave to Sarastro in *The Magic Flute.* Katharine says she shares this vision but knows it has nothing to do with her.

Virginia Woolf's description in "The String Quartet" invokes this patriarchal scene from *The Magic Flute,* where the pillars of Sarastro's castle are plainly antifemale:

> As the horns are joined by trumpets and supported by clarions there rise white arches firmly planted on marble pillars . . . Tramp and trumpeting. Clang and clangour. Firm establishment. Fast foundations. March of myriads. Confusion and chaos trod to earth. But this city to which we travel has neither stone nor marble; hangs enduringly; stands unshakeable; nor does a face, nor does a flag greet or welcome. Leave then to perish your hope; droop in the desert my joy; naked advance. Bare are the pillars; auspicious to none; casting no shade; resplendent, severe. Back then I fall, eager no more, desiring only to go — (HH, 26–27)[15]

The most serious connection between *Night and Day* and *The Magic Flute,* however, is structural, not thematic. *Night and Day* takes from Mozart's opera the Triple Accord (which Mozart took from Masonry and mythology). Among them we note those three knocks on the door repeated as Ralph's *leitmotif* throughout the novel. We also discover myriad repetitions, those manifestations Woolf calls, in *Between the Acts,* the "triple ply" and "the threefold melody." All of them, we may assume can be found in the indelible impression made on Woolf's ear by the "magic number three" in Mozart's music. In Covent Gar-

---

15. See Jacques Chailley, *The Magic Flute: Masonic Opera* (New York: Alfred A. Knopf, 1971).

den, Woolf's ear was educated to an eternal classical rhythm
which she never forgot. Her obsessive trinities were used to
form character, as Mozart had done, to suggest dialectical action, and eventually, in *Three Guineas,* to suggest the boring but
compelling repetitions of human action in history. While most
critics do not credit Woolf's educated ear but recognize the paint-
erly qualities of her eye, I think that she made triangles and
squares on oblongs out of the desire to make visual what her
inner ear heard, as she has shown in "The String Quartet." I also
believe that in *Night and Day* Mozart was a stronger influence
than Roger Fry.[16]

"Stone-breaking" as we shall see, was Virginia Woolf's term
for this classical kind of composition. An appropriately pre-
Masonic process, it suggests breaking down the old structures
and building new ones, both literally and morally. The archetype
of her architecture is different from Mozart's Masonic temple to
the sun. The Queen of Night's temple to Isis is not a fit house,
either, for her modern hero and heroine. When night and day are
at peace with one another, at dusk, their vision is of a cottage in
the country.

The dream house can only be attained, however, by getting
Katharine out of that Chelsea monument to the Victorian family,
the Cheyne Walk temple within a temple to great men. But all
the other dwellings figure importantly in the novel as well —
Rodney's eighteenth-century rooms, Ralph's tower with its rook
in Highgate, Mary's Bloomsbury office, her room of her own in
the City, her family's ancient parsonage in Lincoln, and
the Otways' Stogdon House, a "portly three-decker" nineteenth-century sailing ship. It is Mrs. Hilbery, "the magician"
as Katharine calls her, who embraces all the structures in her
abundant arms. As the female artist and her father's daughter,
she comes back from Shakespeare's tomb refreshed and makes
order out of chaos. She encircles London in her carriage and
abducts the young men from those buildings which are exclusively male, those seats of patriarchal power. She brings
Ralph from Lincoln's Inn and Rodney from Whitehall, passes St.
Paul's and conjures up a fantasy of her daughter's wedding in

---

16. See Allen McLaurin, *The Echoes Enslaved* (Cambridge: Cambridge University Press, 1973) for a fascinating section on repetition and rhythm in Woolf
that compares her writing to the music of Satie. I think the source was
Mozart and Woolf's Cambridge was Covent Garden.

Westminster Abbey. In the temple of art she blesses the two
couples and sends them out. She has been as effective in liberating the young men as the young women. For the economic facts
are such that the women will provide the money to buy Ralph's
pastoral peace in a country cottage and Rodney's Chelsea town
house, in which he can find the intellectual stimulation he needs
to write.

III

Night and Day celebrates, as classically as its title suggests, the
union of the eternal opposites, night and day, nature and reason,
duty and freedom, man and woman. A sweet and comic
Epithalamion, the marriage song is also ironic and melancholy.[17]
The ill-matched couples are sorted out and mated,
blessed, initiated, and brought into society as in Mozart, the
classical master of the celebratory humanistic values to which the
novel constantly refers. In the academic year from fall to spring
which fixes the story in time, William Rodney, the rather pedan-
tic poet, moves from studying the score of *Don Giovanni* to *The
Magic Flute*.

The connections are concretely made. It is that modern Sarastro, Mr. Hilbery, who demands that Cassandra play Mozart.
Like Pamina's uncle in *The Magic Flute* he is also, despite his
wisdom, rather careless about his niece's male associates.
Katharine's presence is "like a strain of music" to Ralph, though
neither listens to Mozart — he is the means of pacifying the family so that they may meet and talk. They "felt an enormous sense
of relief at the license which the music gave them to loosen their
hold upon the mechanism of behaviour." Even Mrs. Hilbery
"charmed herself into good spirits again by remembering the
existence of Mozart." "The melody of Mozart seemed to express
the easy and exquisite love of the two upstairs" (ND, 384, 416,
424).[18]

---

17.   "That's early Mozart, of course — "
      "But the tune, like all his tunes, makes one despair — I mean hope . . ."
      ". . . Sorrow, sorrow. Joy, joy. Woven together, like reeds in the moon-
      light" (HH, 24).
18. See ND, 456, for an evocative picture of an opera house: "The hall re-
      sounded with brass and strings, alternately of enormous pomp and majesty,
      and then of sweetest lamentation. The reds and creams of the background,
      the lyres and harps and urns and skulls . . ."

The thirty-three chapters circle through Katharine's purgatorial sufferings as Angel in the House and Ralph's as Breadwinner, to the infernal betrayals and insecurities of all the characters, to a resolution as a purely human comedy. The descents and ascents suggest the joys and sorrows of love, the hope for Mozart's heaven here on earth. Ralph and Katharine, like Pamina and Tamino, endure both the trial by fire and the trial by water in the last chapter of the novel. In fact, Pamina's "mad scene" is imitated in Katharine's "mad scene" when she fears she has lost Ralph.[19] None of the characters have faith in Isis and Osiris, but rather in the one legacy they can accept from the Victorians, the desire for hard work.

The pastoral idyll, which her sister Vanessa seemed to be living in the country with Duncan Grant, was Woolf's inspiration for the novel. What most impressed her was that their domestic arrangements allowed them the freedom to work. It was a scene of great creative outpouring. The perceptive novelist shows in *Night and Day* a brilliantly accurate historical portrait of the differences in attitudes toward work of middle-class Edwardian men and women. William Rodney begrudges every minute of drudgery in his government office which keeps him from his poetic drama. Ralph Denham chafes at the bonds of domestic responsibility which keep him in his law office. To the women it is another matter altogether. Katharine daydreams about marriage (first to William and then to Ralph), with no thought of sex but with a deep longing for the opportunity to work: "she had come in from a lecture, and she held a pile of books in her hand, scientific books, and books about mathematics and astronomy which she had mastered," and later "fancy the evenings of married life spent thus . . . or with a book, perhaps, for then she would have time to read her books, and to grasp firmly with every muscle of her unused mind what she longed to know" (ND, 138, 282).

And Mary, with her discipline and decision, goes from that time-honored condition of women, volunteer work (even though the cause is women's suffrage), to become the salaried secretary of a movement for greater social change. Margaret Llewelyn Davies, of the Working Women's Cooperative Guild,

---

19. For a fine reading of *Night and Day* and this scene in particular, see Avrom Fleishman, *Virginia Woolf: A Critical Reading* (Baltimore: Johns Hopkins University Press, 1975).

called "Mary Datchet" in Woolf's letters to her, devoted her life to the cause of social justice, and she appears again as Eleanor in *The Years*. She suppresses her personal relationships as well as her writing in a conscious effort to find salvation in work.

When Ralph complains to her about loneliness and his sufferings in love, Mary utters my favorite line: " 'There's always work,' she said, a little aggressively." Ralph thinks that Mary wants him to leave, but she is thinking about Katharine: "She doesn't know what work is . . . But it's the thing that saves one — I'm sure of that . . . Where should I be now if I hadn't got to go to my office every day? Thousands of people would tell you the same thing — thousands of women. I tell you, work is the only thing that saved me, Ralph" (ND, 391–392).

This is one of Woolf's amazing political perceptions: that the ideal of the female utopia was to be in paradise alone, to work. (Work elevated to the status of the highest Christian virtues was what made Masonry appealing to Mozart.) And surely "opera" as "works" tells us of Woolf's own industrious approach to art. Both marriage and the rejection of marriage are for the middle-class heroines of this novel the means to an end, domestic peace and freedom to work. Even the blithe Cassandra views marriage to Ralph as an opportunity to be educated. We expect these marriages to produce not babies, but books.[20] Just as the woman writer, in Woolf's terms, was struggling from the personal to the impersonal, on a different time scale from the male writer, so the aspiring young woman needed work and discipline when her male counterpart was rejecting those Victorian values.

As we move from October to June, we realize that it is not only the year which is academic. (But this "male" academic year is paralleled by a "female" matriarchal year, deriving from Jane Harrison's studies of preclassical Greece and structuring the time sequence of all the novels.) The novel ends with Ralph and Katharine at the half-open door, on the threshold of a new life. They are about to try a new experiment with an old institution, a marriage which will provide peace and respect, a mutual silence so that both can work. Their gentle "good night" suggests that

20. Cassandra is the name of the narrator in "A Society," which ends with one of the members saying, "Oh, Cassandra, for Heaven's sake let us devise a method by which men may bear children! It is our only chance. For unless we provide them with some innocent occupation we shall get neither good people nor good books," *Monday or Tuesday*, p. 39.

most of their passion has been spent opening and closing the doors and windows which have architecturally and symbolically shaped the book into a comedy as surely as they shaped *The Master Builder* into a tragedy. *The Magic Flute* gives us Sarastro's castle in real as well as Masonic terms; unlike Ibsen's dream "castles in the air," it is the model of the patriarchal home.

The score of *Don Giovanni* lies open on William Rodney's piano, dominating the tone of the first half of the novel. His playing Don Juan is amusingly depicted: Katharine calls him "half poet and half old maid," and Ralph thinks, "that little pink-cheeked dancing-master to marry Katharine? that gibbering ass with the face of a monkey on an organ? that posing, vain, fantastical fop? with his tragedies and his comedies, his innumerable spites and prides and pettinesses?" (ND, 68, 303).

By chapter 22 the music master has brought in a new score, *The Magic Flute.* Katharine has become a cold, stargazing sorceress, the Queen of the Night, and Rodney finds himself a more feminine friend in Cassandra. Her "melodious and whimsical temperament" appeals to him. She even plays the flute: "He recalled with pleasure the amusing way in which her nose, long like all the Otway noses, seemed to extend itself into the flute, as if she were some inimitably graceful species of musical mole" (ND, 280). Significantly, Cassandra was the name of Jane Austen's sister, who, by burning her letters, saw to it that she would be "impersonal" forever. It was also the name Florence Nightingale took in her autobiographical fragment railing at the indiscriminate education of girls like Cassandra — which Virginia Woolf's friend Ray Strachey printed in her history of women's suffrage, *The Cause,* and which Woolf recommends to readers of *A Room of One's Own.*[21] Cassandra and Mary, natural

---

21. *A Room of One's Own,* p. 53, n. 3. Of the death of Ray Strachey, Woolf wrote: "that very large woman, with the shock of grey hair, and the bruised lip; that monster, whom I remember typical of young womanhood, has suddenly gone. She has a kind of representative quality, in her white coat and trousers; wall-building, disappointed, courageous, without — what? — imagination?" *A Writer's Diary,* p. 325. Ray Strachey's book ends: "the change in the type of heroine required for 'best sellers' is the real test, and it is not until the 'strong silent hero' ceases to 'dominate' the gentle heroine that the end of the Women's Movement will have arrived"; *The Cause* (1928) (New York: Kennikat Press, 1969), p. 420. Florence Nightingale's fragment "Cassandra" was written in 1859; both Mill and Jowett advised her not to publish. Woolf sustains this critique, describing women like Katharine and Cassandra in terms of an ineffectual versatility: "Now it was socialism, now it was silkworms, now it was music" (ND, 283).

woman and rational woman, then, are in possession of those
magic instruments which the King of Day has left to his "star-
flaming queen" in Mozart's opera. They are given to the questing males, Tamino and Papageno, and are used both to win and
to make joyful the angry rebellious slaves in *The Magic Flute*.

Masonic misogyny and the ancient rituals of patriarchal culture form the structure of the opera, but Woolf's novel has made
the energy of culture a female force embodied in the figure of the
abundant Mrs. Hilbery. And it is Mr. Hilbery as Sarastro, formidable and rational benevolent despot, who is driven from the
temple, "the extravagant, inconsiderate, uncivilized male, out-
raged somehow and gone bellowing to his lair with a roar which
still sometimes reverberates in the most polished of drawing
rooms" (ND, 500). At the same time, Ralph Denham makes a
wonderfully serious recreation of Papageno, bird-catcher and
liar.[22] He keeps a "decrepit rook" in his room, watches birds
instead of shooting them with Mary's brothers in Lincoln, feeds
the sparrows in the park as he lies to Mary and confesses he is a
liar. He sees Katharine as "a bright-plumed bird poised easily
before further flight." It is Ralph, the natural man, not William
the artist, who is Woolf's visionary character:

> an odd image came to his mind of a lighthouse besieged by the flying
> bodies of lost birds, who were dashed senseless, by the gale, against
> the glass. He had a strange sensation that he was both lighthouse and
> bird; he was steadfast and brilliant; and at the same time he was
> whirled, with all other things, senseless against the glass. (ND, 394)

22. Ralph is also very like Leonard Woolf; his voice has "a slight vibrating or
creaking sound" (ND, 17); he is compared to Ruskin and describes himself
as a rebel against "the family system." Katharine calls him "penniless," a
melodramatic Dickensian word not characteristic of Woolf's prose style, but
exactly the word she uses to describe Leonard Woolf in her letters announc-
ing her marriage to her friends. Ralph lives at the Apple Orchard, Mount
Ararat Road, Highgate, in a tower with his rook, which suggests that he is a
Jew, a botanist, an intellectual, and also perhaps like Noah. There is another
mention of Jewishness in the novel. When the aunts come to Mrs. Hilbery to
complain of cousin Cyril living in sin, she casts about for an explanation:
" 'Nowadays, people don't think so badly of these things as they used to do,'
she began. 'It will be horribly uncomfortable for them sometimes but if they
are brave, clever children, as they will be, I dare say it'll make remarkable
people of them in the end. Robert Browning used to say that every great
man has Jewish blood in him, and we must try to look at it in that light' "
(ND, 123). Mrs. Hilbery is always on the side of revolution. When the aunts
fulminate about a third son born out of wedlock, to bear the family name,
Mrs. Hilbery says, "But let us hope it will be a girl" (ND, 122).

These are the only lines in the novel which seem to speak in Woolf's "authentic" voice. Her truth-teller is a liar.

George Bernard Shaw once said that *The Magic Flute* was the music of his humanist and rationalist religion, an allegory of the human struggle for personal goodness and order.[23] It does seem at times like *Pilgrim's Progress* with comic relief.[24] But in *Night and Day* Woolf took up this age-old story and told it from the female point of view. Tamino's question at the end of act I, "O endless night! hast thou no breaking? When dawns the day mine eyes are seeking?" is universal. Woolf, like Mozart, preferred to place her high moral seriousness in a comic setting.

The same, of course, had been done by Shakespeare, and consequently he, too, is one of the heroes of the novel.[25] But even Shakespeare is treated comically. Mrs. Hilbery misquotes and mumbles; one of the aunts carries him in her pocket; Katharine refuses to read him; Rodney impersonates him; tea and dinner conversation are full of him. But the best joke of all is Mrs. Hilbery's pilgrimage to Stratford with her theory that Anne Hathaway wrote the sonnets. She "knows" that this theory implies a "menace to the safety of the heart of civilization itself" (ND, 427– 428). According to Quentin Bell this incident is based on an actual one, as Mrs. Hilbery is based on Virginia Woolf's aunt.[26] She said to Samuel Butler while he was working on his own theories of the *Odyssey's* female author, "Oh, Mr. Butler, do you know my theory about the Sonnets — that they

23. "Music in London," *Major Critical Essays* (New York: W. H. Wise, 1931), II, 275.
24. Robert Moberly calls *The Magic Flute* "the most beautiful and entertaining sermon ever written"; *Three Mozart Operas,* p. 286. Ford Madox Ford called *Night and Day* "a severe love story"; *Picadilly Review,* Oct. 23, 1919, p. 6. Not known for the severity of his own attitude toward love, Ford heard in the novel "the voice of George Eliot . . . who . . . has lost the divine rage to be didactic."
25. For readings of the novel as Shakespearean comedy, see Fleishman, *Virginia Woolf,* pp. 22– 24; Margaret Comstock, "George Meredith, Virginia Woolf and their Feminist Comedy" (Ph.D. diss., Stanford University, 1975); also Comstock's essay on *Night and Day* in the 1976 *Women's Studies* special issue on Virginia Woolf.
26. Quentin Bell quotes from remarks by Virginia Woolf concerning her new novel: "I am the principal character in it & I expect I'm a very priggish & severe young woman but perhaps you'll see what I was like at 18 — I think the most interesting character is evidently my mother who is made exactly like Lady Ritchie [Aunt Annie] down to every detail apparently. Everyone will know who it is, of course"; *Virginia Woolf,* p. 42.

were written by Anne Hathaway?" but he didn't know she was joking.[27]

A musical inspiration may have also come from another direction. Lady Ritchie was Thackeray's daughter and the sister of Leslie Stephen's first wife. Virginia Woolf reviewed her letters in an essay called, oddly enough, "The Enchanted Organ." She describes her aunt's style as musical — "so merry and so plaintive." "The guns are firing," Woolf wrote "and there she sits scribbling brilliant nonsense in her diary about 'matches and fairy tales' " "To embrace oddities and produce a charming, laughing harmony from incongruities was her genius" might be a description of *Night and Day*. Woolf's tribute to her aunt reads: "And the music to which she dances, frail and fantastic, but true and distinct, will sound on outside our formidable residences when all the brass bands of literature have (let us hope) blared themselves to perdition."[28]

The character of Mrs. Hilbery and the novel itself are Woolf's tribute to that music created by the females in her family, truly an "enchanted organ," a hymn to the feminine search for freedom and order as *The Magic Flute* was a hymn to the masculine quest.

For Woolf it is the patriarchs who represent the forces of darkness, while the matriarchs are as sunny as Mrs. Hilbery with her arms full of flowers from Shakespeare's tomb. The vision is one of future creative flowering for women, built on the

---

27. Samuel Butler's *Notebooks* were a source not only for this novel, but for all of Woolf's work. In *Night and Day* it is Rodney who keeps a notebook as Butler's "perfect literary man," as it is Bernard in *The Waves*. See Butler's remark "It is a wise tune that knows its own father," intended to defend borrowing from the classics as a technique of the greatest genius. Also, his passages on unity and separateness seem to me to be the source for Woolf's philosophy: "In the closest union there is still some separate existence of component parts; in the most complete separation there is still a reminiscence of union. When they are most separate the atoms seem to bear in mind that they may have to come together again . . . the two main ideas underlying all action are desire for closer unity or desire for separateness. The puzzle which puzzles every atom is the same which puzzles ourselves — a conflict of duties — our duty towards ourselves, and our duty as members of a body politic. It is swayed by its sense of being a separate thing — of having a life to itself which nothing can share; it is also swayed by the feeling that in spite of this it is only part of an individuality which is greater than itself which absorbs it"; Butler, *Selections,* ed. Geoffrey Keynes and Brian Hill (New York: Dutton, 1951), pp. 211, 142.

28. *Collected Essays,* IV, 73, 75.

strength of the women who have gone before. Katharine is blessed and helped by her mother, "that ancient voyager." She has appropriated to herself the study of Greek, mathematics, and astronomy, stormed the bastion of patriarchal culture by demanding discipline in those closed spheres of learning by which our culture defines its highest values. Ralph, less classbound than William Rodney, has no stake in preserving patriarchy. He is not threatened by her love of the abstract. He hates great men as much as she hates great books. The natural lower-class man is the agent of freedom for the upper-middle-class woman. In *The Magic Flute* that odd duet praising married love as heaven here on earth is sung by Papageno and Pamina.

Men may be mocked in *Night and Day* but they are not murdered. In *The Magic Flute* the male moral order is preserved only when the princess rejects her mother. The patriarchal blessing is bestowed only after the Queen of Night and the slaves have been banished forever. Woolf is not so severe in her reversal. Mrs. Hilbery's blessing is not contingent on Katharine's rebellion against her father. Mrs. Hilbery, the rather muddled matriarch, will mend that breach too.

Woolf had a kind of fondness for Victorian fathers not shared by Samuel Butler and Lytton Strachey in their attacks.[29] If one takes the tragic view of the "flower beneath the foot" in relations between women and men or children and fathers, the result is sheer suicidal anger. Sylvia Plath's Nazi boot in "Daddy" may be an apt metaphor for her sense of oppression, but the writer who plays victim loses the reader, as Virginia Woolf well knew.

The monstrous slippers of the great Victorian poet in *Night and Day* make us laugh. Yet they symbolize effectively his domestic tyranny. Enshrined as they are, and lovingly fingered by his admirers, they expand in the reader's mind. They have that formidable fatherly bulk of the statue in *Don Giovanni*. We wonder, if the poet's biography were ever written, if it would expose the idol's clay feet. We think of the slippers in *Hedda Gabler;* Hedda rejects the role of domestic slavery when she refuses to accept her husband's slippers, piously proffered by his devoted aunt. Surely we are meant to make these connections.

---

29. Woolf also uses Butler's "alps and sanctuaries" as male and female images, here as well as throughout her work.

But it is only possible to do so because the scene is described
with comic irony. Those Victorian slippers clearly will not fit,
and Katharine, with Ralph's help, will not put them on.
Woolf attacks the fathers, as Mozart attacks the mothers. Her
weapons are different from Ibsen's but they do the job. She has
exorcized Victorian family ghosts without once mentioning
syphilis. Her lack of sexual frankness seems to have disturbed
some of her critics. But killing the Angel in the House was a
revolution in itself; she left some work for the women who
would come after her.

Night and Day does not even pay its debt to the author of *The
Master Builder* with quotation marks.[30] But Woolf has invented
no Hilda Wangel. The terms of the novel are female and the
liberating spirit is male and inhabits the person of Ralph Denham, who arrives in the Hilberys' drawing room like a breath of
fresh air. He insists on class distinctions and needs no alpenstock
and hobnailed boots. It is the "alps of his mind" which are
impressive. Mary Datchet's walking stick entwined with ivy
may resemble the glockenspiel only visually, but still it is
appropriately symbolic of the lonely role of peacemaker she has
assumed between the factions of the radical causes she believes
will change the world. Like Hilda's alpenstock in *The Master
Builder*, it also heralds the arrival of "the younger generation
knocking at the door." The magic bell is Ralph Denham on the
telephone.

Ibsen's name is invoked, along with Samuel Butler's, as a saint
in the litany of free love which Katharine supports in her cousin's
life, but eventually rejects for her own, softened by her mother's
definition of love without marriage as "ugly." Significantly, the
grounds for rejection are artistic, not moral.

In conscious imitation of Jane Austen, the opening of *Night
and Day* reads: "It was a Sunday evening in October and in
common with many other young ladies of her class, Katharine

30. The "younger generation knocking at the door" theme is from *The Master
Builder*, as well as the lamps with green shades of Ralph's and Mary's rooms,
those essential props in Ibsen plays which most distressed Henry James.
Woolf recommended that E. M. Forster read Ibsen to understand his
method of combining realism and symbolism, for his achievement of "complete reality of the suburb and complete reality of the soul," like the combination of Pope and Dostoevsky which Rodney recommends to Cassandra.
See *Collected Essays*, I, 346.

Hilbery was pouring out tea" (ND, 9). Irony, wit, and social criticism dissect love and marriage in the English middle classes in the Austen manner. The weapons of the novelist are small and sharp and brightly polished; most of the action takes place in that twilit hour between night and day, when social conventions are alternately preserved and strained over the teacups. Henry James' *Portrait of a Lady* is also recalled here for a portrait of what the feminist Vera Brittain called the making of a "lady into woman." Katharine Hilbery Denham also recalls Katharine Dereham, the heroine of *A Dark Lantern,* reviewed by Woolf in 1905, in which the feminist novelist Elizabeth Robins allows her sensitive female artist to be liberated from a nervous breakdown by a lower-class man.

Ibsen's theme in *The Master Builder* of "the younger generation knocking at the door" is repeated as a theme in a Mozart opera, where the structure demands that there be a happy ending. The eighteenth century is constantly invoked; its literary and political values are a kind of order Woolf wants to impose on the chaos of the contradictions and conflicts between the Victorians and the Edwardians.

All of Ibsen's revolutionary heroines are their fathers' daughters.[31] They slam the doors and break all the windows in the house of the patriarchal family. With no opportunity for education or self-expression they force men to build "castles in the air" for them, as Hilda does in *The Master Builder.* The play is a warning to society about giving women the opportunity to do useful work so their dreams of power do not destroy men. Ibsen saw that it was the male artist who was destroyed by the frustrated woman, in his desire, like the master builder Solness, to build spires to her aspirations.

Katharine confides to Mary her own desire "to beat people down." "I want to assert myself," she exclaims. "Ah, but I want to trample upon their prostrate bodies!" (ND, 58–59). So she would, we feel, if she married William Rodney. But tragedy is avoided when Woolf provides her with a suitable lower-class

---

31. Sally Seale is the self-professed "father's daughter" in *Night and Day.* Her muddle-headedness, her religious fanaticism, and her unswerving devotion to "the cause" are seen as directly deriving from being the uneducated but passionate "daughter of an educated man," as Woolf describes herself in *Three Guineas* and as Ibsen described his nineteenth-century heroines.

man, a comrade who is convinced (with some effort on Katharine's part) that she will neither be exploited nor worshiped. If left alone, she will have no need to live vicariously through him. Like Tamino, Ralph is an exotic "foreigner" and seeks knowledge, not power.

The self-proclaimed fathers' daughters in *Night and Day* are Sally Seale and Mrs. Hilbery. It makes them both romantic and visionary — they seem stuck in the nineteenth century, at odds with Katharine's eighteenth-century rationality and Mary's twentieth-century courage. But as Mrs. Hilbery shakes off her girlish role and pays her debts to the fathers at Stratford, at St. Paul's, and at Westminster Abbey, she seems to realize that she is much more interested in maternal than paternal family history. The reason that the biography of her father never gets written is that Mrs. Hilbery is really much more interested in her mother. It is not revelations about her father's sex life which distress her, but those about her mother's. It is when Mrs. Hilbery and her daughter abandon their roles as priestesses in the temple and speak woman to woman about their ancestress that real communication begins. Her theory about Anne Hathaway writing the sonnets perhaps expresses her own suspicions about the source of her father's poetry. Mrs. Hilbery leaves her father's house at rather a late age for finding her own identity, but Woolf was aware that society makes things more difficult for women. She returns dreaming of her daughter's wedding in the place of her father's funeral.

Hilda Wangel had of course insisted on a complete break with the past; Solness must not only build her a new church but overcome his fear of heights by crowning the spire with a wreath. The act combines sex and death when the view of woman's desire for power is based on fear. He plunges to his death. Ralph, described as one of Woolf's male mountaineers, does not see marriage as a battle of the sexes, a competition with winners and losers. We expect Katharine and Ralph to transform the old institution together, as Virginia Woolf felt she and Leonard and Vanessa and Clive Bell would.

The building metaphors of *Night and Day* reflect Ibsen's concern with social questions and the role of the artist who distinguishes between being an architect and being a skilled laborer ("stone-breaking" and "flying" were Woolf's terms) and

Mozart's Masonic metaphors about building a moral character.
The vision is remarkably like Rhoda's in *The Waves:*

> "There is a square; there is an oblong. The players take the square and
> place it upon the oblong. They place it very accurately; they make a
> perfect dwelling place. Very little is left outside. The structure is now
> visible; what is inchoate is here stated; we are not so various or so
> mean; we have made oblongs and stood them upon squares. This is
> our triumph; this is our consolation.
>
> The sweetness of this content overflowing runs down the walls of
> my mind, and liberates understanding. Wander no more, I say; this is
> the end." (W, 163)

Even Katharine, secret geometrix, would draw "square boxes
halved and quartered by straight lines" (ND, 306).

Unlike Ibsen or Mozart, Woolf does not demand that the old
cities and temples be razed so the "younger generation" can
inhabit them. Let the temples to dead men be opened to living
women, she cries. And not only to heroic women alone, but to
women with men. Let them record not only the history of male
achievement, male work, but women's work as well.

It was a rather optimistic view, surely, and one she had
changed by the time she wrote *Three Guineas.* For those buildings were not so elastic as she imagined, and the cottage in the
country did not satisfy all her desires. But *Night and Day* is as
bent on blessing as is *The Master Builder* on hurling a curse at the
old order. Mozart is clearly the stronger influence.

The characters of *Night and Day* agree in their rejection of the
tragic drama of Ibsen and Wagner. William Rodney, as the new
Shakespeare, chooses his models in Shakespeare's comedies and
Mozart's *Don Giovanni* and *The Magic Flute.* William attempts
the role of Byron's *Don Juan* (Woolf had "fallen in love" with
Byron while writing *Night and Day*) but his paper is about
Shakespeare. His poetic drama, experimental in form, will be
more like *All's Well That Ends Well* than *Don Juan.*

But the plot of his life seems arranged by the author of *Man
and Superman,* for Woolf recognized as Shaw did that Mozart's
comic treatment of the theme had been far more difficult to
execute than Wagner's tragedy. In fact, Shaw felt that Wagner's
concept of love-death was a more dangerous and revolutionary
idea than anything in Marx. Woolf followed Shaw's lead in rejecting a romantic nineteenth-century tragic view of love and
marriage.

Virginia Woolf made the same assertion critically when she compared Jane Austen to the Greeks:

> In Jane Austen, too, we have the same sense, though the ligatures are much less tight, that her figures are bound and restricted to a few definite movements. She too, in her modest, everyday prose, chose the dangerous art where one slip meant death.[32]

That is rather strong language. But it is almost the same language in which Shaw asserts the superiority of the moral allegory of Mozart over Wagner. (Did she find the lovemaking in *Tristan* boring because it was romantically tragic?)

When William Rodney instructed Cassandra "to read Pope in preference to Dostoevsky until her feeling for form was more highly developed" (ND, 280), he was describing what the novelist tried to do in *Night and Day*. The clashes between the old and young, male and female, the workers for and the observers of humanity — are deliberately shaped and orchestrated to produce harmony.

Woolf pounces on his male vanity and his pedantry to reveal not only the folly of being masculine, but how unmasculine it is to be so foolish. Rodney with his mirror, his male props about him (the faded red dressing gown, slippers, pipes, books, photographs of Greek statues) is less a man than someone playing the role of a man. His "rather prominent eyes and the impulsive stammering manner," as well as his angularity, suggest Lytton Strachey. (He did of course admire Pope.) He is not an appropriately androgynous artist. Not Don Juanish, he is merely donnish.

His fussiness about dress and propriety first amuses Katharine, then depresses her. He recommends marriage for her and all women: "Why, you're nothing at all without it; you're only half alive" (ND, 66). In a misogynist mood he boasts to Denham that Katharine is "spoilt" and leads "an odious, self-centered life." Chapter 11 is a farcical representation of the clash between the masculine and feminine, as Katharine cries "My oysters!" and William reads aloud his play. Demonstrating his theory that "every mood has its meter," he asks for her criticism, not of his skill but of his rendering of passion: "I trust you where feeling is concerned" (ND, 140). But Katharine is bored. "Still, she re-

---

32. "On Not Knowing Greek," *Collected Essays*, I, 3.

flected, these sorts of skill are almost exclusively masculine; women neither practice them nor know how to value them; and one's husband's proficiency in this direction might legitimately increase one's respect for him, since mystification is no bad basis for respect" (ND, 140).

William criticizes her coldness, silence, inattention to dress, and lack of respect for her elders and betters; his praise is for her beauty and her French accent. When he criticizes her again at the Otways' she rebuffs him, and her cousin thinks that "women have a peculiar blindness to the feelings of men." Woolf describes Rodney's response in her most Austenish tone:

> Perhaps, for he was a very vain man, he was more hurt that Henry had seen him rebuffed than by the rebuff itself. He was in love with Katharine, and vanity is not decreased but increased by love, especially, one may hazard, in the presence of one's own sex. But Rodney enjoyed the courage which springs from that laughable and lovable defect, and when he had mastered his first impulse, in some way to make a fool of himself, he drew inspiration from the perfect fit of his evening dress. He chose a cigarette, tapped it on the back of his hand, displayed his exquisite pumps on the edge of the fender, and summoned his self-respect. (ND, 203)

His man-to-man talk with Henry repeats the earlier scene with Ralph, where Rodney's man-of-the-world advice about women is a result of a rebuff from Katharine:

> You talk to them about their children, if they have any, or their accomplishments — painting, gardening, poetry — they're so delightfully sympathetic. Seriously, you know I think a woman's opinion of one's poetry is always worth having. Don't ask them for their reasons. Just ask them for their feelings. (ND, 205)

Tamino says the same thing in *The Magic Flute*.

Rodney, as Don Juan, attempts to win Katharine with a patter song enumerating her faults: "Katharine doesn't like Titian. She doesn't like apricots, she doesn't like peaches, she doesn't like green peas. She likes the Elgin marbles and gray days without any sun. She's a typical example of the cold northern nature" (ND, 173). All he does is make herself clearer to herself and, as she gains in self-definition, realizing that her rebellions and dreams have a pattern, she moves further away from him.

When Don Juan suffers hell in this infernal comedy, he deserves it. After telling Mary and Katharine that he has acquired

his knowledge of art from men — "it's a way men have" — he
mocks Katharine in his proprietary way:

> "She pretends that she's never read Shakespeare. And why should she
> read Shakespeare, since she *is* Shakespeare — Rosalind, you know,"
> and he gave his queer little chuckle. Somehow this compliment ap-
> peared very old-fashioned and almost in bad taste. Mary actually felt
> herself blush, as if he had said "the sex" or "the ladies" . . . "She
> knows enough — enough for all decent purposes. What do you
> women want with learning, when you have so much else —
> everything, I should say — everything Leave us something, eh,
> Katharine?" (ND, 175–176)

IV

Sex and the eighteenth century, Virginia Woolf might well
agree with Brigid Brophy, are perennially interesting subjects.
While the brilliant, impersonal, socially ironic style of *Night and
Day* may inspire the reader to congratulate this twentieth-
century writer for the sheer audacity of her tribute to Jane Austen, Woolf confided to her diary that she would rather be
known as the author of *Four Passionate Snails* than as the new
Jane Austen. It was Katherine Mansfield who saw the source in
Austen, but missed it in Mozart: Pamina in *The Magic Flute*
wishes she were a snail to hide from Sarastro.

But Woolf had more in common with "the most perfect artist
among women" than comic wit; for *Night and Day* is as "biting
of tongue but tender of heart" as her model's, as "impersonal"
and "inscrutable." The novelist "wishes neither to reform nor to
annihilate; she is silent," Virginia Woolf praised Jane Austen,
describing her as she herself might be described: "charming but
perpendicular, loved at home but feared by strangers."[33] The
critics berated them both for not writing of war. The little scenes
they describe, like *The Magic Flute,* may be pastoral, even uto-
pian in their expression of the dream of human goodness, of the
possibility of happiness. But the struggle against the fear of
death, which is the drama of the conflicts of the approach to
marriage and the initiation into society, both saw as eternal.
Perhaps *Night and Day* is a comic lie, but it is also as brave and
affirmative an act as marriage itself was in Virginia Woolf's eyes.

---

33. "Jane Austen," *Collected Essays,* I, 154, 145, 146, 149, 144–145.

As Woolf's memoirs of a dutiful daughter, *Night and Day* is remarkably free of resentment. The novel is an act of filial piety and rebellion at the same time. A gift from sister to sister, it celebrates sisterhood. It bows, awkwardly and comically, perhaps, to the women of Woolf's own family through the generous and saintly, funny and eccentric character of Mrs. Hilbery. It enshrines mothers who bless their daughters, who open the doors to love and freedom, preparing and making easier "the way of all flesh."

7. The Form of Fact and Fiction: Jacob's Room as Paradigm

RALPH FREEDMAN

I

Virginia Woolf's response to the tension between fiction and life can be summed up in the well-known title of one of her collections of essays, *Granite and Rainbow*. The need to reconcile the "hard" facts of daily existence with an imaginative vision confronts every artist. Yet Woolf assumed this task with particular clarity and self-consciousness. In her postwar novels beginning with *Jacob's Room*, these two aspects of art are brought together in most striking forms.

As a writer of fiction, Woolf's principal task was to find appropriate patterns that would allow her to project imagery in the high style of the lyric while retaining a tough lineament of concrete facts.[1] In her criticism she often referred to this requirement of her art as a conflict between the "inner" and the "outer," but in her fiction she also focused on these relations in a different way. As she contemplated consciousness at work and sought to analyze its components, she became aware of the need to create adequate forms for the personal and social lives of her characters, her narrators, and indeed of herself. This encompassing vision had to find, in Roger Fry's famous words, its corresponding

---

1. Both Woolf herself and many of her critics have observed this relationship. See Alice van Buren Kelley, *The Novels of Virginia Woolf: Fact and Vision*, as well as my own remarks in the Introduction to this volume. David Daiches pointed to this double strain in her work in his small book on Woolf in the early forties, *Virginia Woolf* (Norfolk, Conn.: New Directions, 1942), p. 36. Compare my discussion in *The Lyrical Novel* (Princeton: Princeton University Press, 1963), pp. 185ff.

design. The novels implementing this need established such visions as artifacts of the imagination.[2]

It is a truism about Virginia Woolf that in spite of the experimental cast of her work she was always at home in the main stream of the English novel. Her fiction explores sensibilities within the context of social relations: they are based on the perceptions that men and women entertain of themselves as individuals engaged in a society whose boundaries have drawn the contours of her art. As we know, a formal history connects Virginia Woolf's novels with Jane Austen's themes, not because of the common sex of the two authors, but because they exemplify the same tradition at similar moments in its development. With their visions of society expressed in the language of largely conventional personal relations, Woolf and Austen both wove the texture of manners by which English fiction has been traditionally defined.[3] At the same time, Woolf's involvement in facts and in the way knowledge functions indicates that she had also turned toward a British tradition in philosophy, incorporating both the empiricism of Locke and Hume and its countercurrents in the eighteenth century and beyond.[4] This mingling of different literary and philosophical traditions to analyze the mind's activity and to recompose its form, accounts for the distinctive shapes of Woolf's novels designed to cast their dual purpose in a new, brilliantly conceived perspective.

In Woolf's universe of fact, as in her universe of fiction, her identity as a moral and social being and her identity as an artist were fused. Her manner of pursuing these two sides of her work is derived from her belief that art resolves the tensions between

2. I am grateful to Jane Marcus, as editor of a forthcoming collection of essays on Virginia Woolf, *Virginia Woolf A/Slant* (London: Macmillan), for making available two essays. The first is an investigation of Roger Fry's adaptation of "sight" in *To the Lighthouse*, which is germane at this point: Sau-ling Cynthia Wong, "Of Flaming Clouds and Kitchen Tables: Roger Fry and the Uses of Sight in *To the Lighthouse*." The other is cited in note 8 below.
3. See Woolf's essay on Jane Austen, *Collected Essays*, I, 144–154. For a discussion of the English vs. the continental novel, and its definition in terms of interpersonal relations as well as of present and pastness, see my essay "The Possibility of a Theory of the Novel," in *The Disciplines of Criticism*, ed. Peter Demetz, Thomas Greene, and Lowry Nelson (New Haven: Yale University Press, 1968), pp. 57–77.
4. Note the title of S P. Rosenbaum's book cited in note 13 below, *English Literature and British Philosophy*; also his essay "The Philosophical Realism of Virginia Woolf."

person and life, since it is only in art, as a form of the imagination, that the self can confront and be united with all other
existents. It is part of the functioning of consciousness: the
simultaneous presence in the mind of those opposites which art
seeks to unify.

These views have made Woolf a "modernist" writer. She
shares a heritage of distinctly Romantic and post-Romantic
probings into the life of the mind not only with Coleridge and
Wordsworth but with Proust, Bergson, Joyce, and others as
well. Her heroes and heroines were "modernist" protagonists,
as R. W. B. Lewis described them in his *Picaresque Saint;* they
were artists who alone could resist the encroachments of deadly
modern life with Platonic effectiveness.[5] Armed with the imagination capable of resolving all oppositions, the artist could bend
reality to his will while remaining impotent in the realm of fact.[6]
Yet precisely because of that impotence, Woolf concluded that
facts must remain; the heights of imagination could be reached
only from an immersion in facts. They are, as she told her
friend, Vita Sackville-West, what one begins with — the diet in
the workhouse, for example — before one considers sunsets and
all the rest.[7] This double perspective, including both the sense
that the artist's vision dissolves all life into mental imagery and
the sense that in the mind's activity the inner collides with a
palpable outer world, constitutes the tension of contradictories
that has gone into the making of Woolf's art.

II

Behind the worlds of Woolf's novels, with their busy sensibilities, stands an omniscient narrator who increasingly turns
into a detached poet as well. Yet that poet's imagination, composed of the facts she had perceived, was dressed in special gar-
ments. The actual writer, whom we have come to know more
and more intimately in recent years, has been transformed. That

5. R. W. B. Lewis, *The Picaresque Saint* (New York: Lippincott, 1959),
   pp. 19–22.
6. Virginia Woolf shared this state with symbolist artists as her protagonists
   shared it with the heroes and heroines of symbolist narratives. See my essay
   "Symbol as Terminus: Some Notes on Symbolist Narrative," *Comparative
   Literature Studies,* IV (1967), 135–143.
7. Cited by Aileen Pippett, *The Moth and the Star* (Boston: Little, Brown,
   1955), p. 209.

soliloquist-figure has been split into several personages, sometimes — like Orlando — even of both sexes, and disguised in various costumes. It is through these figures that facts were converted into visions. And as in Fry and the impressionist and postimpressionist painters Woolf admired, the vision which made the "facts" stand out most clearly also supplied its most congenial form.

The relationships between the living author Virginia Woolf and her tragic and comic personae may sometimes appear close, but her artistry was such that they always took on fresh dimensions and contours. As we have seen, Woolf assumed the tradition of the English novel to show how individual sensibilities would be integrated into social forms that reflected the forms of the novels themselves. But in order to achieve these integrations — in her practical application of her literary and philosophical views — she turned, in addition, to two further genres: lyrical poetry and formal drama.

Woolf's "poetic" style, then, superimposed upon patterns drawn by novels of human relations and sensibilities, was not an end in itself. Unlike more exclusively lyrical prose writers, from De Quincey in *The Opium Eater* to Djuna Barnes in *Nightwood,* her aim was not to develop her essay or story as a form of prose poetry. Rather, her lyrical style — that unique mold of highly physical imagery and elevated diction — was rendered concrete within the confines of recognizably realistic novels. If Paul Valéry's hypothetical protagonist, M. Teste, practiced his artful life as a form of self-variation, Virginia Woolf accomplished that feat by assuming a large number of roles. The appropriate design behind the novel of facts which draws the boundaries of each work is thus not only the lyric (as suggested by imagery and tone) but also the drama, that lends objectivity and coherence to each work.

It is perhaps no coincidence that the last and perhaps most important of her novels, *Between the Acts,* was modeled on the structure of a play which also supplied its plot. It is even more crucial that her greatest artistic accomplishment, *The Waves,* is patterned on a chorus of individual voices which in turn blend into a single "objective" voice, that of a formal narrator. In this latter incarnation, the work is distinctly reminiscent of the formal masque. But at the same time it produced the finest prose poetry rendered with detachment, and ultimately — and paradoxically — the most objective novel of manners. The poet's voice is also that of the effaced narrator, while the individual soliloquists represent different attitudes (by profession, sex, and temperament) which, precisely because each of their monologues is spoken by a single voice, also reflect an identical culture and class. They share the same moment in history. As a chorus they function as individual figures partaking in a single society and vision. This "choral pattern" constitutes the apex of a development that began with *Jacob's Room*.

The form evolved by Virginia Woolf, then, is a form of the imagination which utilizes a variety of available attitudes and techniques borrowed from different genres. It unites the "chorus" of society with the perceptions of the individual mind. This chorus reflects the tragic dimensions in her novels — dimensions that concern the essence of human life: time and the ending of time or death. It is for this reason that *Jacob's Room,* the first work following the end of the war, supplies a paradigm for the way fictions and facts are brought together, and refocused, in Virginia Woolf's later novels.

III

As our contributor B. H. Fussell has shown in this volume, one of the more surprising discoveries about Virginia Woolf is her use of dramatic conventions or forms. But since she did not become famous for writing plays, Elizabethan or otherwise, her dramatic propensities have remained metaphoric. We might therefore find it useful to analyze several routes by which dramatic themes or forms have found expression in Woolf's works and to deduce from them her conception of the imaginative mind.

Virginia Woolf's manner of dealing with the dramatic implications of her subjects was to reflect a tragic vision against a background traditionally viewed as a "comedy of manners." Most of her major novels after 1920 selected war, or a similar disaster, as the counterpoint to daily existence. *Jacob's Room* is about a young man of her class whose promise was cut short by the war. Clarissa's parties in *Mrs. Dalloway* represent a comedy of life counterpointed by the insanity and death of Septimus Warren Smith, for whom the war had played a cruel and tragic role. In *To the Lighthouse* the significant shift occurs during the "Time Passes" sequence, which is highlighted by the Great War

and the deaths it exacted. Even in *The Waves,* where war is
metaphorically treated, it is suggested by the untimely death of
Percival, "the Man of Empire," who fell off a horse in India.
Finally, war is a central image in *Between the Acts.* Within a
historical pageant against which it serves as background, it functions as the core around which the book's comedy of manners
is built.

The components of Woolf's dual concern with vision and fact
can be viewed as a formal dialectic between a "tragedy of life"
and a "comedy of manners," that is, between humanity's wars
and death on the one hand and the surface of life, with its interpersonal relations, on the other. Still, the nagging question continues to plague us: why did the form of the novel remain
Woolf's primary instrument? Her sensibility had been equally at
home in Elizabethan drama, and it would not have been inappropriate had she overtly chosen forms of poetic drama to reflect
her social vision against a background of tragedy. One reason
might have been that she lived in an age of the novel, that she
shared this age not only with Joyce and Proust but also with
Henry James and D. H. Lawrence, with Gide, Kafka, and
Mann, that indeed in her time the novel functioned as the drama
had functioned at the time of Shakespeare. But the principal
reason for her choice of prose fiction remains the realistic
framework of the novel, which was for her the most suitable
form to portray the patterns of the comedy of manners within
the framework of her tragic visions.

This vision involved for Woolf not only the dramatic stage of
events on which her characters moved — a pageantry enacted in
the present tense — but, superimposed upon this display, a vision
that evolved in an epic, that is, a temporally sequential form. As
others in this volume, notably Avrom Fleishman and James
Naremore, have suggested, Woolf's tensions revealed themselves as conflicts between the eternal presentness of each moment (leading to circularity) and the temporal (and ultimately
tragic) linear development that involves both the concept of
pastness and the inevitable reversal in which time, though sequential, is always canceled out with the end of an individual's
existence. Tragedy, then, was not finally rendered as drama: it
was not Sophoclean, but Virgilian. As time spans within the
minds of her characters were rendered in the present, the gradual
unfolding in time and its implied negation gave shape to her total

vision as a novelist, which necessitated the concept of the past. To achieve her purpose, Woolf relied on different types of narrative — epic and romance as well as novel — to present universal above private time and so to mold her narrative.

In *Jacob's Room*, begun in 1920 and published in 1922, the dominant narrative mode was the novel of education. This form was a romantic mode of the novel which was much in use in her own time, but Woolf altered it to conform to the choral patterns that fashioned her "comedy of manners." In a fine essay which has recently come to my attention, Judy Little has enumerated a large number of *Bildungsromane,* parodied and otherwise, with which Woolf was familiar and which she may well have imitated. Examples range from Meredith to H. G. Wells and Dorothy Richardson.[8] One might add the two important novels of education among her own contemporaries: Joyce's *Portrait of the Artist as a Young Man* and D. H. Lawrence's *Sons and Lovers.* But in the curious dialectic Woolf developed in this first, somewhat hesitantly experimental work, the form she chose suggests more of the eighteenth than of the nineteenth or twentieth century.

Woolf's combination of the novel of education and the comedy of manners, which *Jacob's Room* exemplifies, reminds the reader of *Tom Jones,* and indeed Woolf's hero recalls Fielding's in many important ways. He is (initially at least) blind to his own charm and potential. He lacks wisdom, he charmingly attracts women whom he can use and leave behind, and he learns to use his own strengths. The parallel is also apparent in Jacob's lack of connections, which echo Tom's status as a foundling. There are few binding connections for Jacob: women love him, his distraught mother reaches out to him, friends adore him, but basically he remains as free as Tom Jones in the countryside seeking his whole self. *Jacob's Room,* then, echoes the spirit of Fielding's "comic epic." Indeed, viewed in relation to Fielding's work, the structure of *Jacob's Room* emerges with particular clarity. Only in the end is the parallel reversed: Jacob indeed grows as he learns, but he can never find his true connections since, unlike Tom, he is destroyed by the war.

---

8. Judy Little, *"Jacob's Room* as Comedy: Woolf's Parodic Bildungsroman" (forthcoming: see note 2 above). In *Jacob's Room,* Woolf specifically refers the reader to *Tom Jones.* Fielding's novel establishes a bridge between Jacob and Fanny Elmer, who loves him (JR, 207–210).

Displaying the possibility of tragedy, Jacob's life was defined
from the outset as a development which was also cyclical, for the
end was embedded in the beginning. His mother lost sight of the
small boy on the beach just as in the end she lost sight permanently of the young man killed in the war. The first object the
boy held in his hands was a death's head: the sheep's skull cast up
by the sea. But with these indications in mind, the reader soon
notices a series of educational encounters: the copy of Byron
given to Jacob by the departing Reverend Floyd; schooling at
home and in Cambridge; initiations by women; Jacob's friendship with Timmy Durrant and his introduction to society; and
finally the journey to Greece, which culminated in the triangular
relationship with the Wentworth Williams.

On each of these occasions or encounters Jacob added to his
learning and each time he also detached himself. The sheep's
skull that the small boy found on the beach may have signified
death but it also signified freedom, like the coins jingling in his
pockets or left on a mantlepiece.[9] His deliberate distance from
his mother, whose letters he too often forgot to read, was similarly motivated. Yet it might be added that Betty Flanders herself
was marked by tragedy and detachment. She never overcame
her husband's early death to marry another. A similar imprint
can be found on her son: Jacob never allowed himself to establish
a true connection, not with women like Florinda, Fanny Elmer,
or Sandra Wentworth Williams, not with friends like Timmy
Durrant or Bonamy, all of whom loved him. But this detachment does not imply that Jacob's learning was useless. On the
contrary, he learned as much as, if not more than his friends —
scanning the sea as a boy, then Shelley, then Greek poetry as a
young man. In each case, he learned more than just information
and rules of conduct: he learned to be himself in integrity and
freedom.

The dramatic, as well as the ideological point of *Jacob's Room* is
that this integrity of self is always menaced by the possibility of
death — a state providing absolute freedom at the price of existence. Seen in this light, Jacob's growth bears within it its own
negation. Its built-in counterpoint is everpresent: it is the un-

9. For a discussion of coins as a symbol in *Jacob's Room*, see Herbert Marder,
   Feminism and Art: A Study of Virginia Woolf (Chicago: University of Chicago
   Press, 1968), pp. 98–99.

heard leitmotif, the monstrosity of the war, although the fact of war is never mentioned until the end. The hero simply grows and learns while moving freely through a picaresque world. But no reader in 1920–1922 could examine the life of a young man of Jacob's age, who had come to maturity just before the war, and conceivably forget it. The tragic implications of each comic encounter, each social scene, each moment of learning, each erotic episode are always present as the inevitable counterpoints to the human life explored in this novel of education. Tragic implications are thus contained in an epic plot, but the texture on which the plot rests was provided by a drama of social relationships, interpersonal relations that make up the tissue of Jacob's world and compose the aesthetic surface of the book.

IV

The protagonist's evolution toward detachment, in the face of the simultaneous presence of death and war, makes up the tragic component of *Jacob's Room* as it evolves in consecutive time. The dramatic component, on the other hand, functions in the present tense. Consequently, society, which provides the novel's aesthetic texture, is made up of individual relations which Jacob entertains with his friends, teachers, family, and women, and through which his character is discerned.

In this development of the "comedy of manners" two points are remarkable: the protagonist's sex and its importance to the novel as well as to the perspectives in which women are seen; and the interior manner in which all relations, including those with the hero, are enacted. The fact of the protagonist's sex is important because of the immediacy of his perceptions, the directness with which we are acquainted with his inner life. Virginia Woolf drew men superbly, reproducing skillfully figures like her father or her father's colleagues. And she was strenuously aware of her brothers and friends of her brothers' age who existed in a state of pristine innocence and freedom yet were threatened and overshadowed by a fate whose existence they could not know. These figures continued to haunt Woolf even in later years. Still, she also identified with their freedom, with the way they viewed themselves directly, with the way they saw themselves mirrored in their male and female friends, the way

they dealt with their entire society and culture. But she was also
able to view them with some irony and considerable detachment.

Seen from this angle, Jacob turned out to be a most believable
young man, even if she could not view him without the critical
awareness that she as a woman was excluded from his freedom.
Her critique nevertheless was informed by firsthand knowledge
which derived from her identification with him, from her presence practically within his person. Behind Jacob's eye lived the
eye of his author, to perceive precisely the panorama of his
society colored by the vision of his sex. This eyesight was determined by his nonattachment, but it was also colored by a
Byronic confidence that he could reshape the world in the image
of his perception.

Virginia Woolf's power was not confined to her place behind
the retina of her chief protagonist. She existed equally behind the
eyes of his mother, mistresses, and friends. In fact, it is the merit
of her role as the omniscient author — Woolf's brilliance in combining her involvement in consciousness with the tradition of
the objective observer — that she identified herself similarly
with each of her characters and, through these various identifications, wove the texture of her work. It is in this way that the
second aspect of her dramatic method — the analysis of consciousness — must be understood. For in this novel, as in most of
her subsequent work, social relations are viewed as epistemological relations. In her essay on *The Waves* in this volume,
Madeline Moore compares these epistemological relations to
patterns denoting social conflict. They also denote a picture of
manners in which the characters are engaged. Jacob relates to the
world of objects and people around him as a perceiving mind
relates to a perceived object, a pattern which can be observed in
all the relations that characters in the novel engage in with one
another and themselves. Through their intersections a picture or
image of social relations is created.

The emphasis on perception, on eyesight, pervades the entire
novel. A the book opens, Jacob's mother, Betty Flanders, looks
at the ocean while writing a letter:

> Slowly welling from the point of her gold nib, pale blue ink dissolved
> the full stop . . . her eyes fixed and tears slowly filled them. The

entire bay quivered; the lighthouse wobbled; and she had illusions
that the mast of Mr. Conner's little yacht was bending like a wax
candle in the sun. (JR, 3)

As for the little boy Jacob, he had removed himself from mother
and brother and was now looking at "crinkled limpet shells
. . . with locks of dry seaweed." He searched until he saw an
apparition: an enormous man and woman lying in the sun. "The
large faces lying on the bandanna handkerchieves stared up at
Jacob. Jacob stared down at them" (JR, 8).

This interchange of eyesight and eyesight, in which each appears as an object in the other's mind, develops as part of the
dramatic scenery of the novel. For example, an episode, Jacob's
first dinner with the Durrants after he had been sailing with
Timmy on a holiday, is drawn entirely through sighted objects
and colors. He faced his friend's mother and sister, feeling awkward at his initiation and only inadequately protected by the
dinner jacket which "alone preserved him" as it covered with its
civilized black the animal redness of his body. The social scene
was drawn through a moment of sighting:

> The bones of the cutlets were decorated with pink frills — and yester-
> day he had gnawed ham from the bone! Opposite him were hazy,
> semi-transparent shapes of yellow and blue. Behind them, again, was
> the gray-green garden, and among the pear-shaped leaves of the
> escallonia fishing-boats seemed caught and suspended. A sailing ship
> slowly drew past the women's backs. Two or three figures crossed
> the terrace hastily in the dusk. The door opened and shut. Nothing
> settled or stayed unbroken. Like oars rowing now on this side, now
> that, were the sentences that came now here, now there, from either
> side of the table. (JR, 92–93)

Perceived shapes turned into bits of conversation. Even his
companions at table were objects viewed: "Jacob named the
shape in yellow gauze Timothy's sister Clara." And Clara, who
was soon to love him, related to him with her eyes: " 'I've heard
so much of you.' Then her eyes went back to the sea. Her eyes
glazed as she looked at the view" (JR, 93).

Perceptions are registered from many angles. Jacob's relationship with the light-hearted Florinda is first viewed by the reader
at a Guy Fawkes Day bonfire where her face is lit up by the
flames. "By a trick of firelight she seemed to have no body. The

oval of the face and hair hung beside the fire with a dark vacuum
for background" (JR, 122). Soon their entire episode together is
couched in terms of different angles of vision in which Jacob
beheld Florinda as a "brainless" object until, at the end of their
affair, he "sees" her turn up Greek Street on the arm of another
man. Characters love to observe parties (as did Julia Eliot at the
Durrants); they look out of windows. Greece, for example, first
presented itself to Jacob as he looked out of his window, seeing
"three Greeks in kilts; the masts of ships" (JR, 238).

But the book's pattern, that is, its social texture made up of
interlocking minds, is principally determined by the views
characters have of one another, through which they define themselves. As Jacob matures he becomes a man who can look at
persons and objects as equally useful things. An interesting passage late in the book illustrates this point. Just before her protagonist leaves Italy for Greece the omniscient protector reflects:

> For he had grown to be a man, and was about to be immersed in
> things — as indeed the chambermaid, emptying his basin upstairs,
> fingering keys, studs, pencils, bottles of tabloids strewn on the
> dressing-table *was aware.*
>
> That he had grown to be a man was a fact that Florinda *knew,* as she
> *knew* everything, by instinct.
>
> And Betty Flanders even now *suspected* it, as she read his letter,
> posted at Milan . . .

Finally the narrator turns to Fanny Elmer, who loved Jacob
intensely: "Fanny Elmer *felt* it [Jacob's manhood] to desperation.
For he would take his stick and his hat and would walk to the
window, and *look* perfectly absent-minded and very stern, too,
she thought." Fanny responds to this perceiving gesture with a
fatal thought: " 'Anyhow, I can drown myself in the Thames,' "
Fanny cried as she hurried past the Foundling Hospital" (JR,
235– 236, italics mine).

This passage is prophetic of *The Waves.* A dialogue is established through the interchange of different minds engaged in an
act of knowing, perceiving, and feeling. This applies especially
to the view of the maturing Jacob caught in Fanny Elmer's loving perceptions. Seeing him look out on the street (in the transi-
tive meaning of the verb) she also sees him look (intransitively)
"perfectly absent-minded and very stern." The exchange of perceptions is here projected into the same character.

V

The instances of perceptual exchanges which we have examined form a significant movement in *Jacob's Room,* extending from actual sense perceptions to the intellectual perceptions gathered in the process of learning — at home, at Cambridge, and elsewhere — which make up the texture of the book. Their recurrence reinforces the observation that in Woolf's work beginning with *Jacob's Room* perceptual relations become metaphors for transpersonal relations. As each person is an object in the mind of another, each illustrates both the process involved in perception and the actual attempt to relate oneself to another person by viewing that person as an object. Since that object-person is in turn a perceiving consciousness, a kind of conversation, an interchange of relations, ensues. Moreover, anticipating ideas made popular later by Sartre and especially by Simone de Beauvoir, Woolf extended these mutual mirrorings in one another's eyes to relations between the sexes as well. In *Jacob's Room,* as in the other novels, they furnish the drama that counteracts the epic plot, the ironic development from freedom through learning to freedom by extinction, that shapes the structure of the novel.

The epistemological metaphor for transpersonal and sexual relations also illuminates the functioning within consciousness of the perceiving mind. Here we can see how Woolf developed her dramatic situation by stepping behind the retina of Jacob's eye as she stepped behind the eyes of the other characters as well. Observing as gradually her hero was shaped by his perceptions, his learning, she then could subtly guide him while preserving the consciousness of the omniscient author. For example, when Jacob discovers Florinda's betrayal, Woolf intervenes as a playful narrator, much as Fielding intervened in *Tom Jones,* by wondering aloud whether we should follow the disappointed young man to his room. The drama is thus enacted on several stages: in the minds of her personages, individually and collectively, and in that encompassing consciousness of the omniscient narrator and author.

Each dramatic episode, then, finds its reflection in an act of knowledge, in an encounter between minds or between minds and things in which their relations are displayed. This point of intersection Woolf has usually described as a "moment," a privileged point of awareness in which all relations are briefly, and evanescently, apparent. It is an aesthetic and epistemological still point at which the mind focuses on its objects. Moments are thus fraught with all those psychological and philosophical meanings Woolf has consistently applied to the illumination of the mind's activity. Hence she could view her "moment" with an eye trained on Wordsworth and Coleridge, noting that the unconscious "lower mind" perceives unity while the "upper mind" dissipates itself in the facts of the day. But while this description may appear distinctly Wordsworthian, it also suggests Bergson, Proust, Joyce's epiphanies and theories of impressionistic art. It can be seen as an activity telescoping self and world in an image that owes its existence to a single act of apprehension.

In Woolf's famous sketch "The Moment: Summer's Night," her moment is a spatial and temporal instant in which all identities are merged. But, as her work has shown, it can also be seen as a co-presence of mutually distinct relations. During these brief intervals, objects impinge on the minds of the group of friends assembled outdoors at night. Suddenly they are simultaneously aware of themselves and of the things and other selves around them, before the vision collapses and all minds and things become once more separate and distinct.[10] Similarly, objects on beaches, Greek temples, and other people shown in *Jacob's Room* do not derive their existence from their presence in Jacob's or anyone else's mind. Rather they illustrate how relations among people, and between people and objects, existing independently, can be caught in the protagonist's mind in an analogy to the process of knowing. Woolf's dissections of consciousness, then, can also assume a different interpretation.

Although it is widely known that the philosopher G. E. Moore was an important friend of Virginia Woolf's during the "classical" years of Bloomsbury, the significance of his thought to her views of mental activity (which represent such a vital aspect of her ideology and art) was overlooked for a surprisingly long time. For while it was known that Woolf had been fascinated by Moore's ethics, propounded in his famous *Principia Ethica,* the importance to her of his equally famous writings on

10. "The Moment: Summer's Night," *Collected Essays,* II, 293–297.

epistemology was not appropriately considered.[11] This past omission is especially incomprehensible because Woolf's interest in an "idealistic" versus a "realistic" explanation of the process of awareness had been the subject of one of Moore's path-breaking essays, "A Refutation of Idealism" (1903). In that paper, Moore started out from the premise that minds and objects are distinct. Neither can be reduced to the other, and knowledge is, in fact, made possible by their interaction as distinct entities. However, at certain moments, when we introspect our experience, and become acutely conscious of being aware of our awareness, we can behold the objects and contents of our consciousness at the same time. Still, these states are "diaphanous" and cannot endure.[12] As one looks back on this essay and compares it to Woolf's essay "Moment: Summer's Night," it indeed seems as though, with a poet's deft sense for concrete representation, Woolf had turned Moore's formulations into vivid imagery. As we saw, awareness begins with sense impressions — glowing ends of cigarettes in the dark — then turns into a total awareness in which these impressions appear to be momentarily unified before they become separate once more.[13]

This interpretation, viewing knowledge in terms of distinct relations between subject and objects yet providing a brief vision of self-awareness that combines them, illuminates Woolf's art on both a literary and a philosophical plane. While there are also other explanations (including the "realistic" thrust of Roger Fry's "design" to which we have referred), G. E. Moore's analysis of awareness provides a plausible model. It also explains most clearly the analogy between epistemological and social drama which Madeline Moore has described in her reading of The Waves, below, in which each character or episode represents its own particular "moment." Each is diaphanous, none can endure, but together they reflect a constantly changing, alternat-

---

11. See, e.g., J. K. Johnstone, The Bloomsbury Group (New York: Noonday, 1954), pp. 20–45. Compare Quentin Bell, Virginia Woolf, I, 139.
12. G. E. Moore, "A Refutation of Idealism," Philosophical Studies (London: Routledge and Kegan Paul, 1948), pp. 1–30.
13. See my comparison of Woolf's "moment" to Moore's epistemology, The Lyrical Novel, pp. 197–200 and 199n. Compare S. P. Rosenbaum, "The Philosophical Realism of Virginia Woolf," in English Literature and British Philosophy (Chicago: University of Chicago Press, 1971), pp. 316–356; and Madeline Moore in her essay in the present volume.

ing picture, a texture that adheres to the temporal structure of
tragic narrative. In the conclusion of *Jacob's Room,* these two
elements are brilliantly juxtaposed:

> The sound spread itself flat, and then went tunneling its way with
> fitful explosions among the channels of the islands.
> Darkness drops like a knife over Greece.
>
> * * *
>
> "The guns?" said Betty Flanders, half asleep, getting out of bed
> and going to the window which was decorated with a fringe of dark
> leaves.
> "Not at this distance," she thought. "It is the sea."
> Again, far away, she heard the dull sound, as if nocturnal women
> were beating great carpets. (JR, 300)

Greece, the image of nocturnal women beating great carpets —
caught in Betty Flanders' mind — these signify the end of Jacob
as the tragedy of war engulfed him.

In the scene immediately following, the last page of the book,
Betty Flanders and Jacob's friend Bonamy survey his remains:
the things now permanently detached from his existence. A confluence of tragic narrative and the comedy of manners is
achieved, the former reaching the height of its development toward freedom and maturity by exposing the necessity of senseless death which had been concealed all along; the latter by
displaying once more the dialogue of interlocking moments of
awareness, by revealing that texture of relationships, the novel
itself, which is the true furniture of Jacob's room.

VI

If in *Jacob's Room* we still encounter a somewhat hesitant if
successful attempt to project the dialectical play of the tragedy of
life and the comedy of manners, that same tension pervades
Woolf's later, more complex novel, *Mrs. Dalloway.* But in this
book, which confirmed Woolf's reputation as a major writer,
the novel of education we discerned as an underlying structure in
Jacob's Room has been replaced by a dramatic opposition of two
counterpointing figures. She has rendered the tragic dimension
of her novel through a mad symbolic imagination: Septimus
Warren Smith, who acts as Clarissa Dalloway's counterpart
and foil.

Throughout the novel, Clarissa and Septimus are both presented in their "dramatic" present and their "epic" past. But it is
the content of their consciousness, their memories, that places
Septimus into the realm of tragedy and Clarissa into the world of
society and manners. For Clarissa, a defining memory was Sally
Seaton's kiss and the past brought back by Peter Walsh. For
Septimus it was the war in its widest symbolic dimensions. The
tragic and comic elements, then, are not formally distinct ingre-
dients of the novel, as they were in *Jacob's Room*, but are juxtaposed as two distinct forms of the imagination, each treated
with the same weight and complexity: Clarissa Dalloway's
"realistic" as opposed to Septimus Warren Smith's symbolic cast
of mind.

The juxtaposition of social "comedy" and "tragic fate" occurs
in *Mrs. Dalloway* in the present tense created by Clarissa's final
vision at her party. In that diaphanous moment, it is joined with
Septimus' vision at his final moment. Although this novel
avoids the trappings of the *Bildungsroman*, replacing its function
with the figure of Septimus, an opposition persists between the
dramatic presentation of events in the present tense and the conventional narrator's voice speaking of events in the past. Indeed,
in all of Woolf's fiction after *Jacob's Room*, "pastness" (or history)
remains connected with the tragedy of life, whereas the immediacy of perception defines the so-called comedy of manners.

The interplay between scenes denoting points of awareness
which characters share, and the historical sweep in which men
and women are caught, represent Woolf's resolution in art of the
conflicts exacted by life. Here her social and her artistic visions
unfold simultaneously. In Orlando's biography, sweeping him
through time from the Renaissance to the present while he re-
tains an unchanging self (despite even a transformation from
man to woman); in *To the Lighthouse*, where literally, with
Bergson, time "gnaws on things and leaves on them the mark of
its tooth"; and in all of Woolf's later novels — the dual vision of
social presence and tragic or epic past constantly reasserts itself.
This vision, reflecting the opposition contained within consciousness, shaped the collective biography of *The Waves* with
particular clarity: six characters engaged in formal soliloquies in
the present tense (defining their personal and social lives) are
subjected to the times of day, the flow of the seasons, and the
dawn, noon, and dusk of their lives. They become a historical

dream which is always counterpointed by the finitude of death, its necessary negation.

In the historical perspective of *The Years,* as in the "playful" drama of *Between the Acts,* the relation of these two forms (social comedy in the present tense and tragedy in the past) is continually explored. Especially in Woolf's last, unfinished novel, *Between the Acts,* social drama and tragic history are fused with particular clarity. Dramatic plot and the historical narrative are caught in the performance of a play that mirrors both in the shadow of the new world war. Here tragic fate and dramatic present occupy an identical arena that marks the boundaries of the work. In this way, the act of consciousness — that parallel of social and epistemological relations — rendered the form for both fiction and fact. Yet *Jacob's Room* had supplied the paradigm.

8. Mrs. Dalloway:
The Unguarded Moment

LUCIO RUOTOLO

I

In Virginia Woolf's first sketch for what was to become *Mrs. Dalloway*, Clarissa appears walking down Bond Street with the aristocratic assurance one might expect from a woman of her class. Thoroughly at home in a world of smart shops, well-groomed pedestrians, and the governing establishment — couriers are scurrying with messages between Fleet Street and the Admiralty — her pride on this June morning a few years after the end of the first world war keeps her fresh and "upright." A sense of wholeness pervades the scene; "for Mrs. Dalloway the moment was complete." The flag waving above Buckingham Palace (signaling the return of the king and queen), the policeman confidently directing traffic, Big Ben striking the time of day, inspire moreover a condescending ethnocentricity: "it was character she thought; something inborn in the race; what Indians respected."[1]

Woolf's satiric intentions seem clear enough. If, as she puts it somewhat later, she wants "to criticize the social system, and to show it at work,"[2] Mrs. Dalloway appears the vehicle of her reproof. And yet, in the course of this short story, she emerges as something more than a static object of satire.[3] The crux of Woolf's sketch, unsettling Clarissa's classbound self-assurance,

---

1. *Mrs. Dalloway's Party*, p. 21. The sketch entitled "Mrs. Dalloway in Bond Street" was first published in *Dial* (New York, July, 1923).
2. *A Writer's Diary*, p. 56.
3. Alex Zwerdling's "*Mrs. Dalloway* and the Social System" (*PMLA*, XCII [1977], 79) suggests otherwise: " 'Mrs. Dalloway in Bond Street' remains a satiric object . . . utterly loyal to her country, her class, and its leaders."

anticipates the revisions that will transform her from a stiff and tinselly society matron into her author's most famous heroine.

Having stepped into a glove shop (for here it is gloves rather than flowers that call her outdoors) Mrs. Dalloway of the sketch finds herself quite unexpectedly sympathizing with a shopgirl's less privileged life. "When we're in the country thought Clarissa. Or shooting. She has a fortnight at Brighton. In some stuffy lodging."[4]

We can presume that the wife of a distinguished M. P. generally resists such speculations; crossing the boundaries of class invites impulsive, and potentially compromising, acts. Ironically, the fashionable boutique has served to allay disruptive emotions. If passion must exist in human life, let it be for gloves. And how better are we identified than by what we wear? "A lady is known by her gloves and her shoes, old Uncle William used to say."[5] On this visit, however, it proves the setting for a different sort of connection. Probing the affairs of someone outside her world, Mrs. Dalloway discovers a new basis for relationship, derived from an experience shared by all women. Imagining a working girl's feelings (standing as she must all day behind the counter) on "the one day in the month" when the strain might prove particularly agonizing, something more fundamental than the barriers of class momentarily complicates her inherited expectations. Clarissa's imaginative adventure results in contradictory responses: both a generous impulse to help and a no less powerful sense of reservation. "Dick had shown her the folly of giving impulsively."[6]

In "The Russian Point of View," Woolf praises writers such as Chekhov for confronting existential issues that prove illusive and inconclusive. "Nothing is solved, we feel; nothing is rightly held together." English readers are inclined to find such questions a threat to the very basis of their social and literary practice. She suggests further that English novelists, pressured to accept the hierarchical order of a class-structured culture, are "inclined to satire rather than to compassion, to scrutiny of society rather than understanding of individuals themselves."[7] She may well be describing her own struggle with the earlier Mrs. Dalloway.

---

4. *Mrs. Dalloway's Party*, p. 27.
5. Ibid., p. 26.
6. Ibid., p. 27.
7. "The Russian Point of View," *Collected Essays*, I, 241, 244.

Once Clarissa questions her own favored status she invites what is to become with each revision an increasingly liberating form of discord. In the glove store, a series of doubts arise to challenge precisely the ground of her belief: faith in God ("one doesn't believe, thought Clarissa, any more in God"); life's smoothness ("It used, thought Clarissa, to be so simple"); and most centrally, social decorum itself ("Lady Bexborough, who opened the bazaar, they say, with the telegram in her hand — Roden, her favourite, killed — she would go on. But why, if one doesn't believe?")[8]

Mrs. Dalloway falls back on noblesse oblige in answering these questions. One goes on for the sake of the underprivileged. The shopgirl, she would convince us and herself, "would be much more unhappy if she didn't believe." Bound by the limits of her class, Mrs. Dalloway in Bond Street gives up the adventure before it has begun.

While scholars differ over the nature of that "depth" Woolf sought to illuminate through her tunneling discovery, most agree that an altered sense of time past distinguishes her final revisions. *Mrs. Dalloway* is perhaps best described in this regard by J. Hillis Miller as "a novel of the resurrection of the past into the actual present of the characters' lives."[9] Whereas Mrs. Dalloway in Bond Street is revived by that sense of common history she shares with members of her class, in the final version the past arises in the form of less hierarchical and more personal social relationships to disturb her experience of the present or at the very least to complicate it. What was previously exceptional, in the novel becomes the norm. But it is more than the disruptive immediacy of suppressed or disregarded desires, past and present, that transforms Clarissa from an object of social satire to an existential heroine. The subjectivity Woolf's tunneling process discloses remains part of an external world whose kaleidoscopic movement continually uproots and transforms inwardness. We recall the narrator's simile for modern life in "The Mark on the Wall": "being blown through the Tube at fifty miles an hour . . . Shot out at the feet of God entirely naked."

The dynamic of disjunction has a liberating effect. Loosening

---

8. *Mrs. Dalloway's Party*, p. 27.
9. J. Hillis Miller, "Virginia Woolf's All Soul's Day: The Omniscient Narrator in *Mrs. Dalloway*," *The Shaken Realist*, ed. Hardison (Baton Rouge: University of Louisiana Press, 1970), p. 113.

her hold on old supports, Clarissa finds herself with Septimus metaphorically at sea or, to employ a no less applicable cliché, up in the air. Called upon to redefine the moment, she transcends, however tentatively, the constraints of class and hierarchy.

Instinct anchors Mrs. Dalloway in Bond Street to a world of unchanging roles: "there is this extraordinarily deep instinct, something inside one; you can't get over it; it's no use trying."[10] From the opening pages of the novel, however, Clarissa's mind freely ranges over and through inherited assumptions, creating as she does "every moment afresh" (D, 5). If she is not serenely at home in the present, it is because, however timidly, she anticipates change with a mixture of dread and pleasure; even in recollection, as when in Bourton she recalls the solemnity and excitement of something unexpected "about to happen."

While she remains loyally aristocratic, the reader is invited to alternate perspectives. Her words as well as her gestures take on a new transparency. So, initially Woolf picks up the term "upright," which recurred frequently in the short story, and employs it as descriptive of Clarissa's birdlike propensity for flight. On a street corner, "there she perched . . . waiting to cross, very upright" (D, 4). This flightiness, observed by her neighbor, adds ambiguity as well as range to Clarissa's thoughts, an ambiguity she prizes throughout the novel.

The opening pages develop Woolf's analysis of existential anxiety as an added aspect of Clarissa's willingness to question the given. The experience of emptiness and silence in the midst of London traffic — "a particular hush, or solemnity; an indescribable pause" — suspends as well as renews her sense of place and of person. Where Mrs. Dalloway's advisors, the unnamed and impersonal "they," describe the experience as symptomatic of illness, Woolf quickly honors the effects of Clarissa's angst. When in the next instant clock time (Big Ben) begins again its heavy beat, so irrevocable and final, she seems more attuned to the diversity of life around her. Clarissa's perceptions have in fact widened. She responds to the high and the low, the snobbish Hugh Whitbread, a fat lady passing in a cab, a dejected and destitute human being sitting on a doorstep. The events that typified Mrs. Dalloway in Bond Street's narrow, self-justifying

---

10. *Mrs. Dalloway's Party,* p. 20.

response are no longer the source of aesthetic pleasure. Now she celebrates a largely classless pageant:

> In people's eyes, in the swing, tramp, and trudge; in the bellow and the uproar; the carriages, motor cars, omnibuses, vans, sandwich men shuffling and swinging; brass bands; barrel organs; in the triumph and the jingle and the strange high singing of some aeroplane overhead was what she loved; life; London; this moment of June. (D, 5)

Unlike her predecessor, Clarissa derives neither assurance nor stability from her revelatory insights on the streets of London. Such moments, "what she loved was this, here, now, in front of her," pass as quickly as they appear. Since the given remains a problematic reality, existential encounters call for ever-renewed acts of re-creation. No less an aspect of time than the mind which creates them, words must never be allowed to sink into opaque singularity. Throughout Woolf's fictional world, language as well as personality resist the reifying intentions of an acquisitive society. Antithetically, the age's passion for "scientific" definition is treated increasingly as a symptom of collective social madness, an aberration that ironically overshadows Septimus' madness.

II

Toward the close of *A Room of One's Own,* Woolf discusses an instinct of something "real" that inspires her as a writer to look more deeply into her own convictions as well as the appearances of people and of things. The result is often unsettling. Great novelists (Woolf has in mind writers like Hardy, Proust, and Dostoevsky), disrupting the reader's harmony with his world, in an important sense challenge the very conditions of sanity. Injuring our vanity by upsetting our order, such writers seldom tell us the "truth" we want to hear.[11]

While Septimus and Clarissa represent two contrasting visions of truth, "Mrs. D. seeing the truth, Septimus seeing the insane truth,"[12] both reflect what will remain central aspects of Woolf's

---

11. Woolf, "Robinson Crusoe," *Collected Essays,* I, 71.
12. From a page in "The Prime Minister," dated Oct. 16, 1922 (New York Public Library, Berg Collection, ms. 2, p. 82).

iconoclastic assumptions. The truth they witness and enact opposes the conforming aesthetics of what remains for her a paro-
chially narrow culture.

   As Woolf's diaries are published, it will become increasingly
evident how spells of insanity or, more precisely, how her recollections of those spells helped form an aesthetic intention. The
visual distortion that occurs when her mind's hold on things is
threatened prompts her to revise the given. Septimus, reflecting
as he does a central and traumatic part of the novelist's own
personal history, sees the truth, however incoherently, in artistically prophetic terms. His tragedy is that he cannot finally favor
and communicate the explosive immediacy of such visions. He
has received one shock too many.

   To communicate depth in an age systematically incurious
about its own social and personal motivations presupposes a
disposition "to go down boldly and bring to light those hidden
thoughts which are the most diseased." Woolf's essay on Montaigne, with its familiar plea, "Communication is health; communication is truth,"[13] informs the theme of *Mrs. Dalloway*. The
confrontation with disease, however, does not lead her to affirm
the ego's power to face and transcend infirmity. In an important
sense, illness itself becomes a means of renewal. Whether such an
assumption pertains to her personal life as well as to her art
remains an open question.

   Some years later she will suggest the advantage one may derive even from a slight influenza: "How tremendous the spiritual
change that it brings, how astonishing, when the lights of health
go down, the undiscovered countries that are then disclosed,
what wastes and deserts of the soul . . . what ancient and obdurate oaks are uprooted in us by the act of sickness." The mind, as
if on some imperialistic campaign to "cultivate the desert,
educate the native," seeks in health to civilize the body, to maintain its sovereignty over the senses. "With the police off duty,"
the senses are free to roam. Seeing with the eyes of children, "we
cease to be soldiers in the army of the upright."[14]

   If such excursions prove "unprofitable," they urge the mind
from the abstraction of pure thought to a less refined existence
replete with sights and sounds and smells. Lawrence and even
Leavis must surely approve Woolf's plea for a "reason rooted in

13. "Montaigne," *Collected Essays*, III, 23–24.
14. "On Being Ill," *Collected Essays*, IV, 193, 196.

the bowels of earth." The robust society she envisions will sus-
pend its own "dominating" predilections in the expectation that
"life is always and inevitably much richer than we who try to
express it."[15]

On the streets of London, in the grip of his hallucination,
Septimus, like Clarissa, responds with childlike pleasure to
phenomena which the crowd would reduce to objective clarity.
The plane skywriting advertisement urges a multitude of pro-
spective customers to decipher the message. Eager to comply,
they seek answers impulsively. "They were advertising toffee, a
nursemaid told Rezia." Overhearing the woman spelling out the
letters, "K . . . R . . .," Septimus responds to a different
rhythm: " 'Kay Arr' close to his ear, deeply, softly, like a mellow
organ, but with a roughness in her voice like a grasshopper's,
which rasped his spine deliciously and sent running up into his
brain waves of sound which, concussing, broke" (D, 32). Her
voice — it is his newest discovery — "can quicken trees into life."
In touch with an oceanic ground of being (if I may mix a Tilli-
chean metaphor), Septimus experiences the fullness of time as
those around him cannot. Even the space between events strikes
him as important.

Like some foreign visitor, Septimus the outsider sees familiar
objects as if for the first time.[16] At this point of the narrative his
only source of communication is with the omniscient reader,
who, Woolf presumes, shares and relishes his insights; however
disoriented and isolated, his world comes alive for us. We are
reminded again of "On Being Ill" and its somewhat rash pro-
nouncement that "the Chinese must know the sound of *Antony
and Cleopatra* better than we do" — a play that Septimus, with
the ear of a common reader, learned earlier to love.[17] But that
was when he could still share his emotions; with Miss Pole he
had discovered Shakespeare.

In an earlier study of this novel, while acknowledging that
Mrs. Dalloway and Septimus respond creatively to similar detail, I stressed that whereas Clarissa allows the object she perceives to grow in her mind, Septimus, fearing the collapse of

15. "Narrow Bridge of Art," *Collected Essays*, II, 229. Note also Woolf's discus-
    sion of her ideal college in *Three Guineas*.
16. Compare Mrs. Swithin's childlike perception in *Between the Acts*.
17. In the same essay, Woolf suggests that the words of a Donne or a Mallarmé
    reveal an even richer meaning "having come to us sensually first, by way of
    the palate and the nostrils, like some queer odour"; *Collected Essays*, IV, 200.

meaning, retreats from undefined experience. Confronting an existence in flux, he chooses to see and hear no more. To allow himself to indulge further such feelings is to risk going mad.

Septimus' incongruous perceptions prove destructive because he appears unwilling to translate them into an idiom others can tolerate, much less appreciate. While we gain access to his richer vision, Rezia does not. His wife confesses she cannot even sit beside him once he has started to distort familiar objects; he makes "everything terrible," she complains, not without cause. Following the advice of the doctor, she urges her husband to take notice of "real things," of matters not so organically connected with his own feelings. The therapy of self-forgetfulness proves destructive of life as well as of art. Adding to his sense of detached indifference, Septimus, incapable of love or hatred, sees himself as a half-drowned sailor alone on an ocean rock. His problem is not that he feels too much, but too little.

On the battlefront Septimus learned to be upright, to cultivate the same immovable and sustaining indifference that Mrs. Dalloway in Bond Street displayed before the "explosion" of a backfiring car. Trench warfare itself was a study in immobility. Between 1914 and 1918 the Allied lines, with few exceptions, remained essentially fixed, shifting no more than a few hundred yards from the Germans.[18] Four years after the armistice the frozen reality of trench warfare still haunts British life; Septimus finds himself part of an inherited stasis. The gyrations of traffic and pedestrians is movement without motivation or passion, the motion Eliot described in an "Unreal City" of *The Waste Land.*

The first image of Septimus in the novel describes his sense of being blocked by the crowds, unable to pass since "everything had come to a standstill." We recall with irony Clarissa's closing thought in the sketch: "thousands of young men had died that things might go on." The movement his wife Rezia urges upon him — "Let us go on" — is denied him by a world in which movement and change appear aspects of sacrilege. Perception no less than bodily motion seems mesmerized by the ruling deities of state and business, anticipating the sister goddesses Proportion and Conversion who appear later. So the multitude cannot help looking at the Prime Minister's car (Rezia confesses as much) any more than it can resist the blandishments of advertis-

18. Paul Fussell, *The Great War and Modern Memory* (New York: Oxford University Press, 1975), p. 36.

ing. When the car has passed, leaving "a slight ripple . . . all heads were inclined the same way," toward a shop window promoting its wares.

Septimus remains the victim of shock as long as he resists his own eccentric insights, insights that both tempt and terrify him. Schooled in the values of his age long before he becomes a soldier, who can blame him for relying on its authority? (Ironically, in difference — accepting alternate visions of himself and others — resides, as we shall see, his best chance for survival.) His prewar employer, Mr. Brewer, concerned in part by Septimus' health, counsels him in his fatherly way to more manly interests; in place of reading, "he advised football" (D, 130). The war completed the defeminization of Septimus. In the trenches he learned to be a man, winning the respect of his superiors ("he was promoted") and, more significantly, of his closest companion, Evans.

We may presume that on the front he had someone with whom to share his thoughts and at appropriate times, perhaps, even his feelings. The reader learns little of Evans, however. Rezia, having seen him once, describes him as quiet, strong, and "undemonstrative in the company of women" (D, 130). Both men "had gone through the whole show" together. The end of Evans, who is killed just before Armistice, complementing the end of the war, leaves Septimus in fact with neither a sustaining environment nor an ongoing relationship. The battlefront had after all established with brutal simplicity the basis for human survival, the distinction between life and death and the nature of what must be done or, no less relevantly, what must not be done, if one is to go on living.

Thrown back upon himself, Septimus discovers one evening, with panic, "that he could not feel." Not coincidentally it is the evening on which he has proposed marriage to Rezia. The loss of one refuge leads him rather quickly to seek another. Septimus marries, he makes it quite clear, not out of affection but out of the need for "safety." No less pertinent, the panic has come upon him at a time of transition, although at this point what succeeding "show" can inspire the young man to renewed motion is not clear. Moreover a particular time of day inspires unrest: "These sudden thunder-claps of fear," we hear, come "especially in the evening." Septimus fills the empty time by taking a wife. And what attracts him most in Rezia is her assured activity. Making

150   LUCIO RUOTOLO

hats with the other Italian girls — "It is the hat that matters
most" — seems as divinely authorized as the deployment of armies. The sense that the girls are impelled by something other
than feeling or thought for the moment quiets his deeper fear
"that the world itself is without meaning" (D, 133).

Devoid of associative feeling, Septimus does not see, as he will
later, that Rezia's vocation is in fact an expression of love. From
the first description of her hands moving over each hat "like
those of a painter" (D, 132), the beauty she experiences and
urges Septimus to see is an aspect of the objects she creates. Not
until he can begin to participate in her artistic creation does
Septimus move toward health; the doctors, however, make
short shrift of that.

Like some Lawrentian antihero, the early Septimus appears
stirred by the idea people represent to him rather than by their
substantial presence. First Miss Pole serves to reinforce his expectations of literary success ("Was he not like Keats? she
asked") (D, 128). His government appears quick to utilize this
romantic attachment to support a larger and more ominous
abstraction. Septimus went to war to make England safe for
Miss Pole. Evans appears almost totally in abstract terms, his life
no less theoretical in Septimus' mind than his death. Rezia represents the idea of sanctuary. In the course of the novel, Septimus
is shaken, tragically, from his idea of her and thereby finds both
the beginning and the end of his life.

At those moments when Septimus overcomes fear and allows
a vision of exquisite diversity to invade his being, his perceptions, while filtered through the author's consciousness, take on
a creatively poetic form: the quivering of a leaf in the wind,
flying swallows, flies rising and falling, the sound of a motor
horn, "all of this, calm and reasonable as it was, made out of
ordinary things as it was, was the truth now; beauty, that was
the truth now. Beauty was everywhere" (D, 105). Keats has
reemerged. But as in the poet's odes, the temptation is to freeze
the moment and escape time's intransigent slide through life
toward death. Septimus, like Clarissa, "could not look upon the
dead" (D, 105). The sayings he writes down on the backs of
envelopes acknowledging life and change seek also to create a
shockproof world, permanent and self-sufficient, complete as
the wholeness that Mrs. Dalloway in Bond Street expresses on
her morning walk.

The very act of writing would appear an attempt to fix the
moment, to find coherence and sanity in stasis. The world,
however, continually interrupts his artistic and psychological
effort to create a haven; Rezia in particular "was always interrupting," urging him to "look," urging him into a future he has
chosen to avoid. It is no accident that Septimus breaks down
completely as his wife makes plans for children of their own.
Septimus shuns the future as he shuns death. Afraid of change,
afraid to effect change, he capitulates: "Nothing could rouse
him. Rezia put him to bed." The doctor she sends for initiates a
therapy of self-control which only reinstitutes his fear of life.
The final diagnosis of Bradshaw (who is, we have learned, a
specialist on war-inflicted trauma) insists upon total separation
from all sources of future shock, most specifically from Rezia:
"The people we are most fond of are not good for us when we
are ill" (D, 223).

Between the acts of Bradshaw's intended scenario, before Septimus is to be placed in a rest home, he breaks through to the
reality of Rezia's presence. Husband and wife wait in what appears to be a "pocket of still air," on "the edge" of some forest
where "warmth lingers, and the air buffets the cheek like the
wing of a bird" (D, 218). In this suspended moment when, as
with Clarissa in that interim before Big Ben strikes, the processes of civilization are disengaged, Septimus comes to life.[19]

Septimus, driven literally and metaphorically to the edge of
history, finally acts to deny those civilizing forces that would
convert him to "reason." Before he jumps through the lodging
house window to his death, he relaxes his will to remain sane.
Lying on the sofa, he allows the very images of his madness,
a bubbling variety of sights and sounds, to pour like water upon him:

> The sound of water was in the room and through the waves came the
> voices of birds singing. Every power poured its treasures on his head,
> and his hand lay there on the back of the sofa, as he had seen his hand
> lie when he was bathing, floating, on the top of the waves. (D, 211)

For the moment he surmounts his fears. With new courage he
begins cautiously "to open his eyes, to see whether a gram-

19. Woolf's children's story *Nurse Lugton's Golden Thimble* (London: Hogarth
Press, 1966), found in a *Mrs. Dalloway* ms. of the British Museum, plays on
a similar theme: the exotic beasts of the tapestry spring to life once the god
(creator) of their world falls asleep.

ophone was really there" (D, 215). Then, all but miraculously, as
he accepts the reality of things in themselves, things that do not
rely upon his intellectual jurisdiction for their being in space, he
begins to talk with Rezia, responds to her words and her work.
The hat she is making for Mrs. Peters, he ventures, is too small :
"an organ grinder's monkey's hat." Participating in her art, Septimus takes up the ribbons and beads and artificial flowers and
creates a design which Rezia happily sews into a hat. The action,
if commonplace (and it is after all the smallest of events), signifies life at its fullest. Connection is all.

III

The police, however, are not long off duty. Civilization returns with a vengeance to stamp its image on the face of the
weak. And Septimus will have none of it. His suicide is an act
against those like Bradshaw who "make life intolerable." Clarissa's instinctive dislike of this overbearing man leads her finally to
identify with Septimus. Both struggle to preserve a vague and
ill-defined sense of goodness against those "doctors and wise
men" who have long since decided about the nature of truth.[20]
Despite her new capacity for imaginative flight, Clarissa like
her double is tempted continually to absolutize insight, to make
something more permanent of those unsettling moments that
arise in the midst of daily routine. The temptation affects
Woolf's notion of art as much as her character's notion of life.
The "fin" she describes in her diary "passing far out " urges her
to catch the illusive reality, to translate it into something more
than inspired vision. The challenge is to net (Woolf's favorite
verb is "encircle") the fish alive. For the object of art, if it is to
have a life of its own, must be at liberty to grow in the mind of
future viewers.
Clarissa, looking at the passing car at the same time as Septimus, renders the image into an "enduring symbol of the state,"
still the soul of her social identity. The sight of the seal the
footman is holding, "white, magical, circular," conveys a profound basis for the faith of all who watch — all but the dislocated
Septimus. Mrs. Dalloway, standing outside the flower shop,
"stiffened a little" at the thought of her own proximity to this

---

20. "Montaigne," *Collected Essays*, III, 19, 24.

source of majesty. That night she will preside at a grand party. The Prime Minister will be among the guests. Yet there, at her moment of crisis, when she must face the reality of Septimus' death, it will be the absence of such models that leads to her recovery. Here on Oxford Street as the many clocks strike eleven and as Septimus wanders in isolation through an unfamiliar world, bound to a sovereign he cannot see, the object of Clarissa's devotion remains reassuringly immanent. The religion she shares with the crowd of onlookers lifts her "beyond seeking and questing" into a world "all spirit, disembodied, ghostly," a world mirrored in the stillness of St. Paul's Cathedral, where the casual visitor may indulge and glorify permanence. If there is no noise of traffic within, one may presume an extended metaphor; in the presence of authority everything outside, we recall, "had come to a standstill."

Clarissa's sense of belonging as she enters her house is drawn in no less clerical terms: she feels, we are told, like a nun returned from the lordly to a more private realm of worship where death as well as life has lost its sting. "The hall of the house was cool as a vault" (D, 42). Cold and disembodied, her life is shaped by the rhythm of a liturgy that would dull the mind to all but its own calming influence.

> Fear no more the heat o' the sun
> Nor the furious winter's rages.

Even Shakespeare, reduced to opiate, entices the mind to rest. Surrounded once more by "familiar veils" and "old devotions" — the sounds of the Irish cook whistling from the kitchen, a member of the family typing — she feels at once "blessed and purified." Bending over the hall table, "bowed" as if in prayer, Mrs. Dalloway gives thanks to the powers who have allowed this special moment to flower "for her eyes only." If she does not believe in God, she knows to whom to give thanks: "above all to Richard her husband, who was the foundation of it." The table with its message pad, however, interrupts her liturgy: "the shock of Lady Bruton asking Richard to lunch without her made the moment in which she had stood shiver, as a plant on the river-bed feels the shock of a passing oar and shivers; so she rocked: so she shivered" (D, 44).

In her reminiscence "A Sketch of the Past," Woolf offers "the shock receiving capacity" as the catalyst that makes her a writer.

Like Septimus in madness, Clarissa's inclination is to withdraw from shock. Having read the note, she retreats to the privacy of an upstairs bedroom. We learn she has been sick and that her husband "insisted, after her illness that she must sleep undisturbed." Doctor and husband counsel separation as the remedy for disrupted feeling.

But in the process of retiring, Clarissa's mind tunneling into past and present widens the context of her world. In motion she is no longer one thing. If she is a "nun withdrawing," she is also "a child exploring." As on her walk, a variety of incidents arises to engage her attention. Pausing to indulge each new experience — a flash of green linoleum, the sound of a dripping tap — her sense of identity expands again to include that which is not herself. In loosening her hold on things, "seeing the glass, the dressing table, and all the bottles afresh" (D, 54), her grievance against Lady Bruton is all but forgotten.

While her role as wife to Mr. Dalloway is by definition limiting (despite Richard's objection, what can she *do* short of giving parties?), Clarissa has the special talent "of making a world of her own wherever she happened to be" (D, 114). Whether, as Peter Walsh surmises, this is identifiably a "woman's gift" anticipates the question of art's relationship to social function. Women, existing largely outside the world of power, can come in Woolf's view to acquire a more disinterested (as distinct from indifferent) respect for things in themselves. Clarissa's willingness continually to revise her relationship to the extended world of past and present challenges all who surround her to similar acts of re-creation. Her reconstituted moments serve to demythologize the stultifying religiosity of an age that scrupulously avoids redefining its own presumptive formulations. The safe alternative is parodied in that paragon of good taste, Hugh Whitbread, who, avoiding depth, spends his day placidly brushing surfaces.

In the attic room to which she has retired, Clarissa by contrast faces her own presuppositions, ranging from disappointment to envy, and the complexities these emotions bring to consciousness. If her husband has prompted isolation as the basis of recuperation, a narrowing of exposure to others (reflected in the narrowness of her separate bed), she acknowledges a certain coldness of spirit within herself that tempts her from relationships; she prefers reading memoirs.

Her relationship with both men and women speaks of a lack of "something central which permeated; something warm which broke up surfaces and rippled the cold contact of man and woman, or of women together" (D, 46). More than sexual, the failure she confesses involves the inability to move out of herself into the existence of others, to leave the safe confines of her familiar past and present and risk the future. She lacks an "abandonment" of spirit that allows foreigners and only a few Englishwomen (she has in mind her friend Sally Seton) to say and do anything they please. And that presumably is why she married Richard rather than Peter in the first place. Or was there another motive?

As Clarissa tunnels into her past, we are struck by her willingness to raise those fundamental issues her society avoids. Questioning the meaning of "love," "life," and finally "death," she struggles to face these realities as they confront her own existence. "This question of love" leads in her attic room to the insight that her feeling for Sally, unlike her feeling for a man, had been "completely disinterested" (D, 50). In contrast to detachment, disinterest presumes a passion for the thing in itself and the capability (Keats termed it a "negative" virtue) of allowing what is other to remain so — to connect without imposing. Clarissa's objection to Peter's assertive egotism reflects Woolf's critique of larger cultural tendencies.

Had she married Peter she would never know that dignity, the gulf between husband and wife, that underlies one of the author's fundamental convictions about human relationship. So particularly in marriage "a little independence there must be between people living together day in day out in the same house" (D, 10). This Richard has given her while Peter seemed always to lack any notion of another's feelings.

Rezia angers Septimus when, intruding upon his serious thoughts, she exhorts him to take notice of other things or to share his insights with her; she was, we remember, "always interrupting" (D, 36). Clarissa, reflecting on her former life at Bourton, recalls how Peter intruded upon "the most exquisite moment of her whole life," when Sally had kissed her. The shock of his insensitive comment — "Star-gazing?" — was understandably a source of grievance. "Oh this horror! she said to herself, as if she had known all along that something would interrupt, would embitter her moment of happiness" (D, 53).

Peter like Septimus takes himself, which is to say his thoughts, with guarded seriousness. Where fantasies invade the consciousness of either man, they remain largely self-sustaining romances, controlled and directed by the needs vanity prescribes. The important exception for Septimus is of course the narrative event we have just discussed. So Peter, pursuing an attractive woman in Trafalgar Square, remains omnisciently above the self-indulgent scenario he envisions. His adventure leads him finally to stasis, to dream in Regent's Park of some spectral nurse, "champion of the rights of sleepers," who rules and protects him from the "fever of living." If move he must, "let me walk straight on to this great figure, who will, with a toss of her head, mount me on her streamers and let me blow to nothingness with the rest" (D, 87).

But Clarissa's disruptive presence, when Peter visits her home on this same June morning, will awaken him to a renewed desire for experience. Jarred into "idiosyncrasy," Peter finds himself appreciating an infinitely rich and changing environment as he walks through the London streets: "intangible things you couldn't lay your hands on — that shift in the whole pyramidal accumulation which in his youth had seemed immovable" (D, 246). Only when he arrives at the Dalloway party will he revert to old and guarded ways. But this is to come later, after he has intruded upon Clarissa's privacy.

Clarissa's memories of Peter's continued assault on her defects — "How he scolded her" — similarly disturb her inclination to settle into thoroughly derivative and settled roles. Peter, undermining definition as he does, contributes to the healthy ambiguity Woolf develops in her protagonist. After thinking of her relationship with him, Clarissa "would not say of anyone in the world now that they were this or were that . . . she would not say of Peter, she would not say of herself, I am this, I am that" (D, 11). So when he makes his unexpected entrance, having just returned from India, she resists the compulsion to reduce his being to the contours of a past grievance or for that matter to the reality of his own abrasive ideology.

Just before this meeting, however, another interlude suspends the narrative. Returning downstairs from the attic room to mend her party dress, Clarissa seated in the drawing-room falls into the rhythm of sewing. The passage serves to embody Woolf's notion of artistic creation as well as the temptation art offers to withdraw from life into the serenity of a thoroughly satisfying moment. Like some primordial weaver, Clarissa's motions reenact the life of all created beings rising and falling much as waves collect and disperse on a summer beach. A sense of wholeness fills the passage, building as it does toward the penetrating shock of the front door bell ringing and Peter's actual appearance.

The problem for the artist is that the very impulse of such creative action, however therapeutic, serves to isolate her from an ever-intruding and turbulent environment. Art no less than Peter's beneficent nurse or the blandishments of business and politics offers its opiate to all who are world-weary. Clarissa in the motions of her art (and she no less than Rezia is an artist) is lulled into a contentment free of doubt and anxiety:

> That is all. Fear no more, says the heart. Fear no more, says the heart, committing its burden to some sea which sighs collectively for all sorrows, and renews, begins, collects, lets fall. And the body alone listens to the passing bee; the wave breaking; the dog barking, far away barking and barking. (D, 59)

The liturgy plunges her again toward a depth that would obliterate consciousness were she not uniquely responsive to that surrounding pageant of sights and sounds competing for her attention. When the bell rings, "staying her needle," Clarissa though angered by the intrusion is at the same instant "roused" in anticipation of whatever experience is to come.

Reacting to Peter rather than her idea of him, Clarissa allows her impulses freedom to enlarge in the ensuing interview. While the moment is largely fictional — "it was as if the five acts of a play that had been very exciting and moving were now over and she had lived a lifetime in them and had run away, had lived with Peter, and it was now over" (D, 70–71) — her vision is only half made up. She responds with enchantment to those substantial sounds and gestures that reveal her old friend without defining him. If Peter and Clarissa touch each other only shyly — "as a bird touches a branch and rises and flutters away" (D, 64) — separated as they are by time and circumstance, we are moved by their groping effort to reach one another.

IV

What is to be known and loved or hated in another is largely made up of intuitions based on fragments of speech, gestures, or recalled habits such as Peter's half-opening a penknife. Typically for Woolf, human intercourse occurs on the boundary of the mind's knowledge, an instinct of some obscure communion deeper than ideology and more fundamental than sex. The experience tends to point beyond language itself and, insofar as it remains susceptible to description, urges her toward a special rendering of the novel as a vehicle for communication. In this regard, *Mrs. Dalloway* anticipates *The Waves*. With her heroine Woolf considers the English language rich and flexible enough to convey radically disparate notions of human authenticity.

Clarissa's "offering"—the sense, however vague, of her party-giving—seeks a more spontaneous basis for talk as well as other forms of social relationship. Inspired to bring people together for no reason whatsoever, she could never imagine either Peter or her husband acting with such unpremeditated abandon.

The disposition of the party in *Mrs. Dalloway* and Clarissa's role as hostess have led many readers to emphasize its author's satirical intention. If Woolf and her Bloomsbury friends had a preference for parties, and of course they did, only Clive Bell (many of whose personal qualities can be seen in Peter Walsh) had a taste for high society. Can one imagine any character present at the Dalloway party comfortably included at a Bloomsbury Thursday evening? Even so, Clarissa's motives in giving parties, the reality she seeks to create and share, reflect a number of important Bloomsbury assumptions. With G. E. Moore, Clarissa would call her guests to celebrate "the pleasures of human intercourse and the enjoyment of beautiful objects," which is to say the value of things in themselves. No less central, art remains for her an intrinsic good rather than the means to an end. Through her revised protagonist, the novelist struggled to formulate the proper role of the artist, a task that led directly to her representation of Lily Briscoe in *To the Lighthouse* and beyond that to her most experimental novel, *The Waves*.

The problem of making a successful party, like the problem of making a good book, is to create the conditions that will inspire others to collaborate. The good hostess, like the good writer, while technically in charge, remains unseen. Things start to move at the Dalloway party when Clarissa steps back and allows the random talk of people to move at its own course. But first her intention to control events must be thwarted; once again the catalyst is Peter Walsh. The thought of his criticism throws her into confusion: "It was extraordinary how Peter put her into these states just by coming and standing in a corner. He made her see herself" (D, 255). Peter wandering off just when Clarissa would speak to him increases her frustration. At the same time she realizes a failure in her role: everything about the party is "going wrong . . . falling flat." The guests appear walking about aimlessly, bunched in corners and worst of all, like "Ellie Henderson, not even caring to hold themselves upright" (D, 255). The old word signals Clarissa's retreat. Ellie in her "weaponless state," deprived of self-assurance, has cause for poor posture. It is Richard who moves to talk with her as Clarissa, under the spell of grievance, withdraws to the stairs.

At this point the narrative directs us to a yellow curtain designed with exotic birds that is blowing out gently from an open window. In her earlier meeting with Peter, the first recollection of the past they share is "how the blinds used to flap at Bourton" (D, 62). Now, mysteriously, as if the space outside somehow affects the moment, the party suddenly comes to life. The event that inspires this change is merely the image of one undistinguished guest, Ralph Lyon, beating back the curtain as he goes on talking. The gesture is as unpremeditated as Lily Briscoe's impulsive yet decisive act of drawing a line across the center of her canvas. One act signals the beginning of a process, the other its culmination. Clarissa's sense — "It had begun. It had started" — is accompanied by a new impulse that holds her back at the top of the stairs. "She must stand there for the present."

At Bourton, Peter predicted "she would marry a Prime Minister and stand at the top of a staircase" (D, 9). The image fulfilled in his mind her role as "the perfect hostess." So he sees her at this moment (although Richard Dalloway, not even in the Cabinet, has fallen far short of such expectations). But he misreads Clarissa's impulse. Far from some majestic desire to oversee the party, what affects her is the demand to let things be. Having created the festivity, her task is now to allow the party to develop a life of its own.

Descending to her guests, this time in the guise of anonymity, Clarissa celebrates the movement that surrounds her; "one felt them going on, going on" (D, 260). No longer stiffly self-conscious, "her severity, her prudery, her woodenness were all warmed through now." Woolf emphasizes Clarissa's unbridled motion as she glides or more precisely "floats" from one group

to the next. Like a mermaid, "lolloping on the waves and braid-
ing her tresses she seemed, having that gift still; to be; to
exist . . . all with the most perfect ease and air of a creature
floating in its element" (D, 264).

If Clarissa finds it difficult to define the meaning of "this thing
she called life," she has, with Septimus, broken through to the
reality of "something not herself." At the close of the novel she
can imagine his suicide as "an attempt to communicate," because
she transcends, as Mrs. Dalloway in Bond Street could not, the
narrow limits of her social role. Unlike the young guests at her
party, Clarissa will not solidify. A creature of motion and
change, she is at home in a world where nothing remains stable long.[21]

21. Such is the way Woolf describes her own early sense of movement in "A
   Sketch of the Past," *Moments of Being*, p. 79.

9. To The Lighthouse:
Virginia Woolf's Winter's Tale

MARIA DIBATTISTA

I
THE "OLD MAN"

"Books," insists Virginia Woolf in *A Room of One's Own,* "continue each other, in spite of our habit of judging them separately."[1] Like T. S. Eliot, Woolf is intent on tracing literary lines of descent. In his search for origins, however, Eliot needed only select his favorite ancestors in a tradition already established. The female writer is literature's waif. This explains why in surveying the past and present prospects of women and fiction Woolf is faced with the most awesome of spectres — the blank page. While she acknowledges Austen, the Brontës, and George Eliot as great originals, she denies them the status of great originators.[2] The lack of an established tradition for the individual female talent forces Woolf to invent one. In place of the luminous example of Shakespeare, she imagines and then adopts as her literary ancestor Shakespeare's sister, a poet whose distinctive voice was reduced by social conventions and economic necessity to an ignominious silence.

A Room of One's Own, of course, argues persuasively for economic and social independence as the prerequisites for the emergence and survival of women's fiction. But throughout Woolf's often comic polemic, and especially in her peroration, she reminds her audience that, for her, sexual politics functions

---

1. *A Room of One's Own,* p. 84.
2. See ibid., chap. 4.

as a metaphor for literary succession, which establishes itself along patriarchal or matriarchal lines. "For," writes Woolf, "we think back through our mothers if we are women." Woolf's organizing metaphor suggests that the parental structure of literary influence, with all its attendant oedipal anxieties, is not confined to post-Miltonic poets or, more generally, to literature's designated heirs. Fathers have their favorite sons, but they also have daughters, however dispossessed. Moreover, Woolf's analysis helps reemphasize the motive in oedipal literary struggles: rivalry over the mother.[3]

As Woolf's argument develops, her focus shifts subtly but unmistakingly from the poet's relation to the received tradition, to the poet's relation to "the world of reality," and it becomes increasingly clear that she is less interested in the mother as precursor than in the mother as Muse. In this respect, women writers may be more fortunate, since the Muse is one of their own sex, her mysteries closer, finally, to what Woolf deems the mind's essentially feminine "fountain of creative energy." So much, at least, is the belief of Virginia Woolf when, in the final visionary moments of *A Room of One's Own,* she exhorts her female audience to look past Milton's bogey, to "face the fact . . . that our relation is to the world of reality and not only to the world of men and women," so that "the dead poet who was Shakespeare's sister will put on the body which she has so often laid down" (p. 118). That female incarnation of what Woolf sees as the "continuing presences" of past poets is her real hope for assuring the perpetuation of the common life shared by all creative talents, male and female. Thus by a metaphoric sleight of hand, Woolf has translated the central ceremony of literary investiture — the incarnation of the poet — into a truly androgynous phenomenon. Now the dutiful son must share with the dutiful daughter the special privileges of the Muse. In *A*

---

3. Ezra Pound, in a capricious moment, shared such an oedipal joke with T. S. Eliot (*The Letters of Ezra Pound, 1907–1941,* ed. D. D. Paige [New York: Harcourt, Brace, 1950], p. 272):

> Song fer the Muses' Garden
> Ez Po and Possum
> Have picked all the blossom
> Let all the others
> Run back to their mothers
>   Fer a boye's bes' friend iz hiz Oedipus
>   A boy's best friend is his Oedipus.

Room of One's Own, Woolf urges its possibility. But in *To the Lighthouse,* a novel about the liberation of the poetic voice, she had encountered unforeseen complications.

The centrality of Mrs. Ramsay in *To the Lighthouse* would seem to confirm Woolf's habit of thinking back through her mother. The imaginative genesis of the novel, however, proves differently. Having just completed *Mrs. Dalloway,* Woolf records the progress made in expressing her personal vision and foresees a future fiction.

> I feel indeed rather more fully relieved of my meaning than usual . . . Anyhow, I feel that I have exorcised the spell which Murry [John Middleton Murry] and others said I laid myself under after *Jacob's Room.* The only difficulty is to hold myself back from writing others. My cul de sac, as they called it, stretches so far and shows such vistas. I see already the Old Man.[4]

Out of a visionary glimpse of an old man, not a woman, issued Woolf's *To the Lighthouse.* The Old Man is, in one sense, Virginia Woolf's slangy nickname for a disappearing God. It may also be her irreverent, though buried assault on Milton's bogey.[5] Woolf's mockery of the patriarchal, possibly senescent guardians of creation belies the force of her obsession. As her vision clears, the Old Man, the universal father, becomes particularized as her own father, Leslie Stephen.

> This is going to be fairly short; to have father's character done complete in it; and mother's; and St. Ives; and childhood, and all the usual things I try to put in — life, death, etc. But the centre is father's character, sitting in a boat, reciting, We perished, each alone, while he crushes a dying mackerel.[6]

It is, then, as much the ghost of the father as the mother that constitutes the novel's center. Woolf admitted as much in a diary entry dated November 28, her father's birthday.

> Father's birthday. He would have been 96, 96, yes, today; and could have been 96, like other people one has known: but mercifully was not. His life would have entirely ended mine. What would have happened? No writing, no books — inconceivable.
>
> I used to think of him and mother daily; but writing the Lighthouse

4. *A Writer's Diary,* pp. 66–67.
5. See Sandra M. Gilbert's interesting discussion of this peculiar phase in "Patriarchal Poetry and Women Readers," *PMLA,* 113 (May, 1978), 368.
6. *A Writer's Diary,* p. 75.

laid them in my mind. And now he comes back sometimes, but differently. (I believe this to be true — that I was obsessed by them both, unhealthily; and writing of them was a necessary act).[7]

The repeated mention of her father's age suggests how imposing the figure of the Old Man was to Woolf's personal and imaginative life. His continuing life would have augured her creative death: "No writing, no books." For Woolf the passage of thought back through the mother — the creative source — is blocked by the father. The Old Man, the Victorian patriarch, is not so easily dethroned. The daughter must either be silenced or perform the "necessary act." Woolf's belief that the writing of her obsession was essential to her psychic and imaginative health suggests that for Woolf writing initially functions as exorcism, a verbal rite that casts out the resident ghosts haunting the mind. The Woolfian artist is the spiritual medium that mediates between the living and the dead on the hallowed ground where death and life intersect. Her art, hovering in the fictional space (her cul de sac?) between mimesis and invocation, is a summoning of ancestral ghosts.

The emphasis on the relationship between words, writing, and the death of a beloved further suggests that Woolf's novel is linked at its origin to the *consolatio* of the elegiac mode: "I have an idea that I will invent a new name for my books to supplant "novel." A New —— by Virginia Woolf. But what? Elegy?"[8] Woolf's term, elegy, is still the best for describing the experimental form of her novels after the more traditional narratives of her apprenticeship, *The Voyage Out* and *Night and Day*. The narrative ground of *Jacob's Room, Mrs. Dalloway, To the Lighthouse,* and *The Waves* is haunted by memories of the dead.[9] Commemorating the dead is, however, the secondary function of these elegiac narratives. Their primary function is to liberate the elegiac mourner from the dejection of mortality that is death to the imagination. Coleridge's prescription for the decorum of

---

7. Ibid., p. 135.
8. Ibid., p. 78.
9. The sudden death of Virginia Woolf's brother Thoby Stephen is reflected in *Jacob's Room* and *The Waves*, where it is transmuted into the more generalized theme of heroic elegy, the death of the young hero. For the effect of the suicide of Woolf's friend Katharine Maxse on *Mrs. Dalloway,* see Quentin Bell, *Virginia Woolf,* II, 87. It is characteristic and central to Woolf's aesthetic that such private sources of her art inspire but never overwhelm her continuous meditations on death and the experience of loss.

elegy is instructive: "It may treat any subject, but it must treat of no subject for itself; but always and exclusively with reference to the poet himself."[10] *To the Lighthouse* is an elegiac narrative that treats its subject, the dead mother and father, in terms of the surviving daughter, the implied, anonymous narrator of the novel. Woolf's elegy concludes with a double victory: the dead are transfigured (they come back, but differently) and the living descendant discovers an independent voice and a genuine artistic vocation.

II
THE OEDIPAL DREAM

The oedipal origins of *To the Lighthouse* determine not only its subject, but its structure. The form of the novel is contained in the dream of a child. James Ramsay is assured by his mother that, weather permitting, "the wonder to which he had looked forward, for years and years it seemed, was, after a night's darkness and a day's sail, within touch" (L, 9). But Mrs. Ramsay, sympathetic to childhood dreams, does qualify her son's hopes: "If it's fine tomorrow." Yet what she warns as nature's possible constraint on desire is misunderstood. Her words — "If it's fine" — are transposed to "as if it were settled." The novel as a whole vindicates the child's confidence that he will realize his dreams. The expedition does take place after a night's darkness and a day's sail. Yet what to James only seems years and years of waiting actually becomes, in the narrative time of the novel, the ten years that lapse in the section "Time Passes." The illusion of prolonged anticipation becomes a reality, and the night's darkness that intervenes between desire and its fulfillment is protracted in the visionary night of the novel's middle section. Nor is the day's sail without its frustrations; the Ramsay boat is often suspended in its motions by the sea's "horrid calm."

James's expedition, then, like all quests, is completed only after a series of delays, trials, ordeals (the becalmed sea). Yet the most serious threat to the imagination's adventures is the resistance of "facts uncompromising," represented by Mr. Ramsay's abrupt, "But it won't be fine." The father's retort initially frustrates the expedition. Mr. Ramsay, the Old Man, is the anti-

---

10. Coleridge, *Table Talk and Other Omnia of Samuel Taylor Coleridge* (London, 1909), p. 87.

quester who mocks and exposes James's dream as the most infantile form of imagination: daydream. So abrupt and so violent is his initial appearance that the language within the novel responds with reciprocal violence: "Had there been an axe handy, or a poker, any weapon that would have gashed a hole in his father's breast and killed him, there and then, James would have seized it. Such were the extremes of emotion that Mr. Ramsay excited in his children's breasts" (L, 10). Innocent reverie is translated into its opposite — violent (and guilty) patricidal fantasy, a fantasy excited and activated by the extremes of emotion that inform the novel's psychological and creative dialectic. This fantasy relocates the dramatic ground of the narrative. The conflict is no longer between James's desire and the reality that frustrates it — facts uncompromising — but between father and child competing for authority.

For Ramsay's initial act of aggression proves traumatic. The memory of thwarted desire will haunt James when, years later on the final sail to the lighthouse, his childhood dream becomes a nightmare. When the Ramsay boat is becalmed, James becomes anxious that his father will look up and reprove him. "And if he does," James thinks, "I shall take a knife and strike him to the heart" (L, 273). But James, as he sits staring at "that old man reading," realizes that his symbolic role as patricidal avenger is inappropriate to the old man, "very sad," who once inspired his hatred. Without knowing it, James seeks a new oedipal image "to cool and detach and round off his hot anger":

> Suppose then that as a child sitting helpless in a perambulator, or on some one's knee, he had seen a waggon crush ignorantly and innocently, some one's foot? Suppose he had seen the foot first, in the grass, smooth, and whole; then the wheel; and the same foot, purple, crushed. But the wheel was innocent. So now, when his father came striding down the passage knocking them up early in the morning to go to the Lighthouse down it came over his foot, over Cam's foot, over anybody's foot. One sat and watched it. (L, 275)

The name Oedipus in Greek means swollen foot. In the childhood tragedy James stages in his mind, the crushed foot is linked to paternal tyranny. The oedipal encounter between father and son does not take place at the crossroads, but in a garden, romantically linked here to the lost world of childhood. The garden, though happy, is not innocent in desire. As James imaginatively reenters the garden, a figure, distinctly female, begins to emerge:

. . . he could see . . . a figure stooping, hear, coming close, going
away, some dress rustling . . .
    It was in this world that the wheel went over the person's foot.
Something, he remembered, stayed and darkened over him; would
not move; something flourished up in the air; something arid and
sharp descended even there, like a blade, a scimitar, smiting through
the leaves and flowers even of that happy world and making it shrivel
and fall.
    "It will rain," he remembered his father saying. "You won't be
able to go to the Lighthouse."
    The Lighthouse was then a silvery, misty-looking tower with a
yellow eye, that opened suddenly, and softly in the evening.
Now . . . (L, 276)

The faltering rhythms of this interior reverie imitate the motion of James's mind as it struggles to complete the oedipal
"play" of his emotions.[11] The phrases that interrupt the emotional continuity of his thoughts—"like a blade, a scimitar"—
concretize the object of his fixation ("something that stayed and
darkened over him, would not move"). The aggressive, dominating power of the father, metaphorically represented as a
flourishing weapon, is associated with the avenging, punitive
force that makes James's happy world shrivel and fall. The divine father and the natural father become conflated in James's
mind as he attributes the terrible omnipotence of the one to the
other. He now remembers, in the Freudian sense, the traumatic
words of judgment that exiled him from paradise: "But it won't
be fine," words repeating verbatim the father's first words in the
novel. The tyranny of paternal authority runs counter to the
child's instinctual desire for the veiled feminine figure and the
paradise she promises—the "misty-looking tower" with an eye
that suddenly and softly opens. The Old Man has a wife, James
has a mother. In the eternal "now" of his mythic memory,
James is hopelessly divided between them.

---

11. In her notebooks, Woolf plotted the play of James's oedipal emotions as
follows:
                      James hated him
                      felt the vibrations in the air
                      felt the emotion
                      a bad emotion?
                      All emotion is bad
                      felt his mother's emotion
                      What her emotion was
Lighthouse Notebook 1/31/26, quoted in Harvena Richter, *The Inward Voyage*
(Princeton: Princeton University Press, 1970), pp. 225–226.

James's oedipal "complex" of feelings is refracted in the mirror
of the novel's family romance. Lily's painting and Mr. Ramsay's
scrutiny of her progress are posited as "opposing forces" in the
novel's creative dialectic. Minta Doyle, Paul Rayley, even Charles
Tansley, Ramsay's academic heir, have also attached their affections and, in varying degrees, relinquished their power of self-
determination to the novel's archetypal mother and father. The
divided loyalties generated by the oedipal competition to win the
praise and secure the recognition of Mr. and Mrs. Ramsay excites
"extremes of emotion." "I feel," wrote Woolf in "A Sketch of the
Past," "that strong emotion must leave its trace; and it is only a
question of discovering how we can get ourselves attached to it,
so that we shall be able to live our lives through from the start."[12]
It is not the mother or father who bequeathes to the child an image
of its destiny, of its life "lived through from the start." It is the
emotion generated by their compelling, if invisible presence in
the continuing life of the child that discloses the passage into the
past and toward the future (to the lighthouse).

In making this subtle distinction between the oedipal emotion
and the oedipal precursor Woolf is more careful than many of her
critics in analyzing her own anxiety of influence. She never fal-
sifies her oedipal feelings by allegorizing the parental figures as
antithetical principles of imagination and reason. Mr. and Mrs.
Ramsay share, in fact, the same vision of life and nature as essentially hostile realities to be withstood and transformed by the
effort of human will and human imagining. One is the genius of
the garden, the other of the shore, offering their protection against
"the reign of chaos." But like all governing spirits, each assumes a
terrible aspect when its power over life is challenged. Woolf's
elegiac tribute acknowledges both the just and unjust exercises of
parental authority.

III
THE FISHERMAN AND HIS WIFE:
THE MYTH OF EDEN

"But in what garden did all this happen?" wonders James, trying to reconstruct his happy world. His sister Cam, caught between her impulse to submit to her father and her pledge to "resist
tyranny to the death," looks longingly at the receding shoreline

---

12. In *Moments of Being*, p. 67.

and thinks, "They have no suffering there" (L, 253). Both remember worlds free from divisions of feeling, but theirs is not a true remembrance of things past, only a mythification of them. That mythic recovery of the irrecoverable past is articulated by the shape of the novel itself—a circle that contains its end within its beginning. The form of *To the Lighthouse* images fate as the uroborous, the snake with the tail in its mouth, the psychic symbol, as Erich Neumann has argued, "of the origin and of the opposites contained within it."[13] The novel's circular structure represents reality as the "uroboric totality" or Great Round out of which life is individuated and to which it is destined to return.

Presiding over the Great Round of existence is the novel's archetypal mother, Mrs. Ramsay. She is the primary focus of all feeling in the prewar idyll of "The Window," an iconic figure of idealized desire whose "royalty of form" derives not from the authority commanded by her moral being, but from the power of her extraordinary beauty. As a type of the Great and Good Mother who contains and preserves the beauty of the world in a "circle of life," Mrs. Ramsay inspires the novel's pastoral imagery, an imagery emanating from a "naive" vision of a beneficent, prolific, and artful Nature: "The graces assembling seemed to have joined hands in meadows of asphodel to compose that face" (L, 47). William Bankes's homage to her beauty invokes, necessarily, the figure of nature's graces. Such pastoral figures reflect what Neumann designates as "the elementary character" of the eternal feminine that emphasizes the maternal aspect of the archetype and renders all consciousness "whether male or female, childlike and dependent in their relation to it."[14] Only the fully mature artistic consciousness of Augustus Carmichael — the stern classicist who invokes a Vergilian vision of history and nature in the novel — distrusts her beauty and remains outside her sphere of influence. All other social and familial relations in "The Window" find their primary model in the transparent "participation mystique" of mother and child that constitutes "the original situation of container and contained."[15]

Woolf's narrative honors the life-sustaining role of the mother as the foundation of social life; yet it also acknowledges that dependence on the mother is a real threat to the growth and

13. Erich Neumann, *The Great Mother: An Analysis of an Archetype,* trans. Ralph Manheim (Princeton: Princeton University Press, 1963), p. 18.
14. Ibid., p. 26.
15. Ibid., p. 29.

transformation of unreflecting life into autonomous consciousness. Paradoxically, only the estranged, self-reflexive mind can
penetrate into the pathos that always informs the bonds uniting
mother and child, the pathos of inevitable separation and death
embodied in the myth of Demeter and Persephone which, as in
The Winter's Tale, is the underlying season myth in *To the Lighthouse.* The myth of Persephone also projects the mother-child
relation as the primary aspect of nature's Great Round, but represents death as a phase in the self-regenerating cycles of life.
Like *The Winter's Tale, To the Lighthouse* is centered in the relation between the "dead" mother and the "lost" daughter, between things dead or dying and things struggling to be born, a
relation finally revealed and reconciled through art.

The originating relation between mother and child, "objects
of universal veneration" (L, 81), is commemorated in Lily
Briscoe's painting, where it is abstracted and stabilized by Christian iconology. Lily represents the "participation mystique" between mother and child in terms of a third relation, invisible but
implied, to the father. The mother in the Christian family romance is venerated primarily as a figure of intercession, mediat-
ing between the earthly child and the heavenly father who
decides its fate. The double relation of container and contained
that informs the "pagan" archetype of the Good Mother is a
source of ambivalence because it expresses the domination of
nature over spirit. But in the Christian vision, the heavenly
mother is the patron of marriage, of the conscious and moral
relation embodied in the Holy Family.[16] By depicting Mrs.
Ramsay as a triangular shape, Lily interprets her subject in terms
of the mediated or "triangular" desire that, as René Girard
has cogently demonstrated, directs the course of the novel's
"metaphysical desire" and determines its central metaphor for
the devious art of human relationships — the psychological circle.[17] Mrs. Ramsay's role as both the object and mediator of

16. In Mrs. Ramsay's stories about Joseph and Mary, two quarreling rooks who
    settle in the trees outside the Ramsays' bedroom, Woolf makes gentle fun of
    the holy family motif. Mrs. Ramsay's son Jasper, who rather enjoys his
    mother's quaint stories, nevertheless finds great pleasure in shooting at the
    birds, while Rose, "who was bound to suffer," objects to his aggressive
    sport: "Don't you think they mind," she asks Jasper, "having their wings
    broken?" (L, 123).
17. René Girard, *Deceit, Desire and the Novel: Self and Other in Literary Structure,*
    trans. Yvonne Freccero (Baltimore: Johns Hopkins University Press, 1965),
    p. 300. Arguing that all great novels "always spring from an obsession

human desire is stressed throughout "The Window," though the full meaning of her human art is imperfectly understood, even by Lily, until years later when she finally comprehends and transcends the triangular circuits of mediated desire. Mrs. Ramsay's part in effecting Paul and Minta's engagement and her dreams for Lily Briscoe and William Bankes establish her precedence in the social and emotional lives of the community centered around her. The first marriage, of course, is a failure and the second never materializes. As in Joyce's *Ulysses*, Woolf's treatment of the family romance is essentially comic, stressing the imperfect coincidence between her literary figures and their mythic ground, between her "characters" and their informing archetypes, all the while exploiting their psychological force and authority as models of imitation.

Nowhere is the distance separating figure and ground more comic — and ambiguous — than in the transactions Mrs. Ramsay conducts with life:

> A sort of transaction went on between them, in which she was on one side, and life was on another, and she was always trying to get the better of it, as it was of her; and sometimes they parleyed (when she sat alone); there were, she remembered, great reconciliation scenes; but for the most part, oddly enough, she must admit that she felt this thing that she called life terrible, hostile, and quick to pounce on you if you gave it a chance. There were the eternal problems: suffering; death; the poor . . . (and the bill for the greenhouse will be fifty pounds). (L, 92)

Mrs. Ramsay bargains from a position of dread, and from the tone of these parleys one surmises that the great reconciliation scenes negotiated result in precarious balances of terror. To the eternal problems — suffering, death, the poor — she issues her own immutable decrees that "people must marry; people must have children." Lily, a virginal woman who would "urge her own exemption from the universal law" of marriage that Mrs. Ramsay blindly enforces, rebels against Mrs. Ramsay's "simple certainty" that the greenhouse and marriage are the in-

---

that has been transcended," Girard describes the mechanism of novelistic transcendence: "The novelist's self-examination merges with the morbid attention he pays to his mediator. All the powers of a mind freed of its contradictions unite in one creative impulse." Certainly, such is the dialectic at play in "The Lighthouse" as Lily struggles to complete her picture and as Woolf struggles to bring her self-examining, at times morbidly self-searching, narrative to a conclusion.

evitable forms of the female opposition to life: "Then she remembered, she had laid her head on Mrs. Ramsay's lap and laughed and laughed and laughed, laughed almost hysterically at the thought of Mrs. Ramsay presiding with immutable calm over destinies which she completely failed to understand" (L, 79). As the potential mistress of human fate, Mrs. Ramsay incarnates the complementary, if negative, aspect of the eternal feminine which draws us onward. Her serene act of knitting, the sign of her creative urge to unite the separate strands of life into a seamless unity, is also a sign of her terrible power, the willful "deceptiveness of beauty" (L, 78) that entangles human lives in its own artful web.

To emphasize the spiritual traps of the mother, the narrator frames Mrs. Ramsay's reveries with a fairy tale, the Grimms' "The Fisherman and His Wife," which she is reading to her son.[18] The tale is a fable of sexual competition and embattled wills. A fisherman catches an enchanted fish — Mr. Ramsay's dying mackerel — which he releases, but which his wife insists on exploiting to improve their human lot. The plot turns on the successive wishes of the wife, culminating in her desire to be Holy Roman Emperor and then, finally, God. Such may be the implied wish, the reductio ad absurdum of Mrs. Ramsay's dreams of ruling and reforming a world she rightly feels to be unjust. Nor does the masculine will ever approach the daemonic presumption of the imperious feminine will. Even the most prideful masculine fantasies expressed throughout the novel confine themselves to historical and cultural dreams of eminence. Ramsay's preoccupation with human destiny is limited to anxious brooding over the future reputation of the *Waverly* novels and the historical verdict on the character of Napoleon, an emperor whose own titanic will stopped short, as the fisherman's wife in the fairy tale does not, of cosmic divinity. The refrain Mrs. Ramsay unconsciously intones —

> Flounder, flounder, in the sea.
> Come, I pray thee, here to me;
> For my wife, good Ilsabil,
> Wills not as I'd have her will.

---

18. *The Complete Grimm's Fairy Tales* (New York: Pantheon, 1972), pp. 103–112.

— recapitulates and defines the conflict between sexual wills that is the implicit subject of the fairy tale and the novel in which it is absorbed and, finally, transformed.

The self-seeking, self-regarding motives disguised in the apparent beneficence of the maternal will belies the myth of innate feminine altruism. Left to her own devices and her own imaginations, the eternal feminine would, "like God himself" (p. 115), occasionally interfere with Nature's orderly design. Even Lily Briscoe, a more sexually neutral character, is prone to such feminine temptations. Musing over her picture, Lily stirs the plaintains on the lawn with her brush, disturbing the horde of ants crawling among them: "She raised a little mountain for the ants to climb over. She reduced them to a frenzy of indecision by this interference in their cosmogony" (L, 294).

This comic instance of *imitatio dei* ("this interference in their cosmogony") is directly followed by the problem of "seeing" Mrs. Ramsay and tracing the labyrinthine divagations of her will: "Fifty pairs of eyes were not enough to get around that one woman with, she thought. Among them, must be one that is stone blind to her beauty." Lily, blinded by the luminous beauty of the mother, cannot discern that her own unconscious motions provide the best commentary on Mrs. Ramsay's "thoughts, her imaginations, her desires": "What did the hedge mean to her, what did the garden mean to her, what did it mean to her when a wave broke?" (L, 294). The multiple, often antithetical meanings generated by the mother's imagination are expressed in the green world she creates and nurtures ("and the bill for the greenhouse would be fifty pounds" counterpoints Mrs. Ramsay's dialogue with life). The garden, the work of the feminine will, belongs, however, to the tradition of Renaissance gardens of delight, a tradition invoked in the Elizabethan lyric that Mrs. Ramsay casually reads aloud in her husband's presence, unaware that she is singing a siren's song: "Steer, hither, steer your winged pines, all beaten Mariners" (L, 179).[19]

In the novel's interpolation of the Grimms' cautionary tale, Mrs. Ramsay is the wife whose beauty and promise of sheltered life would lure the husband-mariner from his appointed destiny

---

19. The lines are from the "Siren's Song" in William Browne's *Inner Temple Masque* (1615), reprinted in *Elizabethan Lyrics,* ed. Norman Ault (New York: Capricorn, 1960), pp. 462–463.

as the Ulyssean adventurer into the unknown. Mr. Ramsay's insistence that the sea represents the true condition of man complements Mrs. Ramsay's pastoral imaginings. Woolf's portrait of the father represents him as the hero of thought, the rationalist who delineates the boundaries between subject and object that the idealizing maternal will trespasses in its search for unity. Despite the undercurrent of burlesque, Ramsay's agonies in exploring the alphabet of thought, the A – Z that codifies the inexorably linear nature of reality, are signs of an authentic fate:

> It was his fate, his peculiarity, whether he wished it or not, to come out thus on a spit of land which the sea is slowly eating away, and there to stand like a desolate sea-bird, alone. It was his power, his gift, suddenly to shed all superfluities, to shrink and diminish so that he looked barer and sparer, even physically, yet lost none of his intensity of mind, and so to stand on his little ledge facing the dark of human ignorance, how we know nothing and the sea eats away the ground we stand on — that was his fate, his gift. (L, 68–69)

Woolf's vision of the male fate is inevitably Victorian, just as her vision of the sea that comprises our "final destiny" is inevitably Arnoldian. Like the speaker of "Dover Beach," Ramsay stations himself on the shore "where ignorant armies clash by night." The isolation of his outpost contrasts to "the house . . . full of children sleeping . . . shaded lights and regular breathing" that represent "the best of life" to the feminine will. For the female imagination is pietistic and ultimately comic in its faith in regeneration, custom, and transfiguration. The feminine vision absorbs the individuating fact of death in its own ecstatic auguries of transfiguration, even as Lily's knowledge of Mrs. Ramsay's death is transformed into a vision that portends resurrection: "For days after she had heard of her death she had seen her thus, putting her wreath to her forehead and going unquestioningly with her companion, a shade across the fields" (L, 270). The apotheosis of Mrs. Ramsay into a nature goddess, signaled by the royal gesture of self-coronation, is testimony to the feminine faith in transfiguration, a faith beyond the arguments of reason and the evidence of facts uncompromising.

No such transfiguration is conceivable for Ramsay, whose sense of life remains resolutely tragic: "We perished each alone." The real distinction between husband and wife thus lies in the tragic starkness of his vision and the comic abundance of hers.

This is the generic difference between his "fatal sterility" and her "delicious fecundity" — in the "nature" of the world each envisions. Both the fisherman and his wife are united by their common cause against the "fluidity out there." But each responds to the flux differently. Mrs. Ramsay, in the novel's symbolic topography, is at the center of a circle of life which encloses a green world of gardens and marriage. That circle is located at the heart of nature, in a hollow, on an island. Ramsay's station is at the circumference of that circle, on the shore, the very point where the sea is eating the ground we stand on. He positions himself at the edge of the floods, a "stake driven into the bed of a channel." Implied in the figurative relation of fisherman and wife is that Ramsay centers himself in the floods, the flux of life, without being overwhelmed. He demystifies the romantic, essentially feminine mystique of death by drowning. As a male principle he embodies the resistance to engulfment that the maternal will commends. Both he and his wife have destinies linked to the sea, but in the nautical metaphor the novel employs to distinguish the extremes of emotion excited by the fluidity of life, he is the leader of the doomed expedition who would die standing, she the reluctant mariner who "would have whirled round and round and found rest on the floor of the sea" (L, 127). The egotistical man, Mr. Ramsay presses the claims of the individual over the undifferentiated flow. He upholds the authority of "I, I, I" over the anarchy of oceanic feelings.

If the fisherman and his wife have real differences of opinion, they are still married. Differences of will are not as important in *To the Lighthouse* as the love that reconciles those differences. Mr. and Mrs. Ramsay's love is an example of united wills in the private sphere: "Directly one looked up and saw then, what she [Lily] called 'being in love' flooded them" (L, 72). Being in love is an ideal state, like matrimony, of cooperating wills. In the novel's evocation of ideal love, Ramsay's is the responsible vision that makes Mrs. Ramsay's irresponsibility possible.

> . . . she let it uphold her and sustain her, this admirable fabric of the masculine intelligence, which ran up and down, crossed this way and that, like iron girders spanning the swaying fabric, upholding the world, so that she could trust herself to it utterly, even shut her eyes, or flicker them for a moment, as a child staring up from its pillow winks at the myriad layers of the leaves of a tree. (L, 159)

The masculine intelligence is the rational foundation on which human order, dry land itself, rests. This order is inclusive of what is generally called culture: science, mathematics, history, art, the social questions. The female transformative power, which seeks its expressive images in dream and fancy, leans on and trusts to this masculine solidity and can contemplate nature's infinite variety ("the myriad layers") without anxiety (like a child). Once the male organizes the flux and erects that fortress, civilization, nature does seem to murmur a cradle song to soothe the dreaming maternal will.

The love between men and women, husbands and wives is a recurrent metaphor for mental ecstasy and successful creation throughout *To the Lighthouse,* from Mrs. Ramsay's private raptures to the communal feast in honor of Paul and Minta's emerging love. But the novel's most moving celebration of marital love is Ramsay's final benediction of human community, the refrain he intones at the conclusion of the dinner party:

> Come out and climb the garden path,
> Luriana Lurilee.
> The China rose is all abloom and buzzing with
> the yellow bee.

The verse celebrates an Arcadian vision of generation and fecundity. The child's paradise, James's naive dream of a happy garden, does fall before the oppressive figure of the father, but *To the Lighthouse* canonically interprets the child's exile as a *felix culpa.* The child falls, but the garden remains, now purged of profane desire. The father, like Cronos, is a paradoxical figure, a merciless tyrant who eats his children but whose reign is memorialized as the golden age of man.[20]

IV
COMEDY'S AGAPE

Ramsay's is a necessary tyranny, for his authority legitimizes familial love by repressing its erotic, essentially oedipal components. Once the father socializes the libido, love is purged of its destructive desires, and the mother is released to perform her proper function. The father can only maintain order in the pri-

20. See Robert Graves, *The Greek Myths* (Baltimore: Johns Hopkins University Press, 1972), I, 40.

vate sphere. It is the mother who translates private love into communal love — agape. The dinner over which Mrs. Ramsay presides is an expression of the total form of love, a secular equivalent of the love feasts of religious communities. The female toil is to give shape, order, and direction to the community which centers around her but lacks expression: "Nothing seemed to have merged. They all sat separate. And the whole of the effort of merging and flowing and creating rested on her" (L, 126). Resisting creative union in love are the separate selves that compose the party and are not aware of their relation to the social composition. The egotistic "I" that resists the impulse to merge and flow with life is here a negative attribute. In a social context, the male principle of resistance is not the subject of heroic contemplation, but of satiric observation.

The conscious artifices employed by Mrs. Ramsay to mask and merge the self-assertive, dissident impulses of individuals into a unified order of life testify to the pragmatic guile of the feminine imagination. Mrs. Ramsay's social art derives its authority from its generic origin in the comic vision. Her social manner exploits the stylization of speech and gesture that devolve from comedy's filial dependence on its parent forms — rite, pageant, and feast. The language of these social rituals, like the official language of diplomacy, is rooted in a necessary conventionality. To obtain unity, one must "speak French": "Perhaps it is bad French; French may not contain the words that express the speaker's thoughts; nevertheless speaking French imposes some order, some uniformity" (L, 135–136). The acknowledged conventionality of social discourse creates a common ground of exchange in which private utterance is translated into a public speech that may "not express the speaker's thoughts" yet does silence "the strife of tongues" that is the most divisive threat to human dialogue. As the linguistic analogy implies, Woolf trusts to the formulaic properties of language and the inherited conventions of social and literary art to communicate the unapprehended harmonies and agreements that comic art both discovers and creates.

The meaning of this comic work of art is inalienable from the structure of relations it articulates. The community that Mrs. Ramsay brings into existence is not created ex nihilo, in *imitatio dei*. The work of the imagination, like the work of Eden, is to give an ordered and visible expression to the concord wrought by love. The aesthetic composition that discovers the material forms languishing in nature finds its concrete symbol in the fruit bowl prepared by Rose that visually asserts the relationship between nature's boundless fertility and the "delicious fecundity" of the feminine imagination in containing that abundance in a determinate form. This fertile union of art and all-creating nature, of which Eden is the perennial example, is accomplished whenever the external order of nature or society mirrors the internal harmonies of that "unreal but penetrating and exciting universe which is the world seen through the eyes of love" (L, 73). As the artist's agape or unifying power infuses each member of the community, the empty rituals of social life revive their ancient connection with nature's transformative mysteries. The dinner table, previously a masculine symbol of the philosophical problem in discriminating subject, object, and the nature of reality, assumes, in its feminine character, a numinous aspect. It becomes a sacred site, the altar for communion rites by which love is distributed throughout the community of belief.

In the ritual moment of transfiguration, signaled by the radiance of Minta's sexual glow, love gives birth to the illusion that is both the triumph and the mockery of the human community it has brought into being. The doubleness of the novel's social vision is incorporated and inspired by the doubleness of the love the worshippers, under Mrs. Ramsay's aegis, celebrate: "for what could be more serious than the love of man for a woman, what more commanding, more impressive, bearing in its bosom the seeds of death; at the same time these lovers, these people entering into illusion glittering eyed, must be danced round with mockery, decorated with garlands" (L, 151). The mother creates the illusion of self-generating, self-containing life, the great round of existence that bears within itself the "seeds of death." It is not love that dies, but the illusions it generates, and for this reason those out of love can afford to mock the maternal vision they revere. Mockery is also part of ritual, its mode of insuring that the human order will not relapse into the compacted center of unorganized unconscious life. Mockery places the community celebrating the power of love "trembling on the verge" of that circle of life that excludes and is unaware of them. On the threshold between nature and culture that mockery delineates, those out of love can share in the dream of love without being absorbed into it; they can regard the hollowness of the illusion without denying its necessity: "there is nothing more tedious, more puerile and inhumane; yet it is also beautiful and necessary" (L, 155). Only Paul and Minta, whose love will die, and Prue, "just beginning, just moving, just descending" into the dream, are unaware of the fatality of love. For Prue, who will marry and die in childbirth, life is a condensed allegory on the processes of love. But ignorant of the destiny love holds for her, she too greets "the sun of the love of men and women" (L, 164).

That sun soon sets. The mother's twilight vision of a community rescued from impending darkness and division evanesces the moment it is achieved: "it had become . . . already the past" (L, 168). The mother's vision is constrained by its own fixation on surfaces and the cycles of mutability. When Mrs. Ramsay joins her husband in the study after dinner, she needs to "go deeper" than her own vision of life permits, to get, as she says "something" from him. Though they sit in silence, something does communicate itself from him to her. This "something" that extends and deepens her consciousness is "the life . . . the power of it" of Scott's novel *The Antiquary*, which Mr. Ramsay, to his great pleasure, is reading. The episode Ramsay reads concerns the sorrow of Muckelbackit over the death by drowning of his fisherman son, thus summarizing and expanding on the theme of drowning and reabsorption into nature that always accompanies, as if by qualification, the celebration of the maternal will. The central figure in the funeral scene alluded to is not the drowned corpse, nor the bereaved father, but the "crazed old woman" who mourns the loss of the young fisherman.

Like Mrs. Ramsay, the old woman of Scott's novel sits weaving, mechanically "twirling her spindle," either unaware or uninterested in the life around her. The allusion is important, for it uncovers the obsessive force in Woolf's elegy on the lost mother, now remembered and imagined as an old woman, consort to the old man or father. Scott's description of the old woman prefigures Mrs. Ramsay's eventual status in the community she weaves and holds together:

> Thus she sat among the funeral assembly like a connecting link between the surviving mourners and the dead corpse which they bewailed — a being in whom the light of existence was already obscured by the encroaching shows of death.[21]

---

21. Walter Scott, *The Antiquary* (New York: E. P. Dutton and Co., 1906), p. 286.

The child's fixation on the old man, whose death is desired, is transferred to the old woman, whose death is inevitable. In the child's vision of the lost mother, a vision shared by the narrative commemorating her, Mrs. Ramsay is the link between the mystical "body of life" of the community that she has created and that will survive her, and the encroaching shadows of death that will overrun her garden in "Time Passes."

V
THE GRACE OF ANDROGYNY

In "The Window" all life combined to create a sustaining social vision. In "Time Passes" all that remains of that vision are broken fragments, empty forms "from which life had parted" (L, 195). The section begins with the onset of a seemingly endless sleep in which the dream of love becomes a nightmare of death, emptiness, and idiot confusion: "it seemed as if the universe were battling and tumbling, in brute confusion and wanton lust aimlessly by itself" (L, 203). The estrangement between consciousness, which seeks order, and Nature, which languishes in disorder, is symbolized in the ruined garden and rendered in "Time Passes" double narration. The lyrical soliloquies reflect the struggles of the narrative consciousness, the only waking sleeper "tempted from his bed to seek an answer," to reimagine a human order that would "reflect the compass of the soul" (L, 193). The bracketed portions represent the victory of the narrator in rescuing humanly decisive events from the vast stretches of indifferent time that surround them. The death of Mrs. Ramsay, Prue's marriage, Prue's and Andrew's deaths, and the war are recorded in a series of parentheses which typographically enclose and thus preserve historical or human moments from the chaos of undifferentiated existence that threatens to absorb them. The toil of the narrator is reduced to an elementary, yet necessary function: to record or chronicle, to mark time according to the human measure of passage — marriage, childbirth, death, human loss (the death of Mrs. Ramsay) and human achievement (the publication of Carmichael's poems). Such moments are protected from "the insensibility of Nature" that observes only her own relentless rhythms, without aim or direction.

Throughout these nightmarish passages, the narrator's subjective horror has an objective counterpart in the European war. The last word of "Time Passes," *Awake,* ends the sleep that paralyzed the communal mind and reveals the intervening passage of time to be a nightmare, both real and imagined. "Time Passes" is an inversion of the novel's structure, the dream within the dream that constitutes the novel's total form, the nightmare that ruins the dream of peace "the dreamer's dreamt holily, dreamt wisely, to confirm" (L, 213). The dream work of "The Lighthouse" then comes to reconfirm the dream of peace that is the legacy of the mother.[22]

Lily Briscoe, the first to awaken at the conclusion of "Time Passes," is the artist designated to inherit the dream-vision and to penetrate into its meaning: "What does it mean then, what can it all mean" (L, 217). Carmichael, absorbed in his French novel, seems to have succumbed to the contentment of some continuing narcotic dream from which he awakens at the end of the novel like "an old pagan god" dispensing his compassion "over all the weakness and suffering of mankind" (L, 309). Musing on the lawn, Lily tries to recapture the dream of the past in the waking nightmare of the shaken present. "About life, about death, about Mrs. Ramsay": Lily feels that if the three could be brought into conjunction, their relation would reveal the mystery of the world. "If only she could put them together, write them out in some sentence, then she would have got at the truth of things" (L, 219).

That ideal sentence would compose an epitaph, linking life and death in the image of the "one life" of Mrs. Ramsay. But that sentence is never composed, nor are the "sacred inscriptions" that are secured, Lily believes, in the sanctuary of Mrs.

---

22. Technically, the dream work, as Freud defines it in his *Interpretation of Dreams,* consists in translating the latent "dream-thoughts" into the dream's manifest content, a work performed through the condensation, displacement, symbolic representation, and secondary revision of the dream-thoughts. My discussion of "The Lighthouse" is dependent on Freud's useful observation that the dream-content produced through the work of dreaming is "like a transcript of the dream thoughts," a pictographic script (Freud's analogy) in which characters or inscriptions must be read or interpreted according to their symbolic relation and not according to their pictorial value. Lily, as I will demonstrate, clearly thinks of her own painting as a hieroglyphic script which seeks to encode the "dream-thoughts" she attributes to Mrs. Ramsay. See Freud, *The Interpretations of Dreams,* in *The Standard Edition of the Complete Psychological Works of Sigmund Freud,* trans. and ed. James Strachey with Anna Freud, vols. IV, V (London: Hogarth Press, 1953), IV, 277–338; V, 339–508.

Ramsay's soul ever read or decoded. *To the Lighthouse* assumes a more expansive form than epitaph: the elegy, whose primary subject, as Coleridge reminds us, is not the figure of the beloved dead, but the tormented poet who survives.

Ramsay's repeated quotations of the final lines of Cowper's "The Castaway" incorporate this elegiac grief in the novel's underlying myth of the fisherman and his wife. In Cowper's poem, the elegist equates the physical peril of the castaway with the interior condition of the poet, who "of friends, of hope, of all bereft / His floating home forever left."[23] The despairing but courageous self of Cowper's elegy corresponds and illuminates Ramsay's mind as he hears MacAlister's tale of the "great storm" in which three ships were sunk. Ramsay, like the other survivors of "Time Passes," is an emotional castaway whose sole remaining delight is "to trace" the semblance of his grief "in another's case." So Ramsay "relished the thought of the storm and the dark night and the fisherman striving there" (L, 245), because he finds in that story a confirmation of his personal, tragic sense of life. Cowper's emphasis on destiny and fatality dovetails with Ramsay's continuous meditations on our final destiny, how we perish each alone. The sudden reversal that concludes "The Castaway" — "But I beneath a rougher sea / And whelmed in deeper gulphs than he" — redefines the structure and content of tragic destiny. The survivor, not the victim of death, becomes the authentic tragic figure. The tragic fate is not death, but the engulfment of the self by forces that extinguish hope, but not life.

Ramsay, like all honest mourners, mourns for himself. His elegiac lamentations begin in self-pity and conclude in self-justification. Elegy can displace, but it can never disguise its origin in the indomitable egoism of the living. Woolf's understanding of the psychology of mourning accounts for her generally sympathetic portrait of the father as supreme egoist. In the tradition of Meredith, she would and does allow that, for all his petty tyrannies and self-indulgences, the egoist is fundamentally a comic figure who "surely inspires pity."

> He who would desire to clothe himself at everybody's expense and is of that desire condemned to strip himself stark naked; he, if pathos

---

23. William Cowper, "The Castaway," in *Verse and Letters*, ed. Brian Spiller (Cambridge, Mass.: Harvard University Press, 1965), pp. 138–140.

ever had a form, might be taken for the actual person. Only he is not
allowed to rush at you, roll you over and squeeze your body for the
briny drops. There is the innovation [of comedy].[24]

Ramsay's constant demands for sympathy, the immense pressure of his concentrated woe, the horror of his effusive lamentations are tolerated in the novel because, for all his overweening
egoism, Ramsay embodies, as Meredith says, the very form of
pathos. That is why it is to Lily's immense discredit sexually to
stand dumb in the presence of his desolation. But it is also why
her cheerful remark "What beautiful boots!" actually consoles
Ramsay, for the remark, comically inappropriate to the scope of
his self-pity, represents a redeeming innovation of comedy. Mr.
Ramsay smiles at the non sequitur and animatedly protests that
"bootmakers make it their business to cripple the human foot"
(L, 229). The oedipal preoccupation with damaged feet is comically absorbed and displaced in Ramsay's momentary lapse into
the particulars of ordinary existence. Obsession is disguised and
forgotten in this renewed interest in immediate life, ushering
Lily into "a sunny island where peace dwelt, sanity reigned and
the sun ever shone, the blessed island of good boots" (L, 230).
Ramsay's egoism, which, like the oedipal fable, is a source of
the novel's underlying pathos, is transformed through the sane
and peaceful perspectives of comic art. The innovation of comedy is to represent the pathos of egoism, while delimiting its
power to rush and roll over all other life. From the father, the
daughter inherits the egoism and self-concern necessary for her
own survival; from him she learns the potential tragedy of her
own life. But she trusts to her innately comic vision to humanize
her own elegiac self-reflections.

It is by focusing on the pathos of the living, not the dead, that
the turn or reversal of fortune in To the Lighthouse depends: "And
it struck her, this was tragedy — not palls, dust and the shroud;
but children coerced, their spirits subdued" (L, 222). Lily's insight that the tyranny of the grieving father, not the death of the
mother, constitutes the real childhood tragedy is crucial to the
resolution of the novel's elegiac theme. The father's attempt to
subdue the child's spirit is the true threat to life, for it is he who
would block and shut life off from its renewing source — the will

24. George Meredith, "Prelude," The Egoist: The Works of George Meredith
(London: Archibald Constable, 1897), XV, 5.

of children, which is inseparable from the will to futurity. James's and Cam's pledge to resist his tyranny to the death unite them in a rebellious compact against the father who opposes change and obstructs life. Their compact, in turn, designates the terms of a new social contract, a new covenant between the living and the dead, the past and the present. But like all comic romances, *To the Lighthouse* is fundamentally conservative in its vision of a renovated order. James's ascendancy in the novel's final pages marks a successful beginning to a bloodless psychic and social revolution. In the oedipal logic on which the novel relies, the hatred of the father is a measure of the idealization of him.[25] The child must kill in order to become the person he loves. James is both the royal pretender and the authentic heir to his father's kingdom: "Loneliness . . . was for both of them the truth about things."

For when James assumes the symbolic tiller of his father's boat, he inherits the place and the authority of the master mariner. Thus the old man's praise, "Well done," acknowledges James's accession to manhood, while Ramsay, himself reinvigorated by his new alliance with resurgent life, becomes "like a young man" (L, 308). Roles are reversed and exchanged, sealing the familial restoration. The inauguration of a new familial order is mirrored by the vision within. The figure of the "old man reading," the image of James's traumatic fixation on the forbidding father, becomes in Cam's mind an image of the masculine strength and protection on which the trusting feminine spirit can rely: "He read, she thought, as if he were guiding something . . . And she went on telling herself a story about escaping from a sinking ship, for she was safe, while he sat there" (L, 283). Guided and protected by the paternal vision of facts uncompromising, Cam can daydream, make up stories, without being lost in the waters of annihilation. The "rising" of her imaginative power paradoxically involves a "falling" into the sexual roles and attitudes prescribed by the mother. Like her mother before her, Cam defers to and honors her father's vision when, "dabbling her fingers in the water," she murmurs,

---

25. The psychological struggle embodied in the family romance to displace or replace the real father is, as Freud concludes, "only an expression of the child's longing for the happy, vanished days when his father seemed to him the noblest and strongest of men and his mother the dearest and loveliest of women"; Freud, *Standard Edition*, vol. IX (1959), pp. 240–241.

"dreamily, half asleep, how we perished, each alone" (L, 284). Cam's tribute to the father prepares for the reconciliation between father and children; Lily, who observes the family's successful expedition, completes the comic action with the words of divine atonement: "It is finished" (L, 309).

A comic resolution could almost be defined, argues Northrop Frye, "as an action that breaks out of the Oedipus ring, the destruction of a family or other close-knit social group by the tension and jealousies of its members."[26] The novel's linear movement toward the lighthouse represents an imaginative effort to separate its oedipal origins from its psychological end — to break and thus break out of the oedipal ring of anxious and conflicted desire. The narrative action "is finished" when Ramsay steps on the rock, an action that precipitates the completion of Lily's picture. The line Lily draws in the center of her canvas recapitulates Ramsay's movement from vision to fulfillment, but it also expresses a relation between opposite points of reference, connecting and binding them in a determinate, encompassing form. The oedipal ring, a symbol of ritual and imaginative bondage, is transformed into the Great Round, the "uroboric totality" which unites life and death.

Lily's final brush stroke is thus the novel's most positive image of the imagination's leap into liberty, its triumph over anxiety. Despite Lily's fears that "women can't paint, women can't write," she strikes out against the oppressive spectres of self-doubt: "She looked at the steps; they were empty; she looked at her canvas; it was blurred. With a sudden intensity as if she saw it clear for a second, she drew a line there, in the centre" (L, 310). The novel, like "The Winter's Tale," concludes in the *heuresis* or "finding again" of the mother by the daughter. The mother, who had cast a "triangular shadow over the step" (L, 299), is reembodied and brought back to life in the work of art through which "is built up a whole structure of the imagination" (L, 258).

Yet the work of art itself expresses more than this genealogical affinity between Mrs. Ramsay's fecundity and Lily's creative powers. Lily's picture represents the novel's completed effort to reconcile antithetical visions of reality. It captures the light of a

---

26. Northrop Frye, *The Secular Scripture* (Cambridge, Mass.: Harvard University Press, 1975), p. 137.

butterfly's wing — the beauty of the world wrought by the fecund feminine will — burning on a framework of steel, the structure the rational intelligence of the masculine will imposes on the fluidity of nature. The dialectics of plot had previously centered in the conflicting, partial, and contradictory perspectives of embattled sexual wills: mother versus father, father versus son, male versus female. Only in the dream do such opposites attract and merge. As Freud observed, the word "no" does not exist in dreams: "Dreams show a special tendency to reduce two opposites to a unity or to represent them as one thing."[27] To represent opposites as the same thing is the dream work whose product is, like Lily's picture, the thing that endures, even if it leaves no material trace or is hidden from public inspection.

To the Lighthouse, then, concludes as a fable of an artistic *rite de passage* in which Lily, the productive dreamer, masters the female anxiety centered in fears of sexual and creative inadequacy, the fears that earlier had made the creative "passage from conception to work as dreadful as any down a dark passage for a child" (L, 32). Lily is forty-four when her passage from conception to finished work is completed. Virginia Woolf, the daughter victimized by a tyrannical, forbidding, if charming old man, is also forty-four when she moves from her original conception of a novel rooted in the ambivalent memories of childhood, through the dark passages of elegy, to her masterwork on the Victorian family romance.

Appropriately, it is a child triumphant, James Ramsay, the sensitive boy attached to his mother but sharing his father's vision, who solves the oedipal puzzle riddling the novel. It is he who realizes that getting to the lighthouse means arriving at the end of a dark passage where the dream work, the work of representing opposites as the same thing, is finally accomplished. As he looks up at the lighthouse, James understands that as one thing it symbolizes antithetical realities.

> James looked at the Lighthouse. He could see the white-washed rocks; the tower, stark and straight . . . So that was the Lighthouse, was it? (L, 276–277)

27. Freud, "The Antithetical Sense of Primal Words," *Standard Edition,* vol. XI (1957), pp. 153–163.

The father's vision, stark and straight, as austere as that angular table that represents for Lily the energies of Ramsay's splendid mind, "satisfies" James. Yet the knowledge of facts uncompromising no longer opposes, but complements the feminine vision:

> No, the other was also the Lighthouse. For nothing was simply one thing. The other lighthouse was true too. It was sometimes hardly to be seen across the bay. In the evening one looked up and saw the eye opening and shutting and the light seemed to reach them in that airy sunny garden where they sat. (T., 277)

The word "No" in James's reverie provides the rhetorical link between two opposites about to be reduced to a unity. The father's linear and purposive image of the world, by which knowledge is represented in the consecutive alphabet from A to Z, is true. But so is "that other lighthouse" that James and his mother see from their sunny, happy garden, a garden in which thought does not proceed along a keyboard of linearity. Through what Carolyn Heilbrun has aptly called the special "grace of androgyny," the child now sees with the father, but thinks back through the mother.[28]

Woolf's struggles with the ending of her fable indicate her sensitivity to its decorums:

> At this moment I'm casting about for an end . . . The last chapter, which I begin tomorrow, is in the Boat: I had meant to end with R. climbing on to the rock. If so, what becomes of Lily and her picture? Should there be a final page about her and Carmichael looking at the picture and summing up R.'s character? . . . If this intervenes between R. and the lighthouse, there's too much chop and change, I think. Could I do it in a parenthesis? So that one had the sense of reading the two things at the same time?[29]

As Woolf makes clear, Ramsay's character, singled out for summation, both in the original and final stages of composition remained central to her vision of the childhood past. Her decision to discard the proposed "simultaneous" double ending, and to focus instead on the completion of Lily's picture, is structurally consonant with the elegiac priorities of her narrative. Ramsay's

---

28. Carolyn Heilbrun, *Toward a Recognition of Androgyny* (New York: Alfred A. Knopf, 1973), p. 33.
29. *A Writer's Diary*, p. 98.

successful voyage to the lighthouse, undertaken to commemo-
rate his dead wife, concludes the narrative action, but not the
elegiac meditation, which must always refer to the resolutions
achieved in the artists's imagination. The dream work must be
executed in the mind of the narrator, who records, embraces,
and resolves all contradictions in thought and feeling.

The real "grace of androgyny" thus yields a more significant
sign of election: "the recognition," as Heilbrun argues, "of the
daughter as the true inheritor."[30] The work of dreaming and the
rites of mourning are aesthetically transformed into elegy, the
literary form centered in antithesis and contradiction, absence
and presence: "Elegy is the form of poetry natural to the reflec-
tive mind," writes Coleridge. "Elegy presents everything as lost
and gone or absent and future."[31] The either/or of life resolves
itself in the dreamed elegy in which the child lives through her
life from the start. The world of childhood, lost and gone, abides
in the world of the present. *To the Lighthouse* moves from a
dream of childhood through a nightmare of bereavement into
the dream of freedom. That freedom, of course, is the freedom
to continue in the future — writing books. The creative self, the
dutiful daughter, having found her mother and made peace with
her father, no longer mourns, but is free to dream again. Put
another way, books do continue one another in the career of
Virginia Woolf. The bereaved and obsessed self of *To the Lighthouse* becomes the dream self of *Orlando* — the androgyne.

---

30. *Toward a Recognition of Androgyny*, p. 32.
31. Coleridge, *Table Talk and Omnia*, p. 263.

10. Orlando *and Its Genesis:* Venturing and Experimenting in Art, Love, and Sex

JEAN O. LOVE

I
THE GROWTH OF AN IDEA

Orlando emerged from the period in Virginia Woolf's life when she was most experimental and venturesome. Her artistic experimenting resulted in her best novels, *To the Lighthouse* and *The Waves,* as well as *Orlando,* less successful and something of an anomaly among her major fictional works. Her personal venturing was epitomized by her relationship with Vita Sackville-West, in some respects another anomaly. It was the only one of her several intense friendships with women known to have included a physical relationship and thus to have been a testing ground for what she had supposed to be her peculiarity in love — Sapphism. *Orlando* is as much a product of her personal as of her artistic venturing and is her ultimate comment on Vita and the kind of friendship Vita preferred.

Virginia Woolf's diary during the early months of 1927 reveals her "surface mind" at work as she consciously found her way to the conception from which *Orlando* eventually grew. She had finished *To the Lighthouse,* a psychological turning point for her, but it was not yet published. Enduring her customary season of ups and downs while nervously anticipating reactions to a just-completed novel, she deliberately cast about for some new work, almost any new work. On February 21 she asked herself:

"Why not invent a new kind of play . . ."? Evidently she had
not quite finished with some of the themes of *To the Lighthouse,*
for the play she thought of was to be about relationships between a woman and a man. She sketched a possible outline:

> Woman thinks . . .
> He does.
> Organ plays.
> She writes.
> They say:
> She sings.
> Night speaks
> They miss.[1]

A week later she was still casting about for a new work and
was considering biographical memoirs. Perhaps a *Lives of the
Obscure,* based on historical documents she would search out?
Then it occurred to her that it might be wiser not to concern
herself with any book just yet. "After a holiday the old ideas will
come to me as usual; seeming fresher, more important than ever;
and I shall be off again, feeling the extraordinary exhilaration,
that ardour and lust of creation — which is odd, if what I create
is, as it may well be, wholly bad."[2]

While writing in her diary on March 14 Virginia finally conceived an idea, and just a little more, of what would become
Orlando. Her diary notation of that date shows precisely how her
surface mind arrived at a workable conception for the book and
then let her "inner mind" take over the process of creating it.
Her first notion was a story about an unattractive, impoverished
woman who attempted to rescue herself from isolation and
loneliness. A life of an obscure? The woman would stop a motor
to get a ride to Dover and from Dover she would cross the
channel. She dropped that idea when she was suddenly struck,
though only "vaguely," with the thought that she "might write a
Defoe narrative for fun." Her conscious mind began at once to
be less rationally, less reflectively directed, and from her inner
mind there burgeoned a "whole phantasy" for a story, complete
with the title "The Jessamy Brides." From the idea that struck
her in February, 1927, for that play about woman-man relationships, she arrived in March, not yet at her final destination but

---

1. *A Writer's Diary,* p. 103.
2. Ibid., pp. 103–104.

already at the conception of a work about woman-woman relationships. She imagined the possible content: "Two women,
poor, solitary . . . on the ladies of Llangollen . . . Sapphism to
be suggested." She did not say whether she realized at that time
that the idea had originated from her friendship with Vita.

   She made a decision to write the book. She also decided that it
would not come after her holiday but would be the holiday
itself, an escapade before the next "serious, mystical poetical
work." She would write it as she wrote her letters, quickly,
unselfconsciously, thereby resting her head before the exigencies
of the next work. She was ready, she said, to kick her heels and
be off.

   Typically, the scheme and content for a book had ballooned in
Virginia Woolf's mind during a period of incubation, convincing her for the moment that her inner or unconscious mind had
already virtually created a novel. She referred to the experience as
an instance of the "odd horrid unexpected way . . . these things
suddenly create themselves — one thing on top of another in
about an hour. So I made up *Jacob's Room* looking at the fire at
Hogarth House; so I made up the *Lighthouse* one afternoon in the
Square here."[3] Yet her inner mind had not completed its work;
she did not start writing the book until October of that uncertain
year of 1927. The novel *Orlando* that she finally created, though
wild, satirical, and profligate as an experiment, proved in most
other respects to be very different from what she had first imagined. The most significant change was that it became after all a
work about woman-man as well as about woman-woman relationships. There was of course a difference between the
woman-man relationships briefly considered for a play and the
woman-woman relationships envisioned for "The Jessamy
Brides." In *Orlando,* the woman-man relationships are primarily
intrapersonal. The novel is about the feminine and masculine
within an identical person, and about ways in which these may
change and affect interpersonal woman-man relationships as
well. In short, the book became an account of androgyny and
Sapphism, as manifested in Vita, not in Virginia herself. And
that too was part of her comment on Vita and their friendship.

   It is not clear when Virginia knew that Orlando would be
Vita. She acknowledged that fact to Vita only after she had

3. Ibid., pp. 104–105.

started work on the book, wondering, on October 9, how it
would be if Orlando proved to be Vita: What if it would be "all
about you and the lusts of your flesh and the lure of your
mind . . ."?[4]

Orlando, as I said at the outset, is something of an anomaly
among Virginia Woolf's novels. It is not tightly bound to her
other books, not quite as continuous with them as they are with
each other in form and style. Rather, it is marked by its ties to
her life, not her other novels — ties that are even more specific
than those of her other avowedly autobiographical novel, To the
Lighthouse. The most anomalous feature of Orlando, then, came
from the way in which the author wrote about a particular person and episode in her life, fictionalizing, exaggerating both,
even turning them into fantasy, without creating of them the
kind of artful novelistic form one finds elsewhere in her works.

A comparison between Orlando and To the Lighthouse serves as
an illustration. As Maria DiBattista has shown in the previous
chapter, To the Lighthouse transcends particular events — crucial
episodes in Virginia's life with her parents and family —
transforming them while being deeply grounded in them. As a
novel, then, To the Lighthouse is autonomous, disconnected from
these important phases in her personal life, though paradoxically
it also renders the most intimate account of them. For the novel
Virginia Woolf had written remained not merely about herself
and her family but became a work about the human condition.
Orlando, by contrast, was neither conceived nor written in that
way. While it may be read without reference to her life, it does
not quite stand on its own as To the Lighthouse is able to do. In
fact, it cannot be completely understood outside the context of
her friendship with Vita Sackville-West: her most venturesome
and experimental personal relationship. It is best read, I think, as
her ultimate comment on Vita and as her means of gaining
perspective and detachment in order to continue their friendship
on a different basis. To the Lighthouse, too, can be read in that
fashion — as the writer's way of detaching herself from her parents in order to remember them differently from before — but
because of its greater reach and power of transformation it is best
not read thus.

Because Orlando is so peculiarly bound to Virginia's friendship
with Vita, its true genesis is to be sought not in diary entries
early in 1927 so much as in an account of that friendship from its

4. *The Letters of Virginia Woolf,* III (1923–1928), 427–429.

beginnings late in 1922. The novel must have been in the making, must have been developing in her inner mind for several years before she wrote it, possibly from the time she first became acquainted with Vita.

II
ATTRACTIONS AND RESISTANCES

Virginia Woolf met Vita Sackville-West for the first time on December 14, 1922, at a dinner party arranged by Clive Bell, who apparently wanted to bring them together for reasons about which we can hardly speculate. Vita was immediately attracted to Virginia; four days later she entertained her, Clive, and Desmond MacCarthy at dinner.[5] Clive had evidently praised Vita to Virginia for some months before, and Virginia was intrigued before meeting her. On August 10, after seeing Clive, she had written to Vanessa: "Would you be so angelic as to look in Clives [sic] room for The Heir, by V. Sackville-West, and bring it with you? She admires me; therefore I must try to admire her, which, of course, I shan't find difficult."[6]

Virginia did not plunge immediately into a relationship of any kind with Vita. After the initial meetings, the two women had lunch together a few times, saw each other occasionally, and corresponded. The physical relationship did not begin until December 1925, some three years after their first meeting. On Virginia's part at least, love and friendship were slow to emerge. One reason was that at first she had not found Vita as attractive as Clive had led her to expect. "Not much to my severer taste," she wrote in her diary on December 22, 1922. She described Vita as "florid, moustached, parakeet coloured, with all the supple ease of the aristocracy, but not the wit of the artist. She writes 15 pages a day — has finished another book — publishes with Heinemanns — knows everyone." Nevertheless, Virginia tagged Vita "the lovely gifted aristocrat."[7]

Other reasons for the slow start of their friendship were Virginia's shyness, even wariness, and her tendency to vacillate — in brief, a persisting caution about venturing. According

5. Vita Sackville-West and Nigel Nicolson, *Portrait of a Marriage* (New York: Atheneum, 1973), p. 201; Bell, *Virginia Woolf*, II, 235.
6. *Letters*, II, 543– 544.
7. *Portrait of a Marriage*, pp. 203– 205.

to Quentin Bell, Virginia was afraid to become the close friend of someone who had a reputation of being a "frank and unequivocal Sapphist."[8] The reputation did not match the facts, of course: Vita had indeed equivocated and was bisexual, although apparently she much preferred the sexual company of women. Virginia's fear of Vita's reputation, such as it was, seized her mainly during the preliminary phases of their acquaintance. Actually, when she later decided she wanted the affair, the fact that Vita was an experienced Sapphist may have been part of the attraction. And Virginia did decide to let her relationship become sexual. She was not seduced by Vita or, if she was seduced, it happened because she had decided to permit it.

On Vita's part there were also ambivalence and vacillation, attraction and resistance. But her resistance was much weaker than her attraction. It was more in Vita's nature to give in to her attractions than to resist them, and the term "ambivalence" seldom applied to her. She found Virginia exceptionally attractive from the outset. She "simply adore[d]" her, if not from their first meeting, then from their second, as she told her husband. To Harold she summed up Virginia's attractions: "charm and personality"; lack of affectation; a "sort of spiritual beauty." Virginia was detached yet human, she said. Vita also admired Virginia for keeping silent until she had something to say, and then for "saying it supremely well." She had rarely taken such a fancy to anyone. But she criticized Virginia in writing to Harold, telling him that she dressed quite atrociously, that at their first meeting she had worn orange woollen stockings and pumps. At their second, Vita thought she was slightly better dressed: at least she wore yellow silk stockings, although she still wore pumps. Also, she noted that Virginia was "quite old" — forty. Vita was thirty at the time.

As the friendship developed, so did Vita's love for Virginia. Bell described that phase: "Vita was very much in love with Virginia and being, I suspect, of an ardent temperament, loved her much as a man might have loved her, with a masculine impatience for some kind of physical satisfaction — even though Virginia was now in her forties and, although extremely beautiful, without the charm of her youth . . ."[9]

8. Bell, *Virginia Woolf*, II, 116.
9. Ibid., p. 117.

Yet to a degree Vita did resist. Possibly she held back because
of Virginia's resistance and because of the things Virginia said
and did, rather than because of any reluctance to engage herself
in the relationship. Virginia told Vita that she did not want to be
in love, that being in love made everything "a bore," to which
Vita agreed, though perhaps not very sincerely.[10] It was evidently her impression that people and their relationships were
interesting to Virginia not in themselves but mostly because as a
writer she could use them as literary copy. As Vita phrased it,
her friend tended to like people better "through her brain than
her heart." She was of course perceptive, for Virginia was an
inveterate fictionalizer of people and relationships. In fact, she
proved that she liked Vita "through her brain" when she wrote
Orlando — proved it so magnificently that Vita found no sting in
it. But Vita's perception was not wholly accurate, as the history
of their friendship has established. Virginia was also capable of
liking Vita through the heart, of falling in love with her.[11]
Orlando was proof of that too, for as Vita's son, Nigel Nicolson,
has said, it was, among other things, a beautiful love letter.[12]

Vita's resistance was also much weaker than she herself
thought it should have been or than she professed it to be. The
reason she thought she should resist was Virginia's reputation — for madness, not for Sapphism. Vita said in a letter to
Harold: "I am scared to death of arousing physical feelings in
her, because of her madness. I don't know what effect it would
have, you see: it is a fire with which I have no wish to play. I
have too much real affection and respect for her." She added that

> one's love for Virginia is a very different thing: a mental thing; a
> spiritual thing, if you like, an intellectual thing, and she inspires a
> feeling of tenderness, which is, I suppose, owing to her funny mix-
> ture of hardness and softness — the hardness of her mind, and her
> terror of going mad again. She makes me feel protective.

Actually Vita spoke after she had "gone to bed" with Virginia,
although "only twice," thus after she had tried to arouse physi-

10. *Portrait of a Marriage*, pp. 201 – 202.
11. Bell, *Virginia Woolf*, II, 117; to Vita Sackville-West, Aug. 19 and Oct. 4,
     1924, *Letters*, III, 125–126, 137–138; Joanne Trautmann, *The Jessamy Brides:
     The Friendship of Virginia Woolf and Vita Sackville-West* (University Park:
     Pennsylvania State University Press, 1973), pp. 31 – 32.
12. *Portrait of a Marriage*, p. 202.

cal feelings. Harold replied that it was not fire but gelignite with which she played, and urged Vita to be cautious.[13]

As the friendship slowly developed, Virginia reacted to Vita almost as if she had been invented for her pleasure.[14] Her friend proved to have many attributes that impressed Virginia, although her estimation of just what these were tended to change with the stages of their friendship. Eventually Virginia had to realize that Vita had some qualities she disliked, but that came much later. Vita's most fundamental attribute to attract her was her protectiveness. But this acknowledgment too came later, significantly, immediately following the start of their physical relations. Earlier other things stood out more prominently in their friendship. From the beginning Virginia was impressed because Vita was an aristocrat. She called Vita, after their first meetings, a "lovely, gifted aristocrat." Later she called her "my aristocrat."[15] Virginia was also impressed by the accoutrements of Vita's aristocratic background, particularly her family's houses and estates. Above all there was Knole, the huge mansion that had been the Sackvilles' ancestral home and Vita's home during her childhood. One of the great sorrows of Vita's life was that because she was a woman she would not inherit Knole; instead of its descending to her, it was to go to her father's brother.[16] Long Barn was next among the houses associated with Vita's background. The Nicolsons were living at Long Barn when Virginia came to know Vita, and the sexual affair between the two women began there.[17] Finally, there was Sissinghurst, the remnants of an ancient castle that Vita and Harold had bought and restored to a place of exceptional beauty.[18]

Virginia liked the luxury of Vita's houses as well as the sense of history she gained from them.[19] But more fundamental, I think, was the fact that Virginia always had "a nose for houses," and, like Vita, felt an almost mystical attraction for them.[20] Wit-

13. Ibid., pp. 205–206.
14. Bell, *Virginia Woolf*, II, 115.
15. To Jacques Raverat, Jan. 24, 1925, *Letters*, III, 154–156.
16. *Portrait of a Marriage*, pp. 52, 208.
17. Ibid., pp. 203–204; see also Bell, *Virginia Woolf*, II, 117–118, for an exploration of the ramifications of this early phase in their relationship.
18. *Portrait of a Marriage*, pp. 222ff.
19. To Ethel Smyth, Aug. 15, 1930 (New York Public Library, Berg Collection, folder 6).
20. *Letters*, II, xiv.

ness the part played in her own life by Talland House, where she spent her childhood vacations and which she made into the setting of *To the Lighthouse*. Witness also Asham House, Monk's House, and the other Woolf residences, all of which Virginia loved but which seemed a little shabby when compared with the splendor of Vita's houses.[21]

Another attraction was not only the "high lineage" of Vita's family but also their reputation for literary accomplishment.[22] Vita herself was a prodigious author. She had written several books before she and Virginia had met and she continued to write books, publishing some of them with the Hogarth Press. But, as in everything else, Virginia's appreciation of her work was not without the usual ambivalence. Although she did not actually dislike Vita's work, Virginia thought she wrote with "a pen of brass." And she made several other unfavorable comments on her friend's writing, as Vita knew.[23] Perhaps this perception of Vita as a less gifted writer than she was herself may have been an asset for Virginia, however unconsciously, for it reduced the threat of professional rivalry. The further fact that Vita admired Virginia's own work intensely made her, in Quentin Bell's words, appear "irresistible."[24]

Beyond being a writer, Vita was sufficiently intelligent and well informed to impress Virginia and to be an interesting companion and conversationalist. Just as she admired her sister Vanessa for her competence, so Virginia also admired Vita's ability in practical affairs, her ease in running her houses and estates, managing her farms, planting and tending her elaborate gardens.[25] Bell suggests that in some ways Vita was perhaps less intelligent and competent than Virginia thought. He said that she tended to "blunder through life," at times "stupidly."[26] Her

21. Leonard Woolf, *Beginning Again: An Autobiography of the Years 1911–1918* (New York: Harcourt, Brace and World, 1963), pp. 55ff, 166, 171–173; *Downhill All the Way: An Autobiography of the Years 1919–1939* (New York: Harcourt, Brace and World, 1967), pp. 10ff, 153–154; Bell, *Virginia Woolf*, I, 37, 104–105; to Vita, July 6, 1924, *Letters*, III, 117–118; to Ethel Smyth, Sept. 19, 1937 (Berg Collection, folder 74).
22. Bell, *Virginia Woolf*, II, 115.
23. *Portrait of a Marriage*, pp. 208–212; *Letters*, III, xx; diary, Dec. 21, 1925, quoted in Bell, *Virginia Woolf*, II, 117–118; to Jacques Raverat, Dec. 6, 1924, *Letters*, III, 149–150.
24. Bell, *Virginia Woolf*, II, 116.
25. Diary entry, Dec. 21, 1925, quoted by Bell, ibid., pp. 117–118; Angus Davidson, repr. in Joan Russell Noble, *Recollections of Virginia Woolf* (New York: Morrow, 1975).
26. Bell, *Virginia Woolf*, II, 115–116.

husband also thought her a muddler, or at least he used the term
"muddle" to refer to her affairs with women.[27]

Virginia had been somewhat critical of Vita's looks when they
first met but later she came to think her beautiful. She felt at
times, however, as though Vita's beauty were an illusion — that
because she was attracted to her and loved her, she could not see
her objectively.[28] But, except for her hesitancy during the early
meetings and her criticism, at one point, that Vita had gained too
much weight, she usually thought her beautiful. Apparently
others found her attractive, too. Quentin Bell noted her fine
dark eyes and her unselfconscious charm, adding that she was a
"very beautiful woman, in a lazy, majestic, rather melancholy
way . . ."[29] Virginia had first loved Vita for the "beaming
beauty" of her eyes, which was "spoiled when she gained
weight."[30]

Conspicuous among Vita's physical attributes, according to
Virginia, were her legs — an observation which documents the
erotic quality of the attraction. In December, 1924, a year before
the more experimental phase of their friendship began, she told
her friend Jacques Raverat that Vita's "real claim to consideration is, if I may be so coarse, her legs. Oh they are exquisite —
running like slender pillars up into her trunk, which is like a
breastless cuirassier (yet she has two children) but all about her is
virginal, savage, patrician . . ."[31]

If the reference to Vita's legs was coarse, it was a coarseness in
which Virginia persisted. For example, in writing to Vanessa
about a visit to Oxford with Vita in the spring of 1927, she
commented on her friend's attractions, particularly on her "long
white legs." She said that Vita had been bitten by midges and at
dinner had taken down her stockings to apply ointment to her
legs. She liked that about the aristocracy — legs, bites, and the
"complete arrogance and unreality of their minds."[32] Virginia's
awareness of Vita's legs is made into an important image in
Orlando, where her joke about her hero/heroine's beautiful legs
pervades the novel as a recurrent motif.

27. *Portrait of a Marriage,* pp. 187–205.
28. To Vanessa Bell, May 23, 1931 (Berg Collection, folder 77).
29. Bell, *Virginia Woolf,* II, 115–116.
30. To Ethel Smyth, Dec. 3, 1935 (Berg Collection, folder 61).
31. To Jacques Raverat, Dec. 26, 1924, *Letters,* III, 149–150.
32. To Vanessa, May 22, 1927, *Letters,* III, 379–382.

III
THE SEXUAL VENTURE

The experimental phase of the friendship between Virginia
and Vita, their sexual affair, began in December, 1925.[33] It was
preceded for Virginia by increasing emotional involvement with
Vita and, for more than a year, by much thought about love,
especially love between persons of the same sex. Apparently she
was consciously considering where her friendship with Vita,
that frank if not unequivocal Sapphist, might lead, trying either
to talk herself out of her increasing attraction to the idea, or to
persuade herself to act on her attraction. Her slow, hesitating
progress toward a decision can be traced through a series of
letters to Jacques Raverat and a series of diary passages.

In an early letter to Jacques written on October 3, 1924, Virginia professed to find the topic of sexual relations more boring
than she used to and thought love a "disease." She recalled,
however, that she had thought of love differently when she was
younger, particularly when Jacques had become engaged to
Gwen Darwin, one of Virginia's childhood friends. She said —
rather insincerely, for at that earlier time she had doubted that
Jacques loved Gwen — that their love had seemed to her to have
an ecstatic quality, as if they were in a "divine sunset red"
glow.[34] But ten weeks later, in a letter already cited, she praised
the beauty of Vita's legs, which must have tipped him off about
the nature of her attraction.[35]

Another month passed and on January 24, 1925, Virginia
wrote again to Jacques, now more explicitly. She first asked his
opinion about loving one's own sex. Young men so inclined
struck her as "mildly foolish," and she mentioned particularly
Vita's cousin, Edward Sackville-West, declaring that she could
not "respect amours of a creature like *that*." She then turned to
the topic of homosexuality in women and expressed the view
that it could come about either because of "self-protection or
imitation or genuinely." After that rather circumlocutious introduction, she reached her real topic, "my aristocrat." She told

33. *Portrait of a Marriage*, pp. 201–208; *Letters*, III, xxi.
34. To Jacques Raverat, Oct. 3, 1924, *Letters*, III, 135–137. For the earlier
    doubts about Jacques's feelings for Gwen, see letter to Vanessa, Apr. 19,
    1911, *Letters*, I, 462–463.
35. *Letters*, III, pp. 149–150.

Jacques that Vita was "violently Sapphic" and described briefly,
vaguely, and inaccurately Vita's love affair and elopement with
Violet Trefusis. Virginia could not take "these aberrations" seriously; nevertheless, she followed her comment by confiding "a
secret: I want to incite my lady to elope with me next."[36]

Virginia returned to the topic of love once more in a letter to
Jacques on February 5, touching on both love between the sexes
and love for one's own sex. She described Clive Bell and implied
that she had not been able to act on her attraction to him because
she had been "bred a puritan." But since she had had a French
great grandmother to "muddle her," she still liked to warm her
hands "at these red-hot-coal-men." She wished that she had
married a foxhunter, partly out of the need to share in life somehow, which is often denied writers, but, she admitted, she much
preferred her own sex. Young men's conversation was too
monotonous and she resented "the eternal pressure which they
put, if you're a woman, on one string." She intended to cultivate
only women's society in the future. And she concluded poetically, with words reminiscent of the title of her *Night and Day:*
"Men are in the light always; with women you swim at once
into the silent dusk."[37]

The problem of homosexuality, however, continued to concern her. On April 19, 1925, she noted in her diary that she had
had a visit from Lytton Strachey, whose sexual inclinations were
well known. They had discussed "old buggers" (Virginia's
crude slang for aging male homosexuals) and their problem of
being unable to attract the young men they found desirable. The
conversation had revolted Virginia a little. The "pale stare of the
bugger has been in the ascendant too long," she told her diary.
She spoke of her "anti-bugger revolution" that had been round
the world, although she did not make her meaning clear.[38] In
June she again wrote about Lytton and his problems, complain-
ing in her diary that he was neglecting the Woolfs. She thought
he probably stayed away from them because he had found "a
new love." Feeling a little ridiculous as a consequence, he didn't
"relish the company of old cynical friends" such as themselves.
She said that she could only feel "slightly nauseated" upon hearing of his latest amour, of his "agony and entreaty and despair"

36. Ibid., pp. 154–156.
37. Ibid., pp. 163–165.
38. Virginia Woolf, diary holograph, entry of Apr. 19, 1925 (Berg Collection).

that made the young men both pity him and laugh at him. There was, Virginia said, a touch of senility in his thus exposing himself.[39]

Virginia Woolf's letters to Vita during this period, by contrast, did not deal with her thoughts about love and homosexuality. But she did reveal her growing interest in Vita herself, particularly while she was ill during the summer and fall of 1925. Although the symptoms of her illness were primarily physical, they may have also been signs of a threatening emotional breakdown, as suggested, for example, by the nature and vividness of her fantasies. Her illness played a part in her growing attraction to Vita, for when she was ill Virginia was always especially vulnerable to her need for maternal love. But some of her letters to Vita suggest that she was thinking of much more than maternal attentions and that she spent part of her time in bed enjoying her fantasies, especially those surrounding Vita. For example, she wrote on August 24 that the picture in her mind was one of Vita "stamping out the hops in a great vat at Kent — stark naked, brown as a satyr, and very beautiful."[40]

There were times during this illness when Virginia's fantasies and images of Vita were so vivid as to be almost hallucinatory. Vita seemed to be "striding over her head in the moonlight," and Virginia asked that she stop, "exquisitely beautiful though the vision is."[41] At other times, however, she had difficulty calling up any images of Vita. She had tried to "invent" Vita in her mind but had only a few "twigs" and "straws" with which to do so:

> I can get the sensation of seeing you — hair, lips, colour, height, even, now and then, the eyes and hands, but I find you going off, to walk in the garden, to play tennis, to dig, to sit smoking and talking, and then I can't invent a thing you say — This proves, what I could write reams about — how little we know anyone, only movements and gestures, nothing connected, continuous, profound.

The problem of inventing Vita was to be completely solved when she wrote *Orlando*. At this moment, however, Virginia was having difficulty. She could not even talk to Vita, for talk gave her "astonishingly incongruous dreams."[42]

39. Ibid., entry of June 16, 1925.
40. *Letters*, III, 197–199.
41. Ibid., pp. 199–200.
42. To Vita, Sept. 7, 1925, *Letters*, III, 204–205.

By November, 1925, Virginia was well enough to entertain guests and Vita came to visit at least twice. At that time Virginia was still trying to understand the exact nature of her feelings. She wrote in her diary that she was genuinely fond of Vita, but admitted that she was "dazzled" by the "glamour of the unfamiliarity . . . of the aristocracy" as well as by "the flattery." But after "sifting," she was sure much remained of the person she liked for herself. Would she "stay with Vita?" She thought perhaps she might; her illness had "loosened earth at the roots" and had "made changes." Oddly, however, although she was becoming increasingly fond of her, Virginia did not yet count Vita among those people she found essential. Commenting on Madge Vaughan's death and on her "inability to beat up a single tear" for Madge, a woman she had once loved, Virginia said that there were only six people so important to her that her life would "cease" if they should die. She listed Leonard Woolf, Vanessa Bell, Duncan Grant, Lytton Strachey, Clive Bell, and E. M. Forster, but not Vita Sackville-West.

The fact that Virginia asked herself whether she would "stay with Vita" suggests that she was close to a decision to do so, but in November she had not yet made up her mind. By early December, however, she was ready to take the friendship at least a few steps farther. She was assisted in her decision by two or perhaps three factors. The first was Vita's plan to go to Persia in January, where her husband, Harold Nicolson, was on a diplomatic assignment. As Virginia put it, Vita was "doomed" to go. Second, Virginia was motivated by her need to overcome an apparent impasse in their friendship. She complained in her diary just a few days later that she was depressed and wanted to "lie down and weep away her cares," like a "tired child." The trouble was "that devil Vita," who did not write, did not visit, did not invite Virginia to come to stay with her at Long Barn. If she did not see Vita now, Virginia said, then "I shall not —— ever," leaving a blank rather than name what she would never do. By next summer, when Vita returned from Persia, "the moment of intimacy" would have passed.[43] A possible third factor was the advice she received from her husband. Seeing that Virginia was unhappy being out of touch with Vita, he advised her to break the apparent impasse by writing her. Leonard thus

---

43. Diary holograph, entries of Nov. 27 and Dec. 7, 1925 (Berg Collection).

helped Virginia reach her decision by suggesting that she take the initiative, however briefly.[44] He therefore encouraged her unwittingly in allowing the friendship to move into its next phase.

After an exchange of letters, Virginia received the invitation she wanted and went to stay at Long Barn from December 17 to 20, 1925.[45] She was alone with Vita for the first two nights; Leonard joined her on the third. According to Nigel Nicolson, the physical relationship between the two women began on the second night of the visit. He based this conclusion on his mother's diary, where she noted, circumspectly, that she and Virginia had spent a "peaceful evening" on the seventeenth but that they had talked until 3:00 A.M. on the following night, and that it had not been a "peaceful evening."[46] If Virginia had briefly taken the initiative, she now relinquished it to the more experienced Vita.

IV
A PRELIMINARY COMMENT ON THE AFFAIR

Virginia and Leonard Woolf returned home on December 20. The next day she noted in her diary the change that had come over her relationship with Vita, assessing the experience for them both. She was circumspect, though less so than Vita, who in her diary and letters to Virginia was always extremely careful in what she revealed. Nor was Virginia as circumspect in her diary after the affair began as she had been when she left blank her hopes or intentions before the fact. Now she weighed openly the immediate insights she had gained from her "experiment in friendship," which had come to include both passionate love and sex. Most telling, in my view, is the fact that at this very moment, just after her first sexual experience with Vita, Virginia insisted that what she wanted most was maternal protection. It is also significant that she was ever so slightly critical of Vita in that respect. She said that Vita *tried*, in her "rough external way," to give her maternal protection, while Leonard and Vanessa gave it to her completely. Nevertheless, Vita's way of "lavishing" much attention upon her clearly suggested that she tried to do so,

44. Ibid., Dec. 21, 1925, also quoted in Bell, *Virginia Woolf*, II, 117–118.
45. To Vita, Dec. 9, 10, 1925, *Letters*, III, 223–224.
46. *Letters*, III, xxi, 223n.

which was ample reason for Virginia to forgive other shortcomings including her being less organized than Virginia "in brain
and insight."

  Some remarks about Sapphism in this diary passage stand out
as particularly significant because they, too, were made just after
the first sexual encounter. They seem to indicate that even at this
moment Virginia still did not consider herself a Sapphist. "These
Sapphists," she wrote, referring to people like Vita, not people
like Virginia, *"love* women"; "their" — not "our" — friendship is
"never untinged with amorosity."[47] I find no conclusive evidence that Virginia Woolf ever changed her mind and started to
think of herself in that way, although she still admitted "Sapphist
leanings" as late as the thirties.[48] How she did think of herself
emerges from a letter to Vanessa written on July 23, 1927, in
which she said that "poor Billy [Virginia] isn't one thing or
another, not a man nor a woman . . ."[49] And in a letter to Vita
she referred to herself as a eunuch, as someone who "pulls the
shade over the fury of sex."[50] Thus it appears that perhaps one of
Virginia's immediate discoveries after beginning her affair with
Vita was that she could not think of herself as homosexual,
although she had suspected for years that she might be. In fact,
she may have been slightly relieved not to have to characterize
herself as having what she called an "aberration."

  One interpretation of Virginia's initial comments on her sexual affair is to accept her words at face value, as I am inclined to
do. However, another plausible explanation would be that she
could not see herself and her conduct in the most obvious light,
that in her diary she was explaining and justifying herself to
herself. Nigel Nicolson believed that this may have been the case
and noted correctly that no matter how Virginia Woolf may
have characterized herself and her conduct during her affair with
Vita Sackville-West, as long as the affair continued she was acting as a Sapphist.[51]

  Whether relieved because she realized she was not a Sapphist,
or relieved by denying that she was one, Virginia was also
somewhat disappointed and thought she had disappointed Vita

47. Bell, *Virginia Woolf,* II, 117–118.
48. To Vanessa, July 17, 1935 (Berg Collection, folder 90).
49. *Letters,* III, 400–401.
50. To Vita, Jan. 31/Feb. 2, 1927, *Letters,* III, 319–321.
51. Personal correspondence, July 4, 1978.

as well. This was a matter that would worry her frequently in the future. Quentin Bell expressed the view that sexually the experience was relatively unsatisfactory and doubted that it "was of a kind to excite Virginia or satisfy Vita," implying that both felt let down. "As far as Virginia's life is concerned," he added, "the point is of no great importance; what was, to her, important was the extent to which she was emotionally involved, the degree to which she was in love." Bell thought that Virginia was in fact in love, but questioned the depth of her emotion: "One cannot give a straight answer to such questions but, if the test of passion be blindness, then her affections were not deeply engaged."[52] I have already shown that as far as her friend's writing was concerned Virginia was by no means blind, and she may, in fact, have been able to love Vita better because she did not feel professionally threatened.

Virginia Woolf's disappointment, however, may have had deeper roots. It may have arisen from the fact that the experience had done little to develop the sexual aspects of her personality or to clarify her understanding of herself. Her own remarks, expressing concern that Vita might be disappointed in her, suggest that she still felt compelled to think of herself as "cold."[53] At the same time, since she clearly did not find the affair so disheartening and distasteful that she wanted to discontinue it, her disappointment may not have been as extensive as has been supposed. Nigel Nicolson described the affair as "a strange and pleasurable experience, but unintoxicating, terminable."[54] But he also made clear that it was not immediately terminated. He believed that Virginia and Vita continued their affair for perhaps three years, two years longer than he had at first estimated.[55]

There are several reasons why one might think that Virginia was, in fact, not too disappointed and that she was happy during the affair. Her health was better; she wrote with less strain during the physical phase of her friendship and showed no signs of serious regret or guilt. She did not apply to herself any of the terms she had recently used about Lytton Strachey. She was not in a state of "agony, entreaty, and despair," nor was she even slightly nauseated or disgusted. Unafraid to face "cynical

---

52. Bell, *Virginia Woolf*, II, 119.
53. To Vita, *Letters*, III, 231–233, 235–237.
54. *Letters*, III, xxii.
55. Nicolson, personal correspondence, July 4, 1978.

people" like Leonard, her only worry concerned Vanessa. She felt some trepidation about seeing her sister, she wrote, because she herself was still "hung with clouds of glory from Long Barn." Perhaps the best reason to think she was happy was that she said so — that she was far happier than she had been before, and that she was grateful to Leonard for that.[56]

What of Virginia's other reactions when the affair began? As was almost always the case with her, she was ambivalent and could not be totally satisfied or wholehearted about Vita and their relationship. Her friend's criticism of her appearance became a problem for her because her supposed "dowdiness" touched on an area about which she had always been sensitive. Whether or not Vita meant to convey the impression that Virginia was "dowdy" does not matter, nor does it matter whether she actually said that though Virginia was "so beautiful," "no one cared less for personal appearances" or "put on things" as she did. But as a result of these or similar remarks Virginia denigrated herself about the way she dressed and romanticized Vita's attire. Virginia was dowdy; Vita was glamorous, "pink-glowing, grape-clustered and pearl-hung," and stalked on "legs like beech trees."

Virginia also denigrated herself in other ways. Vita was more mature, more capable and confident than she. Vita was a "real woman" as Virginia felt she had never been: she was more voluptuous and she was a mother, although in Virginia's own estimate too "offhand and cool" with her sons. Virginia concluded that there was something "loose fitting" amid all this glamor. She would have to wait to see how much she would really miss Vita when she went to Persia.[57]

V

THE LONG-RANGE LIFE OF THE AFFAIR

Nigel Nicolson's estimate of the duration of the affair was based, in part, on the correspondence between the two women. In her letters to Vita, Virginia implied that they were sexually involved intermittently from December 1925 until at least the fall of 1927, and possibly through much of 1928. However, the

---

56. Virginia Woolf, diary holograph (ms), entry of Dec. 21, 1925 (Berg Collection).
57. Ibid. See also Bell, *Virginia Woolf,* II, 117–118.

letters also continued to suggest that for Virginia the more important attractions of the friendship were the sense of maternal protection; the happy, childlike playfulness; the bantering and teasing; the emotional rather than the sexual intimacy it afforded. She adopted animal nicknames for Vita, an unmistakable sign of intimacy in her relationships. Vita was "Donkey West," "the insect," and sometimes "Dolphin," the name Virginia and others often called Vanessa. Vita was also "dearest creature," "dearest shaggy creature," and "darling honey."[58] Sometimes Virginia referred to herself as "the mole," "the squirrel," and "Bosman's Potto."[59]

The letters also show that the relationship was anything but static. Although Virginia continued to be entranced by and even infatuated with Vita for a long time, she was gradually disillusioned by her Sapphism. Eventually she was hurt and disappointed by her friend's inability to remain committed to her, or to anyone. Vita's husband appeared to be the only exception, but that relationship of course did not involve a sexual commitment or one to which Virginia objected. However, early in their friendship she was primarily concerned that Vita might be disappointed. For example, she wrote soon after Vita's departure for Persia in January, 1926: "As for the people I've seen, I've fallen in love with none — but thats [sic] not exactly my line. Did you guess that? I'm not cold; not a humbug; not weakly; not sentimental. What I am; I want you to tell me." She also hinted that her motives for the affair included curiosity or inquisitiveness. Perhaps she was only a "lively squirrel" with "inquisitive habits," nestling inside Vita's jersey, but a "dear creature all the same."[60] In her next letter she intimated that Vita was disappointed in her, that Vita thought her unable to "feel the things dumb people feel." But, she said, Vita must know that is "rotten rot."[61]

After Vita's return from Persia in 1926 and presumably after further sexual intimacy, Virginia began to speculate that Vita would become tired of her because she was so much older. She

58. For examples see letters to Vita, Jan. 15, 16, Jan. 31/Feb. 2, Nov. 19, 1926; Jan. 31, Apr. 5, May 9, July 4 and 18, and Aug. 7, 1927, *Letters,* III, 228–230, 235–237, 302–303, 319–321, 358–360, 372–373, 395–398.
59. For examples, see Jan. 26, 1926, Nov. 22, 1927, and Feb. 9, 1928, *Letters,* III, 231–233, 440–441, 456.
60. To Vita, Jan. 26, 1926, *Letters,* III, 231–233.
61. To Vita, Jan. 31/Feb. 2, 1926, *Letters,* III, 235–237.

had taken precautions against that eventuality, Virginia said. But
if she did become tired, "Donkey West" would still know that
she had "broken down more ramparts than anyone."[62]

Vita went to Persia again the next year, leaving on January 29
and taking friends with her, including an especially close friend,
Lady Dorothy Wellesley.[63] In her first letter after Vita had left on
that trip, Virginia showed that she considered herself sexually
detached, a fascinated observer, not a participant. She also expressed some annoyance. The great thing about being a "eunuch," Virginia said, was that women confided in her. "One
pulls a shade over the fury of sex, and then all the veins and
marbling, which, between women, are so fascinating, show out.
Here in my cave I see lots of things you blazing beauties make
invisible by the light of your own glory." Yet she missed Vita;
since she had gone, Virginia felt lonely, like "something pitiable
which can't make its wants known."[64] In a later letter, she said
that Vita was solidly lodged in her heart, "such as it is: the cold
heart of a fish . . ."[65]

While Vita was in Persia Virginia began to banter about the
nights they would spend together, writing her playful letters
perhaps suggesting a move toward fictionalizing their relationship. In April she wrote: when Vita returned from Persia, they
would have a merry summer, spending a night at Long Barn,
then a night at Rodmell, writing some nice pieces of prose and
poetry, and snoring.[66] Vita joined in the banter but also hinted
that she had begun once more to resist her attraction to Virginia.
After her return from Persia, she would like to drive to Rodmell
late in the evening and throw gravel at Virginia's window.
Virginia would then let her in and she would stay until five A.M.
She couldn't do that, however, since Virginia was a person with
whom one had to be strict. But the temptation was great.[67]
Virginia wired in response "Come then," but to this gesture
Vita did not reply. In a following letter to Vita, Virginia took the
remark about her strictness as an admonition that Vita thought
her "elderly and valetudinarian," and that by "night" Vita

62. To Vita, Nov. 19, 1926, *Letters,* III, 302–303.
63. *Letters,* III, 319n.
64. To Vita, Jan. 31/Feb. 2, 1927, *Letters,* III, 319–321.
65. To Vita, Mar. 6/8, 1927, *Letters,* III, 342–344.
66. To Vita, Apr. 5, 1927, *Letters,* III, 358–360.
67. To Vita, June 11, 1927, *Letters,* III, 391n.

meant "day."[68] And in yet another letter she called on Vita to "throw over her man," and go with her to Hampton Court, dine on the river, walk in the garden in moonlight, go home late, drink wine, and get tipsy. Virginia would then tell her all that was in her head; she wouldn't stir by day, only by dark on the river.[69]

Did they have a merry summer? Probably not as merry as their letters envisioned although possibly there was sexual intimacy between them. At least they were together overnight several times during that summer. Vita accompanied Virginia to Oxford, where they stayed in a hotel, in May. In July Virginia spent two weekends with Vita at Long Barn. Later in the summer, Vita was Virginia's house guest at Rodmell, although at a time when Leonard was also present.[70]

Virginia's letters to Vanessa implied that the trip to Oxford was "romantic." But Quentin Bell thought that, like other letters in this vein which Virginia wrote to Vanessa about Vita, they were "a form of bravado and sisterly one-up-manship."[71] Possibly that was the case this time also, but possibly it was not. If so, there is again a hint of fictionalization. She wrote first when she was anticipating the trip: "Let us hope for nightingales, moons and love."[72] After the trip she wrote again saying that Vita was splendid and voluptuous but a little absurd. She chided Vanessa for not falling for the charms of her own sex, praised androgyny, and managed to work in a tribute for her sister: "What an arid garden the world must be for you! What avenues of stone pavements and iron railings; greatly though I respect the male mind and adore Duncan (but thank God, he's hermaphrodite, androgynous, like all great artists). I cannot see that they have a glowworm's worth of charm about them — the scenery of the world takes no lustre from their presence. They add of course immensely to its dignity and safety: but when it comes to a little excitement —! (I see that you will attribute all this to your own charm in which I daresay you're not far wrong.)"[73]

68. To Vita, June 14, 1927, Letters, III, 391–392, 391n.
69. To Vita, [1927], Letters, III, 393.
70. Bell, Virginia Woolf, II, 239.
71. Ibid., p. 118.
72. To Vanessa, May 15, 1927, Letters, III, 375–377.
73. To Vanessa, May 22, 1927, Letters, III, 379–382.

One reason for thinking that Virginia and Vita did not have a merry summer and that Virginia was indeed fictionalizing was her growing concern that Vita was interested in other women. Although her friend's inconstancy had been evident to Virginia since the beginning of their relationship, she now seemed to face more serious situations. In July she wrote in a bantering tone, that Vita must be a "careful Dolphin," or else, she continued crudely, she would find Virginia's "soft crevices lines with hooks."[74] There was indeed a concrete basis for Virginia's suspicions. Nigel Nicolson tells that at the time Vita was "becoming deeply involved with Mary Campbell," the wife of the South African poet Roy Campbell, who had taken a cottage near her.[75] Her affair with Mary was to become one of Vita's "muddles," and a particularly unpleasant one at that.

However, during the summer of 1927, Virginia did not yet know about Mary Campbell. Instead she thought that her chief rival for Vita's affections was Dorothy Wellesley, who had accompanied Vita to Persia earlier in the year, and she may well have been right. Moreover, Dorothy, taking advantage of business contacts with the Hogarth Press, also tried to make friends with Virginia, an episode that created some complications.[76] This was not the only time one of Vita's friends also wanted to become a friend of Virginia's. Even Violet Trefusis turned up at one point.[77]

But Virginia did not care for Vita's friends. Rather, she found them a source of turmoil. "Vita had friends — a Sapphist circle — which Virginia found decidedly unsympathetic." Quentin Bell wrote:

> Perhaps Vita found in them a relief from the too-chaste, the too-platonic atmosphere of 52, Tavistock Square and Monk's House, and perhaps Virginia was jealous. At all events Virginia found them second-rate; they engendered a school-girl atmosphere, and although she was conscious of being unkind to Vita she was unable to resist the temptation of telling her what she thought. Poor Vita discovered a certain acidity in her friend's communications . . . And so their friendship was for a time agitated.[78]

74. To Vita, July 4, 1927, *Letters,* III, 395–396.
75. *Letters,* III, 404.
76. To Vita, Sept. 2, 1927, *Letters,* III, 415–417.
77. To Ethel Smyth, Mar. 25, 1935, in Phillippe Julian and John Phillips, *The Other Woman: A Life of Violet Trefusis* (Boston, 1976), pp. 61–63.
78. Bell, *Virginia Woolf,* II, 146.

That fall, Virginia's letters to Vita exuded more and more acidity — or worse. Early in September she wrote about Dorothy, with what appeared to be an ultimatum: "Speaking sober prose . . . I won't belong to the two of you, or to the one of you, if the two of us belong to the one. In short, if Dotty's yours, I'm not. A profound truth is involved which I leave to you to discover. It is too hot to argue: and I'm too depressed."[79]

Soon Virginia learned also about Vita's affair with Mary Campbell and that, if she had a rival in Dorothy Wellesley, there were others still. But she managed to remain rather jocular in expressing disapproval and jealousy in the Mary Campbell affair. She wrote early in October that since Vita had gone "gallivanting down lanes" with Mary, Virginia would not fill her letters with "indiscretions" and "lovemaking unbelievable." She spoke again about the matter a few days later and, still in the guise of humor, delivered another ultimatum. Already at work on her novel about Vita, Virginia told her: "If you've given yourself to Campbell, I'll have no more to do with you and so it shall be written, plainly, for all the world to read in *Orlando*."[80] Later that fall, Vita confided in Virginia and told her more fully about Mary Campbell. She was greatly disturbed because Mary's husband had found out about the affair and had threatened, in his first anger, to kill his wife, and then, cooling off, to divorce her. Virginia was unsympathetic; she chided Vita for "muddling" her life, upon which Vita burst into tears.[81]

Yet even after these ultimatums, and following a fuller knowledge of Vita's involvement with Mary, Virginia continued to vacillate. Thus her attitude toward Vita near the presumed end of their sexual affair was similar to her attitude before it had begun. She still wanted to be with Vita, despite the other women in her life, and she continued to invite Vita to visit when they might have time alone together.[82] That fall her letters continue to hint at sexual contact between them. For example, she characterized one of the times when Vita might see her alone as "the last chance for a night before London's chastity begins."[83] She also said, "we gain in intensity what we lack in sober, com-

79. *Letters*, III, 415–417.
80. To Vita, Oct. 9 and 13/14, 1927, *Letters*, III, 127–130.
81. *Letters*, III, 435n.
82. For examples, see letters to Vita, Oct. 6 and Nov. 16, 1927, June 1, 1928, *Letters*, III, 427, 436–437, 505.
83. To Vita, Sept. 25, 1927, *Letters*, III, 423.

fortable virtues of a prolonged and safe and respectable and chaste and coldblooded friendship."[84]

Letters suggesting that Virginia was still erotically attracted to Vita, or perhaps still sexually involved with her, continued into 1928. How one should best read these letters, however, is problematic, since they may well be further evidence of Virginia's fictionalizing. For at the same time the correspondence between the two women also suggests that Virginia felt a growing detachment, even increasing disapproval and annoyance. She wrote that Vita couldn't help attracting "the flounderers," as she called her friends; it was not Vita's fault, or only partly. Virginia was only "half, or 10th part jealous" when she saw Vita with other women. Yet, despite all these complaints she continued her friendship with Vita and retained a measure of her love. She told her friend: "I'm happy to think that you *do* care: for often I seem old, fretful, querulous, difficult (tho' charming) and begin to doubt."[85]

By the summer of 1928, Virginia had apparently decided that Vita was in fact at fault in attracting and becoming involved with "the flounderers," but she teased her more than she condemned her. Vita was promiscuous and lacked a loving heart. "Thats [sic] all there is to be said of you."[86] Yet Virginia still cared enough to be jealous. In 1929, she recorded her jealousy in her diary and tried to analyze it. She concluded that her intellectual snobbery caused her to resent being linked, through Vita, to Vita's "earnest middle class" "drab and dreary" female companions.[87]

VI
THE ULTIMATE COMMENT

Virginia Woolf's novel about Vita Sackville-West represented a turn from the kind of experimentation in life in which she could not wholly let herself go to the kind of venture in art where she could be wholeheartedly involved. As she put it, the creation of art was both "ardour and lust" to her. The novel *Orlando* which emerged also marked the turning of another

84. To Vita, Oct. 13/14, 1927, *Letters,* III, 429–430.
85. To Vita, Nov. 11, 1927, *Letters,* III, 435–436.
86. To Vita, July 25, 1928, *Letters,* III, 514.
87. Virginia Woolf, diary holograph, Aug. 5, 1929 (Berg Collection).

corner in their friendship. It proved to be the means whereby
Virginia achieved greater detachment from Vita, although
paradoxically at the time she wrote it her novel was an excuse to
be with Vita, to photograph, study, and think about her.[88]

In her afterword to the Signet Classic edition of *Orlando*,
Elizabeth Bowen wrote that the novel was "more irresponsible"
than the rest of Virginia's work, "less considered and more un-
wary." Virginia's usual shyness was absent, and it was in some
ways foolish — a novelist's holiday rather than a novel.[89] This
estimate was correct. Virginia Woolf herself had wanted it to be
a holiday. She also thought that as a novel it was not wholly
successful; she had liked the process of writing it better than she
liked the finished book. Leonard liked it more than Virginia did,
and thought it "in some ways better than the *Lighthouse*,"[90]
probably overestimating it. Others viewed the novel as a very
special experience in the life of the author. Joanne Trautmann
called *Orlando* "the culmination of [the] particular friendship between Virginia and Vita," thereby touching its peculiar nerve.
She also said that even before writing the novel, Virginia Woolf
had virtually created in her own mind the person with whom she
had been allied in this intense and difficult relationship.[91] Nigel
Nicolson pointed out two other conceptions of the book when
he called it both "the longest and most charming love letter in
literature" and "a brilliant masque or comedy."[92]

To some extent *Orlando* is all these things: comedy, satire, and
the transformation of a person into fiction in a brilliant love
letter. But in the reciprocal mirroring between life and art, *Orlando* also retained its function as a catalyst in Virginia's personal
experience. I believe the book shows what its author had learned
from her venture into an intimate physical relationship with
another woman. It also shows what Virginia had concluded
about herself from her intimacy with Vita: that as in all things
she was most herself in friendship when she approached it artistically and made it into the substance of her art. In short, writing
Orlando was Virginia Woolf's way of demonstrating that she

88. *Letters*, III, 427, 434n; to Vita, Oct. 30, Nov. 4, 6, and 11, 1927, *Letters*, III,
    434–436; *Portrait of a Marriage*, p. 208.
89. Elizabeth Bowen, "Afterword," in Virginia Woolf, *Orlando* (New York:
    Signet, 1960), p. 219.
90. *A Writer's Diary*, pp. 125–126.
91. *The Jessamy Brides*, pp. 3, 38–52.
92. *Portrait of a Marriage*, pp. 202, 208.

preferred the role of the artist, of the truly fascinated observer
and commentator, to the role of participant — in sexual as in
other relationships.

The novelist's interpretation of Vita is appropriately complex.
Virginia made it clear that she admired and loved her, though
not without reservations. She expressed her love by according
Vita a kind of immortality. By the time the book ends, Vita, like
Orlando, has been permitted to live through several centuries
without having yet reached middle age. She also demonstrated
her love by in effect magically granting Vita's wishes — at least
as Virginia perceived them. But with her usual ambivalence,
Virginia's interpretations of these wishes also involved a measure
of hostility as well as of love.

The wishes granted in the book included all the license for
Vita to lead whatever sexual life she pleased and to have the best
of both sexes. She also granted her the right to be promiscuous,
or, if Virginia's term is too harsh, to be amoral, uncommitted,
and faithless in sexual relationships, taking pleasure where she
found it. This last right, as it is portrayed in the novel, was
one the aristocracy considered its prerogative. But in addition
Orlando explores the aristocratic attachment to the ancestral
home (and the author's fervent attachment to "houses"). Symbolically, she granted Vita's wish to possess the Sackvilles'
Knole. As Nigel Nicolson has observed, the novel is about
Knole as well as about Vita: in its pages Vita and Knole become
inseparable.[93]

But, as I have suggested, *Orlando* was not all admiration and
love, not all just a magical granting of Vita's presumed wishes. It
was satire after all, and in keeping with that genre, it also contained some rather nasty fun at Vita's expense. In the very conception of the novel, Vita's entire life had after all been turned
into one of Virginia's amusing and clever jokes. And among
hostile interpretations of some of Vita's supposed wishes, the
most unpleasant joke was the author's refusal to grant one of
Vita's most persistent desires: to be a writer of the first rank.
Even after several centuries of life, experience, and prodigious
effort to write, Orlando fails to complete the poem he had been
trying to compose and thus fails to attain a pen of gold rather
than one of brass. This part of the joke was unfair as well as

93. Ibid. See also letter to Vita, July 25, 1928, *Letters*, III, 514.

unpleasant, for Vita was a better writer than Virginia implied in
Orlando.

An illustration of Virginia's gentler satire was the manner in
which she referred to Vita's legs — the legs she had told Jacques
Raverat were Vita's chief claim for consideration. Virginia joked
about Orlando's legs throughout the book. The "old queen"
who knights Orlando can surmise merely from seeing the "dark
head bent so reverently, so innocently before her," that Orlando
has "a pair of the finest legs that a young nobleman has ever
stood upright upon . . ." (O, 23). Sasha (modeled after Violet
Trefusis), in the novel the Russian princess who becomes Orlando's first great romance, praised him "for his love of beasts; for
his gallantry; for his legs" (O, 54). The Archduchess Harriet
(who turns out to be an Archduke after Orlando changes sexes)
adores his legs and sets out to fit them with golden shin cases (O,
116). Nell Gwyn admires his legs, and Orlando is raised by King
Charles to the "highest rank in peerage. The envious said that
this was Nell Gwyn's tribute to the memory of a leg. But, as she
had seen him only once, and was then busily engaged in pelting
her royal master with nutshells, it is likely that it was his merits
that won him his Dukedom, not his calves" (O,125–126).

After Orlando becomes a woman, her legs continue to be the
sign of her beauty and the focus of Virginia's joke. They are so
beautiful as to endanger the lives of men who see them. When
she tosses her foot and shows "an inch or two of calf," a sailor
on the mast "started so violently that he missed his footing and
only saved himself by the skin of his teeth. 'If the sight of my
ankles means death to an honest fellow who, no doubt, has a
wife and family to support, I must, in all humanity, keep them
covered,' Orlando thought. Yet her legs were among her chief-
est beauties" (O, 157). Still almost as much man as woman, and
therefore having "too much stride," Orlando finds skirts and
petticoats too confining. So sometimes she covers her legs with
breeches, disguises herself in men's clothing, and passes herself
off as a man (O, 221), as it was Vita's practice to do during her
affair with Violet Trefusis.[94]

Virginia also used *Orlando* to suggest that Vita was inconstant
and changeable, although she showed a vein of consistency
throughout all alterations. The change from one sex to another is

---

94. *Portrait of a Marriage*, pp. 201–203.

the most obvious illustration. Orlando could make that switch
with relatively little conflict or need for adjustment. He puzzles
about himself from time to time while he lives as a man yet he is
also very much at ease. When he becomes a woman, she has only
minor problems in adjusting to her new life. The reason for her
lack of difficulty is her fundamental androgyny. Orlando had
possessed both masculine and feminine traits as a man, and now
in her new life as a woman both these facets of herself were more
fully developed. She could appreciate life both as a man and as a
woman. She could love her own sex with the masculine side of
her self and the opposite sex with her feminine component.
Sometimes she went about dressed as a man, at other times as a
woman. She married as a woman and gave birth to a son. There
was, then, no reason for Orlando to be in serious conflict about
his or her gender, and much less reason for the two sides of
himself and herself to be in conflict with one another. Virginia
Woolf, by projecting her fantasy, made the general statement
that these oppositions and conflicts are needless and that one
should be frankly and fully androgynous.

Although in theory the sex change was to lead to a more
unified conception of the self, in practice Orlando's changes not
only of sex but also in historical time may point in an opposite
direction. In an important section of the book, Virginia Woolf's
protagonist found it difficult to conceptualize and achieve a unified view of herself. Since Virginia suffered from this difficulty
in her own life, she may have only imagined that Vita endured
it as well. I believe that this was the case. If my judgment is
correct, that section of the novel tells a great deal about Virginia's own profound problems in achieving a coherent perspective of herself and tells very little about Vita. She attributed
Orlando's problems not to her change in sex roles but to the fact
that she had lived so long and experienced so much.

Orlando's ability to live through centuries, if not forever, is
therefore not entirely a blessing. As time passes, her memories
of various people and events change. Too many memories ac-
crue to be easily reconciled; life becomes too much a gigantic
dialectic in time. Worse, as time passes, Orlando changes as a
person; there are too many times ticking in her mind at once. If
there are so many times, the author asks, "how many different
people are there not — Heaven help us — all having lodgment at

one time or another in the human spirit? Some two thousand and fifty-two." With too many "times" and too many "selves," the problem becomes one of finding the right self at a particular time.

> [I]t is the most usual thing in the world for a person to say, directly they are alone, Orlando? (if that is one's name) meaning by that, Come, come! I'm sick to death of this particular self. I want another. Hence, the astonishing change we see in friends. But it is not altogether plain sailing, either, for though one may say, as Orlando said (being out of the country and needing another self presumably), Orlando? still the Orlando she needs may not come . . . (O,308)

Orlando's problem is therefore like but also unlike that of Bernard in the last chapter of *The Waves;* he too calls for self and he too has many selves, but in his case nothing answers, no one comes (W, 279, 283–284).

Orlando was finished on March 17, 1928, and the Hogarth Press published it on October 11 of that year.[95] Virginia sent a copy to Vita on the day of publication and later gave her the manuscript as a present.[96] Her friend was enormously pleased. It did not matter that she had been the object of Virginia's joke and of her satire. She was the hero/heroine of one of Virginia's books, a fact made public by the dedication. Nigel Nicolson relates his mother's reaction:

> Vita wrote to Harold: "I am in the middle of reading *Orlando,* in such a turmoil of excitement I scarcely know where (or who) I am!" She loved it. Naturally she was flattered, but more than that, the novel identified her with Knole forever. Virginia by her genius had provided Vita with a unique consolation for having been born a girl, for her exclusion from her inheritance, for her father's death earlier that year. The book, for her, was not simply a brilliant masque or pageant. It was a memorial mass.[97]

If *Orlando* was also a turning point in the friendship between the two women, its completion and appearance turned them only gradually in a new direction. Virginia continued to be infatuated with Vita for some time, despite her disapproval of the way she lived. In fact, Bell wrote that it was not until 1935 that she realized she was out of love with Vita:

---

95. *A Writer's Diary,* pp. 121–122.
96. *Letters,* III, 543, 544n.
97. *Portrait of a Marriage,* p. 208.

On 10 March [1935] the Woolfs drove in a snowstorm from Rodmell
to Sissinghurst to see Vita. As they took their leave Virginia realised
that their passionate friendship was over. There had been no quarrel,
no outward sign of coldness, no bitterness, but the love affair — or
whatever we are to call it — had for some time been quietly evaporat-
ing, and that particular excitement had gone out of her life, leaving a
blankness, a dullness.[98]

Whatever else it was, as a skillful fantasy and as a work of art,
Orlando, I believe, was the principal instrument Virginia Woolf
used to gain the distance she needed. Work on it had gradually
changed the quality of her love, although she continued to see
Vita and never stopped caring for her as a friend.

In a decisive way, then, the venture into eroticism had ended
with *Orlando* and in a sense the book became a requiem mass for
that part of Virginia's life. Her venturing in art, perhaps inspired
by that spirit of experimentation she had undergone in life, continued to engage her and led to greater creations. Her holiday
behind her, Virginia returned to the mainstream of her fiction to
write *The Waves:* her "serious, mystical poetical work."[99]

98. Bell, *Virginia Woolf,* II, 183.
99. *A Writer's Diary,* p. 104.

11. Nature and Community: A Study of Cyclical Reality in The Waves

MADELINE MOORE

I

Most readers and critics of *The Waves* (1931) think of the novel as asocial.[1] Many also persist in etherializing the impersonal and sometimes violent bases which Virginia Woolf envisioned in nature. In *The Waves,* however, there is an organic and inevitable relationship between Woolf's attitudes toward nature and her attitudes toward community. For in *The Waves* the representative range of human possibilities focuses upon an inevitable cycle wherein individuals are momentarily united with nature, experience both its exaltation and its nothingness, and, in order to preserve their autonomy, reemerge into the present of human effort. The natural cycle is echoed in the social world, where the individual experiences a momentary unity with his companions, recognizes its fleeting and illusory quality, and reasserts his individuality as a means of survival.

---

1. For example, James Hafley says that "the characters of *The Waves* are not examined within a social structure — the author is not concerned with manners as images"; *The Glass Roof* (Berkeley: University of California Press, 1954), p. 154. David Daiches criticizes Virginia Woolf for "keeping her characters on holiday"; *The Novel and the Modern World* (Chicago: University of Chicago Press, 1960), p. 160. Jean Guiguet writes that in *The Waves* "everything is turned inward"; *Virginia Woolf and Her Works* (New York: Harcourt, Brace and World, 1965), p. 379. Harvena Richter in her discussion of the effects of Woolf's stylization in *The Waves* notes that it offers "not the 'social' voice used by most novelists but a deep, sometimes troubling inner voice"; *Virginia Woolf: The Inward Voyage*, p. 145.

Take Bernard for instance. He is finally saved by opting for
the particular, which, though often unpleasant, nonetheless recalls him to his individuality and reminds him of his knowledge
that only in disequilibrium does one experience equilibrium:

> However beat and done with it all I am, I must haul myself up and
> find the particular coat that belongs to me; must push my arms into
> the sleeves; must muffle myself up against the night air and be off. I,
> I, I, tired as I am, spent as I am, and almost worn out with all this
> rubbing of my nose among the surface of things, even I, an elderly
> man who is getting rather heavy and dislikes exertion, must take
> myself off and catch some last train. (W, 296)

It was not Woolf's purpose in *The Waves* to overcome the
phenomenological opposition between subject and object, but
rather to dramatize that conflict.

Even as a child she was constantly preoccupied with nature as
a powerful force and as a catalyst to self-consciousness. In a
recently published retrospective memoir called "A Sketch of the
Past," for example, she reports what was memorable from her
winters at Hyde Park Gate:

> Again those moments of being. Two I always remember. There was
> the moment of the puddle in the path; when for no reason I could
> discover, everything suddenly became unreal; I was suspended; I
> could not step across the puddle; I tried to touch something . . . the
> whole world became unreal. Next the other moment when the idiot
> boy sprang up with his hand outstretched mewing, slit-eyed, red-
> rimmed; and without saying a word, with a sense of horror in me, I
> poured into his hand a bag of Russian toffee. But it was not over, for
> that night in the bath the dumb horror came over me. Again I had
> that hopeless sadness; that collapse I have described before, as if I
> were passive under some sledgehammer blow; exposed to a whole
> avalanche of meaning that had heaped itself up and discharged itself
> upon me, unprotected, with nothing to ward it off, so that I huddled
> up at the end of the bath, motionless.[2]

The description of the walk surfaces twice in *The Waves* and is
emblematic of the horror one feels at recognizing the opaque
nothingness at the core of nature. In the elegiac section of the
novel, for instance, Rhoda repeats Woolf's early trauma:

> "There is the puddle," said Rhoda, "and I cannot cross it. I hear the
> rush of the great grindstone within an inch of my head. Its wind roars

---

2. In *Moments of Being*, p. 78.

in my face. All palpable forms of life have failed me. Unless I can stretch and touch something hard, I shall be blown down the eternal corridors forever." (W, 158– 159)

Woolf's earliest recorded thoughts about *The Waves*, moreover, evoke her childhood experience of paralysis when she stood before the grey puddle in the winter of 1894 at Hyde Park Gate. When she was finishing her revisions of *To the Lighthouse* in 1926, she wrote in her diary:

> Life is, soberly and accurately, the oddest affair; has in it the essence of reality. I used to feel this as a child — couldn't step across a puddle once, I remember, for thinking how strange — What am I? etc. But by writing I don't reach anything. All I mean to make is a note of a curious state of mind. I hazard the guess that it may be the impulse behind another book.[3]

The other book was to be *The Waves*, and in it she would dramatize the impact of those "moments of being" again and again.

Undoubtedly Woolf's "moments of being" have much in common with Heidegger's beliefs. In Heideggerian terms, the experience of anguish and wonder reveals us to ourselves as out in the world without refuge. We are aware of ourselves as "existents" when we traverse certain experiences like anguish which put us in the presence of nothingness from which Being erupts.

Virginia Woolf's familiarity with the otherness of nature is also recorded in her diary. On April 8, 1925, for example, she returns to London after traveling in the south of France for two weeks. As she walks on a London street she sees a woman "pinned against the railings with a motor car on top of her . . ."

> A great sense of the brutality and wildness of the world remains with me — there was this woman in brown walking along the pavement — suddenly a red film car turns a somersault, lands on top of her and one hears this oh, oh, oh.[4]

Sometimes Woolf openly denounces the cruel indifference of nature, for "Nature is at no pains to conceal that she in the end will conquer; heat will leave the world; stiff with frost we shall cease to drag ourselves about the fields; ice will be thick upon

3. *A Writer's Diary*, p. 100.
4. Ibid., p. 71.

222   MADELINE MOORE

factory and engine; the sun will go out."[5] Woolf goes beyond
this existential anguish, however. Whereas in childhood she
thought these sudden shocks were "simply a blow from an
enemy hidden behind the cotton wool of daily life," as an adult
she explained that "the shock-receiving capacity is what makes
me a writer." What is more, she ultimately has faith that out of
the shock will come

> a revelation of some order; it is a token of some real thing behind
> appearances; and I make it real by putting it into words. . . . From
> this I reach what I might call a philosophy; at any rate it is a constant
> idea of mine; that behind the cotton wool is hidden a pattern; that
> we — I mean all human beings — are connected with this; that the
> whole world is a work of art; that we are parts of the work of art.
> *Hamlet* or a Beethoven quartet is the truth about this vast mass that
> we call the world. But there is no Shakespeare, there is no Beethoven;
> certainly and emphatically there is no God; we are the words; we are
> the music; we are the thing itself. And I see this when I have a shock.[6]

Paradoxically, then, Woolf's moments of being are initially experienced as ecstatic and violent shocks. Yet potentially they are
moments of mystical unity, where each person is connected to
the other, and all are part of some inexplicable pattern.

James Naremore has written that there is a problem in all of
Woolf's fiction which springs out of her attitudes toward nature:

> One cannot, at least not in terms of Virginia Woolf's fiction, come to
> a heightened awareness of one's unity with what is 'out there' and at
> the same time conceive of significant individuals. Mrs. Woolf
> suggests that beneath the surface of civilization there runs a current of
> emotion, a general truth that unites all men who submit to it. To
> make oneself fully aware of this current is to subordinate reason to
> feeling, and to lose awareness of the self.[7]

This is a very perceptive statement, but only partially true. Both
in her diaries and in her fiction Woolf differentiates between
a mystical reality with what is "out there" and an active reality involving the autonomous self acting decisively in the
commonplace world. For example, on February 27, 1926, she
writes of

5. Virginia Woolf, "On Being Ill," *Collected Essays*, IV, 198.
6. *Moments of Being*, p. 72.
7. James Naremore, *The World without a Self: Virginia Woolf and the Novel* (New
Haven: Yale University Press, 1973), pp. 25–26.

the infinite oddity of the human position; trotting along Russell
Square with the moon up and these mountain clouds. Who am I,
what am I, and so on; these questions are always floating about in
me: and then I bump against some exact fact — a letter, a person,
and come to them again with a great sense of freshness. And so it
goes on.[8]

The same Virginia Woolf who in the early years of World War II
yearns for oblivion in the flooded fields near Rodmell also writes
in her diary: "I'm terrified of passive acquiescence. I live in
intensity. In London, now, or two years ago, I'd be owling
through the streets. More pack and thrill than here. So I must
supply that — how? I think book inventing."[9] One can take any
period of Woolf's life and see these "contradictory" impulses
toward, now, an affirmation of one's mystical reality and, then,
an affirmation of one's active reality. Thus I believe that a dialectical relationship between a spiritual being and a social self is the
irreducible given from which Woolf and her protagonists understand their existence.

Though she hinted at this dialectic in her earlier novels, Woolf
did not find an adequate form for this vision until she wrote *The
Waves*. There her protagonist, Bernard, does momentarily live
in a universe of opposites, but his community with the natural
world is possible only when he is in a state of *being*. His *self* must
reemerge from this temporary mystical state, for although man
may long for the freedom of the purely natural world, he is
incapable of remaining in it. And though nature's impersonal
rhythms of life and rebirth point to the continuation of the
world, individuals live in a time-bound and imperfect way.
One's selfhood finally capitulates to these rhythms in death. In
the end, then, man's allegiance will be to the imperfect world he
knows. The *self* experiences reality as a series of willed acts
which stand out from a being half in love with the easeful forget-
fulness of the cosmos. Because we are born into a divided world,
we never finally escape a dualistic existence. Nevertheless Woolf
is suggesting that aspects of the paradigmatic mystical experience might be transformed into the active world. Two questions
arise for Woolf in *The Waves*. First, how can a spiritual unity be
duplicated in the social world? Second, how to render her pro-

8. *A Writer's Diary*, pp. 84– 85.
9. Ibid., p. 341.

tagonist's state of consciousness in such a way as to reveal that he is both a child of the cosmos and a child of the divided world? Though Woolf's feelings about nature emerged from personal experiences, G. E. Moore's philosophy made her more aware of the process of perceiving nature. When Virginia was twenty-three and living in Gordon Square with Thoby and Vanessa, G. E. Moore was often the center of their Thursday evening gatherings. Moore was, in fact, a central figure to the early Bloomsbury thinkers, largely because of his theories of friendship. We know from Quentin Bell's biography that in 1908 Woolf read *Principia Ethica* with great admiration: in fact, her correspondence for the next few months is studded with testimonials to Moore.[10] Moreover, Leonard Woolf tells how he and many of his friends at Cambridge were "deeply affected by the astringent influences of Moore and the purification of that divinely cathartic question . . . 'What do you mean by that?' "[11] He believed too that the clarity so characteristic of Virginia Woolf's literary style was due in part to Moore's influence.

In Moore's essay "The Refutation of Idealism" (1903), he insists on the dualism of consciousness and its objects:

> The point I had established so far was that in every sensation or idea we must distinguish two elements, (1) the "object" or that in which one differs from another, and (2) "consciousness" or that which all have in common — that which makes them sensations or mental facts.

He illustrates what he means by this in the same essay:

> The term "blue" is easy enough to distinguish, but the other element which I have called "consciousness" — that which the sensation of blue has in common with the sensation of green — is extremely difficult to fix. That many people fail to distinguish it at all is sufficiently shown by the fact that there are *materialists,* and, in general, that which makes the sensation of blue a mental fact seems to escape us: it seems, if I may use a metaphor, to be transparent — we look through it and see nothing but the blue; we may be convinced that there is something but what it is no philosopher, I think, has yet clearly recognized.[12]

---

10. See *The Letters of Virginia Woolf,* I, 347–368.
11. Leonard Woolf, *Beginning Again,* pp. 24–25.
12. G. E. Moore, "The Refutation of Idealism, *Philosophical Studies,* p. 20. See the discussion of Moore's epistemology in relation to *Jacob's Room* in Ralph Freedman's essay "The Form of Fact and Fiction" in the present volume.

Though Moore's description of the exact nature of consciousness later in the essay is simply to call it "diaphanous," he is nonetheless, like Bertrand Russell and William James, a philosopher of consciousness.

Virginia Woolf's critical theories testify to the relevance of Moore's ideas on perception and consciousness for her fiction. For example, in "Modern Fiction" (first published in 1919) Woolf uses the same term Moore does to criticize Arnold Bennett, H. G. Wells, and John Galsworthy:

> If we fasten, then, one label on all those books, on which is one word, *materialists*, we mean by it that they write of unimportant things; that they spend immense skill and immense industry making the trivial and the transitory appear the true and enduring.

These writers have ignored the diaphanous quality of life:

> Life is not a series of gig lamps symmetrically arranged; life is a luminous halo, a semitransparent envelope surrounding us from the beginning of consciousness to the end. Is it not the task of the novelist to convey this varying, this unknown and uncircumscribed spirit, whatever aberration or complexity it may display, with as little mixture of the alien and extreme as possible?[13]

In "Phases of Fiction" (first published in *Bookman* in April, May, and June, 1929), Woolf described how the good novelist frees the reader to be aware of the process of consciousness:

> Then we see the mind at work; we are amused by its power to make patterns; by its power to bring out relations in things and disparities which are covered over when we are acting by habit or driven by the ordinary impulses. It is a pleasure somewhat akin, perhaps, to the pleasure of mathematics or the pleasure of music.[14]

Many of Woolf's early short stories, like "The Mark on the Wall" and "The Lady in the Looking Glass," are sketches of the way consciousness combines to evoke a proper fictional reality. And in the early manuscript version of *The Waves*, the narrator also describes the very processes of consciousness — the ability to isolate after experiencing the multiplicity of natural events: "But it was only when the thing had happened and the violence of the shock was over that one could understand, or really live; only

13. Virginia Woolf, "Modern Fiction," *Collected Essays*, II, 105, 106.
14. Virginia Woolf, "Phases of Fiction," ibid., II, 82.

when one had left the room and was walking home at the dead of night."[15]

But if the posi゙ ve moment becomes a vision in which nature is bracketed and "we see the mind at work" and are "amused by its power to bring out relations in things," there is also the negative moment when one becomes aware of the obduracy of matter and material objects. Then the natural world impinges upon and sometimes overcomes the individual. For example, in "The Moment: Summer's Night" Woolf says:

> Let us do something then, something to end this horrible moment, this plausible glistening moment that reflects in its smooth sides this intolerable kitchen, this squalor; this woman moaning . . . Let us smash it by breaking a match. There —snap.[16]

There is no pleasure in this dualistic moment; instead it is often apprehended as an absorbing or paralyzing force which can be broken only by intense effort or violence.

II

It is inherent that human beings in a divided world experience nature dualistically: they usually perceive it as an alien force, and only rarely do they understand its spiritual unity. For example, early in The Waves, Neville recalls how he felt "about the dead man through the swing door last night . . . The apple tree leaves became fixed in the sky; the moon glared; I was unable to lift my foot up the stair . . . I shall call this stricture, this rigidity, 'death among the apple trees' for ever" (W, 24). In fact, the underlying reality of nature in the novel is generally felt to be chaotic, but it is countered by the equally forceful and particularistic movements of those who oppose it. In a diary entry in 1930, Woolf says:

<hr>

15. The manuscript of The Waves, New York Public Library (Berg Collection), I, 17. The manuscript consists of seven bound volumes and a small looseleaf notebook which begins the second draft. The pagination for my essay has been supplied by the authorities of the Berg Collection. Each volume is numbered separately beginning with the title page. The seven volumes contain two complete holograph drafts, the first running from vol. I to p. 76 of vol. IV; the second goes to p. 43 of vol. VII. Subsequent references will appear in my text in parentheses following the quotation, with Roman volume and Arabic page numbers.
16. Probably written in 1931; in Collected Essays, II, 296.

It occurred to me last night while listening to a Beethoven quartet that I would merge all the interjected passages into Bernard's final speech and end with the words O solitude; thus making him absorb all those scenes and having no further break. This is also to show that the theme effort, effort, dominates: not the waves . . .[17]

And in *The Waves,* not only Rhoda and Neville, but all six of the characters become aware of their identities as they experience sometimes a separation from and sometimes an opposition to nature. Aesthetically Woolf achieves this in the form of six soliloquists verbalizing their perceptions in a phased series of common episodes from dawn to dusk of their lives. "The six are concerned not only with the impingement of others and the sea on their consciousnesses but also with their individual identities, their separate developing selves that are distinguishable from their consciousnesses."[18]

Virginia Woolf illuminates the text of the six soliloquists' voices by opening each new section with a symbolic description of the beach as it changes from dawn to night. These italicized prologues mirror the entire natural movement of the novel and infer the perceptual changes which the soliloquists articulate as they live their lives. This is partially borne out by the common structure of the passages themselves: the first paragraph describes the sea's appearance and the waves' motion; the second evokes the effects of light in a garden and the birds' response to it; and the third is a passage of light through a house and over household objects. Moreover, by encompassing the scope of an entire life within a single day, these passages, like "Time Passes" in *To the Lighthouse,* suggest the powerlessness of human life before the final authority of nature. They also provide a set of images drawn from the natural world, and when these images reappear in the soliloquist's speech, the reader sees how each one responds to his natural world and, by inference, his social world.

Because the scenes and characters are so elaborately interrelated in *The Waves,* it is fruitful to approach the novel horizontally rather than vertically. Many critics have done this within a certain framework. For example, Alice Van Buren Kelley traces each character's attempt to balance vision with fact throughout

---

17. *A Writer's Diary,* p. 159.
18. S. P. Rosenbaum, "The Philosophical Realism of Virginia Woolf," in *English Literature and British Philosophy,* p. 349.

the novel's nine sections,[19] and Jean O. Love describes a "movement from diffusion to partial differentiation and back to diffusion."[20] While both of these approaches lead to a better understanding of the novel, I feel that in a comprehensive analysis one sees that the epistemological conflict acts as a paradigm for the social conflict. Thus each character becomes conscious of his separation from nature and then begins a quest for identity or self-consciousness; as a group, the failure of the six to establish communion around the charismatic unity of Percival sends them searching for the enactment of a real community among themselves. I maintain then that the novel makes a social statement which, though embedded within a philosophical construct, is social nevertheless. As the narrator in the early manuscript of *The Waves* says: "I am not concerned with the single life, but with lives together" (I, 17).

In her diary Virginia Woolf testifies to the social elements in *The Waves*:

> The poets succeed by simplifying: practically everything is left out. I want to put practically everything in: yet to saturate. That is what I want to do in *The Moths* [*The Waves*]. It must include nonsense, fact, sordidity; but made transparent.[21]

One remembers that in "The Refutation of Idealism" Moore used the word "transparent" as a metaphor for the act of consciousness. Woolf's statement about characterization is also revealing in terms of the social content of the novel. She believes that the essentials of a person's character "should be done boldly, almost as caricature." This does not mean that realistic concerns are absent in *The Waves*, but rather they are crystallized and universalized. *The Waves* is both a sustained examination of the nature of selfhood and a sustained postulation of the possibilities of community.

III

In the first prologue prior to the children's birth, the creative force of nature is anthropomorphized as a great mythic woman

19. Alice Van Buren Kelley, *The Novels of Virginia Woolf: Fact and Vision*.
20. Jean O. Love, *Worlds in Consciousness: Mythopoetic Thought in the Novels of Virginia Woolf* (Berkeley and Los Angeles: University of California Press, 1970), p. 209.
21. *A Writer's Diary*, p. 136.

who is the source of all creation. She is the symbolic figure out of which Woolf establishes a cosmogony in *The Waves*. She holds a lamp in her hand, and when she turns the lamp the light reveals a chaos which holds a reservoir of all the elements of the world — the matrix of all life. This mysterious and self-contained force looks down upon everything with equanimity and acceptance.

In the first chapter of the novel each child seems enclosed in his or her own undifferentiated world. For the most part, the relationship between the soliloquists in the first section is limited to a series of exercises in perception. Occasionally they achieve "moments of contiguity,"[22] when they share an object of perception:

> "Here is the garden [said Susan]. Here is the hedge. Here is Rhoda on the path rocking petals to and fro in her brown basin."

> "All my ships are white," said Rhoda. "I do not want red petals of hollyhocks or geranium. I want white petals that float when I tip the basin up . . . I will now rock the brown basin from side to side so that my ships may ride the waves. Some will founder. Some will dash themselves against the cliffs. One sails alone." (W, 18–19)

But even at this early age they distinguish between the independence of the thing perceived and the action of perceiving. The petals are only petals to Susan, but Rhoda exercises the full power of her consciousness on them. They must be white and they are ships contained within a certain space where Rhoda can enact the drama of her own consciousness within a safe place.

As the children grow older they no longer exist in an undifferentiated state. They experience nature as an impingement rather than a benevolent force; and as they become more social, the simultaneous formation of a separate identity becomes a necessary defense against other people. As Bernard first leaves home for boarding school, he says: "I must make phrases and phrases and so interpose something hard between myself and the stare of housemaids, the stare of clocks, staring faces, indifferent faces, or I shall cry" (W, 30). Words and stories help him attain that state of strength which alleviates for a time the terrifying spectacle of pure phenomena. Bernard forms his identity in the very processes of creation and by his extreme effort to bracket

22. Ralph Freedman, *The Lyrical Novel*, p. 252.

out the shock of pure phenomena. Even the most elemental form of communication in *The Waves* — the relationship between two friends — is purchased with pure effort and force. Jinny kisses Louis, shattering his absorption in nature; and though he would like to forget this event, it alters him permanently. Bernard feels Neville's hostility toward his Byronic posing and he relinquishes the pose. Neville remarks:

> How useful an office one's friends perform when they recall us. Yet how painful to be recalled, to be mitigated, to have one's self adulterated, mixed up, become part of another. As he approaches I become not myself but Neville mixed with somebody — with whom? — with Bernard? (W, 83)

Louis, on the other hand, neither depends upon nor trusts the influx of other personalities in the formation of his own. As an outsider, he invariably insists upon a reality based on the ultimate separation of one from the other: "Children, our lives have been gongs striking; clamour and boasting; cries of despair; blows on the nape of the neck in gardens" (W, 39– 40).

It is no accident that Louis and Rhoda, both strangers to the English upper classes, voice the most direct criticism of the society in which they live. As young children, these outsiders are the first to become self-conscious, that is, to be aware of a self independent of their communal being. Woolf accentuates the fact that their epistemological self-consciousness is basic to their social consciousness. Even in the dawn of their lives, wisdom brings disillusionment and pain to them.

> "I will not conjugate the verb," said Louis, "until Bernard has said it. *My father is a banker in Brisbane and I speak with an Australian accent.* I will wait and copy Bernard. He is English. They are all English. Susan's father is a clergyman. *Rhoda has no father.* Bernard and Neville are the sons of gentlemen. Jinny lives with her grandmother . . . I know more than they will ever know . . . But I do not wish to come to the top and say my lesson. My roots are threaded, like fibres in a flower-pot, round and round about the world . . . Jinny and Susan, Bernard and Neville bind themselves into a thong with which to lash me. They laugh at my neatness, at my Australian accent." (W, 19– 20, italics mine)

Louis' consciousness is embedded in the past. Part of him embodies that magical unity of past and present which characterizes the mystical experience. But he is aware of a present self

which is stereotyped by neatness and an Australian accent.[23] As
the son of a Brisbane banker and a "colonial," Louis is always
aware of his alien position in English society, and he consoles
himself by claiming "I know more than they will ever know."
Nevertheless when faced with the problem of working out Latin
translations, Louis secretly acknowledges his superiority, but
waits for Bernard to speak so he can imitate Bernard's accent and
obliterate his own. Yet even as a child he hopes that the harsh-
ness and discontinuity in their present lives will not always persist: "The time approaches when these soliloquies shall be
shared. We shall not always give out a sound like a beaten gong
as one sensation strikes and then another" (W, 39). He sees very
clearly that the traditionally heroic order embodied by Percival
and the ambience of a public school is exciting yet cruel:

> How majestic is their order, how beautiful is their obedience! . . .
> But they also leave butterflies trembling with their wings pinched
> off; they throw dirty pocket-handkerchiefs clotted with blood
> screwed up into corners. They make little boys sob . . . (W, 47)

Rhoda on the other hand lives in a world of dreams. Her
experience at school is perhaps the female counterpart to Louis'
condemnation of his peers:

> This great company, all dressed in brown serge has robbed me of my
> identity. We are all callous, unfriended. I will seek out a face, a
> composed, a monumental face, and will . . . wear it under my dress
> like a talisman . . . (W, 33)

Fatherless, Rhoda embodies that aspect of rootlessness which so
characterized Woolf's illnesses. As a young child, Rhoda describes the sensations which finally drive her to suicide; for her
the attainment of consciousness without identity is ultimately
unbearable:

> Now I spread my body on this frail mattress and hang suspended. I
> am above the earth now. I am no longer upright, to be knocked

23. Louis bears some resemblance to T. S. Eliot, a bank clerk and "colonial,"
whose combined businessman mentality and intellectualism were always
puzzling and sometimes comic to Virginia Woolf. In fact, Bloomsbury's
compounded condescension and awe of Eliot can be heard in Bernard's
description of Louis, whom he finds to be a "strange mixture of assurance
and timidity." Eliot, whose father was a successful businessman in St. Louis,
was very sensitive to the taunts of Lytton Strachey, who used to insist that
Eliot's business trips were excuses for him to meet quaint characters in the
isolated countryside of England.

against and damaged. All is soft, and bending. Walls and cupboards whiten and bend their yellow squares on top of which a pale glass gleams. Out of me now my mind can pour. I can think of my Armadas sailing on the high waves. I am relieved of hard contacts and collisions. I sail on alone under white cliffs. Oh, but I sink, I fall! . . Let me pull myself out of these waters. But they heap themselves on me; they sweep me between their great shoulders; I am turned; I am tumbled; I am stretched, among these long lights, these long waves, these endless paths, with people pursuing, pursuing. (W, 27–28)

Rhoda, like Louis, seeks her identity by imitation; and so she attaches herself to names and faces and saves them "like amulets against disaster." Because the external world is so alien to her, Rhoda finds it more difficult than do the other six to form an identity. Consequently she sometimes longs for anonymity, but the anonymity which night brings also threatens her with dissolution: she falls into nothingness and must bang her head against something hard to recall her physical self. Like Louis also, Rhoda is aware of social anomalies. She sees the great gap between the potential community among the girls in a private school and the real isolation which that institution enforces. Though we know few facts about Rhoda's background, we do know that "she has no father" and no friends. Both epistemologically and socially, then, she is the orphan of the novel. She longs for a home among them, yet is always outside the loop.

Her vision reaches toward the future and will not be harbored in the earth. Yet in her voice, we hear Woolf's own yearning for a real community — something more than the momentary bracketing which Bernard scaffolds against the world's chaos. For Rhoda says, "I will bind flowers in one garland and advancing with my hand outstretched present them — Oh! to whom?" (W, 57).

Although it is momentary, the six characters do unify around Percival in the Bond Street dinner scene prior to his departure for India. Bernard says, "We have come together at a particular time, to this particular spot. We are drawn into this communion by some deep, some common emotion. Shall we call it, conveniently, 'love'? Shall we say 'love of Percival' because Percival is going to India?" (W, 126). In their immature vision, the children saw Percival as an embodiment of charismatic unity. For example, at boarding school Neville said of Percival, "He is remote

from us all in a pagan universe. But look — he flicks his hand to
the back of his neck. For such gestures one falls hopelessly in
love for a lifetime" (W, 36). Louis adds, "His magnificence is
that of some medieval commander. A wake of light seems to lie
on the grass behind him" (W, 37). Yet his unity is neither
spiritual nor moral, for Percival is finally illusory and impene-
trable. He casts no shadow for himself; but casts shadows for the
other six. He says no words, but in his silence the others hear
their own words.

The dinner party marks the noon of each character's youth
(they are in their late twenties). Then, in their very queries about
the nature of Percival's unity, the characters pierce through their
own youthful experience of unity and project into the future. It
is possible to be a seven-sided flower only momentarily. Significantly, only the outsiders, Rhoda and Louis, actually converse
with one another. They look for signs of a future community,
yet their projection into the future points to its eventual failure, at least its failure with Percival as catalyst. Louis knows that
if there is unity among them, it is their common experience of
violence in the world, for "there is a chain whirling round,
round, in a steel-blue circle beneath" (W, 137). Rhoda envisions
a column or a fountain with the sea roaring in the background.
"It is beyond our reach. Yet there I venture. There I go to
replenish my emptiness, to stretch my nights and fill them fuller
and fuller with dreams." She realizes, however, that this vision is fragile and depends upon "these lights, from Percival and
Susan, here and now" (W, 139). Embodied in Louis' metaphor is
a startlingly primitive funeral ritual: the ring of blue steel is like
the dance of savages and the death-directed procession around a
unity which cannot persist:

> "Look, Rhoda," said Louis, "they have become nocturnal, rapt . . .
> Like the dance of savages," said Louis, "round the campfire. They
> are savage; they are ruthless. They dance in a circle, flapping blad-
> ders. The flames leap over their painted faces, over the leopard skins
> and the bleeding limbs which they have torn from the living body."

> "The flames of the festival rise high," said Rhoda. "The great proces-
> sion passes, flinging green boughs and flowering branches . . . They
> throw violets. They deck the beloved with garlands and laurel leaves,
> there on the ring of turf where the steep-backed hills come down.
> The procession passes. And while it passes, Louis, we are aware of

downfalling, we forbode decay. The shadow slants. We who are
conspirators, withdrawn together to lean over some cold urn, note
how the purple flame flows downwards."

"Death is woven in with the violets," said Louis. "Death and again
death." (W, 140–141)

Louis and Rhoda see that Percival's unconscious charisma
evokes a unity only among the young, and only momentarily.
With the crystallization of self-consciousness comes the need for
a real community, and the characters transcend their childish
hero worship. For Percival has neither self-consciousness nor a
sense of ethics. He should "have a birch and beat little boys for
misdemeanors,"yet he is "allied with the Latin phrases on the
memorial brasses" (W, 36).

If Percival is symbolic of mute unity, then Bernard, like Lily
Briscoe, represents the self-conscious unifier. His success as a
unifier results from his immersion into storytelling. Even in his
imaginary Elvedon, however, it is as important that Bernard
asks Susan to share his fantasy as it is that he elaborate the story
itself. For as they look down on Elvedon they still the confusion
of their imaginary adventure and become comrades in their
shared perception: "That is Elvedon. The lady sits between the
two long windows, writing. The gardeners sweep the lawn with
giant brooms. We are the first to come here. We are the dis-
coverers of an unknown land" (W, 17).

And if Percival sometimes seems like a comic god of the sun,
he must be constantly destroyed, for his death, like the death of
Mrs. Ramsay, sets all movement in action again and reaffirms
the character's necessity to "oppose ourselves to this illimitable
chaos . . . this formless imbecility" (W, 226). Percival's heroism
is effective only in a nonreflective world. As Bernard says: "Percival rides a flea-bitten mare, and wears a sun-helmet. By applying the standards of the West, by using the violent language that
is natural to him, the bullock-cart is righted in less than five
minutes" (W, 136). The kind of action which Percival embodies
is not a working model for a just community. It is hemmed in by
"standards of the West" and violent language. Bernard, on the
other hand, can look squarely at violence, yet not become violent himself.

In their maturity the characters turn to Bernard, for he alone is
both diversified and integrated. At least momentarily, moreover, his mind is like the androgynous mind which Woolf de-

scribed in *A Room of One's Own* because he is capable of fusing opposites. "Coleridge perhaps meant this when he said that a great mind is androgynous."[24] Bernard's perception that things in themselves are often chaotic is married to his ordering process. Like Neville, he has experienced that amazement and rigidity which Neville called "death among the apple trees," but he can look directly at the "thing that lies beneath the semblance of the thing" without bitterness. Like Mrs. McNabb's chant, Bernard's storytelling is filled with the persistence which Woolf called the "life principle."

In his attitude toward words, Bernard is capable of experiencing opposing realities. Words and stories help him to attain that state of impersonality which alleviates for a time the terrifying spectacle of pure phenomena. He acknowledges, however, both the fragile and the playful quality of words, and he has a humility about their efficaciousness in achieving lifelong solutions. Words are alive for him: "They flick their tails right and left as I speak them . . . now dividing, now coming together" (W, 20). "But how describe the world seen without a self?" Seemingly there are no words. In order to become whole, he must look squarely at the "world without a self," and realize that "a little language such as lovers use" is a proper language in a world with no divisions, but it is ineffectual against the deathlike fate inevitable in a dualistic world. After the Hampton Court reunion Bernard undergoes a harrowing experience which makes him aware of the epistemological paradox of self-reflection. Words fail him and movement ceases and he completely loses his identity:

> "I spoke to that self who has been with me in many tremendous adventures . . .
> This self now as I leant over the gate looking down over fields rolling in waves of colour beneath me made no answer. He threw up no opposition. He attempted no phrase. His fist did not form. I waited. I listened. Nothing came, nothing . . . No fin breaks the waste of this immeasureable sea. Life has destroyed me. No echo comes when I speak, no varied words. This is more truly death than the death of friends, than the death of youth." (W, 283–284)

Thus "joined to the sensibility of a woman" are the physical prowess and spiritual leadership which should have been Percival's, but which belong to Bernard. In addition to the play on the

---

24. *A Room of One's Own*, p. 102.

name (which echoes, of course, the Percival in the King Arthur legends), Woolf succeeds in mocking Percival's unconscious charisma for public school boys and adoring Indians. Bernard, on the other hand, both imagines the parameters of a real community and tries to effect a unity in his friends' lives.

We have seen that in *The Waves* a pastoral sensibility is impossible because nature in the divided world cannot give peace, but only death. On the other hand, Woolf was apparently attracted to the idea that although the primary imagery of the city is one of fragmentation, for some writers the city replaces the magic of past pastoral longings because it has the capacity to provide a sense of community and protection which the former world possessed.[25] Bernard, for instance, sees the city as a possible place of protection and community:

> "How fair, how strange," said Bernard, "glittering, many-pointed and many domed London lies before me under mist. Guarded by gasometers, by factory chimneys, she lies sleeping as we approach. She folds the ant-heap to her breast. All cries, all clamour are softly enveloped in silence. Not Rome herself looks more majestic. But we are aimed at her. Already her maternal somnolence is uneasy."
> (W, 111)

Bernard and his fellow passengers do experience a "splendid unanimity" en route to London because they are connected by one desire: to arrive at the station. "Our community in the rushing train sitting together with only one wish to arrive at Euston was very welcome." But when they arrive in the city ". . . individuality asserts itself. They are off. They are all impelled by some necessity. Some miserable affair of keeping an appointment, of buying a hat, severs these beautiful human beings once so united" (W, 112–113). The potential values of protection and community are shattered by their needs for assertion

---

25. In two of Virginia Woolf's letters to Ethel Smyth, she praises London: once on August 12, 1930, she claims that London keeps her braced, gives her the tension she needs. Again in January, 1941, she talks of London as her only patriotism — the place which evokes Chaucer, Shakespeare, and Dickens. Several of her diary entries are an apotheosis to the city. For example, on May 25, 1924, she writes: "One of these days I will write about London, and how it takes up the private life and carries it on, without any effort. Faces passing lift up my mind; prevent it from settling, as it does in the stillness at Rodmell . . . And I like London for writing it [Mrs. Dalloway], partly because, as I say, life upholds me; and with my squirrel cage mind it's a great thing to be stopped circling. Then to see human beings freely and quickly is an infinite gain to me. And I can dart in and out and refresh my stagnancy"; *A Writer's Diary,* p. 61.

and individuality: "We are about to explode in the flanks of the city like a shell in the side of some ponderous, maternal, majestic animal" (W, 111). In the manuscript version of *The Waves* the narrator pinpoints this conflict less poetically, but exposes the seams of Woolf's political fabric. The city must be seen as an enemy; its potential for social unity cannot be realized in a world which honors only its values of force and self-assertion:

> Then indeed, such was the force of the walls with their legal bark, in the windy shop, where they sold theater tickets, in the office with its knotty desks and the emphatic, irregular typewriters, in the great shop with the submissive men handling rolls of stuff, that whatever there was of identity and oddity and idiosyncrasy became sharper, made visible by fire and sun, brought out, hardened — like a mark held to the fire . . . I am I. I don't wish to be other than I am, welcoming the advent of I. A feeling that I was to be supported and enforced at whatever cost. (II, 183)

Bernard, like the reader, is left with the yearning but not the fact.

Thus in situation after situation in *The Waves,* Woolf postulates a social unity only to undercut it. In the Hampton Court reunion scene Louis and Rhoda continue the search for social community they began at the first dinner party:

> "If we could mount together, if we could perceive from a sufficient height," said Rhoda, "if we could remain untouched without any support — but you, disturbed by faint clapping sounds of praise and laughter, and I, resenting compromise and right and wrong on human lips, trust only in solitude and the violence of death and thus are divided." (W, 231)

But because their world is unjust, Louis is diminished by social alienation and Rhoda by the very hypocrisy of those who reject her.

The fleeting quality of social unity in *The Waves* is apparent in narration as well as situation. It is as if Woolf, striving after an impersonal narrative voice, has not allowed her characters any real participation in their common pursuit of human history. In the early manuscript version of *The Waves,* the first narrator, who is nature embodied as a woman, speaks with an interesting mixture of detachment and longing:

> I am telling myself the story of the world from the beginning. I am not concerned with the single life, but with lives together. I am trying to find, in the folds of the past, such fragments as time, having

broken the perfect vessel, still keeps safe. The perfect vessel? But it
was only when the thing had happened and the violence of the shock
was over that one could understand, or really live; only when one had
left the room and was walking home at the dead of night. Then in
that darkness, which had no limit, very dark, whose shores were
invisible, whatever had happened, expanded, and something
dropped away. Then without a companion one loved; spoke with no
one to hear; and carried on an intercourse with people who were not
there more completely than [when] one's chair was drawn close to
theirs. (I, 17)

The search of this early narrator for the perfect vessel is
metamorphosed into Bernard's quest for the complete story of
his friends' lives. Accompanying this quest is his preoccupation
with process, his sense of longing and by implication of loss, for
some unity which can finally only be enumerated as a series of
specific events elaborated from a retrospective point of view.

Bernard never fully participates in or accomplishes social
unity; yet embedded in his efforts to bracket the world is a
yearning for something like a true community where the agony of
autonomy might be lost. Just as in "The Niece of an Earl," Woolf
asked, "The art of a truly democratic age will be what?"[26] Here in
The Waves she seems to be asking what the world would look like
if the social ideal were realized. If this question can be answered,
the answer comes from a projection into the future. In trying to
imagine a more democratic art form, Woolf, in *A Room of One's
Own,* constructed several examples of the "masculine" sentence.
But she did not give examples of the counterpart. We have to
build our own feminine sentence in opposition to the masculine
one, which will not do. In order to live through our mothers we
must take hold of our yearnings and boldly imagine a feminine art
form. We must also imagine a just community.

In spite of Bernard's attempts to ease his friends' loneliness by
ordering some kind of human unity, he fails. In recounting the
stories of his friends' lives to an unnamed "you," in the final
section, he seeks "some design more in accordance with those
moments of humiliation and triumph that come now and
then . . ." (W, 239). Yet this does nothing to change the pain and
isolation of the lives of his friends, all of whom are absent and
many of whom are dead. There is a detached and abstract tone in

26. *Collected Essays,* I, 223.

most of his narration. He "is telling the story of the world from the beginning." As John Graham has pointed out, Bernard, like the omniscient narrator in the early manuscript version:

> narrates it in the past tense and comments on it in the present; like her he is seated at a table with the conscious purpose of recovering from the past such fragments as time, having broken the perfect vessel, still keeps safe; and like her, he finds that the scrutiny of his past forces him to deal not with single lives but with lives together.

Graham goes on to comment on the importance of Bernard's single narration in the final chapter, suggesting that "The most common image of communion is that of one body, of which the communicants are members; and since the only 'body' given to the *dramatis personae* of *The Waves* is speech, the one voice Bernard in the summing up *is* that body."[27]

Now, this interpretation is very compelling, but it raises some difficult questions. If Bernard's summing up *is* the body of all its members, it is only insofar as he collects their *representational nature* into an "omnipresent, general life." Bernard does fuse the multiplicity of human beings within his androgynous personality. At least he can do this in the retrospective manner in which all artists tell stories:

> Here on my brow is the blow I got when Percival fell. Here on the nape of my neck is the kiss Jinny gave Louis. My eyes fill with Susan's tears. I see far away, quivering like a gold thread, the pillar Rhoda saw, and feel the rush of the wind of her flight when she leapt. (W, 289)

His art captures a momentary unity which verbally echoes the female creator's mystical unity. Yet his subjects are individual as well as representative. They experience loss and death, and it would be impossible to ignore the fact that Rhoda's and Louis' overwhelming longing for community is unfulfilled. Action is necessary to community in the social world. The process of individualization in *The Waves* is both personal and representative, so that the summing up which Bernard performs is bittersweet and melancholy. The tension between social and contemplative impulses apparent in the novel is resolved formally only when Bernard elevates his vision of the six to a

27. J. W. Graham, "Point of View in *The Waves*" in *University of Toronto Quarterly*, 39 (April, 1970), 208.

sufficient height; then he can bracket their pain into a retrospective whole; but the ring is very fragile indeed: "It quivers and hangs in a loop of light."

Significantly, in the final pages of the novel, Bernard's narration reemerges in the present tense. His final words are not contemplative or retrospective, but are filled with the energy of opposition which signifies his effort for survival. "It is death against whom I ride with my spear couched and my hair flying back like a young man's, like Percival's when he galloped in India. I strike spurs into my horse. Against you I will fling myself, unvanquished and unyielding, O Death!" (W, 297). Thus, in spite of the social impulses which are omnipresent in *The Waves,* Woolf's characters do not achieve their potential community. Instead, community is experienced symbolically or in moments of ecstatic longing. These moments alternate with the neverending experience of social alienation, a cycle not unlike Bernard's inevitable cyclical alternation between a momentary absorption in nature and the necessary emergence from it into the present of particularization. That cycle evokes a faithful yet poignant fatalism, a tantalizing reality which binds us to Woolf's vision as to no other.

12. Nature and History in The Years

JAMES NAREMORE

I

One of Virginia Woolf's most famous remarks is that "in or about December, 1910, human character changed." Scholars have offered several possible reasons for her choice of that date: the postimpressionist exhibition had opened, King Edward was dead, and a general election had taken place; December, 1910, is very close to the time historian Ralph Fox has marked for the "strange death of liberal England"; and in fact, 1910 was the year Woolf herself made a commitment to the Adult Suffrage Movement, doing political chores on behalf of women's rights.[1] Obviously, social and artistic change was everywhere in the winds in those days; nevertheless Woolf's view of "character" is such that one must ask if her remark means exactly what it says. Did she mean that history had somehow transformed consciousness at its deepest levels, or that a crisis in bourgeois culture had led artists to the discovery of new levels of personality?

Her fiction suggests the latter view. In *Orlando* and *Between the Acts,* for example, history manifests itself as a kind of fashion, creating important changes in manners and morals, even in people's sexual identities, but leaving the underlying human nature untouched. Ultimately, the significance of Virginia Woolf's comment appears to be that she, like most of the finest writers of her time, had sensed in the early twentieth century a profound conflict between the inner, instinctive needs of the psyche (which she presented as more or less unchanging, like the cycles

1. Quentin Bell, *Virginia Woolf,* I, 161.

of nature or the sea) and the outer lineaments of the society
(which do change). In roughly the same historical period, Freud
had described this conflict as a battle between what he called the
id and the superego; among novelists, Lawrence had spoken of a
breakdown in the "old stable ego" of his fictional characters, and
Joyce had taken Leopold Bloom through nighttown. By the
mid-thirties, E. M. Forster was to remark that there is something "unstable in each of us," which is capable at any moment
of "rising to the surface and destroying our normal balance." In
other words, social contradictions in the world at large were
being mirrored in the prevailing theories of human personality,
theories which described consciousness as a battleground between instinctive needs and institutional repressions.

Virginia Woolf was to provide her own distinctive vision of
this split between society and individual, and that vision is the
source of the celebrated quarrel with Wells, Bennett, and
Galsworthy. Her chief complaint against the Edwardian novel
was that its "materialist" bias rendered an untrue picture of personality, depicting the physical trappings of character while ignoring the deeper essences. Furthermore, when Woolf said that
"life" in such novels was like a "series of gig lamps symmetri-
cally arranged," she was indirectly suggesting a link between a
society's material possessions (the carriages of the *haute
bourgeoisie,* lined up on a fashionable curb) and the "unrealistic"
shape of its fictions. It follows that if the traditional novel was
incapable of describing character, then the society which gave
rise to that novel had set up barriers against the biological and
spiritual needs of its people. To perceive life differently was to
place oneself in opposition to the social status quo; to change the
form of the novel, or to write fictions which in many ways do
not seem like novels at all, was to challenge the prevailing European social order and its methods of defining humanity. Hence,
contrary to the way most people have described it, Virginia
Woolf's program for modern fiction was an aestheticism which
was also deeply political.

Political implications such as these are found everywhere in
the artistic revolution known as "modernism," and they are at
the heart of European romanticism in general. But within the
larger movement individuals took different positions — some
reactionary; some progressive; some, like Joyce, extremely difficult to assess. Woolf's own politics were quite far to the left, a

fact which I emphasize because she has customarily been described as an experimental novelist who was sheltered by her privileged class. Clearly she was in many ways a product of her birth and station; intellectually, for example, she was attracted to theories of significant form and to a kind of romantic mysticism. Even so, there is another side to her life and work. She was also a cheroot-smoking feminist whose ideas were deeply influenced by the horrors of the first world war, and who remained in sympathy with socialist ideas throughout her career as a novelist. For all the emphasis she placed on the aesthetic quality of life, she recognized a connection between spirit and substance, a link between ideas and economics. And because she was a woman, her response to social change was different from that of her contemporaries; indeed she is virtually alone among the classic moderns in her lack of nostalgia for the old, predemocratic order of things. It was Woolf, after all, who argued that women would need the power of the vote, a good income, and rooms of their own if they expected to write as well as men; and it was Woolf who once optimistically prophesied that a political force would break down the old class and sex distinctions "and melt us together so that life will be richer and books more complex, and society will pool its possessions instead of segregating them."[2]

This last quotation should remind us that one of the major efforts of Virginia Woolf's novels is to disclose the possibility of a "community of feeling with other people," in which, as Mrs. Ramsay says, life is "all one stream, and chairs, tables, maps, were hers, were theirs, it did not matter whose." In every respect, from her love of watery metaphors to the peculiarly ambiguous, multipersonal quality of her narrative style, Woolf tries to overcome boundaries, insisting upon an ideal unity in life; but she also recognized, especially in her later novels, that her longing for unity was bound to be frustrated. At the most fundamental level, the continuity of life is split up by the necessities of time and space, which cut people off from one another and eventually lead to death; at the level of social intercourse, the unified life is threatened by a patriarchal, capitalistic society, which individualizes people and insists upon the private ownership of things. To defend against these problems, Woolf had two re-

2. "Memories of a Working Woman's Guild," *Collected Essays*, IV, 141–142.

sponses: in the face of the inevitable tragedy of time and death, she offered the consolation of nature seen from a cosmic perspective, as in the interchapters of *The Waves,* where individuals are subordinated to a life spirit. In regard to social disunity, she vaguely suggested that the whole of what she called the "materialist" world should be changed, to be replaced by a classless, nonsexist, purely communal existence, a life where, in its ideal and probably unattainable form, history itself would come to a stop.

Nowhere are these themes more evident than in her ambitious historical novel *The Years* (1937), which was written at a time of political crisis in Europe, and which shows the relationship between Woolf's formal experiments and her politics more clearly than any of her other writings. One obvious subject of *The Years* is the historical change away from an old patriarchal order. But the book also poses a problem; for even though Woolf was predisposed to welcome social change, the late thirties left her uncertain whether the world was moving in the direction of greater unity or greater totalitarianism. Therefore her typical ambivalence over the life process — the passing of time that leads us all closer to death — was doubled and intensified by a more immediate ambivalence about history. This uneasiness gives *The Years* its remarkably complex tone; and the merging of a transcendent, elegiac theme with a social radicalism helps to make the novel one of Woolf's most comprehensive statements.

II

To understand Woolf's attitude toward social change or indeed to understand her politics in general, it is necessary to read *The Years* in conjunction with *Three Guineas* (1938), the long polemical essay which, as she herself suggested, serves as a companion to her novel. Her original intention was to make *The Years* an "essay novel," but *Three Guineas* appears to have absorbed much of the analysis and rhetoric which might have found its way into the fiction. Unfortunately, however, *Three Guineas* has been the most undervalued of Woolf's writings and until recently has been neglected almost as much as the book it illuminates. From the beginning it was not much liked, and became the subject of the most vitriolic of all the attacks by the *Scrutiny* group: Q.D. Leavis' "Caterpillars of the Commonwealth Unite," an influential essay which maintained, among

other things, that Woolf was "quite insulated by class," that she
was "silly and ill-informed," and that she had written a tract
characterized by a "deliberate avoidance of any argument."[3]
Woolf's friends and admirers were not much more sympathetic.
One of her most scholarly critics has called *Three Guineas* a
"neurotic" book; and Quentin Bell has said that it failed because
Woolf attempted to discuss two issues which seemed at the time
to have only a tenuous connection: women's rights and the war
against fascism.[4]

But in fact there is a profound connection between these two
issues, a connection Woolf brought out with great lucidity. Unlike most of her critics, Woolf was no conventional liberal, and
she did not view the rise of fascist dictatorships in the thirties as a
simple aberration or as a case of the "good" British versus the
"bad" Germans. Though she confessed a deep, nonrational loy-
alty toward England like that of a child for a parent, she looked
beyond the old European patriotisms, seeking the causes of war
at a deeper level — in the very structure of middle-class, liberal
democracy. To Woolf the treatment of women under such a
democracy was symptomatic of the society's basic contradictions, its inability to live up to the ideals it professed; furthermore, she argued that the Spanish Civil War, and the dictators of
the right who were the immediate causes of that war, were the
direct outgrowth of the very system the British were trying to
preserve. Such a perception naturally left her feeling uneasy.
British democracy was preferable to fascism, but it maintained
the same sexual and class divisions, the same proprietary modes
of thought, the same masculine militarism which had given rise
to the fascists in the first place.

Caught in a dilemma, Woolf ultimately gave a guinea to a
barrister who had written asking her advice and support in pre-
venting war, and she contributed two more guineas to support

3. *The Importance of Scrutiny,* ed. Eric Bentley (New York: George Stewart,
1948), pp. 382–391. "The years change things," Woolf had written in *Three
Guineas,* and indeed they have changed things to the point where it is Mrs.
Leavis, not Woolf, who seems insulated by class. In regard to Woolf's claim
that the society kept women at a disadvantage, Leavis commented, "I feel
bound to disagree . . . that running a household necessarily hinders or
weakens thinking." "The onus is on women," she wrote, "to prove that they
are going to be able to justify (emancipation), and that it will not vitally
dislocate . . . the framework of our culture." Elsewhere she hinted darkly
that Woolf's proposals for changing the schools and family had something in
common with the "Soviet system."
4. See Herbert Marder, *Feminism and Art,* p. 174; Bell, *Virginia Woolf,* II, 204.

women's colleges and women's entry into the professions. But at
the same time she pointed out that all the committees to prevent
war, all the colleges and all the professions, were either beside
the point or themselves a part of the problem; the society and its
values would have to be radically changed before humane goals
could be achieved. Under present circumstances, she wrote,
people were forced to choose between bad institutions and an
essentially private life as "outsiders." This split between public
and private worlds—a split which is embodied throughout
modernist literature and in all of Woolf's novels—was ultimately destructive. "For such will be our ruin," Woolf said, "if
you in the immensity of public abstractions forget the private
figure, or if we in the intensity of our private emotions forget the
public world. Both houses will be ruined . . . the material and
the spiritual, for they are inseparably connected." What was
needed, and what at present could be found only in the voices of
the poets, was "that capacity of the human spirit to overflow
boundaries and make unity out of multiplicity." But such a unity
is only a dream, Woolf said, "the recurring dream that has
haunted the human mind since the beginning of time."[5]

In writing *The Years,* Woolf tried to give a concrete dem-
onstration of the split between private and public worlds, the
conflict between a timeless, transpersonal human nature and a
divisive, changing social structure. She also provided intima-
tions of that "dream" of unity which haunts the mind, and
envisioned history moving toward a potential resolution of
people's inner conflicts. Interestingly, however, she chose to
write a book which was superficially similar to the family
chronicles of John Galsworthy himself, and that may explain
why a few of her critics have wrongly described *The Years* as one
of her more conventional works. In fact the novel is strikingly
unorthodox, and in every respect serves to undermine the assumptions of traditional "realist" fiction.

Although history is one of the book's manifest subjects, *The
Years* subordinates public events to a series of domestic scenes or
dinner parties, taking us into people's cell-like homes or rented
rooms, where sounds can be heard drifting in through windows,
or where characters repeatedly gaze outside, noting symbolic
details in the environment. The novel is never tendentious, and

5. *Three Guineas,* p. 143.

it does not offer a comprehensive view of social classes; Woolf's progress from chapter to chapter is determined simply by the passing of time, and while Eleanor Pargiter comes close to being a central personage, she hardly qualifies as the agent of the basic change or *parapataea* which gives shape to most plots. The story arises not out of action or exposition but out of a web of family relationships and the collective memories of various characters. We are given not so much a narrative history as a montage, an irregular succession of meaningful but undramatic moments which reveal the quality of daily life.

In her typical fashion, Woolf organizes the material according to a roughly musical form, repeating certain motifs (such as a pigeon cry heard throughout), and establishing thematic echoes between chapters. And yet despite the rigor with which it is executed, *The Years* has a somewhat diffuse surface. Compared to other novels by Woolf, such as *The Waves,* it is striking in its lack of symmetry, its refusal to present an obvious pattern; even the nature descriptions which preface each chapter are not given a sequential rhythm. Such features of the novel may account for the remarks of Basil de Senancourt, whose early review pleased Woolf a great deal. Senancourt noted especially the writer's "instinct . . . towards disjunction," together with a "poetical" movement of consciousness which seemed to pull unity out of chaos.[6] This double tendency is indeed the basis of Woolf's later writings, where she is always challenging her view of unity and continuity in human experience by choosing to render the dislocations caused by passing time, by death, or by the mind's conversations with itself. In *The Years,* her problem is posed explicitly by Eleanor, who wonders if there is a "pattern" to life, "a theme, recurring, like music; half remembered, half foreseen? . . . But who makes it? Who thinks it?" (Y, 369). Ironically, the same idea has just been rejected by Eleanor's niece Peggy, who bitterly contemplates the chatter of her relatives and feels that even if there were a pattern it would be meaningless, like a "habit," or a "kitten catching its tail" (Y, 359–360).

Throughout *The Years* Woolf's mood seems to waver precariously between Eleanor's turn-of-the-century optimism and Peggy's "present day" pessimism, so that feelings of unity,

6. The review is reprinted in *Virginia Woolf: The Critical Heritage,* ed. Majumdar and McLaurin, p. 373.

communion, and significant form are always threatened. The threat is felt not simply at the level of content — as in those passages where characters meditate inconclusively upon the meaning of life — but in the technique itself; the blank spaces between scenes act as signifiers of some gap, some fissure in experience which the imagination of both author and reader seeks to close up.

The Years therefore shares with Between the Acts a fragmented, asymmetrical form, and it also has in common with Woolf's last novel a constantly shifting tone, moving effortlessly between lyricism, satire, and perverse ugliness, rather like Eliot in his Waste Land period. Clearly the atmosphere of political engagement in thirties' literature affected The Years profoundly, even though the book takes place in a private sphere and does not give much sense of an industrial England. In none of Woolf's previous works is there so powerful a sense of urban poverty and violence, or of economic disparities within and between the social classes. These qualities persist throughout the novel, even at the close, when the Edwardian culture is in ruins and Woolf has a clear sense of what the new world ought to be like; Woolf even predicts, through Eleanor, the possible advent of that world, but she has been so unremittingly honest in confronting the capitalist wasteland of the present that she leaves the novel poised, reflecting the tension of doubt. Because she is writing out of a deep knowledge of injustice, her vision of unity and meaning in life is not easily won.

Woolf's uneasiness about the ultimate meaning of history is reflected not only in individual episodes, but in the whole shape of the book. At first glance even the years themselves seem to have been chosen randomly, with little regard to historical significance or official importance to the characters' lives. Except for the death of Mrs. Pargiter in 1880, the dramatic events take place offstage; the first and last years of the world war are given, but the 1914 section takes place in spring, a little in advance of hostilities, whereas the very brief 1918 section is meant to indicate the meaninglessness of "victory" — the Pargiters'ex-servant Crosby simply pauses to hear the guns booming in the distance, then queues up at the grocer's shop as usual. The novel alludes to historical incidents (including the deaths of Parnell and King Edward, the Irish Civil War, the emancipation movement, the rise of Mussolini, and so on), but people seldom comment on the relation between their lives and these events. Even the nar-

rator of the book, that ghostly persona so common to Virginia
Woolf's work, tries to direct attention away from social or political facts. The evocative but generalized descriptions of landscape at the opening of each chapter suggest that nature has
transcended both history and the unsatisfactory conditions of
individual lives, the weather becoming more significant than
social change.

The descriptions of landscape, however, are not so much a
negation of history as an attempt to give the novel a firm
grounding in what I have already described as the "eternal"
natural process. Thus the consciousness of the characters is influenced not only by their social class and their economic needs, but
also by their natural instincts and their desire for communion.
Nearly all the people in the novel are powerfully affected by the
conflict between social institutions and some deeper human nature; and the corollary to such a proposition is that true happiness can be attained only when civilization is brought into
harmony with *bios,* or with what Lawrence, in another context,
called the "deepest self." In the society as Woolf perceives it,
however, this harmony is continually frustrated; especially in the
earlier parts of the novel, one senses a battle between the characters' instincts and the social forms which dictate their behavior.
Here, for example, is the scene where Delia Pargiter watches her
mother's burial:

> Earth dropped on the coffin; three pebbles fell on the hard shiny
> surface; and as they dropped she was possessed by a sense of some-
> thing everlasting; of life mixing with death, of death becoming life.
> For as she looked she heard the sparrows chirp quicker and quicker;
> she heard wheels in the distance sound louder and louder; life came
> closer and closer . . .
>
> "We give thee hearty thanks," said the voice, "for that it has
> pleased thee to deliver this our sister out of the miseries of this sinful
> world ——"
>
> What a lie! she cried to herself. What a damnable lie! He had
> robbed her of the one feeling that was genuine; he had spoilt her one
> moment of understanding. (Y, 87)

Obvious as these social impediments to Delia's "understanding" may be, they are not commented upon until fairly late in
the book, when Eleanor and Nicholas Pomjalovsky have a conversation during a blackout in World War I:

> "I was saying," he went on, "I was saying we do not know our-
> selves, ordinary people; and if we do not know ourselves, how then

can we make religions, laws, that——" he used his hands as people do
who find language obdurate, "that——"

"That fit — that fit," she said, supplying him with a word that was
shorter, she felt sure, than the dictionary word foreigners always
used . . .

". . . that fit," she repeated. She had no idea what they were talking about. Then suddenly, as she bent to warm her hands over the
fire, words floated together in her mind and made one intelligible
sentence. It seemed to her that what he had said was, "We cannot
make laws and religions that fit because we do not know ourselves."

"How odd that you should say that!" she said, smiling at him,
"because I've so often thought it myself!"

"Why is that odd?" he said. "We all think the same things; only we
do not say them." (Y, 281–282)

Nicholas and Eleanor are able to achieve a tentative, halting
perception, a shared insight, because they are both "outsiders."
Eleanor is one of those "daughters of educated men" who do not
participate as full members of the society, whereas Nicholas is a
foreigner and a homosexual who, as Sara ironically puts it,
"ought to be in prison." We are asked, however, to regard these
two as "ordinary people," because Virginia Woolf is suggesting
that at the deepest levels of biological necessity we all share the
same needs, feel the same discontent, "think the same things."
Nicholas elaborates on this issue, arguing that under present
conditions there is no way to achieve harmony and wholeness,
no way for what he calls "the soul" to express itself:

"The soul — the whole being," he explained. He hollowed his
hands as if to enclose a circle. "It wishes to expand; to adventure; to
form — new combinations?"

"Yes, yes," she said, as if to assure him that his words were right.

"Whereas now," — he drew himself together; put his feet together;
he looked like an old lady who is afraid of mice — "this is how we
live, screwed up into one hard little, tight little — knot?"

"Knot, knot — yes, that's right," she nodded.

"Each is his own little cubicle; each with his own cross or holy
book; each with his fire, his wife . . ." (Y, 296)

Significantly, Nicholas' vision of a selfish, proprietary society
is centered not in public institutions, but in the same private
realm of family life that Virginia Woolf's novel has sought to
describe. As Woolf had said in *Three Guineas,* "the public and the
private worlds are inseparably connected . . . the tyrannies and

servilities of the one are the tyrannies and servilities of the other." Indeed, the suppression of the "soul" by social forms is nowhere more evident than in Woolf's depiction of people's "own little cubicle" of marriage, which in *Three Guineas* is called "the one great profession open to [women] since the dawn of time."[7]

Every chapter of *The Years* contains some reference to marriages of property or to unrequited loves. The first, most vividly satiric example of the latter theme is in the early episodes involving Abel Pargiter's niece Kitty Malone, a handsome young woman who is the daughter of an Oxford don. Kitty's conservative, snobbish father is a man who, "had a frame been set round him, might have hung over the fireplace" (Y, 77), whereas her mother is contrasted unfavorably with the American visitor Mrs. Fripp, a lady who wears makeup and eats ices instead of making the customary tourist's visit to the Bodleian. Kitty feels frustrated and imprisoned in Oxford, where it always seems to be raining and where she is being forced to read Dr. Andrew's "The Constitutional History of England." (We are told that she once inadvertently spilled ink over one of her father's manuscripts — a history of the college — obliterating "five generations of Oxford men." Dr. Malone's only reply had been, "Nature did not intend you to be a scholar, my dear.") Kitty's mother intends her to marry a suitable man, and cannot understand her daughter's unhappiness; after all, her own convenient marriage has represented an escape of sorts from the tedious country life of Yorkshire. The irony is that Kitty would actually prefer an empty countryside to the college. She contemplates the "barber's block," Edward Pargiter, with distaste, and her only impression of one of the famous scholars who has visited the house is the "damp feel of a heavy hand on her knee" (Y, 66). Her attraction to Jo Robeson becomes the one moment when her life holds out the possibility of romantic liberation, but just when her story seems to be taking a hopeful turn Virginia Woolf concludes the chapter, leaping over several years and casually remarking that Kitty has made a prosperous marriage with Lasswade, a mate approved by her mother.

Actually, the theme of frustrated, misplaced, or hypocritical alliances has been introduced even earlier, and Kitty's essential

7. *Three Guineas*, p. 6.

loneliness is echoed in the lives of nearly everyone we meet. Somewhat in the manner of Eliot, Woolf is describing a sexual wasteland, but unlike Eliot she implies that the causes of love's failure are more social than metaphysical. Thus the book opens with Abel Pargiter's clandestine, grotesque visit to his mistress in a street of "dingy little houses" near Westminster. As his amputated fingers fumble at the neck of his lover, Woolf calls attention to sordid details: an eczemous dog; a creaking staircase; the sounds of children outside jumping in and out of "white chalk marks on the pavement" — this last a recurrent motif in the early parts of the novel, and an image used in *Three Guineas* to signify "a monstrous male . . . childishly intent upon scoring the floor of the earth with chalk marks, within whose mystic boundaries human beings are penned, rigidly, separately, artificially" (p. 105).

Meanwhile, Abel Pargiter's wife Rose lies dying in their huge house in Abercorn Terrace, where the children of the family, particularly the females, are quite literally "penned, rigidly . . . artificially," becoming virtual prisoners of Edwardian respectability. Here we are introduced to the four Pargiter daughters: Rose, the adventurous little girl who will grow up to become a suffragette, and who will one day have painful memories of "a certain engagement" when "her happiness, it seemed . . . had fallen" (Y, 161); Delia, the romantic, rebellious teenager who daydreams about Parnell, and who will reject the Pargiter household only to end her life married to a conservative Anglo-Irish landlord; Milly, a self-conscious, unremarkable young woman, who will marry a rustic Devonshire gentleman and live contentedly producing his children; and Eleanor, the eldest and most sympathetic, who neither marries nor rebels against her father, but who wishes for one painful moment in her old age that she had been able to find a companion: "I should like to have married," she thinks suddenly, almost surprising herself, resenting "the passage of time and the accidents of life which had swept her away" (Y, 299).

Companionship is obviously a necessity for all these characters, but in the world of *The Years* marriage is rarely presented as a satisfactory alternative to isolation. The daughters of Digby Pargiter, Maggie and Sara, seem to represent the two possible extremes in life: because their side of the family is relatively poor, they grow up to share a shabby apartment in Hyams Place; Maggie ultimately finds a relatively happy, unconventional marriage with a foreigner, and Sara, who is frequently compared to Antigone, becomes totally isolated and harmlessly insane — indeed, her speeches are examples of what Woolf, in the context of *Mrs. Dalloway,* called the "mad truth."

The Pargiter sons, on the other hand, have the advantage of "Arthur's Education Fund," that money which throughout British history had been set aside for the education of males. Edward Pargiter becomes a classical scholar at Oxford, Morris enters the law, and Martin joins the army — three institutions Woolf had taken special pains to attack in *Three Guineas.* In *The Years* we see just enough of this public world to understand how it is related to the domestic lives of the characters. The deadly Oxford environment, with its prejudice against women and its complacent snobbishness, is treated in some detail in the Kitty Malone section of the first chapter; the horrors of militarism and war are suggested at various places, most obviously in the 1917 chapter; and the courts of law are depicted in an early scene when Eleanor goes to see Morris perform. At first she admires the wise looks of the presiding judge, but then remembers having met him socially: "And it was a sham. She wanted to laugh" (Y, 111). But even though Woolf points to the social inequity between men and women, she does not suggest that the men have fuller lives; on the contrary, a profound feeling of frustration and lost possibility is felt equally by both sexes. Morris makes a prosperous marriage to a daughter of the Chinnery family and lives on their estate, but he grows old before his time, and Eleanor at one point feels guilty because she urged him to go to the bar (Y, 202). Martin wishes he had been an architect, "but they sent me into the Army instead, which I loathed" (Y, 230). Even Edward, the vain but successful scholar, becomes supercilious, reserved, and secretly homosexual; his nephew North tries to speak with him at Delia's party, but ends up thinking "It's no go . . . He can't say what he wants to say; he's afraid" (Y, 414).

"When shall we be free?" Eleanor wonders as she listens to Nicholas, "When shall we live adventurously, wholly, not like cripples in a cave?" (Y, 297). The book never answers this question and none of the years marks a liberating change in either society or character. Even when Woolf records events from 1910, they are less momentous than we might expect. The announcement of King Edward's death, which Maggie Pargiter hears out the window of her flat, is clearly a symbolic event and is followed closely by an important moment in the lives of the Abel Pargiter family: in the 1913 chapter, Eleanor sells the house in Abercorn Terrace, and Martin thinks back on his childhood. "It was an abominable system . . . family life," he notes, "there all those different people had lived, boxed up together, telling lies" (Y, 222–223). But the collapse of the old Edwardian order does not seem to have created a healthy new day. The years are still pervaded with an atmosphere of futility and lost opportunity; every level of the Pargiter family, from the poor rooms at Hyams Place to the Lasswade seats at the opera, has been shown suffering in quiet desperation. People are still "boxed up," unable to express their feelings, and the death of the king seems merely in keeping with the theme of mortality which is found everywhere in the novel.

If *The Years* has a most important year, it is not 1910 but a date which is never inscribed in the text. We are shown the lives of the Pargiter family between 1880 and 1918, and then Woolf leaps into the "present day," leaving 1919 as an unstated boundary between old and new. The significance of that year is apparent in *Three Guineas,* where it is repeatedly cited as a watershed in the history of women's emancipation; for in 1919, as Woolf notes, women were admitted legally to the professions. This event, however, tended only to liberalize British life, not to change it fundamentally. Although Woolf believed 1919 was an important date, she regarded the new power of women with some irony, pointing out the dangers of being admitted to equal partnership in an evil system.

> Now that the Civil Service is open to us we may well earn from one thousand to three thousand a year; now that the Bar is open to us we may well earn 5,000 a year as judges, and any sum up to forty or fifty thousand a year as barristers. When the Church is open to us we may draw salaries of fifteen thousand . . . When the Stock Exchange is open to us we may die worth as many millions as Pierpont Morgan, or as Rockefeller himself . . . In short, we may change our position from being the victims of the patriarchal system . . . to being the champions of the capitalist system.[8]

The playfulness of these remarks does not conceal the seriousness of Woolf's convictions. She admits that women seeking to

8. Ibid., p. 67.

enter the universities might think her arguments niggling, but she cautions that her readers should look at the photographs of dead bodies and ruined houses that the Spanish government sends almost weekly.[9] In her view, as we have seen, there is a direct connection between patriarchy, capitalism, and fascist dictatorship; indeed the historical period covered by *The Years* shows the society moving from the first of these stages into the second, with the third brooding on the horizon as the book closes. Woolf therefore opposed any compromise which would allow women to participate even marginally in the British system while at the same time preserving its unjust features. And it is precisely such a compromised social condition that we find in the "Present Day" section of *The Years*. Peggy, the daughter of Morris Pargiter, has become a doctor, but this important change in the status of women does not lead to personal happiness, nor does it heal the split between old and young, between social classes, between individuals and the community. The last section does suggest the dawning of some new world, as indeed throughout the novel we have been given the sense that the movement of history might ultimately redeem everyday life from its sadness and futility. But the new day is not yet arrived as the novel ends, and the chief representatives of the "Present Day" are just as dissatisfied as their forebears had been.

Clearly certain hopeful changes have taken place in the texture of middle-class relationships: Delia Pargiter's elaborate family reunion, which is the setting for most of the action of the final chapter, takes place not in a home, but in a flower-bedecked estate agent's office, with people sitting on stools or on the floors, dining off every kind of table. Delia thinks that this "had always been her aim . . . to do away with the absurd conventions of English life" (Y, 398). But her attempt to dissolve the old formalities and bring people together has not been completely successful. North remarks sardonically to himself that everyone present makes a good income, and both he and his sister feel a sharp division between their own generation and Delia's. Of the two younger Pargiters, Peggy is especially isolated and embittered; now thirty-seven years old and beginning to turn grey, she lives what she herself calls a "suppressed" life, a frustrated existence different in kind but not in quality from the one we saw earlier in the daughters of

---

9. Ibid., p. 10.

Abel. Bored and distressed by the habitual chatter of her older
relatives, she is equally upset by the conversation of an egotistical
young man. She does not participate in the dancing, and spends
much of the evening brooding alone. She is made especially uncomfortable by the difference between herself and her aunt, and
notes sourly that Eleanor can still believe in "freedom" and "justice," "the things that man had destroyed" (Y, 331–332).

Peggy's dissatisfaction is given its most vivid and painful expression early in the chapter, when, en route to the party, she
and Eleanor take a cab through London's entertainment district.
Peggy is struck by the grotesquerie of the streets:

> The light fell on broad pavements; on white, brilliantly lit-up public
> offices; on a pallid, hoary-looking church. Advertisements popped in
> and out. Here was a bottle of beer: it poured: then stopped: then
> poured again . . . Cabs were wheeling and stopping. Their own taxi
> was held up. It stopped dead under a statue: the lights shown on its
> cadaverous pallor.
> "Always reminds me of an advertisement of sanitary towels," said
> Peggy, glancing at the figure of a woman in a nurse's uniform hold-
> ing out her hand. (Y, 336)

The remark shocks Eleanor, who momentarily feels that a knife
has sliced her skin. But Peggy's description of the "figure of a
woman in a nurse's uniform" is still more unsettling if we recognize the London landmark to which it refers, a monument
that Woolf has carefully avoided naming. We are told simply
that the figure makes Eleanor think of Peggy's brother, "a
nice . . . boy who had been killed."

> "The only fine thing that was said in the war," she said aloud,
> reading the words cut on the pedestal.
> "It didn't come to much," said Peggy sharply.
> The cab remained fixed in the block. (Y, 336)

The statue which evokes this brief exchange is dedicated to
Nurse Cavell and in 1937 was one of the four best-known
monuments to women in London. Erected in St. Martin's Place
in 1920, the Cavell statue was given an inscription by the Labor
government in 1924; the words on the pedestal read "Patriotism
is not enough."[10] Typically, Eleanor has read the motto as a kind

---

10. See *An Encyclopaedia of London,* ed. William Kent (New York: Macmillan,
    1951), p. 524. Kent remarks of the statue: "The figure is an admirable one,
    but the background is unsightly."

of lesson learned in the war, whereas Peggy regards it cynically. Hence at a later point in the novel Eleanor will comment that things have changed for the better: "We've changed in ourselves," she says, "We're happier — we're freer." But Peggy can only wonder what "freedom" and "happiness" mean (Y, 386).

At Delia's party, Peggy tries to explain to North that she perceives a "state of being" in which there might be real happiness; but then she insults him by predicting that he will marry and "make money" instead of "living differently" (Y, 390). Actually, North is almost as isolated as she, and has begun his drift toward marriage only because he cannot find a satisfactory alternative. Having spent years in the army and then on an African sheep farm, he returns to London feeling oddly out of place, a stranger to his relatives, his thoughts during the day and evening turning around the problem "Society or solitude, which is best?" — a topic he has heard Nicholas Pomjalovsky discussing at Eleanor's apartment.

North's own feelings seem to pull him toward solitude. His favorite poem, for example, is Marvell's *The Garden,* and he enjoys quoting the lines, "Society is all but rude / to this delicious solitude." At the same time, however, his bachelorhood has grown oppressive, and he has come to London partly out of a vague longing for a mate. While in Africa, he wrote a letter to Sara containing the message that "this is Hell. We are the damned." But now that he has returned to London, he shares an almost surreal luncheon with Sara in her apartment at 52 Milton Street, "near the Prison Tower," and he seems not much happier. In one of the more comic passages of the final chapter, he sits at Delia's party and meditates on the marriage between Hugh Boggs and Milly. An overweight, bovine couple, they make sounds like the "munching of animals in a stall," and North wonders if this is what marriage comes to, where the men go out to hunt and the women "break off into babies." For a moment he contemplates revolution and dynamite, wondering if his sister Peggy could invent a potion that would exterminate the Gibbses of the world. "They're not interested in other people's children," he observes, "Only in their own, their own property . . . How then can we be civilized?" (Y, 375–378). While Eleanor comments on the "miracle" of life, which she calls "a perpetual discovery," North can only say, "I don't know what I want" (Y, 382–383).

Even more clearly than Peggy, North perceives the split between his desires and the objective conditions of the society.
Looking about Delia's party, he thinks, "What do they mean by
Justice and Liberty? . . . all these nice young men with two or
three hundred a year. Something's wrong . . . there's a gap, a
dislocation, between the word and the reality." Gazing into his
champagne glass, he imagines what life ought to be and un-
knowingly echoes Nicholas' and Eleanor's thoughts from an
earlier chapter:

> For them it's all right, he thought; they've had their day; but not for
> him, not for his generation . . . Why not down barriers and
> simplify? But a world, he thought, that was all one jelly, one mass,
> would be a rice pudding world, a white counterpane world. To keep
> the emblems and tokens of North Pargiter — the man Maggie laughs
> at; the Frenchman holding his hat; but at the same time spread out,
> make a new ripple in human consciousness, be the bubble and the
> stream, the stream and the bubble — myself and the world to-
> gether — he raised his glass. Anonymously, he said, looking at the
> clear yellow liquid. But what do I mean, he wondered — I, to whom
> ceremonies are suspect, and religion's dead; who don't fit, as the man
> said, don't fit in anywhere? He paused. There was the glass in his
> hand; in his mind a sentence. And he wanted to make other sen-
> tences. But how can I, he thought — he looked at Eleanor, who sat
> with a silk handkerchief in her hands — unless I know what's solid,
> what's true; in my life, in other people's lives? (Y, 410)

North's meditation in this passage is crucial not only to an
understanding of The Years, but in a more general way to appreciation of Virginia Woolf's entire work. For at virtually every
level of her writing she is preoccupied with the distinction she
feels between the inner self and the outer world, between solitude and society, between "the bubble and the stream." Like
North, she wishes to harmonize two kinds of existence: on the
one hand are the timeless recesses of being, where one feels a loss
of personal identity and a communion with nature; on the other
hand is the time-bound social world of day-to-day relationships,
where people assert their identity and relish their differences.
The difficulty presented in The Years — and by implication in all
of Woolf's novels — is that the two kinds of existence will not
"fit," partly because the society will not allow people to translate
their private dreams of unity into public relationships. As a re-

sult the characters feel torn between two worlds, doomed if they choose either one exclusively.

As a novelist, Virginia Woolf seems to have faced a similar difficulty. In "Mr. Bennett and Mrs. Brown," for example, she confronts the problem of reconciling the inward essence of character with the outer shell; as Peggy says when she tries to describe Eleanor, "Where does she begin, and where do I end? . . . two sparks of life enclosed in two separate bodies" (Y, 334). Always Woolf tried to capture some transpersonal human essence, some "spark of life" which unites individuals. In passages like the "Time Passes" section of *To the Lighthouse,* she actually attempted to write about a pure life process, a stream without bubbles, where unity has become so complete that there is no distinction between seeing and seen. In most cases, however, she felt torn between a visionary mode of writing and a more public approach, which she identified with the hated orthodoxies of the society. She recognized the ultimate unsatisfactoriness of these alternatives, which forced her to experience life purely at extremes, and she often felt compelled to choose between what she called the novel of "vision" as opposed to the novel of "fact." Hence in *The Waves* she attempted a purely visionary work, but she was no sooner finished than she felt a positive need to write about an opposite kind of experience, to make a solid, "factual" counterpart such as *The Years.*

What makes the later novels like *The Years* and *Between the Acts* so interesting, however, is that they will not settle for one mode of existence over another. Woolf was actually seeking a synthesis of extremes, a dialectic between "female" and "male," between "thou" and "I," between "stream" and "bubble." As North Pargiter recognizes, a world of pure unity and vision would be a "rice pudding world, a white counterpane world," whereas a world of pure individuality must inevitably make people feel that they are "boxed in," cut off from essences. The problem is to develop a human consciousness and a manner of writing which is able to express both kinds of existence simultaneously. In *The Years* Woolf suggests that this problem has social and historical causes and will not be solved by an act of individual will. The split between the two kinds of existence is related to all those artificial boundaries set up between people, all those petty tyrannies of the household, all those economic inequities which

260   JAMES NAREMORE

have been shown indirectly throughout the novel; and the reconciliation is not possible until the society itself is fundamentally changed.

This dissociation between public and private worlds helps explain why characters in The Years have so much difficulty expressing their feelings to one another, or even to themselves. Repeatedly, especially in the last chapter, people experience North's difficulty of trying to "make other sentences," an anxiety Woolf the novelist must have felt as strongly as her imagined characters. The problem is most obvious when the characters try to ask large questions. When Peggy asks if there is any "standard" for human behavior, the issue is dropped while Eleanor tries to recall something she wanted to say; when North asks whether society or solitude is best, Sara's reply is washed away by the chaotic sounds outside her window; when Nicholas tries to make a significant speech at Delia's party, his comments become slightly drunken and incoherent. "Directly something got together, it broke," Peggy thinks (Y, 392), and her observation is reinforced when Nicholas accidentally shatters a champagne glass while he is trying to make his most important statement.

And yet, underneath these elliptical, unfinished attempts to give life meaning, underneath the apparently random fragments of the text, Virginia Woolf suggests a kind of unity, a potential for harmony. This unity is expressed partly by the fact that, despite their surface differences, the characters in the novel at least feel the same discontent across generations — indeed, the elder Pargiters do not conform to the easy stereotypes given them by Peggy and North in the final section. Given this possibility of human community, Woolf is able to provide the novel with a conclusion which strikes a balance between hope and irony. In the last scene, Eleanor looks out the doorway of the estate agent's office, echoing all those times before when characters have looked out unhappily on the streets, and sees a young couple entering the house across the way, a symbol for the sexual accord and fulfillment which has been denied nearly everyone else: " 'There,' Eleanor murmured . . . 'There,' she repeated, as the door shut with a little thud behind them" (Y, 434).

Like the couple Woolf notices out the window in A Room of One's Own, the man and woman in this scene represent "a force in things which one had overlooked," a potential for unity in life. At the same time, however, they are going inside a house, where the door shuts with a little thud. Are they not "boxed in," like so many of the characters we have seen elsewhere in the novel? Clearly the image is not a satisfactory representation of happiness, because it returns us to the same kind of domesticity which has been a center of trouble throughout. As if in compensation for this final scene, Woolf closes the novel with an explicitly optimistic statement: We are told that "the sky above the houses wore an air of extraordinary beauty, simplicity, and peace." Understandably, some critics have felt that the exaltation in these lines is not congruent with the tone of the novel as a whole.[11] But it seems to me that we are not intended to read Woolf's last words as a sort of "Happy ever after"; she is not saying that the problems of the novel have been solved, only that a certain natural harmony is potentially within the grasp of humanity.

Actually, Woolf does not know what the future will bring, and in the moment when she tries to predict tomorrow, her essential optimism is tinged with fear. Only a few pages before the conclusion of the novel, Delia's party is interrupted by the entry of a group of children of the building's "caretaker," who are not members of the class who make up the party. "Speak!" Martin Pargiter commands, taking up the role of his father before him, and when they do not reply Peggy remarks sardonically that the younger generation "don't mean to speak" (Y, 429). Instead, the children nudge one another and break into song:

> Etho passo tanno hai,
> Fai donk to tu do,
> Mai to, kai to, lai to see
> Toh dom to tuh do —
> (Y, 429)

It is a new and strange language, understood by none of the adults. One of the more conservative members of the party suggests it is a "Cockney accent," but no one is quite sure. We are told that the "distorted sounds rose and sank as if they followed a tune" (Y, 429), and that there was "something horrible in the noise they made. It was so shrill, so discordant, and so

---

11. See, for example, Josephine O'Brien Schaefer, *The Three-Fold Nature of Reality in Virginia Woolf* (London: Mouton, 1965), pp. 167–185.

meaningless" (Y, 430). Typically, only Eleanor can find something good to say about the performance:

> "But it was . . ." Eleanor began. She stopped. What was it? As they stood there they had looked so dignified; yet they had made this hideous noise. The contrast between their faces and voices was astonishing; it was impossible to find one word for the whole. "Beautiful?" she said, with a note of interrogation, turning to Maggie.
> "Extraordinarily," said Maggie.
> But Eleanor was not sure that they were thinking of the same thing. (Y, 430–431)

The curious mixture of admiration and sinister terror in this episode is rather like the final scene in *Between the Acts,* where a husband and wife approach one another across the darkness, about to commit an "act" which will determine the future. We may safely assume that Virginia Woolf herself felt such emotions when, in the late thirties, she tried to think about the movement of history. Unlike T. S. Eliot, she did not cling to a tradition, but at the same time she was appalled at what liberal democracy (identified with the masculine ego) had done to the human spirit. She was therefore fearful: Would the inevitable changes to come lead humanity toward some higher plane, or were the years moving in a downward spiral, each stage as frustrating as the one before? Her novel leaves us waiting for the answer, poised for an apocalypse. And yet what is so remarkable about *The Years* is the tenacity with which it keeps faith in "beauty, simplicity, and peace," despite so much social and sexual frustration. Although Woolf is not in league with Blake or Lawrence, she does suggest that a radical change in human consciousness is due; by offering the vision of a peaceful landscape, even if tentatively, she partly overcomes the feelings of despair and solitude which are characteristic of so much modernist literature, helping us believe that human nature might eventually triumph over history.

13. *Woolf's Peculiar Comic World:* Between the Acts

B. H. FUSSELL

> This world is contingency and absurdity incarnate, the oddest of pos-
> sibilities masquerading momentarily as a fact.
> — George Santayana, *Soliloquies in England and Later Soliloquies.*

I

" 'Curse! Blast! Damn 'em!' " rages Miss La Trobe at the
climax of the first scene of her pageant, for "here was her
downfall; here was the Interval" (BA, 94). Miss La Trobe, the
dramatist, curses the tyranny of the audience and its demands for
tea just as Virginia Woolf, the novelist, often cursed the reader
and his demand for "fact." Of the many self-portraits executed
by Virginia Woolf, Miss La Trobe is her most satiric. Here is a
Portrait of the Artist as old Bossy, a squat spinster who celebrates her moment of failure and glory in the local pub, alone,
drowned in beer and words — "Words without meaning —
wonderful words" (BA, 212). Woolf's caricature of the artist
dominates a work that caricatures Woolf's own kind of art, for
Between the Acts is a novel that burlesques a play that burlesques a
poem that burlesques a novel. In this circular generic mix Woolf
achieves the apotheosis of what she called the "play-poem idea,"
at the same time as she demolishes it.[1] Further she cannot go in
rendering absurdity incarnate. *Between the Acts* is a kind of
epitaph to her pervasive and peculiar kind of comedy, which is
both funny and odd.

The comedy of Virginia Woolf has been largely overlooked, I
believe, partly as a result of the problem of dramatic distancing

1. *A Writer's Diary* (Saturday, June 18, 1940), p. 107.

noted by Wayne Booth in *The Rhetoric of Fiction*. In pointing to "the price of impersonal narration" paid by modern novelists, Booth instances the misreadings of Joyce's *Portrait of the Artist*. Not until the publication of *Stephen Hero* (1944), Booth claims, did readers begin to see the degree of Joyce's intended satire and irony in the revised work.[2] Woolf shares with Joyce the problem of misreading as she shared his concern to make the personal narrator impersonal by various means of dramatic objectification. Both detractors and admirers tend to mistake the degree of Woolf's satiric and ironic tone. She is still critically patronized and extolled not as a comic writer but as a novelist of sensibility or, even worse, of female sensibility — a Sensitive Plant[3] drooping in a Bloomsbury hothouse.

One of the difficulties for contemporary readers is that her satiric arena *is* the Bloomsbury hothouse and drawing-room. Like Jane Austen, she chose to limit her scene to the particular domestic and social milieu in which she lived. Here the trouble begins. Woolf is condemned for both social and literary snobbery: condemned for not having rebelled from the particular social class in which she was born, and which is in current disfavor; condemned for a snobbish aestheticism which scorns the many for the few. Ironically, Booth while elucidating Joyce's satire failed to see Woolf's. He specifically attacks Woolf for "a retreat to a private world of values"[4] and admonishes novelists, with her example, to worry less about techniques of surface "objectivity" and more about actual objectivity through self-detachment.

Woolf's attitude is far more complex, ironic, and toughly realistic than the populist assumptions of Booth's condemnation. Her own attitude toward the satire of Jane Austen is illuminating here. Had Austen lived longer and known more of the wider, disruptive world of London, Woolf writes, most likely "her comedy would have suffered" but "her satire . . . would have been more stringent and severe."[5] She would have distanced herself more from her characters "and seen them more as a group, less as individuals." The distance of satire provoked by a

---

2. *The Rhetoric of Fiction* (Chicago: University of Chicago Press, 1961), p. 333.
3. Denis Donoghue's term for Stephen Daedelus, cited by Booth in ibid., p. 333.
4. Ibid., pp. 392ff.
5. "Jane Austen," *Collected Essays*, I, 153.

less secure world would have made her, Woolf concludes, the forerunner of the group of modern writers among whom Woolf placed herself — James, Proust, Forster, Lawrence, Eliot, and Joyce.

In praising Joyce for his "realism" in "Modern Fiction" (1919), Woolf calls upon the new young writers to discard the old conventions of the Edwardian novel of "fact" and to record the "reality" of the modern world: "Let us record the atoms as they fall upon the mind in the order in which they fall, let us trace the pattern, however disconnected and incoherent in appearance, which each sight or incident scores upon the consciousness."[6] The "reality" of a universe and consciousness disjunct exposes "ordinary waking Arnold Bennett life" as fictive.[7] The real world is contingency masquerading momentarily as a fact, a world which can be expressed only by negatives and apprehended only in fragments. Woolf shares Joyce's and Eliot's vision as she shares their methods of ironic juxtaposition and dramatic distancing. But unlike Joyce and Eliot, she eschews the mythic and portentous for the common and domestic within a narrowly prescribed social scene. Accustomed to the scale and grandeur of Joyce's *Ulysses* or Eliot's *Waste Land,* readers are apt to overlook Woolf's tough-mindedness because her scale is so small and her setting so ordinary, but she does in little what they do at large. Her self-imposed limitation is precisely her strength because it provides the basis for her satire: the gap between the cozy little scene and an appalling universe.

The stringent severity of Woolf's satire springs precisely from her capacity to distance herself from her characters. The capacity for self-detachment was one which she had supremely, according to those who knew her personally, and it was the source of that fun and gaiety they all remark as her most identifying characteristic. Elizabeth Bowen recalls her "whoops of laughter," while Clive Bell affirms that "she was about the gayest human being I have known."[8] E. M. Forster writes, importantly, that she escaped mere aestheticism "because she liked writing for fun" and because "she was tough; sensitive but tough." Christopher Isherwood remembers her "delicate malice" in parodying

6. *Collected Essays,* II, 107.
7. *A Writer's Diary,* (Wednesday, May 31, 1933), p. 201.
8. See *Recollections of Virginia Woolf* (ed. Joan Russell Noble): Bowen, p. 49; Bell, p. 71; Forster, pp. 185, 187; Isherwood, p. 178; Macaulay, p. 165.

others. She was no less incisive in parodying herself. "I think I
shall prepare to be the Grand Old Woman of English Letters,"
she said once to Rose Macaulay, "Or would you like to be?"

It would be remarkable if this mocking gaiety were not also a
primary quality of her work. As Woolf distanced herself further
from her characters than Joyce did, so her characters are more
explicitly parodic, especially of artists and their art. For Woolf
the struggle of the artist to engage "this formidable ancient
enemy . . . this other thing, this truth, this reality," as she writes
in *To the Lighthouse* (L, 236), is a dramatic one, but the drama is
not tragic. It is mock-heroic. Her hero is not a mythic artificer,
but a Miss La Trobe or a Lily Briscoe. Lily, portrait of the artist
as painter, in the midst of her anguish over an empty canvas
knows she is all the same "a skimpy old maid, holding a paint-
brush" (L, 269). Old Carmichael, portrait of the artist as poet,
doesn't write but dozes in alcoholic slumber. Jacob Flanders,
portrait of the Joycean aesthete, wanders about the Parthenon
having epiphanies, completely unaware of the "hook" of Sandra
Wentworth Williams "dragging in his side" (JR, 147).

Woolf's Bernard in *The Waves* repudiates the grand overview
of the divine creator evoked by Joyce's Daedelus. "It is the
panorama of life, seen not from the roof," Bernard explains,
"but from the third story window that delights me" (W, 242).
Bernard seeks the limited perspective of a third-story man for
whom "the little language is enough." The little language is the
language Woolf demonstrates in action in *Between the Acts*. The
Joycean device of a hidden narrator, what Woolf calls "the other
voice speaking, the voice that was no one's voice" (BA, 181),
Woolf comically unmasks as the "megaphonic, anonymous"
bray (BA, 186) of Miss La Trobe hidden in the shrubbery. Miss
La Trobe is a portrait of the artist as dramatist.

Rather than the triumphs of art, here as elsewhere Woolf de-
picts the failures of art in man's endless struggle with meaning.
While glory possesses Miss La Trobe for an instant, her triumph
is only in the giving, not the gift — and after? " 'A failure,' she
groaned, and stooped to put away the records" (BA, 209).
Armed in his seedy weaponry of words, man confronts the universe. For Woolf the moment is terrifying, touching, and
ridiculous. Woolf's comedy is more satiric than Austen's, for she
sees her characters as a group in a grotesque universe. As
Woolf's "realism" is the basis of her satire, so her pessimism is

the basis of her gaiety. To incarnate the contingent and absurd in the most humble and commonplace object or most ordinary moment of daily life is Woolf's artistic task and one which she regards with wry amusement.

II

Finished with the "huge burden" of *The Years* and launched on her biography of Roger Fry, Woolf notes in her *Diary* (April 26, 1938) an idea for a new novel:

> But to amuse myself, let me note: Why not *Poynzet Hall:* a centre: all literature discussed in connection with real little incongruous living humour: and anything that comes into my head; but 'I' rejected: 'We' substituted: to whom at the end there shall be an invocation? 'We' . . . the composed of many things . . . we all life, all art, all waifs and strays — a rambling capricious but somehow unified whole — the present state of my mind? And English country; and a scenic old house — and a terrace where nursemaids walk — and people passing — and a perpetual variety and change from intensity to prose, and facts — and notes; and — but eno'![9]

The novel that became *Between the Acts* began with the wish "to amuse myself" and to distill all literature into "real little incongruous living humour." True to this aim, Woolf caricatures the process of writing a play and a novel and in so doing changes the title from a place to a pun. She then structures her novel on the pun of the Interval, on what happens *between* the acts.

By punning on several meanings of the Interval as a pause or gap, Woolf exposes impossible likenesses between unlike things. First, the Interval means the dramatic intermission between pageant scenes, which enables Woolf to equate performances on the stage and off, to equate the staged melodrama of the pageant and the soap-opera lives of the people at Pointz Hall. Second, the Interval equates dramatic and narrative modes so that, by framing a play within a novel, Woolf makes each mode of action an "Interval" of the other. The peculiarity of both actions, however, is that while everybody comes and everybody goes, nothing happens — several times. Third, the Interval equates action and inaction by suggesting a permanent intermission where nothing *can* happen. Finally, the Interval in its musical sense

---

9. *A Writer's Diary,* pp. 279–280.

equates melody, or a distance in pitch between notes sounded successively, with harmony, where notes are sounded simultaneously. By punning on the musical meanings of the Interval, Woolf equates opposite organizing systems, systems of time, of narrative, and of language. All these meanings conflate in the Interval as a punning symbol of the inherent gap between the word and reality, a gap Woolf images as an abyss of emptiness and silence at the center.

Woolf makes the entire theatrical pageant into a structural pun which exposes the gap between nature and art. Nowhere is the comic incongruity of human existence better exposed than in "the pageant of the theater" envisaged earlier by Bernard in *The Waves:*

> The clay-coloured, earthy nondescript animal of the field here erects himself and with infinite ingenuity and effort puts up a fight against the green woods and green fields and sheep advancing with measured tread, munching. (W, 270)

The village pageant of *Between the Acts* is just such a ludicrous drama, staged against a pastoral backdrop that renders the posturings of the human animal comically and pathetically irrelevant. In *Between the Acts* Woolf renders the pageant in a ludicrous mixture of voices, "a mellay; a medley" (BA, 93), as if she had picked up a cue from Santayana's description of existence in *Soliloquies* as "a medley improvised."[10] Her pageant is also a ludicrous mixture of dramatic kinds in which she burlesques the entire tradition of English pastoral tragicomedy. By presenting pastoral drama enacted by real village yokels and real munching sheep, she satirizes her own "mungrel" form.

Woolf's instinct for drama is rooted in the same instinct for detachment that generates her comedy, but not until this last novel does she exploit fully the idea of the drama to objectify what she refers to as "the present state of my mind." Throughout her novels Woolf's imagination is "dramatic." She sees life as conflict and art as dialectic: she orders oppositions in the way that drama does by juxtaposing opposite points of view, opposite styles, and opposite worlds. Her mode is the mode of

---

10. Santayana, *Soliloquies in England and Later Soliloquies* (New York: Scribner's, 1922), p. 142. Another of Santayana's formulations in this essay seems especially relevant to *Between the Acts:* "All nature is lyrical in its ideal essence, tragic in its fate, and comic in its existence."

tragicomedy in which detachment counters involvement, laughter counters tears. In *The Waves* Bernard explains that "on the outskirts of every agony sits some observant fellow who points" (W, 248), so that we are never fully merged in our own experiences. The observant fellow may be the narrator who points overtly, as in the little dramatic scene with which Woolf ends *The Years*. Here the children of the caretaker sing an unintelligible song in an accent so hideous that "the grown-up people did not know whether to laugh or to cry" (Y, 430). Or the observant fellow may be objectified in dramatis personae. In *Between the Acts* the audience does not know whether to laugh or cry at the amateur performers and so it does both.

"Real little living incongruous humour" is the nature of the dramatic act since, as Shakespeare never tires of reminding us, even the best in this kind parody in performance the drama they enact. Since the gap, or interval, between a live performer and his symbolic role is the inherent limitation and glory of the drama, amateur theatricals merely expose what professionals attempt to conceal. In Woolf's village pageant, infant England is ludicrously embodied in little Phyllis Jones, who forgets her lines and thrice repeats *"England am I"* until Mrs. Swithin is provoked to ask, " 'England? That little girl?' " (BA, 79). When Eliza Clark the tobacconist impersonates Queen Elizabeth, the audience at Pointz Hall naturally laughs, just as the audience at Theseus' court laughed at performers very like Eliza the tobacconist, Budge the publican, and Hilda the carpenter's daughter. From the nursery entertainments of the Stephens' children performed for the downstairs maids — "Denizens of the kitchen, Come in your thousands!!"[11] — to Woolf's adult entertainment *Freshwater: A Comedy in Three Acts,* Woolf saw in dramatic performance an emblem of comic incongruity. In *Between the Acts* she makes dramatic performance a metaphor for every human action.

III

Woolf exposes the innate absurdity in any dramatic convention in the gaucheries of La Trobe's performers. Her pageant, which misrepresents the history of England through its drama in

---

11. See Bell, *Virginia Woolf,* I, 22 – 29.

four merry and tragical, tedious and brief acts, is funny and awful and touching, all at once. It moves by fits and starts; it aborts in every scene and as a whole. The comic climax of the pageant, which occurs in the first scene of Merry England, dissolves in such a roar of " 'Laughter, loud laughter' " (BA, 85) that neither words nor plot can be understood. We are told that the plot is nothing, and it is clear that satiric allusion is everything. The Elizabethan device of the play-within-the-play is squeezed into a moment's "recognition scene," where an old beldam sees the mole on her child and drops dead. The dancing spheres of the Elizabethan cosmos are reified in the dancing of the village clodhoppers about the still point of Mrs. Clark: "Hands joined, heads knocking, they danced round the majestic figure of the Elizabethan age personified by Mrs. Clark, licensed to sell tobacco, on her soap box" (BA, 93). While La Trobe the dramatist agonizes, Woolf the narrator points. She points to exaggerated pastoral conventions that make birds chuckle like people and people laugh like startled jays.

Through the second scene of Restoration burlesque, "Where There's a Will There's a Way," Woolf enlarges her parody of dramatic conventions in the manner of John Gay's *What D'Ye Call It? A Tragical-Comical-Pastoral Farce*. Again La Trobe agonizes at the tea break which interrupts the plottings of Lady Harpy Harraden and Sir Spaniel Lilyliver and causes someone to remark, " 'All that fuss about nothing!' " (BA, 138). La Trobe suffers death because the illusion failed. But Woolf the narrator points to the way in which Nature steps in to fill the gap, not with sheep munching but with cows bellowing: "The cows annihilated the gap; bridged the distance; filled the emptiness and continued the emotion" (BA, 140–141). Woolf then points to the fallaciousness of the "pathetic fallacy" in her bovine chorus: "It was the primeval voice sounding loud in the ear of the present moment" (BA, 140).

In the Victorian melodrama which furnishes the third scene, Woolf sends up the same plot in the mode of sentiment and aborts La Trobe's dramatic climax spectacularly. In the midst of the patriarch's prayer, Nature grossly intrudes: Albert the idiot, impersonating the rear end of a donkey, gives too real a performance — "Intentional was it, or accidental?" (BA, 171). La Trobe's dramatic climax similarly aborts when she holds real mirrors up to Nature. The extended emptiness and silence of

" 'the present time. Ourselves,' " in which the playwright "douches" the audience with its own "present-time reality" (BA, 178–179), prove that reality is too much for both audience and playwright: "Blood seemed to pour from her shoes. This is death, death, death, she noted in the margin of her mind; when illusion fails" (BA, 180). Nature in sympathy "douches" the audience with a thundershower to salvage the failures of fiction with real rain: "Down it poured like all the people in the world weeping. Tears, Tears, Tears" (BA, 180). Communal laughter of the past is displaced by communal tears of the present. But this is tragicomedy in the little language. The anonymous voice that bridges the gap between comedy and tragedy, as between art and nature, is the sound of the gramophone, and the gramophone plays a nursery rhyme:

> The King is in his counting house
> Counting out his money,
> The Queen is in her parlour . . .

By flagrantly baring the devices of drama, Woolf satirizes her own devices of narrative. She ridicules her own shaping rhythms in the gurgling of the gramophone. She ridicules her own distorting images in the fragments of tin cans and scullery glass. She ridicules finally her own structural analogies between play and poem in the figure of the Rev. G. W. Streatfield: "Of all incongruous sights a clergyman in the livery of his servitude to the summing up was the most grotesque and entire" (BA, 190). As the climactic action of this pageant is one in which nothing happens, so the peroration is delivered by one incapable of speech. He is thus a fit spokesman for mankind: "their symbol; themselves; a butt, a clod, laughed at by looking-glasses; ignored by the cows, condemned by the clouds . . . an irrelevant forked stake in the flow and majesty of the summer silent world" (BA, 190–191). Unaccommodated man is not Lear but a village curate who gives over the struggle with language and submits to "the natural desire of the natural man" for tobacco.

IV

Acting out their own unacted parts, the inhabitants of Pointz Hall invest themselves in theatrical roles as incongruous as those of the rustic performers. Vulgar Mrs. Manresa, oversexed and overdressed, commands the terrace as Great Eliza does the stage: "Radiating royalty, complacency, good humour, the wild child was Queen of the Festival" (BA, 79). Isa, incapable of passion, stages her own Keatsian drama in the greenhouse: "And from her bosom's snowy antre drew the gleaming blade. 'Plunge blade!' she said. And struck" (BA, 113). Mrs. Swithin, called Old Flimsy and sometimes Batty by the villagers, cries at the play's end, " 'I might have been — Cleopatra' " (BA, 153).

Like the stage performances, their lives abort ludicrously, not tragically. At the center of Pointz Hall there is also a gap — a permanent stasis: "They were all caught and caged; prisoners; watching a spectacle. Nothing happened" (BA, 176). Each is caught in a polarity of love and hate. Old Bart and Lucy, brother and sister, act out eternally the arguments of Reason and Faith. Giles and Isa, husband and wife, act out eternally the dialectic of Flesh and Imagination: he violent, without words or metaphor; she all scraps and tags of poetry, disembodied and disengaged — " 'Abortive,' was the word that expressed her" (BA, 15). The diagram of complementary and warring opposites which distances the family members as a group is completed by the outsiders. Mrs. Manresa is "all sensation" (BA, 202), all erotic sexuality, while William Dodge is all aesthetic and homoerotic.

For the audience the Intervals of the pageant constitute a comic-pathetic waiting, as if for Godot. William wishes to kneel before Lucy and receive absolution, but Lucy cannot even remember his name. " 'I'm William' " (BA, 206), he repeats, as little Phyllis Jones had repeated " 'England am I.' " Isa and Dodge long for some kind of intimate encounter but can only chatter in the greenhouse. Frustration, failure, incompletion, regret — these are the ties that bind the characters in their mutual and inevitable separation from cradle to grave. Distinctions between cradle and grave are illusory, as Woolf makes clear in an image for Old Bart's regret at the departure of Mrs. Manresa: in her passing she "ripped the rag doll and let the sawdust stream from his heart" (BA, 202). Distinctions between time are also illusory, as Woolf in this same image condenses and completes an aborted action which opened her narrative. Wearing a beak of paper, Old Bart had intended to make his grandson laugh. Instead, the joke aborted and George cried. Another tragicomedy in the little language.

In portraying the tragicomic performances of the spectators, Woolf exposes the arbitrary conventions of life as she had those of the stage. "Surely it was time someone invented a new plot, or that the author came out from the bushes . . ." (BA, 215). The center of the house, like the center of the play, is a terrifying vacuum:

> Empty, empty, empty; silent, silent, silent. The room was a shell, singing of what was before time was; a vase stood in the heart of the house, alabaster, smooth, cold, holding the still, distilled essence of emptiness, silence. (BA, 36–37)

The vase, symbolic of art, within a room, symbolic of life — both distill images of the abyss at the center of consciousness and of reality. It is the death suffered by Miss La Trobe "when the illusion fails." It is the death the maid sees in the lily pond at Pointz Hall: "It was in that deep center, in that black heart, that the lady had drowned herself" (BA, 44). It is the death of individual consciousness and meaning imaged by Woolf in the darkness of a stony sky: "blue, pure blue, black blue; blue that had never filtered down; that had escaped registration" (BA, 23).

Woolf uses Pointz Hall as an organizing metaphor, like the metaphor of the play, to embody a symbolic center and a symbolic moment. Her method here of using an actual place or social occasion as a symbolic point for illuminating and unmasking a reality empty of content is one she employs throughout her fiction. There is Jacob's empty room, Mrs. Ramsay's empty house, the emptiness at the center of Mrs. Dalloway's dinner party or the family reunion of the Pargiters. Aborted lives and violent deaths are at the center of these particularized places and gatherings. A place, an occasion, a dramatic scene are ways of objectifying that interior center which Woolf calls "a knot of consciousness."[12] In her *Diary* entry of January 19, 1935, Woolf wrote that she had "an idea for a 'play.' Summer's night. Someone on a seat. And voices speaking from flowers." In her brief piece "The Moment: Summer's Night," she projects a moment of illumination; but she doesn't carry out the idea of the play to dramatize the disparities that characterize her knot of consciousness until *Between the Acts*.

The play, and drama's peculiar way of misrepresenting the symbolic by the actual, furnishes Woolf with a model for other

---

12. *Collected Essays*, II, 294.

forms of misrepresentation. Human perception of time and its changes involves similar misrepresentations of "mind time" by "actual time." History for Woolf is a form of fiction like the drama, for it is subject to the particular insight and blindness, the deforming interpretations, of each generation. Here is how the narrator of *Orlando* explains the Elizabethans: "Of our crepuscular half-lights and lingering twilights they knew nothing. The rain fell vehemently, or not at all" (O, 27). In *Between the Acts* Woolf splits up the knot of consciousness in differing characters in order to register the comic and horrible disparities of perception. Isa, for example, can see and hear only eternal recurrence: "Isa heard the first chime; and the second; and the third — If it was wet, it would be in the Barn; if it was fine on the terrace. And which would it be, wet or fine?" (BA, 46). Old Lucy, on the other hand, reading her Outline of History, can imagine only an eternal present, which creates odd juxtapositions: "There were rhododendrons in the Strand; and mammoths in Piccadilly" (BA, 30).

V

Woolf's continued experimentation with fictional form springs from her desire to render the conflicts of daily life fully, in their odd mixture of the actual and the imaginary. While writing *The Years,* she asks, "I mean how give ordinary waking Arnold Bennett life the form of art?" She wanted the novel to embody in its own form the heightened oppositions of drama, to express both "immense breadth and immense intensity," both the "I; and the not I; and the outer and the inner."[13] While the prose novel leisurely accumulates the prosaic details of ordinary life, the poetic drama contracts, generalizes, and heightens through its more rigorous artifice.[14] She thought she had found a model for her lyric and dramatic narrative aims in the language of the Elizabethan play, because to her the play combined the symbolic density of poetry with the flexibility and speed of living speech.

Each of her novels presents a partial solution to her need to construct a mongrel form of fiction that, like the mongrel form

13. *A Writer's Diary,* pp. 191, 201, 250.
14. "Notes on an Elizabethan Play," *Collected Essays,* I, 58.

of tragicomedy, would connect incongruous fictive modes without sacrificing the unique advantages of each. After finishing *To the Lighthouse,* she writes in her *Diary* that she wants to invent a new kind of play: "Away from facts; free; yet concentrated; prose yet poetry; a novel and a play." This new kind becomes the "play-poem idea," which she first mentions while mulling over the story that became *The Waves.*[15] The "play-poem idea" as she works it out in her final three novels incorporates the organizing rhythms of poetry with the objectified personae of drama, splitting up the emotion and incarnating it in "dramatic" voices, though they necessarily remain narrative voices.

The Waves and *The Years,* the one leaning toward poetic "fiction," the other toward prosaic "fact," represent nearly opposite versions of the final satiric synthesis of *Between the Acts.* Despite the "dramatic soliloquies" of *The Waves,* this novel is perhaps the least "dramatic" of her fictions since each of the characters is isolated in narrative monologues. She has split up the act of narration into characters, but each character tells his own story or writes his own novel in succession.[16] *The Years,* in contrast, presents a succession of dramatic scenes, but again the novel as a whole is "undramatic" because the narrative chronicling of the family dynasty is far too long to strike the single definite impression that drama or even "dramatic" narrative must do through compression. Not until *Between the Acts* does she structure her narrative wholly on the incongruities of dramatic performance and on the incongruous juxtaposition of "dramatic" voices.

In *Between the Acts* she flaunts the element of fictional masquerade by pretending that her fictions are "facts." In rejecting the narrative "I" for the dramatic "we," she finds a device for registering the quiddity of each separate thing and at the same time for unifying the "mellay" by giving each queer thing its own queer voice:

---

15. *A Writer's Diary,* pp. 103, 107.
16. In *The Waves,* Woolf carries out the dramatic idea less by juxtaposing one soliloquy with another than by juxtaposing narrative monologues with the interludes of lyric prose. Curiously, she repeats the device of Sidney's *Arcadia* that she notes in her essay "The Countess of Pembroke's Arcadia." She remarks there that Sidney uses prose for the generalized, expanded emotions and settings of his romance; he uses verse when he wishes "to sum up, to strike hard," so that his verse performs "something of the function of dialogue in the modern novel"; *Collected Essays,* I, 24.

276 B. H. FUSSELL

> For me Shakespeare sang —
> (a cow mooed. A bird twittered)
> (BA, 84)

Translating these disparate things into lyric voices, she first organizes them in the "regular, recurrent beat" of poetry and then dramatizes them by the pretense of an objective voice that is "no one's voice" because it is everyone's voice.[17] Through the encompassing rhythm of these voices, she makes the inner world of the imagination and the outer world of actuality reciprocal. But she also satirizes the oddity of her own device. The cough of cows and the chuckle of birds, for example, merge in the "chuff, chuff, chuff" (BA, 195) of the gramophone. The music of the spheres and the voice of the bard are sounded by a machine wheezing in the bushes, a machine which runs down with aggravating frequency and which reduces the music of time to a meaningless stutter. Woolf's gramophonic rhythm is that "rhythm of beauty" by which Stephen Daedelus defined art — the cry, cadence, or mood which "finally refines itself out of existence." In Woolf's parody, the rhythm of beauty is the sound of God paring his fingernails with blunt scissors.

Through the jogging metrics of La Trobe's play, Woolf creates a playful and parodic universe of rhyme. Like the structural puns on "Interval," the sustained rhymes uncover surprising "identities" in radically unlike things. Sights are made to rhyme with sounds: "The view repeated in its own way what the tune was saying" (BA, 134). The pageant is made to rhyme with the landscape, and the audience is made to rhyme with the view. People rhyme with cows: the cows "lowered their heads, and began browsing. Simultaneously the audience lowered their heads and read their programmes" (BA, 141).

Woolf's rhyming rhythm is a highly self-conscious device of wit to bridge the gap between play and poem: the play acts out the poem, the poem voices the play. Woolf's trick is to expose the figurative basis of language on which art and perception of any kind depend. La Trobe's perception is governed entirely by the trope of drama, wherein she automatically converts the grounds of Pointz Hall into " 'the very place for a pageant!' " Isa's perception is governed entirely by the rhymes of poetry:

---

17. In "How Should One Read a Book?" Woolf notes how quickly a reader tires of novels of "fact" because "facts are a very inferior form of fiction"; Collected Essays, I, 6.

"But somewhere, this cloud, this crust, this doubt, this dust —
She waited for a rhyme, it failed her . . ." (BA, 61). As Woolf
parodies the art of the play through La Trobe, so she parodies the
art of the poem through Isa.

Woolf's rhyming of the emotional with the banal, the gran-
diose with the trivial, produces some curious effects. Lucy, noting the resemblance of Mrs. Sands's name to the cook's action of
cutting sandwiches, remembers her mother's warning: " 'Never
play . . . on people's names' " (BA, 33). But the play on names
is part of the narrated action: "Mrs. Sands fetched bread; Mrs.
Swithin fetched ham. One cut the bread; the other the ham" (BA,
34). As they fetch and cut, Lucy's associative mind links yeast to
alcohol to inebriation to Bacchus; Sands's more empirical mind
links the tick of a clock and the sight of a cat to the buzz of a fly.
Inner and outer worlds, facts and fictions, are thus impossibly
linked: when Mrs. Sands remarks on the misbehavior of her
nephew, Mrs. Swithin responds, " 'That'll be all right' . . . half
meaning the boy, half meaning the sandwich" (BA, 35).

This incongruous rhyming produces effects of horror as
well as wit. A single example may serve to illustrate Woolf's
somewhat Proustian method of clustering associations around
a concrete object of daily use. She links a number of seemingly disconnected passages by associating savage violence with
an ordinary household tool, the hammer that Lucy first uses to
nail the placard to the barn. When later Isa reads about a girl
attacked by a trooper, she imagines the scene so vividly that she
sees on the library panels the girl screaming and hitting her
attacker — "when the door . . . opened and in came Mrs.
Swithin carrying a hammer" (BA, 20). Next, when Lucy puts
the hammer back in the cupboard by the fishing tackle, she
remembers how her brother had made her take a fish from a
hook and how "the blood had shocked her" (BA, 21). Moments
later Isa hears beneath the chime of bells another sound: " 'The
girl screamed and hit him about the face with a hammer' " (BA,
22). The hammer becomes an objectified symbol of violence like
a dramatic property on a stage. The blows of a hammer link the
quarrels of Lucy and her brother ("once more he struck a blow at
her faith" [BA, 25]) to Mrs. Manresa's sexual aggression ("so
with blow after blow, with champagne and ogling, she staked
out her claim to be a wild child of nature" [BA, 41]). Similarly,
the action of repeated striking links the brutality of Giles, who

stamps on a snake until his tennis shoes are soaked with blood,
to the brutal destruction of artistic illusion experienced by La
Trobe when she felt blood pouring from her shoes.

VI

In analyzing the demands of the play, Woolf writes that "the
play demands coming to the surface — hence insists upon a reality which the novel need not have . . ."[18] This objective "surface," where everything is made public and physical, belongs to
"the intolerable restrictions of drama"[19] which provide at the
same time drama's special privileges: "Always the door opens
and someone comes in. All is shared, made visible, audible,
dramatic."[20] While the stage demands a preposterous embodiment in the actual, it is granted the special illusion of immediacy,
contracting imaginary times and places into a specific here and
now. As all plots can seem to be reenacted in the plot fragments
of the pageant and all English history condensed into its scenes,
so all performers and audiences can seem to be reassembled at
Pointz Hall: " 'Adsum; I'm here, in place of my grandfather or
great-grandfather' . . . At this very moment, half-past three on
a June day in 1939 . . ." (BA, 75). Woolf uses the analogy of
dramatic "surface" to contract into narrative the glories of an
imagined past shrunk to the dimensions of the present. The
result characterizes her satiric style as mock-epic.

To translate the inner world of the imagination into a public
and physical reality is to embody the visionary in feet of clay —
specifically, as in The Years, in "two large feet, in tight shoes, so
that the bunions showed."[21] Or in Jacob's Room in the pair of old
shoes that Mrs. Flanders brings in to interrupt Bonamy's contemplation of eighteenth-century architecture. In other words,
the anomalies of mock-epic are like the anomalies of performed
drama. One indecorum reflects another: the indecorum of ele-

18. A Writer's Diary, pp. 208–209.
19. "On Not Knowing Greek," Essays, I, 5. In this important essay, Woolf
    claims that the novelist seeks devices for replacing the chorus of Greek
    drama and describes the chorus as an anonymous voice: "The undifferen-
    tiated voices who sing like birds in the wind."
20. "Notes on an Elizabethan Play," Essays, I, 61.
21. In The Years, p. 390. Peggy's vision of an owl's white wing in the evening
    with country people singing "became distinct" in these feet in these shoes.

gant architecture and old shoes reflects the larger indecorum of civilization's artifices and nature's gross actualities.

Through such indecorums Woolf creates a series of parlor pastorals and domestic heroics. Her strategy allows a double effect: seriocomic deflation and ennoblement, both at once or separately. In *Jacob's Room,* which is an extended Ode to the City of London, she both apostrophizes the city at dawn and places it in a comic perspective by alluding to the dawn of civilization: "The Bank of England emerges; and the Monument with its bristling head of golden hair" (JR, 163). A similar effect occurs in Jacob's meditation on Clara Durrant: "A flawless mind; a candid nature; a virgin chained to a rock (somewhere off Lowndes Square) . . ." (JR, 123). Andromeda squeezed into Clara Durrant exploits the indecorum of mock-epic simile which Woolf employs fully in *Mrs. Dalloway,* as in the reunion of Clarissa (aptly named) with Peter Walsh:

> 'Well, and what's happened to you?' she said. So before a battle begins, the horses paw the ground; toss their heads; the light shines on their flanks; their necks curve. So Peter Walsh and Clarissa, sitting side by side on the blue sofa, challenged each other. (D, 66)

So consistently does Woolf use the formula of Homeric simile in this vein that she can invest Clarissa's every act with Argive allusion:

> Now it was time to move, and, as a woman gathers her things together, her cloak, her gloves, her opera-glasses, and gets up to go out of the theatre into the street, she rose from the sofa and went to Peter. (D, 71)

The trivia of ordinary waking reality bear willy-nilly the enhancing and humiliating burden of the imagined past. But so it has always been. Past and present share alike in the vast disproportion between change and essence crystallized in any single moment. This is the oddity of consciousness that Woolf attempts to capture by shuffling continuously between sympathy and irony in order to render "the moment whole." So Betty Flanders, hearing the boom of the guns which have killed Jacob, thinks to herself,

> There was Morty lost, and Seabrook dead; her sons fighting for their country. But were the chickens safe? Was that someone moving

downstairs? Rebecca with the toothache? No. The nocturnal women
were beating great carpets. Her hens shifted slightly on their perches.
(JR, 75)

Mingling chickens with dead sons, toothaches with mythic
shadows, Woolf amalgamates the imaginary and the actual to
reveal the oddities of both. The same peculiar mixture of tone
colors the ending of *To the Lighthouse,* when Mr. Ramsay at last
completes his Odyssean voyage to the island and demands
of his children an ultimate sacrifice — " 'Bring those parcels' "
(L, 308). Completing the submerged classical-Christian allusion,
Lily Briscoe completes the comic irony, " 'He has landed,' " she
says, " 'It is finished' " (L, 309).

Because incongruity is the source of both deflation and enlargement, Woolf can turn the same weapon of the grotesque
toward comedy or tragedy. In *Mrs. Dalloway,* for example, Peter
Walsh is comic when he yokes people to vegetables: " 'I prefer
men to cauliflowers' " (D, 4); but a similar yoking provokes
quite different effects when Septimus finds terror in "the plate of
bananas on the sideboard" (D, 220). The humblest item is revealing. So Bernard at the end of *The Waves* finds "disorder, sordid-
ity and corruption" in breadcrumbs, stained napkins, and the
remains of dead birds: "It is with these greasy crumbs, slobbered
over napkins, and little corpses that we have to build" (W, 292).
In Woolf's little tragicomedies, the struggle with the enemy includes calling the waiter and paying the bill.

VII

In her final novel Woolf compresses and enlarges these earlier
effects to create monstrosities. The summer's night and the
voices of "The Moment" reappear in the opening scene of *Between the Acts,* but the people talking are transmogrified into
creatures like Mrs. Haines, "a goosefaced woman with eyes
protruding as if they saw something to gobble in the gutter"
(BA, 3) and what the people are talking about is —— "the
cesspool." The words of people talking undergo the most
grotesque metamorphoses of all. Words become actors in the
pageant of existence: "Words this afternoon ceased to lie flat in
the sentence. They rose, became menacing and shook their fists
at you" (BA, 59). Words are threatening, comic, and hopelessly

inadequate: " 'We haven't the words — we haven't the words' " (BA, 55). The gap "between the word and the reality" that Nicholas perceives in *The Years* broadens in *Between the Acts* to a wordless sound that follows the command of the anonymous voice to "break the rhythm and forget the rhyme" (BA, 187). The machine of the gramophone is a deus-ex-machina providing a mock resolution: "from chaos and cacophony measure; but not the melody of surface sound alone controlled it; but also the warring battle-plumed warriors straining asunder . . ." (BA, 189). Cacophonous harmony in heroic imagery, yes, but typically Woolf concludes with a fall into animal reality: "And some relaxed their fingers; and others uncrossed their legs."

Satiric deflation informs the simile which follows the uncrossing of legs:

> As waves withdrawing uncover; as mist uplifting reveals; so, raising their eyes (Mrs. Manresa's were wet; for an instant tears ravaged her powder) they saw, as waters withdrawing leave visible a tramp's old boot, a man in a clergyman's collar surreptitiously mounting a soapbox. (BA, 189)

In the image of the clergyman as an old boot left by the tide, Woolf brings together two of her major symbols for Nature and art, the sea and the play. The sea, like Pointz Hall, is a symbolic center analogous to that of the play, but it is a more ominous center of darkness from which the artist compels measure by language. "As if," Woolf says of the Elizabethan dramatists, "thought plunged into a sea of words and came up dripping."[22] The sea provides an underwater world which corresponds to the autonomous worlds of the play and the poem.

In *Between the Acts,* Woolf turns comic metamorphoses into terrifying ones through a sort of universal "fish rhyme." Isa at her dressing table murmurs, " 'Flying, rushing through the ambient, incandescent, summer silent' " — the rhyme, she thinks, was " 'air' " (BA, 15). But she leaves the rhyme incomplete and instead picks up the telephone: " 'What fish have you this morning? Cod? Halibut? Sole? Plaice?' " Her inner voice completes the order, " 'Soles. Filleted.' " Filet of sole ludicrously "rhymes" with air. Mrs. Swithin makes a fish rhyme when she traces the sequence of her thoughts and counts on her fingers, " 'The Pharoahs. Dentist. Fish' " (BA, 31). Isa, while lunching on the

---

22. *Collected Essays,* I, 60.

sole, remembers falling in love with Giles when "the salmon had leapt, had been caught, and she had loved him" (BA, 48). Fish "rhymes" with love.

Symbolic of Nature, the sea subsumes the play, symbolic of art. The sea is that obdurate enemy, reality, that escapes human registration. When La Trobe images the terror of her artistic isolation in a vision of drowning ("from the earth green waters seemed to rise over her" [BA, 210]), she seeks consolation in the pub:

> Words of one syllable sank down into the mud. She drowsed; she nodded. The mud became fertile. Words rose above the intolerably laden dumb oxen plodding through the mud. Words without meaning — wonderful words. (BA, 212)

In this cycle of exhaustion and renewal of the creative act, the mud that is man ludicrously imitates the initial act of his own creation from primeval mud. The mud in which old Bossy struggles is the mud of night primeval and of chaos old — "the night that dwellers in caves had watched from some high place among rocks" (BA, 219) and that resurfaces in the ancient drama of love and hate enacted by Giles and Isa "in the heart of darkness, in the fields of night."

The mud made fertile begins the cycles anew — the cycles of the human drama ("then the curtain rose. They spoke" [BA, 219]), of day and night, of civilization and chaos. Woolf alludes by satiric indirection to those correspondences of little and larger worlds that the Elizabethan age mirrored in its drama and that, by contrast, confirm the loss of a shared vision in the present. Woolf attempted to simulate a shared vision by invoking the Elizabethan play, but the actuality of such a vision was impossible.

In her *Diary* of February 26, 1941, she writes: "My 'higher life' is almost entirely the Elizabethan play. Finished Pointz Hall, the Pageant; the play — finally *Between the Acts* this morning."[23] Her successive retitling of her final novel suggests that she had in the process of writing it refined herself out of existence. Her struggle to escape the isolation of the artist in a solipsistic universe was no less intense than that of Joyce before her or Samuel Beckett after. The extremity of the modern dilemma has seemed to provoke extreme "solutions," both in art and in life. Joyce

23. *A Writer's Diary*, p. 351.

ended with the logorrhea of *Finnegan's Wake,* Beckett composed the 60-second silence of *Breath.* Woolf ended with the emptiness and silence of the Interval between the acts. "The writing 'I' has vanished," she wrote in her *Diary* while completing the novel, "No audience. No echo. That's part of one's death."[24] The struggle to bridge the gap between art and life and to live in both spheres was, as Woolf put it, "a strain."[25] Though she ended the strain by translating the imagined actions of her fiction into tragic fact, she did so with an irony that is gay as well as grim. In the final entry of her *Diary* on March 8, 1941, before the green waters rose above her, she "rhymed" fish with art. "Haddock and sausage meat," she wrote. "I think it is true that one gains a certain hold on sausage and haddock by writing them down."[26]

---

24. Ibid., p. 323.   25. Ibid., p. 203.   26. Ibid., p. 351.

Contributors

MARIA DiBATTISTA has written on Cervantes and Molière and has recently completed a book-length study of problems of narrative authority in the major novels of Virginia Woof which will be published by the Yale University Press. She teaches English at Princeton University.

AVROM FLEISHMAN is Professor of English at Johns Hopkins University and the author of several books on Victorian and modern literature. His *Virginia Woolf: A Critical Reading* won the Explicator Prize as the best work of explication for 1975–76. His latest book is *Fiction and the Ways of Knowing: Essays on British Novels,* to be published in 1979.

RALPH FREEDMAN has written *The Lyrical Novel: Studies in Hermann Hesse, André Gide, and Virginia Woolf,* a biography, *Hermann Hesse: Pilgrim of Crisis,* and numerous articles on modern English and continental literature and criticism. He teaches comparative literature at Princeton.

B. H. FUSSELL, who teaches at the New School for Social Research, has written on the relation between comedy and dramatic form in contemporary literature in *Hudson Review,* the *New York Literary Forum, Sewanee Review, ELH,* and elsewhere.

JAMES HAFLEY is the author of *The Glass Roof: Virginia Woolf as Novelist* and a number of other studies in English and American literature. He is Professor of English at St. John's University in New York.

JEAN O. LOVE is Professor of Psychology at Lebanon Valley College in Annville, Pennsylvania. She is the author of several books on Virginia Woolf, including *Worlds in Consciousness: Mythopoetic Thought in the Novels of Virginia Woolf* and the first volume of a two-volume work, *Virginia Woolf: Sources of Madness and Art* (1978). Her contribution to the present book forms part of the second volume, which will appear in 1979.

JANE MARCUS was a Research Fellow of the National Endowment for the Humanities in 1977–78. She is an editor of and frequent contributor to the *Virginia Woolf Miscellany,* and has written on Woolf's politics for *Women's Studies, Feminist Studies,* and other journals.

She is the editor of a forthcoming collection of feminist essays on Virginia Woolf, *Virginia Woolf A/Slant*, and is currently editing the letters of Ethel Smyth.

FREDERICK P. W. MCDOWELL is Professor of English at the University of Iowa and has published widely on George Bernard Shaw, E. M. Forster, and many other nineteenth- and twentieth-century British and American writers; one of his titles is *E. M. Forster: An Annotated Bibliography of Writings about Him* (1977). He has been particularly active in promoting the study of early twentieth-century British literature.

MADELINE MOORE teaches nineteenth- and twentieth-century English and American literature at the University of California, Santa Cruz, where she was one of the founders of the Women's Studies major. She has published articles on Norman Douglas, Joseph Conrad, Jane Austen, and Virginia Woolf, and one of her essays on Woolf, "*The Voyage Out* and Matriarchal Mythologies," will be included in the forthcoming volume edited by Jane Marcus. She is currently completing a book, *The Mystical and the Social in the Works of Virginia Woolf.*

JAMES NAREMORE is the author of *The World Without A Self: Virginia Woolf and the Novel* (1973), as well as numerous articles on literature and film. His latest book is *The Magic World of Orson Welles* (1978). He is Professor of English and Film Studies at Indiana University.

HARVENA RICHTER is a novelist, poet, and critic who has published in many national and international journals. Her books include a novel, *The Human Shore,* and *Virginia Woolf: The Inward Voyage,* originally published in 1970. She teaches a course in Virginia Woolf, as well as creative writing, at the University of New Mexico.

LUCIO RUOTOLO is Professor of English at Stanford University. His book *Six Existentialist Heroes* won Harvard University's Thomas J. Wilson Prize in 1973. He is a founding editor of the *Virginia Woolf Miscellany,* and in 1976 he edited Woolf's comedy *Freshwater* for Harcourt, Brace, while living in Monk's House, Rodmell.

Selected Bibliography

Compiled by MARIA DIBATTISTA

VIRGINIA WOOLF: PRINCIPAL WORKS

The Voyage Out. London: Duckworth, 1915; New York: Doran, 1920; Harcourt, Brace, 1926.

Night and Day. London: Duckworth, 1919; New York: Doran, 1920; New York: Harcourt Brace Jovanovich, 1973.

Monday or Tuesday. Richmond: Hogarth, 1921; New York: Harcourt, Brace, 1921.

Jacob's Room. Richmond: Hogarth, 1922; New York: Harcourt, Brace, 1923.

Mr. Bennett and Mrs. Brown. Hogarth Essays. London: Hogarth, 1924.

The Common Reader. London: Hogarth, 1925; New York: Harcourt, Brace, 1925.

Mrs. Dalloway. London: Hogarth, 1925; New York: Harcourt, Brace, 1925. With Introduction by Virginia Woolf. New York: Random House, Modern Library, 1928.

To the Lighthouse. London: Hogarth, 1927; New York: Harcourt, Brace, 1927. With Introduction by Terence Holl; New York: Random House, Modern Library, 1937.

Orlando: A Biography. London: Hogarth, 1928; New York: Crosby Gaige, 1928; Harcourt, Brace, 1929.

A Room of One's Own. London: Hogarth, 1929; New York: Fountain Press, 1929; Harcourt, Brace, 1929.

The Waves. London: Hogarth, 1931; New York: Harcourt, Brace, 1931.

A Letter to a Young Poet. Hogarth Letters no. 8. London: Hogarth, 1932.

The Common Reader: Second Series. London: Hogarth, 1932; New York: Harcourt, Brace, 1932 (entitled *The Second Common Reader*).

Flush: A Biography. London: Hogarth, 1933; New York: Harcourt, Brace, 1933.

The Years. London: Hogarth, 1937; New York: Harcourt, Brace, 1937.

Three Guineas. London: Hogarth, 1938; New York: Harcourt, Brace, 1938.

Roger Fry: A Biography. London: Hogarth, 1940; New York: Harcourt, Brace, 1940.

Between the Acts. London: Hogarth, 1941; New York: Harcourt, Brace, 1941.

The Death of the Moth and Other Essays. London: Hogarth, 1942; New York: Harcourt, Brace, 1942.

A Haunted House and Other Short Stories. London: Hogarth, 1943; New York: Harcourt, Brace, 1944.

The Moment and Other Essays. London: Hogarth, 1947; New York: Harcourt, Brace, 1948.

The Captain's Death Bed and Other Essays. London: Hogarth, 1950; New York: Harcourt, Brace, 1950.

A Writer's Diary, ed. Leonard Woolf. London: Hogarth, 1953; New York: Harcourt, Brace, 1954.

Virginia Woolf and Lytton Strachey: Letters, ed. Leonard Woolf and James Strachey. London: Hogarth Press with Chatto and Windus, 1956; New York: Harcourt, Brace, 1956.

Granite and Rainbow: Essays. London: Hogarth, 1958; New York: Harcourt, Brace, 1958.

Contemporary Writers, ed. Jean Guiguet. London: Hogarth, 1965; New York: Harcourt, Brace and World, 1966.

Collected Essays. 4 vols. London: Hogarth, 1966–1967; New York: Harcourt, Brace and World, 1967.

Mrs. Dalloway's Party: A Short Story Sequence, ed. with an introduction by Stella McNichol. London: Hogarth, 1973; New York: Harcourt Brace Jovanovich, 1975.

The Letters of Virginia Woolf. Vol. I: 1888–1912 (1975); Vol. II: 1912–1922 (1976); Vol. III: 1923–1928 (1977); Vol. IV: 1929–1931 (1978). Edited by Nigel Nicolson and Joanne Trautmann. New York: Harcourt Brace Jovanovich, 1975 –1978.

Freshwater, ed. Lucio P. Ruotolo. New York: Harcourt Brace Jovanovich, 1976.

Moments of Being: Unpublished Autobiographical Writings, ed. Jeanne Schulkind. Brighton: Sussex University Press, 1976; New York: Harcourt Brace Jovanovich, 1976.

The Waves / Virginia Woolf; The Two Holograph Drafts, transcr. and ed. J. W. Graham. London: Hogarth, 1976.

Books and Portraits, ed. Mary Lyon. London: Hogarth, 1977.

The Pargiters; The Novel-Essay Portion of "The Years," ed. Mitchell A. Leaska. New York: New York Public Library, 1977. London: Hogarth, 1978.

The Diary of Virginia Woolf, ed. Anne Olivier Bell. Vol. I: 1915 –1919 (1977); Vol. II: 1920–1924 (1978). London: Hogarth, 1977–1978; New York: Harcourt Brace Jovanovich, 1977–1978.

Note: The Hogarth Press, London, has kept up to date its Uniform Edition of Virginia Woolf in sixteen volumes.

CRITICAL WORKS

Albright, Daniel. *Personality and Impersonality: Lawrence, Woolf and Mann.* Chicago: University of Chicago Press, 1978.

Alexander, Jean. *The Venture of Form in the Novels of Virginia Woolf.* Port Washington, N.Y.: Kennikat, 1974.

Auerbach, Erich. "The Brown Stocking," *Mimesis,* tr. William Trask. Princeton University Press, 1953.

Bazin, Nancy Topping. *Virginia Woolf and the Androgynous Vision.* New Brunswick, N.J.: Rutgers University Press, 1973.

Beja, Morris, ed. *Virginia Woolf: To the Lighthouse.* London: Macmillan, 1970.

Bell, Quentin. *Virginia Woolf: A Biography.* 2 vols. New York: Harcourt Brace Jovanovich, 1972.

Bennett, Joan. *Virginia Woolf: Her Art as a Novelist.* Cambridge: Cambridge University Press, 1945; 2d ed., enlarged, 1964.

Blackstone, Bernard. *Virginia Woolf: A Commentary.* London: Hogarth, 1949.

Brewster, Dorothy. *Virginia Woolf's London.* London: George Allen and Unwin, 1959.

———. *Virginia Woolf.* London: George Allen and Unwin, 1963.

Chambers, R. L. *The Novels of Virginia Woolf.* Edinburgh: Oliver and Boyd, 1947.

Chastaing, Maxime. *La Philosophie de Virginia Woolf.* Paris: Presses Universitaires de France, 1951.

Daiches, David. *Virginia Woolf.* Norfolk, Conn.: New Directions, 1942 (rev. ed. 1963).

Dolle, Erika. *Experiment und Tradition in der Prosa Virginia Woolfs.* Munich: W. Fink, 1971.

Fleishman, Avrom. *Virginia Woolf: A Critical Reading.* Baltimore: Johns Hopkins University Press, 1975.

Forster, E. M. *Virginia Woolf: The Rede Lecture, 1941.* Cambridge: Cambridge University Press, 1942. Reprinted in *Two Cheers for Democracy.* New York: Harcourt, Brace, 1951.

Freedman, Ralph. *The Lyrical Novel: Studies in Hermann Hesse, André Gide and Virginia Woolf.* Princeton: Princeton University Press, 1963.

Guiguet, Jean. *Virginia Woolf and Her Works.* Translated by Jean Stewart. London: Hogarth, 1965.

Hafley, James. *The Glass Roof: Virginia Woolf as Novelist.* English Studies no. 9. Berkeley: University of California Press, 1954.

Hartman, Geoffrey H. "Virginia's Web," Chicago Review, 14 (1961). Reprinted in Beyond Formalism: Literary Essays, 1958 – 70. New Haven: Yale University Press, 1972.

Holtby, Winifred. Virginia Woolf. London: Wishart, 1932.

Johnstone, J. K. The Bloomsbury Group: A Study of E. M. Forster, Lytton Strachey, Virginia Woolf, and Their Circle. New York: Noonday, 1963 (1954).

Kelley, Alice van Buren. The Novels of Virginia Woolf: Fact and Vision. Chicago: University of Chicago Press, 1973.

Kirkpatrick, B. J. A Bibliography of Virginia Woolf. London: Hart-Davis, 1967.

Leaska, Mitchell A. Virginia Woolf's Lighthouse: A Study in Critical Method. New York: Columbia University Press, 1970; London: Hogarth, 1970.

——. The Novels of Virginia Woolf. New York: John Jay Press, 1977.

Lewis, Thomas S. W., comp. Virginia Woolf: A Collection of Criticism. New York: McGraw-Hill, 1975.

Love, Jean O. Worlds in Consciousness: Mythopoetic Thought in the Novels of Virginia Woolf. Berkeley and Los Angeles: University of California Press, 1970.

——. Virginia Woolf: Sources in Madness and Art, I. Berkeley and Los Angeles: University of California Press, 1977.

McLaurin, Allen. Virginia Woolf: The Echoes Enslaved. Cambridge: Cambridge University Press, 1973.

Majumdar, Robin. Virginia Woolf: An Annotated Bibliography. New York: Garland, 1976.

Majumdar, Robin, and Allen McLaurin. Virginia Woolf: The Critical Heritage. London: Routledge and Kegan Paul, 1975.

Marder, Herbert. Feminism and Art: A Study of Virginia Woolf. Chicago: University of Chicago Press, 1968.

Miller, J. Hillis. "Virginia Woolf's All Soul's Day: The Omniscient Narrator in Mrs. Dalloway," The Shaken Realist: Essays in Honor of F. J. Hoffman. Edited by O. B. Hardison, Jr., et al. Baton Rouge: Louisiana State University Press, 1970.

Modern Fiction Studies, 18 (1972). Special edition devoted to Virginia Woolf.

Moody, A. D. Virginia Woolf. Edinburgh: Oliver and Boyd, 1963; New York: Grove, 1963.

Naremore, James. The World without a Self: Virginia Woolf and the Novel. New Haven: Yale University Press, 1973.

Nathan, Monique. Virginia Woolf par elle-même. Paris: Seuil, 1956. Translated by Herma Briffault as Virginia Woolf. New York: Grove, 1961.

Newton, Deborah. *Virginia Woolf.* Melbourne: Melbourne University Press, 1963.

Noble, Joan Russell, ed. *Recollections of Virginia Woolf.* New York: Morrow, 1972.

Novak, Jane. *The Razor Edge of Balance.* Coral Gables: University of Miami Press, 1975.

Pippett, Aileen. *The Moth and the Star: A Biography of Virginia Woolf.* Boston: Little, Brown, 1955.

Rantavaara, Irma. *Virginia Woolf and Bloomsbury.* Helsinki: Annales Academiae Scientiarum Fennicae, 1953.

———. *Virginia Woolf's The Waves.* Port Washington, New York: Kennikat, 1969 (1960).

Richter, Harvena. *Virginia Woolf: The Inward Voyage.* Princeton: Princeton University Press, 1970.

Rose, Phyllis. *Woman of Letters: A Life of Virginia Woolf.* Oxford: Oxford University Press, 1978.

Rosenbaum, S. P. "The Philosophical Realism of Virginia Woolf," *English Literature and British Philosophy.* Chicago: University of Chicago Press. 1971.

Ruddick, Lisa. *The Seen and the Unseen: Virginia Woolf's To the Lighthouse.* Cambridge (Mass.): Harvard University Press, 1977.

Schaefer, Josephine O'Brien. *The Three-Fold Nature of Reality in the Novels of Virginia Woolf.* London: Mouton, 1965.

Sprague, Claire, ed. *Virginia Woolf: A Collection of Critical Essays.* Englewood Cliffs, N.J.: Prentice Hall, 1971.

Thakur, N. C. *The Symbolism of Virginia Woolf.* New York: Oxford University Press, 1965.

Trautmann, Joanne. *The Jessamy Brides: The Friendship of Virginia Woolf and Vita Sackville-West.* University Park: Pennsylvania State University Press, 1973.

Vogler, Thomas A., ed. *To the Lighthouse: A Collection of Critical Essays.* Englewood Cliffs, N.J.: Prentice Hall, 1970.

Woodring, Carl. *Virginia Woolf.* New York: Columbia University Press, 1966.

Woolf, Leonard. *Sowing: An Autobiography of the Years 1880–1904.* London: Hogarth, 1960.

———. *Beginning Again: An Autobiography of the Years 1911–1918.* London: Hogarth, 1964.

———. *Downhill All the Way: An Autobiography of the Years 1919–1939.* London: Hogarth, 1967.

———. *The Journey, Not the Arrival Matters: An Autobiography of the Years 1939–1969.* London: Hogarth, 1969.

Index

Aestheticism, 4, 8, 136, 242, 243, 264, 265
Aesthetics (of VW): and artist-characters, 18, 43, 158, 234, 263, 266; and artistic identity, 6, 8–10 passim, 78, 124–126 passim, 158, 186, 188, 214, 229, 234–235, 283; and attitudes toward art, 18, 32, 33, 43, 92, 117–118, 124–125, 152–158 passim, 177–178, 185–186, 264–267, 273, 283
Anderson, Sherwood, Winesburg, Ohio, 46
Androgyny, 20, 21, 21n15, 35, 119, 126, 131, 175–176, 180, 188, 191, 215–216, 234–235, 239. See also Feminism; Homosexuality; Sapphism
Austen, Jane, 38n5, 42, 99, 102, 110, 115, 119–121 passim, 124, 161, 264, 266; Emma, 38n5, 42; Pride and Prejudice, 99

Barnes, Djuna, Nightwood, 126
Beauvoir, Simone de, 135
Beckett, Samuel, Breath, 283
Beethoven, Ludwig van, 222
Bell, Clive, 78, 85, 97, 103, 117, 158, 193, 200, 202, 265
Bell, Vanessa Stephen, 17, 103, 108, 117, 197–209 passim
Bennett, Arnold, 225, 242, 265
Berg Collection (New York Public Library), 6, 23n20, 197n21, 198n28, 198n30, 200n38, 202n43, 204n48, 206n56, 212n87, 226n15

Between the Acts: artist-characters in, 263, 266; comic vision in, 272, 279; and drama, 126, 267–270 passim, 274–282 passim; dual vision in, 140; history in, 241; language in, 276, 280–281; mixed modes in, 263, 267, 280; and Mrs. Dalloway, 147n16; musical forms in, 267–268; narrative voice in, 264, 266, 269, 275; satire in, 263–266, 276, 281, 282; as synthesis of The Waves and The Years, 275; as tragicomedy, 269, 271, 273, 275; tragic vision in, 101, 273; and war, 128, 140; and The Waves, 269, 275; and The Years, 248, 262, 281
Bildungsroman, 9, 10, 76, 129, 139
Blake, William, 262
Bloomsbury, 3, 4, 77, 101, 136, 158, 224, 264
Booth, Wayne, The Rhetoric of Fiction, 264
Bowen, Elizabeth, 213, 265
Brontë, Charlotte, 161
Brontë, Emily, 84, 161; Wuthering Heights, 84
Browne, Sir Thomas, 15
Butler, Samuel, 112, 113n27, 114, 114n, 115; Notebooks, 113n27
Byron, Lord George Gordon, 118, 130, 132; Don Juan, 118

Campbell, Mary, 210, 211
Campbell, Roy, 210
Chekhov, Anton, 44–46 passim, 142; Notebooks, 44

Circular form, 52n16, 53, 53n, 59–69 passim, 128. See also Dialectic

Coleridge, Samuel Taylor, 34, 47, 125, 136, 165, 182, 188, 235; "Dejection: An Ode," 34; on elegy, 181–182, 188; Table Talk and Other Omnia, 165, 188

Comedy of manners, 9, 53n, 127, 128, 131, 138–139. See also Comic vision

Comic vision, 10, 41, 42, 53n, 59, 97–123, 140, 176, 177, 182–185 passim, 268, 272, 279, 280. See also Circular form; Comedy of manners; Dialectic; Pastoral; Satire; Tragicomedy

"Countess of Pembroke's Arcadia, The," 275n16

Darwin, Gwen, 199

Davies, Margaret Llewelyn, 108

"Death of the Moth, The," 17n8, 27

DeQuincey, Thomas, Confessions of an English Opium-Eater, 126

Dialectic, 7, 8, 10, 12, 40, 69, 106, 123n, 125, 138–139, 170n17, 185, 223, 247, 259, 268–269. See also Time; Tragicomedy

Diaries (of VW), 6, 146. See also A Writer's Diary

Dickens, Charles, 41

Dickinson, Goldsworthy Lowes, 99, 120; The Magic Flute: A Fantasia (1911), 99–101 passim, 112

Dostoevsky, Fyodor, 145

Drama, 126, 128, 275–278 passim. See also Elizabethan, drama

Dreadnought Hoax, 98

Dual vision. See Dialectic

"Duchess and the Jeweller, The," 59

Edel, Leon, 4

Edwardian: age, 101, 108, 116, 248, 252, 254, 282; novel, 242, 265

Elegy, 164–165, 168, 179–183 passim, 186–188 passim, 220, 244

Eliot, George (Mary Ann Evans), 47, 47n8, 48, 73, 112n24, 161; Middlemarch, 35n; "Notes on Form in Art," 47

Eliot, T. S., 3, 11, 15, 50, 97, 148, 161, 231n, 248, 252, 262, 265; The Waste Land, 148, 248, 252, 265

Elizabethan: age, 270, 274, 282; drama, 127, 128, 268–270 passim, 274, 281, 282; lyric, 173

"Enchanted Organ, The," 113

Epic, 53n, 128, 135; mock, 229, 278

Epiphany, 45, 48–51 passim. See also Moment, the

Epistemology, 11, 36, 132–137, 140, 155, 160, 230, 232, 235. See also Moore, G. E.; Mysticism; Philosophy, British

Essays (of VW). See individual titles

Fairy tale, 172, 173

Faulkner, William, 50

Feminism, 4, 7, 98–122 passim, 161, 238, 241–245 passim, 253–254. See also Androgyny

Fielding, Henry, 129, 135; Tom Jones, 129

Flush, 98

Formalism, 46, 47, 52n15, 52n16. See also Circular form; Linear form

Forster, E. M., 97, 100, 115n30, 202, 242, 265

Freshwater: A Comedy in Three Acts, 269

Freud, Sigmund, 51, 167, 181n, 184n, 186, 242; The Interpretation of Dreams, 181n

Fry, Roger, 100, 106, 123, 124n2, 126, 137, 267

Galsworthy, John, 225, 242, 246

Garnett, Constance, 45

Gay, John, What D'Ye Call It? A Tragical-Comical-Pastoral Farce, 270

Genres, literary. See Literary genres and modes

Girard, René, 170n17

Granite and Rainbow, 123

Grant, Duncan, 103, 108, 202, 209

Grimm, the Brothers, (Jakob and Wilhelm), "The Fisherman and His Wife," 172

Hardy, Thomas, 35, 43, 145; "During Wind and Rain," 43

Harrison, Jane, 109

"A Haunted House," 34, 35, 38, 62–63, 68

A Haunted House, 53

Heidegger, Martin, 221
Heilbrun, Carolyn, 187
Hemingway, Ernest, 46, 50
Hesse, Hermann, 5, 6
Hogarth Press, 19, 27, 44, 197, 210, 217
Homosexuality, 189, 194–206,
211–212. *See also* Androgyny;
Sapphism
"How Should One Read a Book?"
276n
Hume, David, 124

Ibsen, Henrik, 99, 102, 110, 114,
115–118 *passim; Hedda Gabler,* 114;
The Masterbuilder, 99, 110, 115n, 116
Imagery, 78, 185–186, 227, 273,
278–282 *passim;* moth, 13–28
passim, 35
Impressionism, 126, 136. *See also* Fry,
Roger; Postimpressionism
"Introduction, The," 67
Isherwood, Christopher, 265

Jacob's Room: as *Bildungsroman,* 129,
129n; coin symbolism in, 130n;
comic vision in, 42, 278–279; dual
vision in, 123; as elegy, 16; genesis
of, 191; London in, 279; moth
symbolism in, 13, 16; narrative
voice in, 42, 126–127, 132, 135;
perception in, 132–135; and Thoby
Stephen, 16, 164n9; and *Tom Jones,*
129n; tragic vision in, 127, 130–131,
138–142 *passim;* and war, 127, 131,
138; and *The Waves,* 134; and
Woolf's later fiction, 138–140;
mentioned, 9, 14, 16, 17n8, 18, 26,
41, 74, 163, 273
James, Henry, 4, 26n30, 73, 102, 115n,
116, 128, 171, 265; *Portrait of a Lady,*
116
"The Jessamy Brides," 190, 191
Joyce, James, 3, 5, 6, 11, 35, 45–50
passim, 97, 125, 128, 129, 136, 171,
242, 243, 264–266 *passim,* 276,
282–283; "Araby," 51n; "The
Dead," 45, 49; *Dubliners,* 45;
Finnegan's Wake, 283; "A Painful
Case," 50; *Portrait of the Artist as a
Young Man,* 129, 264, 279; *Stephen
Hero,* 45, 264; "Two Gallants," 50;
Ulysses, 171, 242, 265

Keats, John, 30, 36, 150, 155, 271;
"Ode on a Grecian Urn," 30
"Kew Gardens," 35, 37, 42, 46, 56, 57,
69
Koteliansky, S. S., 44

"Lady in the Looking Glass, The,"
60, 69, 225
"Lapin and Lapinova," 59
Lawrence, D. H., 83, 128, 129, 146,
150, 242, 262, 265; *Sons and Lovers,*
129
"Leaning Tower, The," 22
Leavis, F., 146
Leavis, Q. D., 244, 245n3;
"Caterpillars of the
Commonwealth Unite," 244
"Legacy, The," 59–60
Lesbianism. *See* Sapphism
Letters of Virginia Woolf, The, 6, 75n,
190–218 *passim*
Lewis, R. W. B., *The Picaresque Saint,*
125
Linear form, 53–58, 69, 128, 161–168
passim. See also Dialectic
Literary genres and modes (in VW),
126, 127, 274–275. See also
Bildungsroman; Comedy of
manners; Drama; Elegy; Fairy tale;
Lyric poetry; Parody; Pastoral;
Romance; Satire; Tragedy;
Tragicomedy
Literary tradition (and VW): English,
12, 36, 236n, 270; novel, 124, 126,
242, 246, 265; mentioned, 4, 161,
162, 242. *See also* Literary genres
and modes; Modernism
Little, Judy, 129
Locke, John, 124
Lukacs, George, 46–47
Lyric poetry, 123, 126, 180, 274–276,
275n16

Macaulay, Rose, 266
MacCarthy, Desmond, 193
"Man Who Loved His Kind, The," 58
Mansfield, Katherine, 44–51 *passim,*
46n5, 55, 97, 101, 121; "The Aloe,"
45; "At the Bay," 49; "Bliss," 46;
"The Doll's House," 49; "The
Garden Party," 46; "The Prelude,"
44, 49

"Mark on the Wall, The," 35, 42, 45, 53, 69, 143, 225
Marvell, Andrew, "The Garden," 257
Maxse, Katharine, 164n9
"Memories of a Working Woman's Guild," 243
Meredith, George, 97, 101, 129, 182
Milton, John, 162–163
"Modern Fiction," 31, 225, 265
Modernism, 3, 7, 7n, 11, 47, 97, 125, 125n6, 126, 138, 241, 242, 246, 262, 265, 282–283
Modes, literary. *See* Literary genres and modes
Moment, the, 91, 135–139 *passim,* 221, 226. *See also* Epiphany; Epistemology
"Moment: Summer's Night, The," 136, 137, 226, 273, 280
"Moments of Being," 60–62, 68, 69
Moments of Being, 220, 222
"Monday or Tuesday," 63–64, 69
Monday or Tuesday, 29, 30, 40, 41, 46
Monologue. *See* Narrative voice
"Montaigne," 146, 152n
Moore, G. E., 136–137, 158, 224, 225, 228; *Principia Ethica,* 136, 224; "Refutation of Idealism," 137, 224, 228
Mozart, W. A., 10, 28, 28n, 29–31 *passim,* 67, 84, 99, 101–102, 103n9, 104n14, 106n16; *Don Giovanni,* 107, 110, 114, 118; *Magic Flute,* 10, 84, 97–107 *passim,* 110–118 *passim,* 120
"Mr. Bennett and Mrs. Brown," 31–35 *passim,* 258
Mrs. Dalloway: artist-characters in, 158; autobiographical element in, 24, 164n9; and *Between the Acts,* 147n16; comic vision in, 42; dual vision in, 138–139; as elegy, 164; language in, 145; London in, 141, 144, 148, 156, 236n25; narrative voice in, 42; as satire, 141–143; tragic vision in, 42, 144–146; tragicomic vision in, 280; and *The Voyage Out,* 87; and war, 127, 138–139, 141, 148–149; and *The Waves,* 158; mentioned, 10, 18, 163, 164n19, 273
Mrs. Dalloway's Party, 46, 58, 59n, 62n, 68, 142, 144

Murry, John Middleton, 163
Music (and VW), 80–84 *passim,* 100–107, 110–113 *passim,* 247, 267, 268. *See also* Beethoven; Mozart; Satie; Wagner
Mysticism, 20, 51, 80, 83, 88, 93n13, 158, 169, 170, 222, 223, 232, 239, 243. *See also* Epistemology; Moment, the; Nature, view of; Religion; Self, concept of; Time
Mythology: mythic figures, 23, 24n26, 25, 27, 169–176 *passim,* 179–181 *passim,* 185, 228–229; 236; mythic structures, 11, 20, 22–25 *passim,* 87n, 97, 98, 228–229, 236, 280. *See also* Oedipal myth

Narrative voice, 11, 23, 30–43 *passim,* 126, 132, 135, 163–164, 237–239, 243, 248, 264–269 *passim,* 275, 275n16, 278n19. *See also* Aesthetics, and artistic identity; Persona
"Narrow Bridge of Art, The," 147
Nature, view of (in VW), 219–226 *passim,* 229, 244, 249, 259, 261, 270–271, 282. *See also* Mysticism
Neumann, Erich, 169
"New Dress, The," 54, 55
Nicholson, Harold, 194, 196, 202
Nicholson, Nigel, 6; *Portrait of a Marriage,* 192–199 *passim,* 203–206 *passim,* 213–217 *passim*
"Niece of Earl, The," 238
Night and Day: autobiographical element in, 17; critical views of, 97, 98–108 *passim;* and feminism, 98–122 *passim;* music in, 100–107, 110–113 *passim;* myth in, 97–98; and *Orlando,* 98; as satire, 97–102; as traditional narrative, 164; and war, 97, 100–102 *passim;* and *The Waves,* 118; mentioned, 10, 200
Nightingale, Florence, "Cassandra," 110n
"Notes on an Elizabethan Play," 274
Novel, English (and VW), 124, 126, 242, 265. *See also* Literary tradition
Novels (of VW). *See individual titles*
"Nurse Lugton's Golden Thimble," 151n

O'Connor, Frank, 50
Oedipal myth, 165–168, 183, 184n, 186–187
"On Being Ill," 19, 146, 147, 222
"On Not Knowing Greek," 119, 278n19
Opera. *See* Mozart; Music; Wagner
Organicism, 47, 47n8, 48
Orlando: androgyny in, 21, 126, 188, 191, 215–216; dual vision in, 139; perception in, 14; history in, 241; moth symbolism in, 19, narrative voice in, 35, 42; and *Night and Day*, 98; as satire, 214; the self in, 216–217; and *To the Lighthouse*, 188, 192; and *The Waves*, 24, 217; mentioned, 24, 274. *See also* Sackville-West, Vita

Pankhurst, Sylvia, 98, 98n4
Parody, 10, 129, 266, 269, 276, 277. *See also* Satire
Pastoral, 121, 161, 169, 178–179 *passim*, 188, 236, 268, 270, 279. *See also* Comic vision
Pater, Walter, 40, 79; *The Renaissance*, 40
Persona, 6, 19, 74, 126, 239, 248, 269, 275. *See also* Aesthetics, and artistic identity; Narrative voice
"Phases of Fiction," 225
Philosophy, British, 124, 125, 136, 137, 225. *See also* Moore, G. E.
Poe, Edgar Allan, 49
Political views (of VW), 4, 6, 7, 8, 141, 145, 146, 152, 154, 241–262 *passim. See also* Androgyny; Feminism; War
Postimpressionism, 126, 241. *See also* Fry, Roger; Impressionism
Pound, Ezra, 3, 50
Proust, Marcel, 50, 125, 128, 136, 145, 277

Raverat, Jacques, 196n15, 197n23, 198, 199
"Reading," 14, 16, 18
Religion (and VW), 154, 163, 177, 222, 280. *See also* Mysticism
Restoration comedy, 270
Richardson, Dorothy, 129

Ritchie, Lady (Annie Thackeray), 103, 112n26, 113
Robins, Elizabeth, *A Dark Lantern* (VW's review of), 116
"Robinson Crusoe," 145
Roger Fry: A Biography, 267
Romance, 129; family, 171, 186. *See also* Pastoral
Room of One's Own, A, 21, 26, 110, 145, 161, 162, 235, 260
Ruskin, John, *Modern Painters*, 33
"Russian Point of View, The," 142

Sackville-West, Edward, 199
Sackville-West, Vita, 11, 125, 189–218 *passim; The Heir*, 193
Santayana, George, *Soliloquies in England and Later Soliloquies*, 263, 268
Sapphism, 189, 194, 195, 199, 204, 207, 210. *See also* Androgyny; Homosexuality
Sartre, Jean Paul, 135
Satie, Erik, 106n
Satire, 10, 75, 97–102, 141–143, 214, 263–266 *passim*, 278, 281, 282. *See also* Comedy of manners; Parody
Schriener, Olive, 101
Scott, Sir Walter, 43, 172, 179; *The Antiquary*, 179; *Waverly* novels, 172
"Searchlight, The," 66, 69
Self, concept of, 36, 84, 87–92 *passim*, 93n13, 130, 155, 158, 160, 216, 217, 219–223 *passim*, 227–231 *passim*, 237, 242, 246, 249–250, 258–259. *See also* Androgyny; Epistemology; Mysticism
Senancourt, Basil de, 247
Shakespeare, William, 43, 102, 112, 112n25, 118, 128, 147, 153, 161, 170, 185, 222, 236n, 269; *The Winter's Tale*, 11, 170, 185
Shaw, G. B., 68, 112, 118; *Man and Superman*, 118
Shelley, P. B., 130
"Shooting Party, The," 38, 65, 69
Short stories (of VW). *See individual titles*
Short story, 9, 44–70 *passim*, 225. *See also* Circular form; Linear form
Sidney, Sir Philip, 275n16

298 Index

"Sketch of the Past, A," 93, 153, 160n, 168, 220, 222
Smyth, Dame Ethel, 99, 103, 236n
"Society, A," 98
"Solid Objects," 54
Soliloquy. See Aesthetics, and artistic identity; Narrative voice
Spanish Civil War, 245, 255
Stephen, Leslie, 113, 163, 164, 186
Stephen, (Julian) Thoby, 16, 17, 90, 164n9
Stephen, Vanessa. See Bell, Vanessa Stephen
Stevens, Wallace, 3, 33, 35, 36, 37; "The Poems of Our Climate," 36
Strachey, Lytton, 77, 114, 119, 200, 202, 205, 231n
"String Quartets, The," 29, 31, 34, 36, 37, 67, 68, 105, 106
Suffrage movement. See Feminism
"Summing Up, A," 49, 64

Three Guineas: critical response to, 244; and feminism, 245; thesis of, 245–246, 250; and The Years, 244–246, 250–254 passim; mentioned, 101, 106, 116n, 118, 147n15
Time, 9, 10, 128, 143, 216, 272, 274, 278, 279. See also Dialectic; Mysticism
"Together and Apart," 57, 58
To the Lighthouse: androgyny in, 20, 188; artist-characters in, 158, 159, 188; autobiographical element in, 18, 163, 186, 187, 188; comic vision in, 176–177, 182; dialectic in, 166, 170n17, 185; dual vision in, 139, 188; as elegy, 164–165, 168, 179, 180–182, 183, 186–188; and Roger Fry, 124n2; genesis of, 191; lyric in, 173; as mock-epic, 200; myth in, 167–188 passim; narrative voice in, 42, 163–164; and Orlando, 188, 192; pastoral in, 161, 169, 173, 174, 177, 179, 188; revisions of, 221; tragic vision in, 101, 174, 182–183; and The Voyage Out, 87; and war, 127, 180–181; and The Waves, 227, 234; mentioned, 11, 18, 35, 43, 79, 89, 231, 273, 275. See also Oedipal myth

Tragedy, 128. See also Tragicomedy; Tragic vision
Tragicomedy, 268–275 passim, 278–279, 280. See also Comic vision; Dialectic; Tragic vision
Tragic vision, 9, 41, 42, 127–128, 130, 131, 138–139, 144–146, 174, 182–183, 240, 273, 275. See also Linear form; Tragicomedy
Trefusis, Violet, 200, 210, 210n77, 215
Two Stories, 45

"Unwritten Novel, An," 37, 38, 57, 69

Valery, Paul, 126
Vaughan, Madge, 202
Victorian: age, 104, 116; family, 115, 186; fathers, 114, 174; males, 174; melodrama, 270; values, 109
Voyage Out, The: autobiographical element in, 16, 17, 73, 90; as Bildungsroman, 76–77; critical reception of, 73n; genesis of, 73; literary allusions in, 84n; moth symbol in, 16; and Mrs. Dalloway, 87; music in, 80–84; mysticism, 80, 83, 88–96; myth in, 82, 87n; and Thoby Stephen, 16; and To the Lighthouse, 87; as traditional narrative, 164; tragic vision in, 41, 42, 89–96 passim; and The Waves, 74, 79–80, 83–96 passim; and Woolf's later works, 74, 74n2; mentioned, 9, 16n, 24, 41

Wagner, Richard, 84, 100, 101, 118, 119; Tristan, 84, 100, 119
War, theme of, 100, 101, 127, 131, 138, 148–150 passim. See also Spanish Civil War; World War I; World War II
Waves, The: androgyny in, 234–235, 239; artist-characters in, 158, 222, 229, 234–235; autobiographical element in, 17, 26, 164n9; and Between the Acts, 269, 275; comic vision in, 268; critical views of, 219; dual vision in, 129, 133; epistemology in, 132, 134, 224, 228–235 passim; genesis of, 275; imagery, 227; and Jacob's Room, 134;

London in, 236, 236*n*, 237; manuscript of, 23*n*20, 226*n*15; moth symbolism in, 13, 35; and *Mrs. Dalloway*, 158; musical structures in, 105; mysticism in, 20, 80, 83, 222–223, 232, 239, 243, 244, 259; myth in, 20, 228–229; narrative voice in, 23, 126, 137, 237, 239, 275, 275*n*16; and *Night and Day*, 118; and *Orlando*, 24, 217; pastoral in, 236; as poetic fiction, 259, 275; the self in, 219–223 *passim*, 227–231 *passim*, 237; and *To the Lighthouse*, 227, 234; tragicomedy, 42, 85, 89, 101, 269, 280; and *The Voyage Out*, 74, 79–80, 84–96 *passim*; and war, 128; and *The Years*, 247, 259; mentioned, 9, 11, 18, 20, 21, 24, 38, 79, 86, 189, 218
Wellesley, Lady Dorothy, 208, 210, 211
Wells, H. G., 129, 225, 242
West, Rebecca, 99
Woolf, Leonard, 6, 27, 34, 44, 45, 59, 68, 98*n*4, 100, 111*n*, 202, 203, 205, 209, 213, 224. *See also* Hogarth Press
Woolf, Virginia: critical revaluation of, 3–6, 7, 7*n*, 11, 125–126
— Literary heritage. *See* Aestheticism; Literary genres and modes; Literary tradition
— Literary methods. *See* Dialectic; Imagery; Literary genres and modes; Music; Mythology; Narrative voice
— Personal history: childhood, 9, 13, 15, 17, 18, 131, 163, 186–188 *passim*, 192, 197, 220–224 *passim*; illnesses,

13–19 *passim*, 24, 146, 153, 195, 201; relationships, *see names of individuals;* residences, 196–197; youth, 14, 98, 100, 224
— Philosophical perspectives. *See* Aesthetics; Comic vision; Dialectic; Epistemology; Tragic vision
— Political perspectives. *See* Androgyny; Feminism; Political views; War
— Works. *See individual titles*
Wordsworth, William, 36, 125, 136
World War I, 16, 90, 97–102 *passim*, 112, 127, 138, 141, 148–149, 180–181, 243, 249, 256–257
World War II, 223, 245, 248
Writer's Diary, A, 18–24 *passim*, 96, 110*n*, 141, 152, 163, 164, 189–191 *passim*, 213–223 *passim*, 236*n*, 263–268 *passim*, 273–278 *passim*, 282, 283

Years, The: and *Between the Acts*, 248, 259, 262, 275; comic vision in, 43; critical response to, 246, 261; dual vision in, 140, 259; and elegy, 244; and daily life, 274, 275; and language, 281; mixed modes in, 259; as mock-epic, 278; musical form in, 247; mysticism in, 258; narrative voice in, 42, 248, 275; and social radicalism, 244, 248–262; technique in, 247–248; and *Three Guineas*, 244, 246, 250–254 *passim*; and *To the Lighthouse*, 259; and *The Waves*, 247, 259; mentioned, 10, 38, 42, 109, 273, 278*n*21
Yeats, William Butler, 3, 64

Designer: Jim Mennick
Compositor: Viking Typographics
Printer: Vail-Ballou Press, Inc.
Binder: Vail-Ballou Press, Inc.
Text: VIP Bembo
Display: Phototypositor Weiss
Cloth: Joanna Arrestox B44000
Paper: 55 lb. Antique Cream